AF605812

Eulogy for Burying a Crane and the Art of Chinese Calligraphy

LEI XUE

A McLellan Book

UNIVERSITY OF WASHINGTON

SEATTLE

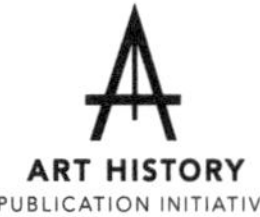

Eulogy for Burying a Crane *and the Art of Chinese Calligraphy* was made possible by a collaborative grant from the Andrew W. Mellon Foundation.

This publication was also supported by grants from the Metropolitan Center for Far Eastern Art Studies and the Center for the Humanities at Oregon State University.

Additional support was provided by the McLellan Endowment, established through the generosity of Martha McCleary McLellan and Mary McLellan Williams.

Design by Laura Shaw Design
Composed in Arno Pro, typeface designed by Robert Slimbach; and Avenir Next, typeface designed by Adrian Frutiger

23 22 21 20 19 5 4 3 2 1

Printed and bound in the United States of America

UNIVERSITY OF WASHINGTON PRESS
uwapress.uw.edu

LIBRARY OF CONGRESS CATALOGING-IN-PUBLICATION DATA
Names: Xue, Lei, 1975– author.
Title: Eulogy for burying a crane and the art of Chinese calligraphy / Lei Xue.
Description: Seattle : University of Washington, [2019] | Includes bibliographical references and index.
Identifiers: LCCN 2019018139 | ISBN 9780295746364 (hardcover) | ISBN 9780295746357 (ebook)
Subjects: LCSH: Yi he ming. | Calligraphy, Chinese.
Classification: LCC NK3634.Z6 Y539 2019 | DDC 745.6/19951—dc23
LC record available at https://lccn.loc.gov/2019018139

The paper used in this publication is acid free and meets the minimum requirements of American National Standard for Information Sciences—Permanence of Paper for Printed Library Materials, ANSI Z39.48–1984.∞

Contents

Acknowledgments

I started writing these acknowledgments at Beijing Normal University in early 2019, where I was invited to give a series of lectures. About two decades before, I was a student of literature there and had the great fortune to study with Qi Gong (1912–2005), who eventually guided me to the field of art history and calligraphy, encouraging me to pursue a further study in a very different culture and scholarly tradition. This book has been inspired by his insights in numerous aspects, and, more fundamentally, by his confidence in a curious student.

My other mentor, Robert E. Harrist Jr., patiently converted me into an art historian and taught me how to explain calligraphy—quite the esoteric subject, even within the field of Chinese art—to an audience who usually reads little Chinese. Many ideas in this book were produced during my discussions with him before and after my studies at Columbia University. The reader may easily recognize his great influence in this book.

Similarly, I wish to acknowledge David Ake Sensabaugh, Alfreda Murck, Amy McNair, Dawn Ho Delbanco, Matthew McKelway, and Li Feng for their guidance in different stages of research leading to this book. Alexandra Tunstall and Johanna Seasonwein helped edit drafts and final versions of the manuscript. Yang Yuanhui of Jiaoshan Stone Inscription Museum has accompanied me every time I visited the site and generously shared images and other materials with me. Merry Yue Cai provided me convenient access to library resources. My colleagues at Oregon State University—Lee Ann Garrison, director of the School of Arts and Communication; Dean Larry Rodgers; Kirsi Peltomäki; Julie Green; and Doug Russell, among many others—have continued to support this project. Thanks are also owed to Susan Shih-Shan Huang, Timothy Davis, Jonathan Pettit, Peter Sturman, Hui-Shu Lee, Lu Hui-wen, Dorothy Wong, Tom and Patricia Ebrey, Itakura Massaki, Lai Guolong, Eileen Hsu, Michael Cherney, Zhu Yuqi, Xu Man, Risha Lee, Chen Li-wei, Chelsea Foxwell, Yasuko Tsuchikane, Chun-Yi Joyce Tsai, and Sandrine S. Larrivé-Bass for their support and help in various ways.

My research and writing benefited from two fellowships and a publication grant at the Center for Humanities at Oregon State University; the Freeman Postdoctoral Fellowship at the College of William and Mary; and the Humanities Foundation Visiting Scholarship (Renwen Jijin) at Peking University. Material that contributed to the book was presented in annual meetings of the American Oriental Society, the

Association of Asian Studies, the College Art Association, and the European Association for Asian Art and Archaeology, as well as many other venues at Columbia University, the Jordon Schnitzer Museum of Art at the University of Oregon, the University of Kansas, the Colloquy on East Asian Art History at the University of Heidelberg, the Center for Chinese Studies at UCLA, the Center for Research on Ancient Chinese History at Peking University, and the Department of Chinese Language and Literature at Tsinghua University. I have learned a great deal from hosts, panelists, and other participants. Material for chapter 1 first appeared in "The Enigma of *Yi he ming*: Is It a Real Epitaph?" *Artibus Asiae* 73 (2012): 53–90.

This book could not have been completed without the encouragement and guidance of executive editor Lorri Hagman. My gratitude also goes to Richard Feit, Neecole Bostick, Julie Van Pelt, and other people of the University of Washington Press for their meticulous work during the production of this book. And I want to thank two anonymous readers, who pointed out many errors in the manuscript and offered numerous suggestions. All errors remain mine, of course.

Finally, I am grateful for the understanding and love of my family. It is so meaningful that I finished the project in my parents' old apartment, where I spent my teenage years and discovered my dream to be a scholar, a dream that they have never questioned. My wife, Hu Juan, has always been my critical reader and gone through all the joy and pain of writing with me. And our son, Xiao Shu, although being disappointed that it was not a fairytale ("except the first paragraph," he groaned), still wishes his dad will get rich by publishing this book. My life has been so enriched because of you. This book is dedicated to you all.

Chronology of Chinese Dynasties

- Shang ca. 1600–ca. 1046 BCE
- Zhou ca. 1046–256 BCE
  - Western Zhou ca. 1046–771 BCE
  - Eastern Zhou 770–256 BCE
    - Spring and Autumn 770–ca. 470 BCE
    - Warring States ca. 470–221 BCE
- Qin 221–206 BCE
- Han 206 BCE–220 CE
  - Western Han 206 BCE–9 CE
  - Xin 9–23
  - Eastern Han 25–220
- Three Kingdoms 220–280
  - Wei 220–265
  - Shu 221–263
  - Wu 222–280
- Jin 265–420
  - Western Jin 265–316
  - Eastern Jin 317–420
  - Sixteen Kingdoms 304–439
- Northern and Southern Dynasties 420–589

Northern Dynasties	*Southern Dynasties*
Northern Wei 386–535	Liu Song 420–479
Eastern Wei 534–550	Southern Qi 479–502
Western Wei 535–557	Liang 502–557
Northern Qi 550–577	Chen 557–589
Northern Zhou 557–581	

- Sui 581–618
- Tang 618–907
- Five Dynasties and Ten Kingdoms 907–960
- Liao 916–1125
- Song 960–1279

Northern Song 960–1127
Southern Song 1127–1279
Western Xia 1038–1227
Jin 1115–1234
Yuan 1271–1368
Ming 1368–1644
Qing 1644–1912

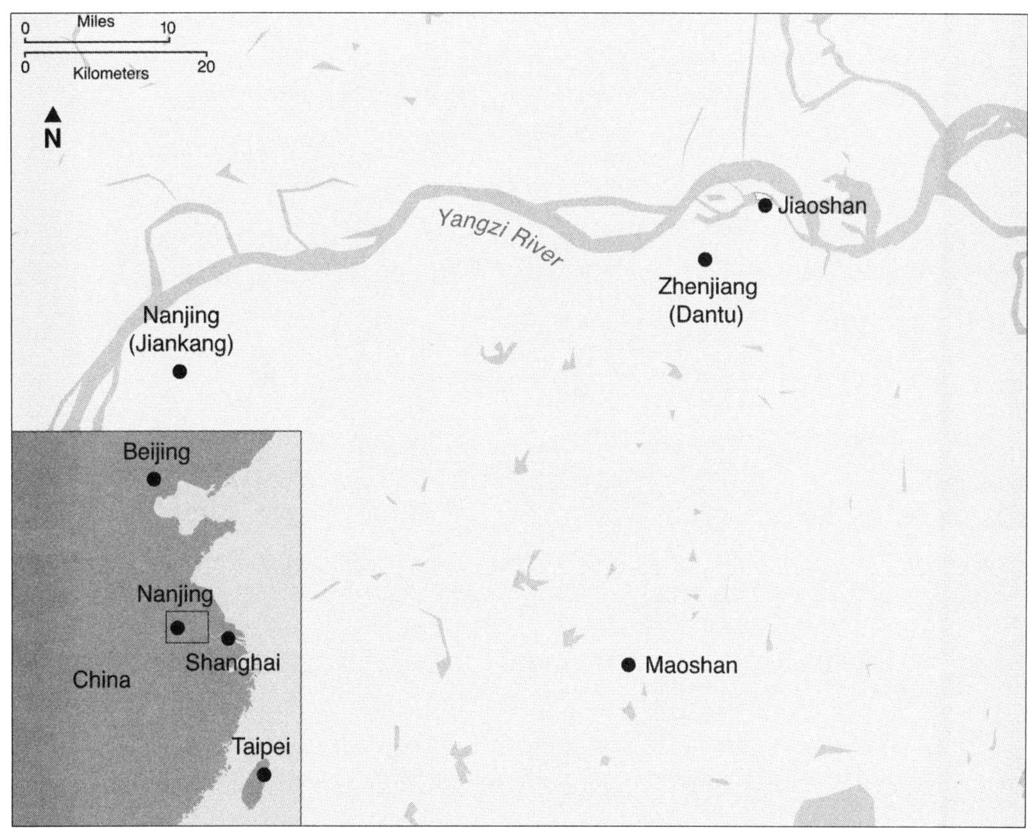

MAP 1. Nanjing-Zhenjiang-Maoshan region

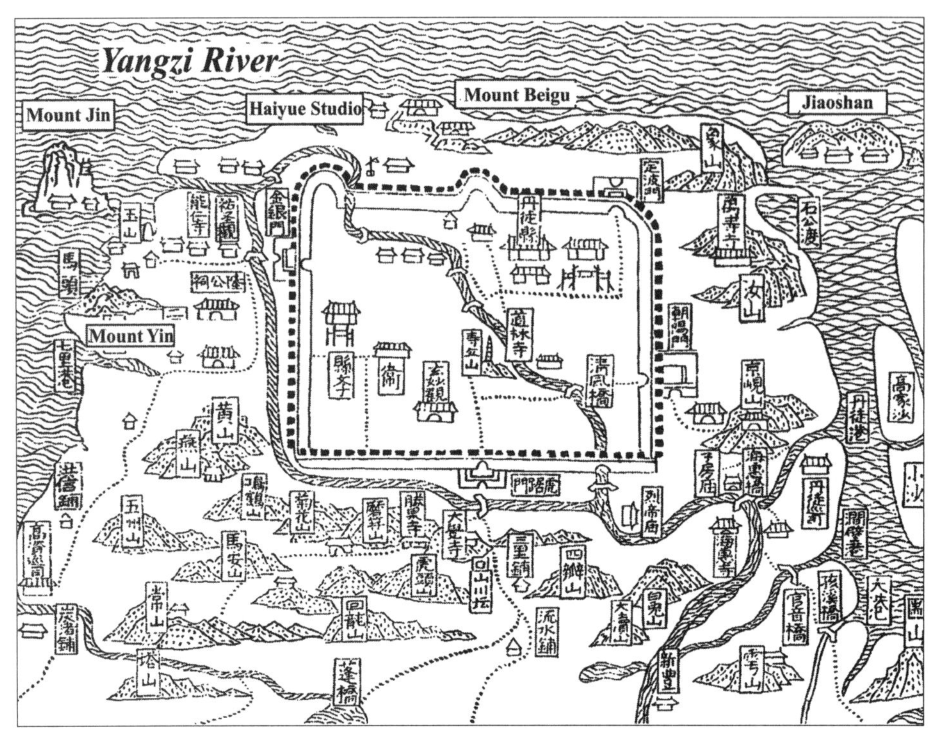

MAP 2. Major historical sites at Zhenjiang, adapted from a map from *Gazetteer of Zhenjiang in the Zhengde Era* (Zhengde Dantu xianzhi, 1521). Courtesy of Peter Sturman.

Eulogy for Burying a Crane and the Art of Chinese Calligraphy

Introduction

Once upon a time, a gentleman traveling in southern China visited Jiaoshan, a small island in the Yangtze River near today's Zhenjiang, Jiangsu (plate 1). There, he found a pair of cranes dancing in the courtyard of a temple. The dance was so elegant and swift that the gentleman was inspired to write calligraphy in the air with his finger, following the rhythm of the moving birds. Before leaving, he purchased the cranes from the temple and arranged to collect them when he returned from his journey. After a few months, during which he thought constantly of the cranes and the calligraphy he had imagined writing, he returned to Jiaoshan, only to learn that the birds had died. Heartbroken, he was guided to a cliff beneath which the cranes had been buried. He then composed an epitaph for the birds in a calligraphic style inspired by their dance and had this carved in stone above the tomb.[1]

The gentleman in this strange tale, part of the folklore of Jiaoshan, was Wang Xizhi (ca. 303–ca. 361), known as the Sage of Chinese Calligraphy. The epitaph the story attributes to him is known as *Eulogy for Burying a Crane* (Yi he ming). The "tombstone" was discovered early in the eleventh century at the foot of Jiaoshan, where the carved rock had partially collapsed into the muddy waters of the Yangzi River and broken into pieces. Only during the winter months, when the water level of the river was lower, were curious adventurers able to see the inscription on the fragmentary rocks. However, the unusual calligraphy of the *Eulogy* and the story of its heartbroken creator fascinated generations of visitors to the island—a fascination that was only heightened by the difficulty of accessing the inscription. In 1713, after a few unsuccessful attempts, five fragments of the inscription were painstakingly chiseled off the rocks, hauled from the river, and placed on view on the island. Today they are exhibited in a dedicated hall of the Jiaoshan Stone Inscription Museum (plate 2).[2]

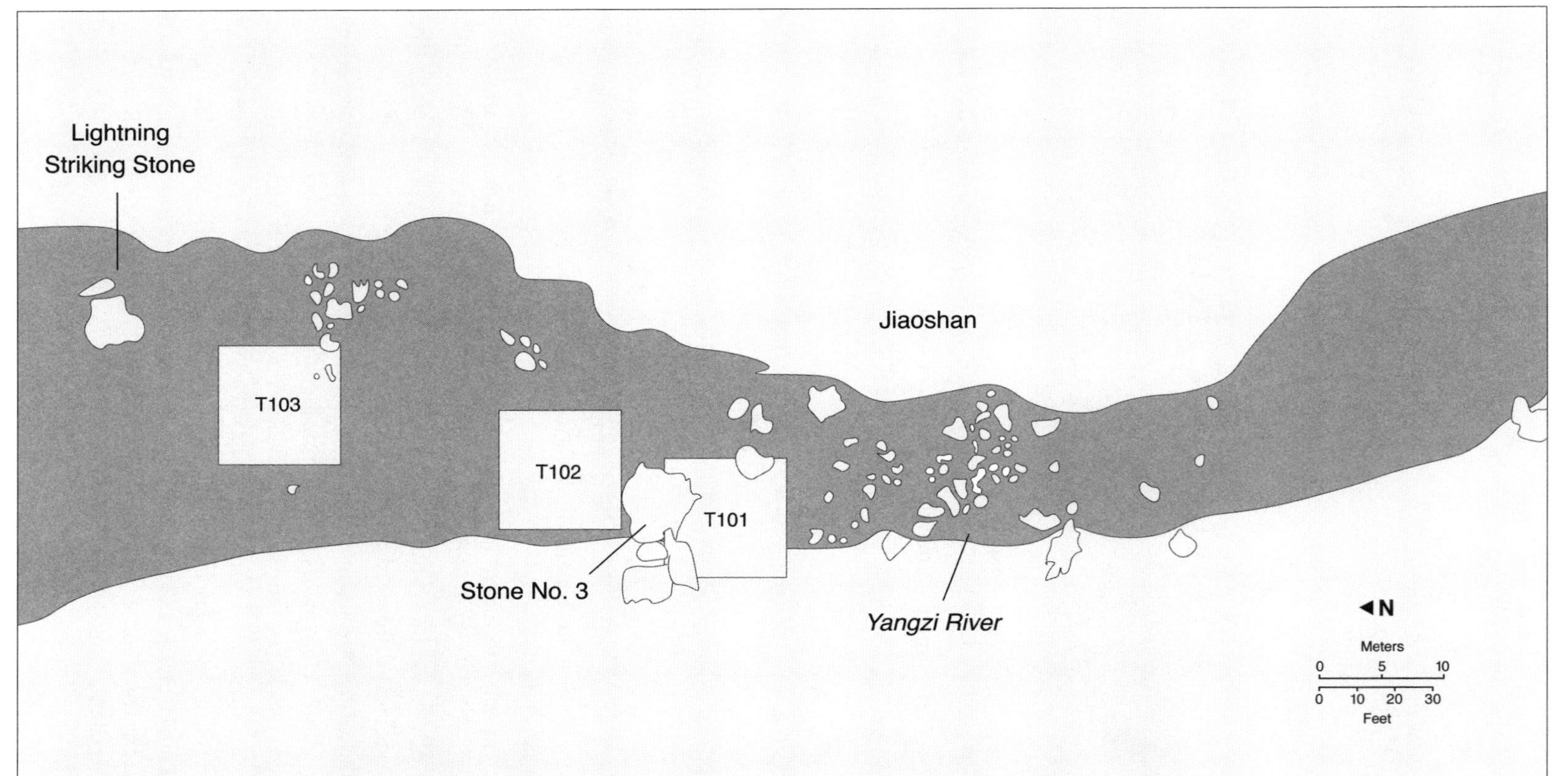

FIGURE I.1. Plan of Excavation at Jiaoshan in 1997. Courtesy of Jiaoshan Stone Inscription Museum. Redrawn by Mary Yang.

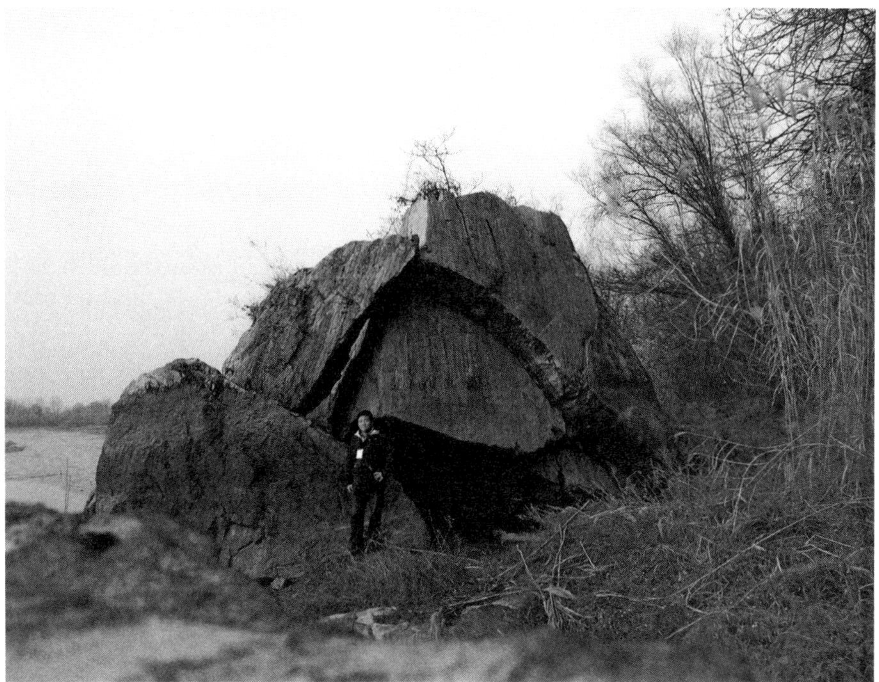

FIGURE I.2. Boulders at the shore of Jiaoshan. Author's photo, 2007.

There is no record of the *Eulogy*'s original location on the mountainside. The shattered rocks that remain on the shore, however, do provide some clues. In 1997, an archaeological survey was conducted at the west foot of Jiaoshan, focusing on three areas (marked T101, T102, and T103 in figure I.1), in particular the large boulders (figure I.2) between T101 and T102. These investigations yielded a positive identification of the locations of the inscription before the removal of the fragments from the water; traces of cutting and chiseling are still clearly visible on the largest boulder (stone no. 30 in figure I.1; on the right in figure I.2).[3] Given the size of the boulder, it is unlikely that it was brought to the site by water. The *Eulogy*, therefore, was perhaps originally located on the cliff right above these boulders, on the west side of Jiaoshan (as marked on the contour map in figure I.3), somewhere above Luohan Rock (Luohanyan; figure I.4).

Over the centuries, visitors to Jiaoshan left their own inscriptions on the cliff or the rocks along the mountainside (figure I.4). Some of the authors did so to pay tribute to the *Eulogy*, while others celebrated their own visit (see appendix 1 for a list of these inscriptions, as recorded in textual sources), and many of them survive on the island, mainly located at Luohan Rock and Floating Jade Rock (Fuyuyan; see their locations in figure 1.4). The list may only reflect a small portion of the inscriptions that have been carved in the island—many more were probably destroyed by frequent landslides and floods over the last millennium. These inscriptions are important witnesses to the history of the island and *Eulogy for Burying a Crane*.

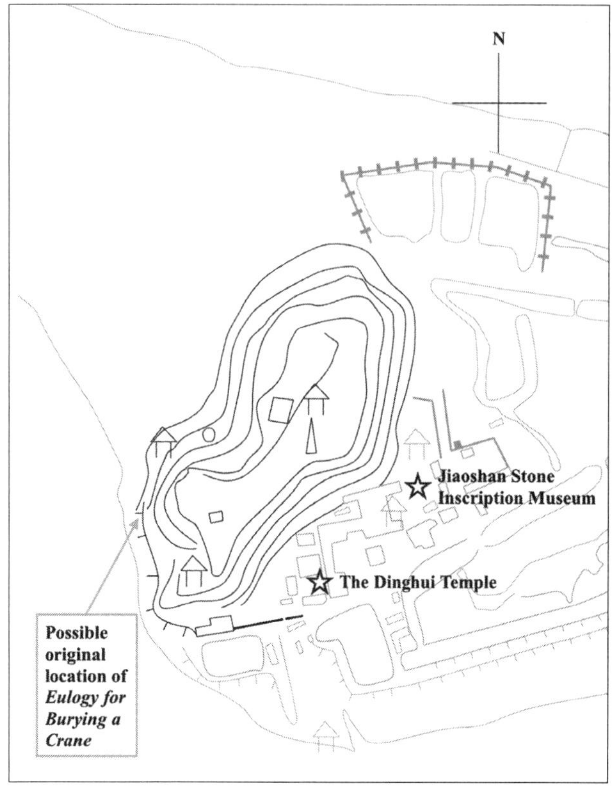

FIGURE I.3. Contour map of Jiaoshan. Courtesy of Jiaoshan Stone Inscription Museum. Redrawn by Li Bin.

The Enigma of the *Eulogy*

Although the Wang Xizhi story suggests that there were two birds, nothing in the inscription supports this idea, and it appears that the monument refers to only a single bird. The epitaph begins with a short biography of the crane from birth to death, continues with an elaborate eulogy alluding to the history and mythology of the crane, and ends with emotional condolences. Names of the mourners were inscribed on the far right side of the epitaph, though none of them are real. Instead, all are titles of Daoist immortals, which only increases the mysterious aura surrounding the inscription.

The story has no basis in historical fact; there is no evidence that Wang Xizhi visited Jiaoshan, and the calligraphy of the inscription looks nothing like other writings attributed to him. Although it appears to have been invented, the story has had enduring appeal—especially for the denizens of Jiaoshan and the surrounding area—for two reasons: the fame of Wang Xizhi added to the luster of local history, and, more significantly, the story satisfied a desire, widespread among connoisseurs and antiquarians in China, to associate notable works of art with the names of famous people, however fanciful these attributions may have been.

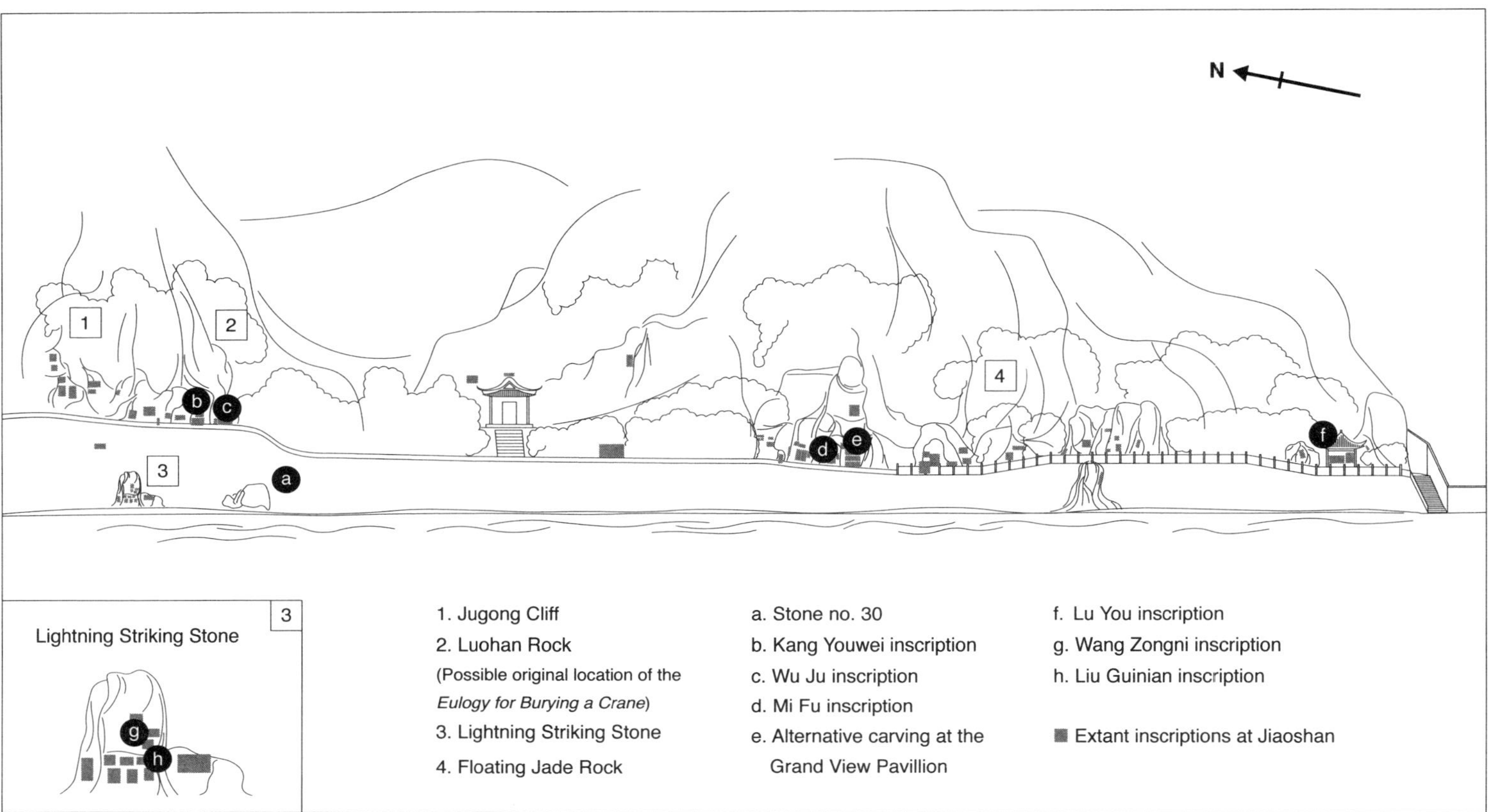

FIGURE I.4. Westside of Jiaoshan and locations of major inscriptions mentioned in the book. Adapted from a drawing provided by Jiaoshan Stone Inscription Museum. Redrawn by Mary Yang.

Since the eleventh century, skeptical scholars who have focused on textual evidence and calligraphic style have asked this central question: Who was the author of this work, if it was not Wang Xizhi? The only clues are the names, both clearly aliases, that appear next to the title of the inscription, identifying the author as the Perfected Recluse of Mount Huayang (Huayang Zhenyi) and the calligrapher as the Woodcutter of Mount Shanghuang (Shanghuang Shanqiao). Opinions vary widely over the significance of these names and the periods in which the individuals thus identified might have lived.[4] Today, most scholars accept that the inscription dates to 514 CE and was perhaps created by Tao Hongjing (456–536), the prominent scholar, calligrapher, and Daoist master at nearby Maoshan (see map 1 at beginning of book), a thriving Daoist community.[5] Tao left almost no reliably attributable surviving works that would enable a comparison of calligraphy.[6] As some scholars point out, however, contemporary inscriptions on stone wellheads and bricks discovered at Maoshan suggest what engraved calligraphy within the orbit of Tao Hongjing and the Maoshan community might have been like.[7] Other candidates have been proposed, but they have received less support.[8] Barring the discovery of new evidence, the question of the identity of the *Eulogy*'s calligrapher will probably remain unanswered.

Many things about the crane's tombstone are unique. First, to my knowledge, it is the only monument in Chinese history dedicated to an animal or bird. True, many literary compositions about birds and other creatures have been transmitted to us, some of them in the form of eulogies or epitaphs, but such works appear to have been literary concoctions that were never intended to be carved in stone, still less to mark an actual place. Although the text of the *Eulogy* belongs to this literary tradition, it was transformed into a physical stone monument, placed directly on the surface of the earth and embedded in the landscape of the island of Jiaoshan. Second, within the known corpus of medieval stone inscriptions, the design of the inscription is also highly unusual. The texts of almost all carvings were arranged in strictly ordered rows and columns, and the characters for these highly formal inscriptions display an equally measured decorum of compositional structure and brushwork. In comparison with these, the crane's epitaph displays an unusual freedom of design in the characters' layout and their unpredictable changes in size and compositional orientation.

Finally, the status accorded *Eulogy for Burying a Crane* in the history of Chinese calligraphy and the frequency with which later calligraphers imitated this work are puzzling. Having been submerged in the water for centuries, the stone carving was difficult to see, and rubbings taken from the stones varied widely in quality and reliability. In spite of these impediments, the *Eulogy* emerged at various times in history as a source of inspiration for calligraphers, particularly at moments of change. Two paragons in the history of Chinese calligraphy, Huang Tingjian (1045–1105) and Dong Qichang (1555–1636), admired the *Eulogy* and studied the calligraphy seriously. It entered the calligraphy canon thanks to its inclusion in a popular calligraphy model book in the early seventeenth century. Ironically, a couple of centuries later, it was during a fervent attack on the traditional canon that the *Eulogy* was elevated to become one of the best-known calligraphy models.

This book is a cultural biography of this stone, building upon the meticulous scholarship on the subject over the last millennium, recent archaeological finds in the region, my fieldwork at the site, and a reexamination of textual and visual materials ranging from the fifth century to modern times. The story I tell in the following pages, however, is by no means a transparent and straightforward one. The origin of the *Eulogy* is obscure and its reception controversial, and both demand a fresh look. More broadly, the inquiry into each episode of the stone's story reveals the diversity, complexity, and, sometimes, the paradox of the cultural practices that have been generalized as "Chinese calligraphy."

Historiography of Chinese Calligraphy

Traditionally, the history of Chinese calligraphy has often been divided into two phases: the art of writing and the art of the calligrapher. In the first phase, the artistic potential of writing—its visual form, color, materiality, and placement—was fully recognized and explored as early as the second millennium BCE, as demonstrated by extant oracle bone inscriptions, and continued to be experimented with in later engraved monuments. What distinguished Chinese calligraphy from its counterparts in other cultures, however, is the second phase, believed to have begun in the Eastern Han dynasty (25–220 CE), when calligraphy evolved to be a vehicle of self-expression, an embodiment of personal character, and a tool for social cohesion among cultural and political elites. After the fall of the Han, during the time of division, the art was refined and perfected in the south by Wang Xizhi, the protagonist of the folk story, and his son, Wang Xianzhi (344–386). The north, ruled by consecutive dynasties of nomadic origins, was believed by later scholars to have been left behind in the development of the art form until the reunification of China in the great Tang dynasty (618–907). The works of the Two Wangs (as they were later called), codified as the imperial standard, became the core of the classical tradition of Chinese calligraphy in subsequent centuries. Alternative approaches have emerged throughout the history of Chinese calligraphy, such as the monumental style of the Tang statesman and calligrapher Yan Zhenqing (709–784), the individualistic pursuits of the Northern Song literati, and the antiquarian calligraphers in the late Qing. However, it is believed that the core values initiated by the Two Wangs have remained unchanged. Such a belief sustains the transhistorical notion of *shufa* (literally, "the method of writing"), the Chinese word for calligraphy.

This received historical narrative, while persuasive in many other situations, is less so when trying to make sense of many of the episodes in the story of *Eulogy for Burying a Crane*. The date of the inscription falls between the lifetime of the Two

Wangs and the codification of their works in the seventh century. Its calligraphy, however, bears little sign of an inevitable trajectory in the historical progression, as was formerly believed. Instead, this and other contemporary specimens of writing reveal an unfamiliar picture of calligraphy during the Southern Dynasties. Furthermore, the canonization of the *Eulogy*'s calligraphy in later times entailed a wide range of contradictory discourses, disoriented debates, and curious artwork that does not easily fit into a linear historical narrative. These paradoxes in the story of the *Eulogy*, all demanding a contextualized interpretation, prompt us to rethink both the definition of calligraphy as a "fine art" and the collective term "calligrapher"; these terms' actual connotation and denotation can be revealed only in specific social and historical contexts.

The historiographic problems require us to reexamine historical writings on calligraphy that have often been cited as "evidence." For example, the Tang critic Zhang Huaiguan's (fl. early eighth century) *Evaluation of Calligraphy* (Shu duan, preface 727 CE) has been the major source for studying pre-Tang calligraphy. However, in addition to the textual corruptions that have inevitably taken place over the centuries, caution is called for on at least three other levels when using these sources. First, the text is a mixture of earlier sources and a later account of an earlier history and thus not free from Zhang's mid-Tang projection. Second, the text was edited and included in *Essential Records on Calligraphy* (Fashu yaolu, preface 847 CE) and may therefore reflect editor Zhang Yanyuan's (815–907) personal view—or even his own political agenda—in the mid-ninth century.[9] Third, as the original copy of *Essential Records on Calligraphy* has been long lost, its contents were collected and published in the late-eleventh-century *Ink Pond Compilation* (Mochi bian). That publication, whose text is now mixed with that of *Evaluation of Calligraphy*, was not free from the new aesthetic values and historical perceptions of the literati and antiquarian scholars at the time.[10] Given the layers of possible editing and interpretations, therefore, historians have to select carefully from the sources and read them critically, although their judgments often risk revealing their own self-serving biases.

Furthermore, an additional challenge for art historians is that these critical and historical discourses may be visualized and materialized in their own corpus of images, which, in turn, often present themselves as "visual evidence" to support the discourses themselves. Many of the extant Two Wangs specimens, for example, are the later products of the imaginations of the elusive fourth-century masters—yet they are still treated as visual evidence that sustains the historical narrative of the formation of the Two Wangs tradition. Moreover, to challenge the traditional canon, the calligrapher-theorists of the nineteenth century systematically formed their own canon, mostly of long-ignored anonymous ancient stone inscriptions, to justify their revisionist narratives. Thus, the visual materials we will encounter in this book are not value free and always require cautious examination.

Last but not least, the study of calligraphy—or any Chinese literati art—calls for special attention to be paid to the literary nature of the written sources. Appropriation, parody, and sarcasm, among many other literary and rhetorical devices, often appear in historical and critical writings and can even be present in works of calligraphy, creating endless intertextual games and constantly shifting meanings. Sometimes, a specific social context plays a decisive role in decoding the language. For example, when Dong Qichang, the arbiter of taste in his time, called something "authentic," he did not necessarily mean it thus. He may have just wanted to save face for a peer collector, support a business partner, or put forward his own art theory. His true motive can be carefully uncovered only in the context of the immediate social, economic, and political environment.

Terms for Calligraphy: The Character, Script Types, and Styles

A Chinese character can be imagined as a matrix of individual strokes. The character *yong* 永 is traditionally used to illustrate the fundamental elements (figure I.5); each stroke has its own name and is executed in a certain direction—generally speaking, from top to the bottom, like *shu* (3), *pie* (6 and 7), and *na* (8); or from left to right, like *heng* (2) or the slightly slanted *ti* (5). A hook, *gou* (4), is an exception in that it goes in the opposite direction. *Zhe* (2–3 and 5–6) or *wan* (3–4) is the name for one turn that joins two continuous strokes. The most diverse stroke is *dian* (1), or dot, which can go in any direction, depending on the structure and flow of writing. There are many variations of strokes, often with fancy names, which do not need to be elaborated upon for the purposes of our discussion.[11] The sample character *yong*, meaning "eternal," represents the basic form, or *duti zi*. Most Chinese characters, however, are combined of two or more compounds, which are called *pianpang*, or radicals.

To compose a character, the strokes are written down in a prescribed order (as shown in numbers 1 to 8). Sometimes the pattern (starting from either the top or the center part of the character) follows one's instinct, yet it is largely the result of conventions that must be memorized through consistent practice. Although the modulated quality of brush-written strokes is lost in modern pen writing, the directions and orders are still imposed in the classroom. It is in the dynamic balance between

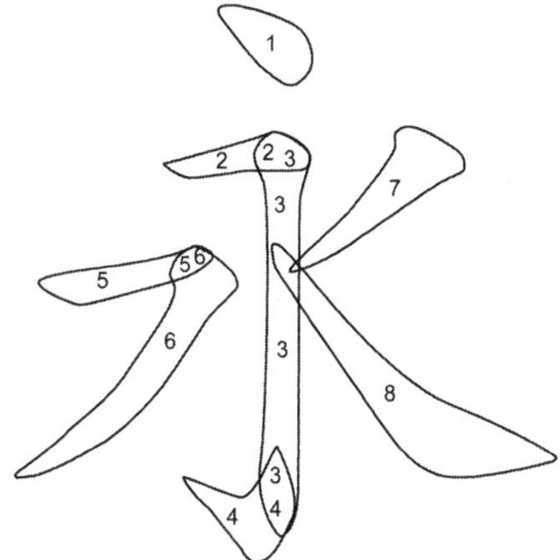

FIGURE I.5. Strokes of the Chinese character *yong*. The numbers indicate the sequence in which the individual strokes are made. Drawn by Li Bin.

all these elements and in the energy flow throughout the writing that the calligrapher demonstrates skill and personal style.

When studying the history of Chinese calligraphy, the first lesson always begins with script types (figure I.6):

Standard script (*kaishu, zhengshu,* or *zhenshu,* "true script") is the most commonly seen script for printed materials. The strokes are executed with consistent thickness and moderate variation. The compact and square structure gives the alternative name to the Chinese characters, *fangkuai zi,* or "square character," that every primary school student must memorize and practice.

Running script (*xingshu*) has an irregular composition, often tilting to one side, but still maintains the consistency of stroke width of standard script. Strokes vary in thickness and are sometimes connected to each other for faster writing. Because of its expressive power, running script was favored by aristocratic calligraphers and, later on, literati scholars.

Cursive script (*caoshu*) has the appearance of being created more quickly than running script and with many more lined strokes; sometimes, as in the given example, it is completed with one continuous move. The shapes of characters vary greatly, as strokes were often abbreviated or even omitted. The structure is open, making it easy to connect one character to the next, which creates an unbroken flow of writing. As opposed to what is commonly believed, however, the cursive character follows a quite strict formula.

Clerical script (*lishu*) is an archaic formal script type featuring squat composition, as if compressed vertically, and modulated strokes. Horizontal strokes are often elongated and ended with a distinctive wavy upward tail.

Seal script (*zhuanshu*), a more archaic formal script, is distinctive for its even thickness of strokes (often called "lines" for their wire-like quality). Unlike the clerical and standard scripts, which feature sharp and angular turns, seal script can be easily identified for its smooth and curvy turns. Its structure is regular and closed.

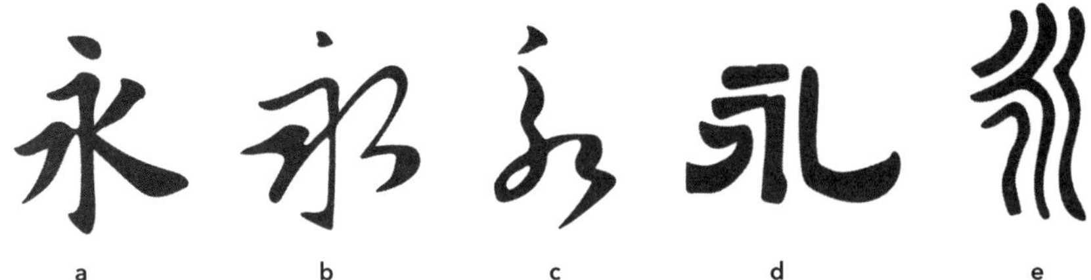

Figure I.6. Major script types of Chinese characters: (a) standard script, (b) running script, (c) cursive script, (d) clerical script, (e) seal script. Drawn by Mary Yang.

Here I have given the most straightforward definitions that are based on the form and without any historical connotations. Generally speaking, standard script was "evolved" from clerical script, and clerical from seal script, which came from more ancient scripts that trace back to oracle-bone inscriptions.[12] Nevertheless, the older script types were preserved and often reused in later times, juxtaposed with newer script types, for formal ritual purposes or artistic expression.[13] Cursive and running scripts evolved in parallel with the formal scripts. Historically, all these scripts were used for everyday writing, depending on the occasion. Today, however, besides standard script, which is still practiced by every student learning Chinese, other script types are reserved for calligraphy, either as a fine art or for decorative purposes. Technically, anyone could write in a self-fashioned "running" or "cursive" script, but they would immediately be dismissed for their script's lack of the "method," a schema of structure and brushwork formed over the course of history.

The seemingly objective categories of script types are inseparable from certain established historical styles (*ti*) that are often attributed to individual calligraphers. Even a beginner of calligraphy may recognize that, for example, the first character in figure I.6a is more or less in *Liu ti*, or the style of Liu Gongquan (778–865), the prominent Tang dynasty calligrapher whose writing specimens have served as the most popular models for school students. A more informed reader might speculate that the last character, in the seal script shown in figure I.6e, might be a modern reinterpretation of ancient script. It is these historical and cultural connotations that transform a piece of writing (*xiezi*) into a work of calligraphy (*shufa*).

It should be noted that these categories are artificial, made for the convenience of students of calligraphy. When we try to apply them to historical examples, we may encounter problems. The terminology may cause confusion for today's reader; the two terms *kaishu* and *lishu*, for example, were interchangeable when referring to contemporary standard script during certain time periods and were not differentiated by those who used them. More fundamentally, the "evolution" of scripts, more or less based on a biological analogy (an easily written script replaced an older and more difficult one because it was better adapted to social use), is often accepted at the cost of overlooking historical specificities and complexity. In the following discussion, we will use the script types for descriptive purposes, but the reader should be aware that these categories are themselves historical constructs and cannot be applied uncritically to our analysis.

Media for Calligraphy: Rubbing and Model Letters

The calligraphy works discussed in this book were executed in a wide range of media and materials. One major genre, and perhaps the most complex, is rubbing. The word "rubbing" encompasses many different types of artifacts. In the field of calligraphy, there are two major categories: *taben* (rubbing copies), which are made directly from stone inscriptions (collectively called *bei*, or "stele"); and *fatie* (model letters), which replicate ink-written works (generally called *tie*, or "letter").[14] (The word "letter" is derived from the earliest collected calligraphy works, which are often in the form of short handwritten messages.[15] Unlike self-titled steles like the *Eulogy*, most of the "letters" bear no original title and thus are traditionally named after the first few characters of the text.) Whereas *taben* are mainly for documenting historical materials (and later for calligraphy study) and are also found in other cultures, *fatie* are intended to reproduce calligraphic works and thus can be treated as a unique kind of publication.

To make *fatie*, the original (a handwritten work, a tracing copy, or sometimes even another rubbing) first needed to be carved into a stone (or woodblock, in some cases). The process entailed at least four major steps: first, the original was traced on a thin piece of paper (*goumo*); then the other side of the tracing copy was covered with cinnabar (*tianzhu*), creating a reversed image; before it dried, the cinnabar image was impressed on the surface of the stone (*shangshi*); and finally, the stonecutter chiseled away the cinnabar characters (*tuizao*), creating an intaglio (an incised carving).[16] This was followed by the rubbing process (which was the same for making *taben*): a wet piece of paper was laid on the stone and smoothed and pounded until the paper was pressed into the engraved strokes; ink was then carefully applied to the paper. The ink covered only the space around the characters, which remained as blank paper, thus creating a negative black-and-white image.[17] A set of rubbings could be cut, trimmed, and mounted in the form of a book or album, and several volumes could be placed in a case to create a multivolume compendium.

Critics and connoisseurs of rubbings are known for their meticulous studies and sometimes heated debates on the authenticity of the original ink-written works, accuracy of reproduction, chronology and lineage of rubbings from different times, appraisal of the *shanben* (better or earlier editions), and their ability to distinguish between the rubbings from *chongke* (the recarved inscription, if the original is lost), *fanke* (the replicated inscription, if the original still exists), and *weike* (a forged inscription).[18] Because of limited access to rubbing objects, art historians must rely heavily on the judgment of rubbing specialists. The latter's knowledge is not always reliable, however. Before the widespread use of photography and digital images, such appraisals were often based on specialists' comparisons with what they remembered of other examples or on brief "cheating notes" about the physical traits of datable rubbings. Furthermore, in most cases, the absolute date of a rubbing is almost impossible to know. To my knowledge, it is unusual for a rubbing maker to add a date and signature on a rubbing. Most rubbings, including those considered in the present study, are dated to a certain early time (like so-called *Song ben*, or Song dynasty editions) merely according to collectors' colophons or seals, which themselves are often problematic.

Dimensions of This Study

In reconstructing the biography of the legendary *Eulogy*, my approach is largely based on my visual analysis of transmitted works, including both brush-written calligraphy and ink rubbings, in the context of archaeological materials and a critical reading of historical writings. This book delves into issues in the established field of calligraphy, such as the meaning and context of individual calligraphic works, the problem of canon formation, and other historical dimensions of calligraphic practices and discourses. Following a small number of exemplary studies of Chinese calligraphy in English, as well as much more extensive scholarship in China and Japan, I opt to focus on micro-historical case studies and sociopolitical interpretations.

This book also explores the gray zone between calligraphy and what may be called the visual culture of writing. Calligraphy is fundamentally writing. The manner of displaying and viewing writing has dictated whether it is deserving of the term "calligraphy"; this, in turn, has permeated the very fabric of everyday life and profoundly shaped social and psychological spaces in traditional and modern China. This issue has been explored in an edited volume, *Writing and Materiality in China*, which includes Wu Hung's insightful article on rubbings.[19] Robert E. Harrist's research into *moya*, or cliff-carving inscriptions, provides a new perspective that combines the history of writing/calligraphy and "place studies."[20] Craig Clunas's recent publications concern the visuality of writing/calligraphy in Ming society.[21] These studies, among many others that broaden and reveal historical issues that have often been muted or tamed, have informed the present study.

This book deals with two different kinds of "history" of the *Eulogy*. It begins by situating the *Eulogy* within the literary and visual cultures of the early sixth century, recovering a long-forgotten memory once crystallized in the monument. Concentrating on the symbolic nature of the inscription, it analyzes metaphoric writings and imitative genres in Chinese literary history and reconsiders the status of the *Eulogy* as a work of public writing intended to transform the island of Jiaoshan into a virtual tomb. The efficacy of displaying writings developed in conjunction with Daoist beliefs at the time and added a new dimension to the culture of Chinese calligraphy. Careful reading of its text and visual form suggests that the inscription was erected by a Daoist community to mourn their suffering during a period of imperial proscription.

The following chapters trace the afterlife of the *Eulogy* by focusing on two pivotal and lively moments in Chinese cultural history: the late Northern Song (960–1127) and the late Ming (1368–1664). Historical records, colophons, and art criticism on the rediscovery of the stone of the *Eulogy* and other ancient artifacts during the eleventh century were generated by the rise of antiquarianism, a mixture of fascination with antiquity and a deep cultural anxiety on the part of Northern Song literati scholars. Paradoxical intellectual attitudes regarding the *Eulogy*, represented by the conflicting views among major scholars of the time, shaped later writings on the

Eulogy and many other canonical works. Recarving and replication of the inscription ironically expressed the search for antiquity, and the boundary between the original, the copy, and the forgery becomes blurred.

The canonization of the *Eulogy*'s calligraphy through its reproduction and transmission in the complex late Ming cultural milieu was characterized by a dynamic interaction between continuing antiquarianism, commercialization of model-letters publication, and experimentation in calligraphy in the transition to a modern visual culture. Interest in the *Eulogy* resurged thanks to a burgeoning taste among the urban elite for leisure, spectacle, and a taste for strangeness. A close examination of model-letters productions in the context of contemporary print culture reveals how the *Eulogy* and other historical calligraphic works became accessible to a larger audience of diverse social classes and gained canonic status. Against this background, elite theory and practice in calligraphy interacted with contemporary popular culture.

The book concludes with a review of the material history of the *Eulogy* stone from the late seventeenth century to our own time, in which investigation, restoration, and enshrinement of the inscription's fragments again sparked antiquarian interest and imperial cultural propaganda, leading to further appropriation and commodification of the *Eulogy* among calligraphy theorists and practitioners who encompass traditional literati circles and the early twentieth-century art market in Shanghai, as well as to archaeological excavation, cultural promotion, and media consumption of the *Eulogy* through the last decades.

Altogether, this study explores the historical construct—which is still ongoing—of Chinese calligraphy through the microscopic lens of an individual stone monument. It by no means offers a comprehensive survey of calligraphy history; for example, I do not discuss every important historical period, such as the Tang dynasty (618–907). The noncontinuous timeline, partly reflecting the nature of the story of the stone itself, may help us escape the traditional linear narrative and seek an alternative contextualization of calligraphic works and events. To do so, however, we may first need to unlearn and defamiliarize ourselves from many prescribed notions, concepts, and historical narratives about calligraphy. One advantage of the present case study is that *Eulogy for Burying a Crane*, the strange tombstone for a bird, has consistently revealed its paradoxes to viewers, readily inviting controversies and problematizing what we have learned about calligraphy, the most revered art in China.

CHAPTER 1

Inscribing the Island

In 2018, there were about 780,000 visitors to the small island of Jiaoshan.[1] Many of them were calligraphy lovers who came to worship the stone carving of *Eulogy for Burying a Crane.* Housed in a traditional-style building in the garden of the Jiaoshan Stone Inscription Museum, the five fragments are pieced together in a kind of faux cliff intended to approximate the appearance of the original site (plate 2, figure 1.1). To help the visitors see the characters in the dim lighting, each stroke is filled in with white plaster.

Despite its dilapidated status and large size (approximately 235 × 204 cm), it is clear that the rectangular layout was like that of stone epitaphs from medieval China. However, unlike the characters on those artifacts (or those on freestanding stone steles, which are carefully polished before the writing is added), the characters were carved directly into the rough surface of the unquarried rock. The calligrapher adapted the characters to the irregularity of the stone, making some larger than others and avoiding a strict regularity of columns or rows. Whereas some characters show clear strokes, others display odd shapes that make the viewer wonder if they reveal the original brushwork or are rather the result of natural erosion or numerous campaigns of recarving and alteration. Still, it can be ascertained that the strokes were carved from the two edges, creating a wide-open V-shaped groove on the stone, as shown in figure 1.2.

These fragments, traditionally numbered one through five (hereafter noted as F1–F5, as marked on the rubbing in figure 1.1), vary in size, shape, and texture. F1 (plate 3), the smallest stone, has lost most of its characters and shows many signs of scraping and other abrasions. F2 (plate 4) is rectangular and has a relatively smooth surface; the carving of the characters on this fragment is shallower than that on the other stones, which makes some scholars suspect that it was a later recarving. F4

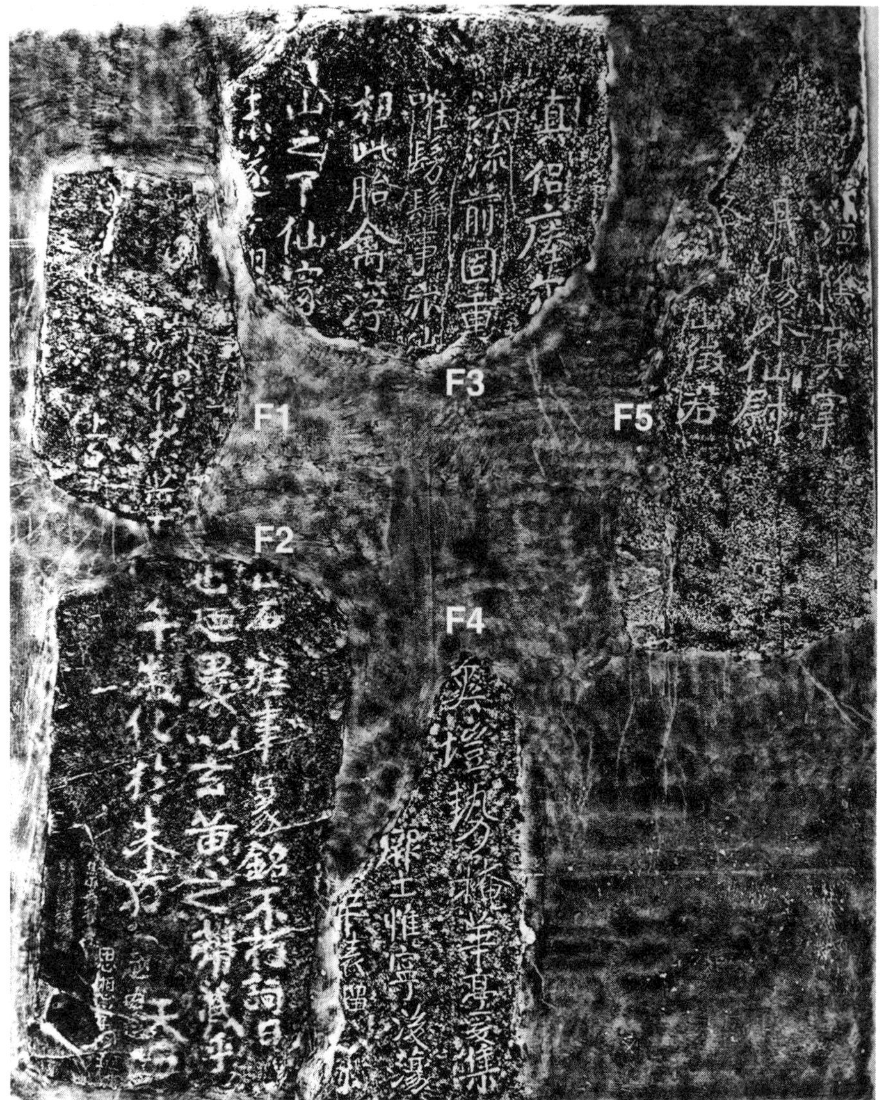

FIGURE 1.1. Overview of *Eulogy for Burying a Crane*. Ink rubbing, approx. 235 × 204 cm. Courtesy of Jiaoshan Stone Inscription Museum. The numbers F1–F5 refer to the extant fragments.

(plate 6) presents the same problem and has the most irregular surface, marked by several deep indentations. Characters are deeply carved and possibly the result of late modification. F3 (plate 5) and F5 (plate 7) appear quite different in texture from the other fragments. Numerous tiny pockmarks on their surfaces (figure 1.2) show the effects of natural erosion that are often found on limestone (similar to those on the porous Taihu stones that adorn traditional Chinese gardens). Although it is reported that the inscription was heavily damaged after it was removed from the water in 1713 (see conclusion), F3 and F5 seem well preserved; the location and shapes of dents and pores match their traces (referred to as "stone flowers" by

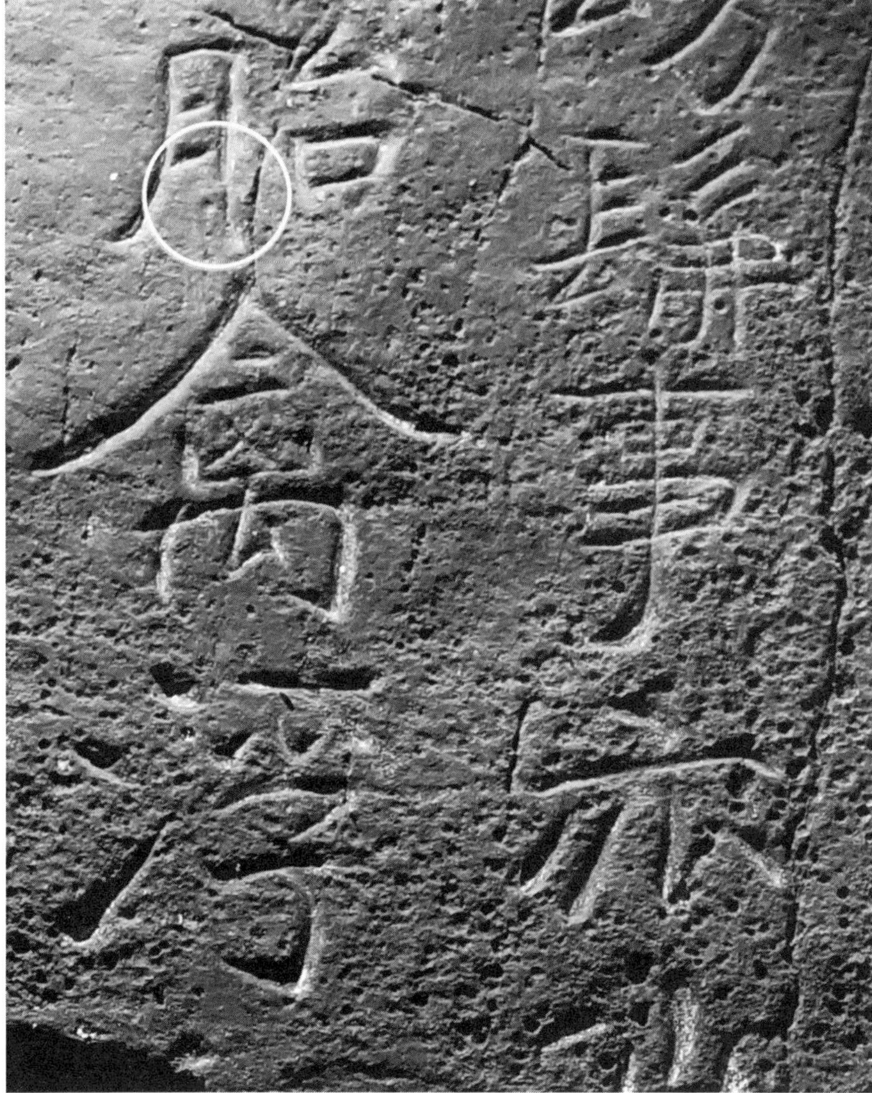

FIGURE 1.2. Detail of Fragment no. 3 of *Eulogy for Burying a Crane*. The circle indicates the worn strokes discussed in the text.

rubbing connoisseurs) left on the early rubbing (figure 1.3; see full image in figure C.9), which is arguably dated to the Song dynasty.[2]

Even so, the engraved strokes are hardly intact. Take the example of the character *tai* 胎, which appears complete and crisp on the rubbing. On today's stone, however, the bottom of the *shu* stroke in the *yue* 月 radical (figure 1.2, marked with a circle) is almost worn away. Oddly enough, the top section of the same stroke is still deeply carved, even lower than the worn area—very likely a result of rechiseling. The modification even causes the entire *yue* radical to pull away a little from the right radical. Looking closer at the *yue* radical, one can find traces of modification in the double

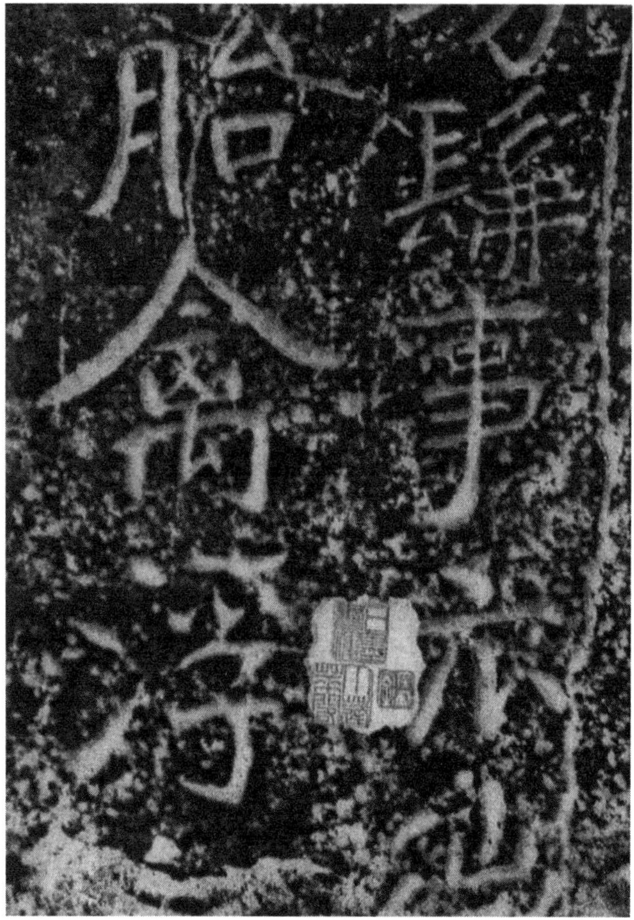

FIGURE 1.3. Rubbing of *Eulogy for Burying a Crane*. Detail. Palace Museum, Beijing. From *Zhongguo meishu quanji: Shufa zhuanke bian* 2:142.

lines at the bottom of the *pie* stroke (figure 1.2). Whereas these possible modifications (and even alterations) may not affect our reading of the text, we shall proceed with great caution in the discussion of the "original" stone of the *Eulogy*—indeed, of any original stones of famous monuments from ancient times. Instead, our analysis of the calligraphy will be based mainly on the rubbing images, even though they are not free from similar problems.

The Text: Reconstruction and Translation

The ninety total characters on the extant stones (including twelve partly damaged characters) constitute only about two-thirds of the original inscription (plate 8; early accounts report characters in yellow that no longer survive on today's fragments). Other characters in the chart were reconstructed by Zhang Chao (1625–1694) and Wang Shihong, the latter of whom combined the characters extant in his time with an earlier reconstruction of the text, said to have been made before the stones completely fell into the river (see the concluding chapter for details). Some characters (noted in the translation below and also marked in red in plate 8) were added to make the text coherent, but these were pure speculation.[3] The inscription reads from left to right, a format unusual but not unique in traditional Chinese writing. Full of literary allusions and tropes, the text is cryptic to modern readers without annotations, and the fragmentary status only increases the challenge of reading:

Eulogy for Burying a Crane, with Preface
Composed by the Perfected Recluse of Mount Huayang[4]
in the calligraphy of the Woodcutter of Mount Shanghuang[5]
No one knows the age of this crane.
I acquired him in the year *renchen*[6] in Huating.[7]
He transformed in the year *jiawu* at Zhufang.[8]
Did Heaven not allow me to soar about the cosmos as I wish?[9]
Why take away the crane so quickly?
I therefore wrapped him in [Daoist ceremonial] black and yellow silk[10]
and buried him at the foot of this mountain.
The immortals do not hide . . .[11]
. . . my . . .
I then set up a stone to honor his virtues
and carved a eulogy so that the crane will not be forgotten.
The eulogy reads,
To judge the physiognomy of the "viviparous bird,"[12]
[The immortal] Master Fuqiu wrote the *Crane Classic*.[13]
I do not wish to say anything more.
You [the crane] have hidden the spirit.[14]
At the Thunder Gate you departed the drum;[15]
on the *huabiao* pillars you left behind your shadow.[16]
The meaning is obscure and subtle;
these events are elusive and mysterious.[17]
Where is it that you will go?
Released and transformed[18] . . .
to the west bamboo grove, the sacred place.[19]
The land is quiet and peaceful.[20]
Behind flows the raging torrent;
in front stand firmly the double-layered gates.[21]
The left side reaches to the Kingdom of Cao;[22]
the right side is fenced with a thorny gate.[23]
The shady side of the mountain is dry and lofty.
The height of the place overlooks Huating [the crane's home].[24]
Therefore, I have gathered my perfected companions,[25]
buried you here, and written this eulogy.

The Recluse of Mount Jiang[26]
The Outer Immortal Commandant of Danyang[27]
The Perfected Steward of Jiangyin.[28]
(1A)[29]

At first glance, the literary form of the *Eulogy* text is no different from that of countless medieval epitaphs surviving today. It opens with the title and the name of the author (though the calligrapher is rarely mentioned in other cases). Next comes a prose biography of the deceased, here the crane (lines 4–10). The prose section is followed by a eulogy in tetrasyllabic verse praising the bird by likening it to notable cranes of antiquity (lines 15–24). The *Eulogy* closes with the description of its landscape setting (lines 25–33)—an indispensable part of an epitaph to announce the safe and auspicious burial location to both the living and the underground world. What would be unusual for a common epitaph is the names of three witnesses who presumably attended the burial (lines 36–38).

Traditionally, scholars have read this poem as evidence that Daoists actually buried and mourned a pet crane at the foot of Jiaoshan. Based on this assumption, they have spilled much ink decoding place names and aliases in the text, confident that—in spite of its strangeness—the carving was a *real* epitaph for a *real* crane. This assumption, however, more or less overlooks the place of the *Eulogy* within the history of early medieval Chinese literature and material and visual culture.

The complex allusions and poetic language mark the text as part of a tradition of writing about birds and other animals as a way to metaphorically express feelings about human misfortunes. The "epitaph" also appropriates medieval funerary objects in multiple dimensions; the text may be read as a literary parody imitating mortuary writing, while the physical form, though appropriating that of entombed medieval epitaphs, distinguishes itself from a real epitaph by its public visibility. Furthermore, the placement of this unprecedented epitaph near the base of Jiaoshan took advantage of the topography of the island and transformed it into a symbolic monument.

Imagery of the Crane

Cranes are a family of bird that includes many species, but the most distinctive kind, or at least the type most often represented in Chinese visual art, is *Grus japonensis*—*danding he* in Chinese—the red-crowned crane. As its Latin name suggests, its habitat is in northeastern Asia. This is a tall, regal bird with shiny white plumage trimmed with black feathers along its primaries (the wing's outer flight feathers). It has a black face and throat and a striking vermillion cap on the top of its head. These large, beautiful birds are known for their elegant dance and clear singing. They migrate south in winter. Such a seasonal appearance must have made people wonder about the remote country they traveled from and associate the crane with the otherworld. Such

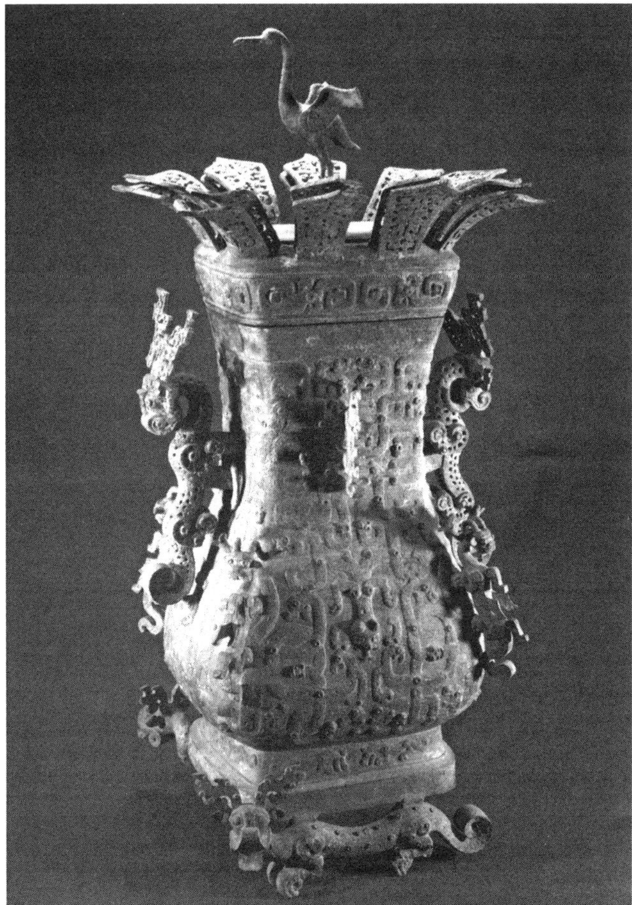

FIGURE 1.4. Bronze *hu* vessel. Eastern Zhou dynasty. 118 cm (height). From Xinzheng, Henan. Palace Museum, Beijing. From *Zhongguo meishu quanji: Gongyi meishu bian* 5: plate 13.

an imagination might have been materialized in the dancing crane atop an exquisite bronze *hu* (figure 1.4) dating to the sixth century BCE.[30] For the *hu*'s creator, who lived in the heartland of China, the exotic bird, like the mythical beasts crouching on the side of the vessel, might have represented a mysterious place where immortals were also believed to live.

On the other hand, cranes might have been kept as pets, since they are fairly easy to tame and highly intelligent. Since time immemorable, they have wandered in palaces and gardens, turning the mundane world into an immortal land, and have become the subject of poems and prose. An early visual representation can be found in a literal "burial" of cranes (actually bronze sculptures) that was discovered in the necropolis of Qin Shihuangdi, the First Emperor of the Qin (r. 220–210 BCE).[31] These bronze birds, along with geese, ducks, and other birds, appear to be real-life building decorations. However, buried with the emperor, perhaps they were believed to exert their magical power even in the afterworld.

The imagery of immortals riding the crane can be traced to Eastern Han writings, if not earlier, and is certainly attributable to the spread of Daoism and the impact of Daoist beliefs. *Biographies of Exemplary Immortals* (Liexian zhuan), the oldest surviving text of its kind, records the legendary Wangzi Qiao (ca. 565–ca. 549 BCE), also known as Prince Jin, a son of King Ling (d. 545 BCE) of the Zhou dynasty (ca. 1046–256 BCE), who left his home at an early age to seek the immortal way. When his family sent a messenger to find him in the mountains, Wangzi Qiao told them that he would present himself on the seventh day of the seventh month on the top of Mount Goushi (in today's Yanshi Henan). When that moment arrived, the biography text recounts,

> [Wangzi Qiao,] riding a white crane, appeared on top of the mountain. People were able to see him but not able to reach him, as Qiao was waving his hand to greet the people. [The scene lasted for] a few days before he departed.[32] (1B)

Tomb decorations from the fifth and sixth centuries that depict immortals riding on the back of a crane might reference this story. In one scene, discovered in a painted tomb (figure 1.5), a slim immortal, surrounded by flying clouds or currents of mystic energy and wearing a strange tall hat, rides on a large white crane (the figure has his own wings too—perhaps a reference to *yuren*, the mythic winged man in Daoist lore). Although there is no red cap on the head of the crane, its wings and legs are marked with touches of red color. Holding a long staff and turning back, the immortal may be waiting for the soul of the tomb's occupant to follow his direction to the otherworld. The tomb's location in today's northeastern China, then the northern border of the Korean Goguryeo Kingdom (37 BCE–668 CE), may be more than coincidental, as the region is the major habitat for red-crowned cranes.[33]

This imagery of a crane-riding immortal was part of the lore inherited by the *Eulogy*'s author; the latter's wish to "soar about the cosmos" (line 7 of the *Eulogy* text), for example, was derived from the old beliefs. And the allusion to the ancient immortal Ding Lingwei riding the crane over a *huabiao* pillar (line 21) in many ways resembles the Wangzi Qiao story.[34] Nevertheless, the place of cranes in Daoist mythology should not deflect attention from a different role played by the crane in early Chinese literature. More than other creatures, birds and their sounds were often used since antiquity to symbolize human feelings, especially those of sorrow and regret. On the words of a dying man, Zengzi (505–436 BCE), one of Confucius's disciples, made a famous analogy with birds: "When a bird is about to die, its notes are mournful; when a man is about to die, his words are good."[35] An association between birds and the expression of human sorrow was developed in the literature of the Han dynasty, especially in the genre of *fu*, or rhapsody.[36] Famous examples include Jia Yi's (200–168 BCE) "Rhapsody on the Owl" (Funiao fu), which, though ostensibly about the bird, was intended to express the sorrows and political dissatisfactions of the author when he was banished from the court.[37]

Despite its multivalent meanings and associations in early literature, the crane's association with human sorrow seems more intense than any other avian subject, in

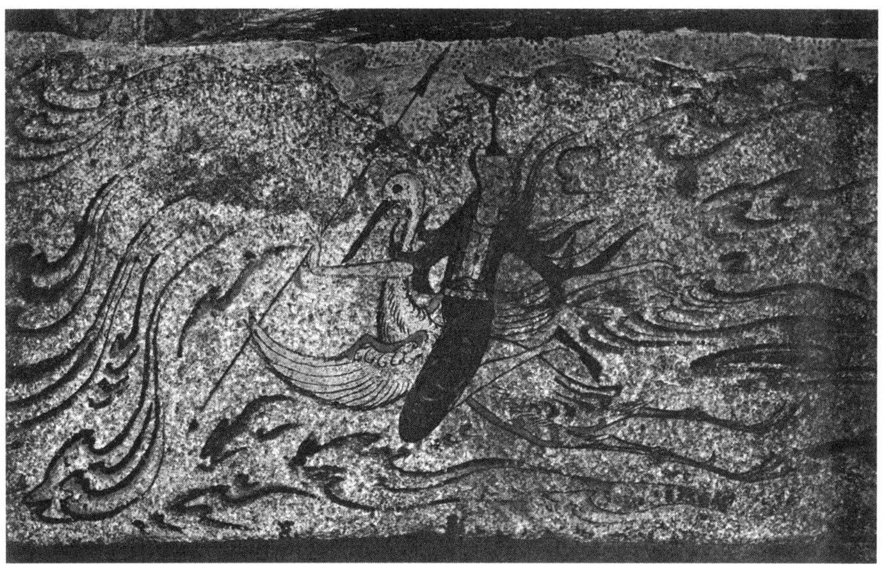

FIGURE 1.5. Immortal riding on a crane. Fifth century. Tomb mural at Tonggou, Jilin. From *Zhongguo meishu quanji: Huihua bian* 12: plate 82.

particular in writings from the Wei and Jin periods (220–420), when themes of anxiety and loneliness caused by political isolation were popular.[38] Cao Zhi (192–232), a famous literary prodigy, wrote two works on cranes, "Pair of Cranes" (Shuang he) and "Rhapsody on a White Crane" (Baihe fu). The closing lines of the latter describe the painful isolation of a crane:

> [The crane] sorrows at betraying his nature,
> lamenting about leaving the flock and staying alone.
> He flees [from predators] and roosts in hiding all the time,
> crying sadly and folding his feathers.[39]
> (1C)

According to many later explications, what Cao Zhi expresses here are feelings of anxiety and desperation induced by his tense relationship with his brother, Cao Pi (187–226), the founder of the Wei Kingdom (220–265).[40] The poet's anxiety was also tinged with a longing for personal freedom:

> Hoping that the net will come loose,
> Then he can fly into the far distance.[41]
> (1D)

Cao Zhi's allusion to a net recalls the historical fact that because of their beauty and intelligence, cranes were often captured and put into cages as pets, becoming, in turn, symbols of humans subjected to external restraints. According to an anecdote in *A New Account of Tales of the World* (Shishuo xinyu), in order to keep a pair of pet cranes from escaping, the scholar-monk Zhidun (314–366) clipped their pinions. Responding to the reproaches implicit in the birds' cries, he finally allowed their feathers to grow back and then set the birds free.[42] This anecdote became a popular allusion used by writers in later periods, perhaps including the author of the *Eulogy*, to evoke the freedom and dignity they desired but rarely obtained.

Although they lived in somewhat more settled political environments, many writers of the Southern Dynasties continued to use the crane as a symbol of spiritual freedom. Examples of this can be found in works such as Bao Zhao's (414–466) "Rhapsody on Dancing Cranes" (Wuhe fu), Shen Yue's (441–513) "Hearing a Crane Crying at Night" (Wen ye he), and Yu Xin's (513–581) "In Praise of Cranes" (He zan), to name a few.[43] The theme of the mournful, crying crane reappears in literary works in the Tang and later periods.[44]

Eulogy for Burying a Crane was not the first example of mortuary writing dedicated to a crane. Zhan Fangsheng (fl. early fifth century), a poet of the Eastern Jin (317–420), composed "Dirge for a Crane" (Diao he wen), which informs the *Eulogy* in so many ways that it is worthy of full translation. This passage is dedicated to a lonely crane that was probably dying in captivity. It starts with a preface:

> On a long night in the deep winter, I suddenly heard a crane singing in front of the stairway. The pure and sharp sound penetrated the chilly wind. The sorrow mounted as the bitter atmosphere was felt. I listened carefully and was deeply moved before the song ended. Then I composed a text to lament it. (1E)

Then the author continues to imagine the life of the crane using the form of a dirge:

> Here is a marvelous bird from the other end of the sea,
> born with the vigorous pneuma.
> He can vie with a phoenix and fly with it together,
> and has a spirit superior to other feathered creatures.
> He has washed himself in the pure ice and frost,
> and uttered a unique sound from the deepest wetland.[45]
> He has pecked the remaining grains from the "wild court,"[46]
> and drunk water from the remote river.
> He has rested the feathers when seeing clouds spreading,
> and departed again for a journey, facing toward the morning glow.
> (1F)

After praising the divine bird's past glories, the author turns to the bird's suffering when it loses its freedom:

> After escaping from the Wangzi [Qiao]'s sacred reins,
> he was captured by the gardener with a rope;

After leaving the immortal friends in caves of the elixirs [*danxue*],
he has to stay in the court with other common birds.
He wants to soar about the sky as he wishes,
and is still frightened when he turns to look at the nets and cages.
In the deep of the night his heart is heavier,
And he begins to sing when the sharp frost sets in.
Although he has strong feathers allowing him to soar in the sky,
now he is not different from other birds.
Although he has a long life like the mythical *mingling* tree,
he is withering like autumn foliage.
It is not the bird itself that deserves my sorrow.
It is fate itself that stirred me to write [this poem].[47]
(1G)

Due to the lack of historical information, it is difficult to speculate on the context in which Zhan Fangsheng wrote. The loneliness and desperation of the crane can only be read metaphorically as the physical or psychological state of the man, as Zhan makes clear at the end of his dirge. Furthermore, to anyone familiar with the Chinese poetic tradition, the tone of the dirge is unmistakably derived from Qu Yuan's (ca. 340–ca. 278 BCE) classical poem "Encountering Sorrow" (Li sao), which conveys an exiled poet's desolation and yet unchanged loyalty and dignity.[48]

Seen in the context of a rich literary tradition of writing focused on cranes, *Eulogy for Burying a Crane* no longer stands alone as a literary composition dedicated to a bird. The imagery of a dead crane echoes the description of the captive crane and the dying birds in the works noted above, in particular in "Dirge for a Crane." It draws from the same storehouse of allusions and symbols used in earlier works, which often express human sorrows.[49] Thus, when understood within the literary tradition of writing about cranes and the concomitant use of allusions, the text of the *Eulogy* can be read less as a eulogy for a real bird than as a literary concoction inspired by the author's feelings and personal history. The latter is revealed in two emotional lines in the *Eulogy* (lines 7–8):

Did Heaven not allow me to soar about the cosmos as I wish?
Why take away my crane so quickly?

While the rest of the text seems to concern the bird and the burial, these two lines, echoing the ending of Zhan Fangsheng's work, hint at another subtext altogether: the fate not of the birds but of the subjects who mourned them.

We will return to the symbolism of the *Eulogy* and the possible historical event behind it soon. For now, the dense literary references and the poetic sentiment in the lines of the *Eulogy* prompt us to a more urgent question: Is it a real epitaph? To better answer this question, we need to consider both the textual and material aspects of epitaph in its historical context.

Epitaph as Literary Genre

The character *ming* in the title of *Eulogy for Burying a Crane* (Yi he ming) is a short form of *muzhiming*, or inscription on marking the tomb—the Chinese equivalent of the Western epitaph. A literal translation of the *Eulogy* could thus be "Inscription on Burying a Crane." More precisely and narrowly defined, *ming* refers only to the verse section of the epitaph text (the prose section is *xu*, or "preface," as we read in the *Eulogy* text). At any rate, the term *ming* or *muzhiming* has a double meaning: it designates not only a highly conventionalized genre of writing but also the artifact on which such a text is carved. A close examination of its textual and physical form reveals that though *Eulogy for Burying a Crane* evidently takes the form of a medieval epitaph, it distinguishes itself at both levels from real epitaphs as an *imitative* work. The interpretation of the work should therefore go far beyond a literal reading.

It should be noted, however, that the English translation of "epitaph" for the Chinese term *muzhiming* may be misleading, since unlike their Western counterparts, which were displayed in cemeteries or churches, epitaphs in medieval China were not put on view for public reading but were buried *inside* tombs.[50] The origin of these entombed artifacts remains unclear. Based on archaeological finds, scholars have traced the prototype of entombed epitaphs to the Qin dynasty (221–206 BCE), when bricks and tiles inscribed with the names of the deceased were placed in the graves of prisoner-workers.[51] These inscriptions were used to identify the bodies for later reburial. Another important precursor to the entombed epitaph was the miniature stele found inside tombs during the Western Jin (265–316 CE).[52] In the following century, the custom of burying epitaphs was known in southern China, though the forms of these objects were different, usually consisting of inscribed bricks or cheap stones; the writing and carving was very casual and thus lack any ceremonial significance.[53]

By the end of the fifth century, epitaphs were consistently placed in tombs. A more elaborated form of epitaph was developed, carved on square or rectangular limestone slabs. The texts on these slabs were much longer than earlier epitaphs and normally documented the family history and career of the deceased in a formulaic pattern of prose and verse—the form from which the *Eulogy* derived. Epitaphs were usually placed in the underground tomb corridor near the tomb chamber or in front of the coffins. Once the tombs were sealed, the readership of the entombed epitaphs was restricted to the world of the spirits, and texts helped the deceased to resume their identity in the afterlife.[54]

In the south, the best examples of elaborate epitaphs are those made for the imperial families. The epitaphs of the prince of Guiyang, Xiao Rong (472–501), dated 502, and his wife, Wang Qishao (473–514), dated 514, are typical.[55] Both have lengthy texts (528 and 696 characters, respectively) carved in standard script in an elegant calligraphic style. In the north, then ruled by the Tuoba Wei dynasty (386–535, known also as the Northern Wei), the making of epitaphs was taken to another level. These epitaphs incorporated elements from other tomb artifacts and gained a more important ritual function. The calligraphy and carving is highly refined, and the text is sometimes protected by an inscribed ornamental cover.[56]

On the other hand, by the sixth century, epitaph writing had become such a mature literary genre that it often occupies an independent section in noted writers' anthologies.[57] Most texts of this category bear titles such as "*Muzhiming* of . . ." (followed by the name of the deceased). Normally, the text consists of a prose introduction setting forth the genealogy, place of origin, career, and notable achievements or virtues of the deceased; this section is followed by tetrasyllabic verses that elaborate on the information in the preface, often praising the dead in effusive language. Take, for example, the epitaph for Xiao Rong. The text was composed by Ren Fang (460–508), one of the most noted writers of his time. The preface elaborates on Xiao Rong's family history and career; this is followed by an account of his death:[58]

> In his thirtieth year the prince died on the twelfth day of the twelfth month in the third year of the Yongyuan era [501 CE]. In the second year of the Zhongxing era [502 CE] he was posthumously granted the titles "executive assistant" and "gentleman attendant at the Yellow Gate." His August Highness with divine martial prowess dispelled the disorder and greatly benefited the people; [with these actions] the grievances and shame [of the past] were cleansed and the posthumous glory was granted.[59] (1H)

The preface then rephrases an imperial decree to commemorate Xiao Rong and concludes with the execution of the epitaph, including its formal title and the author's name and official title:

> On the *yimao* day, the first day of the eleventh month in the first year of the Tianjian era [502], when the year-star was in *renwu*, he was entombed near Mt. Yipi [according to proper] ritual. Alarmed that bronze and stone can become corrupted, and hills and valley do not stay put, we venture to compose an account of his lingering conduct, [and place] a model inscription in his chamber by the [Yellow] Springs.
>
> The entombed epitaph inscription of the Liang dynasty's late cavalier attendant-in-ordinary and grand general controlling the armies, the prince of Guiyang, [Xiao] Rong, posthumously canonized as the Guileless Prince.
>
> Composed in accordance with imperial decree by the probationary gentlemen of the interior for the Ministry of Personal in the Secretariat, Minister Ren Fang. (1I)

The lengthy and elaborate *ming* eulogizing the deceased begins with the following lines:

Oh! How brilliant is the imperial lineage!
It enjoys an exclusive claim on the excellence of former kings.
[Its destiny foretold in] green charts and cinnabar records,
[And manifest on] gold writing strips in jade cases.
The royal shrines have multiplied, blessed by the heavenly order,
and the [imperial] enterprise flourished under Ji Chang.[60]
[Its members] continued ceaselessly to be written about in cinnabar,[61]
[Their reputations] are stainless and long lasting.
Illustrious, indeed, and resolute,
[Xiao Rong] opened a wide path to spread wisdom.
Exhausting [his study of the] lacquered documents of literary arts,
He completed his learning [by mastering everything] that has been
written on silk.[62]
He was affectionate toward his filial brothers;
There is no room for gossip [in his family].
(1J)

As part of a text used in a funeral ritual, these lines of the epitaph adhere to a formal rhythm and display deliberately archaic and extremely ornate language (barely reflected in the plain English translation) appropriate to their solemn function.

There is no doubt that in form, *Eulogy for Burying a Crane* follows conventions detectable in Xiao Rong's epitaph: the self-referential title indicates that it was an epitaph for a crane; the preface recounts the life and death of the bird; and the rhymed *ming* (in its narrow definition) eulogizes the deceased crane and expresses the sorrow of the living. Nevertheless, there are some differences between conventional epitaphs and the one expressed in the *Eulogy.* First, the subject matter is odd; to my knowledge, there was no known tradition of erecting epitaphs for animals in any period of Chinese history. Second, the rich literary symbolism and allusions would not have been considered suitable for the formal language of epitaph writing, which, although highly decorative, was not supposed to stir the literary imagination. Last—and most important—is the lyrical language and self-expressional nature of the text, which is subtly but profoundly different from the ritualized expression in an actual epitaph.

What we encounter in the *Eulogy*, thus, is a work of parody, a phenomenon not unusual in literary works from the fifth and sixth centuries. Parodies were based on the vocabulary and form of established genres, especially those usually reserved for formal ritual use, but they were enlivened by new meanings, satirical or not.[63] Zhan Fangsheng's "Dirge for a Crane," cited above, easily falls into such a category; his imitation of the mortuary genre of a dirge makes sense only when understood as an expression of mourning for the fate of human beings. This combination of parody and symbolism can also be found in the *Eulogy*—a written parody appropriating the form of a medieval epitaph.

Transcending the Epitaph

As a parodic epitaph, *Eulogy for Burying a Crane* was not alone among sixth-century writings. "Inscription on Thinking of the Past" (Si jiu ming), a work by Yu Xin, the most prominent literary figure of his time, seems to have been written in the same manner. Identical in its formal structure to an epitaph, this work is ostensibly a lament for the author's dead friend Xiao Yong (d. 558), a nobleman of the Liang imperial family who served the Northern Zhou (557–581) after the Liang dynasty (502–557) collapsed. The piece begins conventionally with a "preface":

> In the year of *sheti* [the year of the tiger], when the star is located in *guoshou* [early in the fifth month], the marquis Guanning of the Liang, Xiao Yong, died. Oh, how sorrowful it is! How a man's annihilation can be avoided [even if his name is inscribed on] the metal and stone [monument]? How the laments of the gentlemen can be different between the past and present?[64] (1K)

Following the passage is a dazzling array of literary allusions to occasions of all kinds evoking feelings of sorrow in ancient history: the tragic suicide of Xiang Yu (232–202 BCE), the warlord who toppled the Qin empire, and the bitter exile of Li Ling (d. 74 BCE), the Han dynasty (206 BCE–220 CE) general who had been distrusted by his home country, among others. The long list ends with the famous Lu Ji's last word about cranes singing at Huating, which we have read in the *Eulogy* (line 5, note 7). What has been omitted, in a complete departure from the convention of epitaph writing, is the biographical information about the deceased.

Moreover, whereas a conventional *ming* section is often concluded with a generic mourning, Yu Xin's piece ends with another series of literary images that refer to the personal and intimate perspective of the surviving widow:

> After the farewell in the south of the mountain,
> there survived the old person [widow] alone.
> On her loom remained only horizontal threads.
> She is living like a single crane or a lonely phoenix.
> In the inner chamber in the quiet night,
> wind and moon feel chilly.
> Her life has come to the end,
> Yet her remembrance will last forever.
> In the box she keeps the broken zither strings;[65]
> From the neighbor comes the sad flute music.[66]
> The general's former official tent
> now has been converted into the curtained funeral setting.[67]
> (1L)

Yu Xin uses these many allusions to compel the reader's sympathy, and the direct expression of personal grief far overshadows the ritual decorum of a real epitaph, which is represented in the archaic phrases and liturgical language that we found in the epitaph for Xiao Rong. Yu Xin's composition may be read, therefore, as an imitation or literary representation of mortuary writing.[68] As Ni Fan (1637–1704), the later commentator on Yu Xin's writings, correctly pointed out, rather than a lament for his dead friend, "Inscription on Thinking of the Past" may be better understood as an expression of Yu Xin's own homesickness.[69]

The significance of the *Eulogy* is illuminated when its text is read in this literary historical context. In addition to the lyrical expression, Yu Xin's work finds other striking parallels with *Eulogy for Burying a Crane*: in both works, dates are indicated by *ganzhi* compounds only. This avoidance of a precise date may be intended to distance the work from any practical function. Whereas Yu Xin's writing deliberately leaves out biographical details, *Eulogy for Burying a Crane* is also ambiguous about the crane's actual life: its age was unknown, the date vague, its story "elusive and mysterious" (line 23). Although one poem was composed for a deceased man and the other ostensibly for a bird, both works transcend the formulaic compositions they imitate. And both serve the purposes of their lyrical expression beyond the face value of the genre.

Paradox in the *Eulogy*

It seems unlikely, however, that Yu Xin's "Inscription on Thinking of the Past" would have been carved in stone and buried in his friend's tomb, although it was apparently dedicated to a real person. At least, no such archaeological example has ever been found, to my knowledge. This differentiation may be reflected in the later compilation of Yu Xin's collected works; two entire volumes, labeled "*zhiming*," consist of real epitaphs that follow all the conventions of the genre. They were very likely carved in stone and actually placed in tombs, though none of them has been discovered so far.[70] "Inscription on Thinking of the Past" is instead found in a different volume, labeled "*ming*," which consists of a miscellaneous group of commemorative eulogies. Some of them are ritual inscriptions, but many of them, though so titled, are more likely literary compositions that were not supposed to be actually inscribed.[71]

Eulogy for Burying a Crane, however, presents a paradox: whereas it shares the lyrical quality of "Inscription on Thinking of the Past," it, like the real epitaphs we saw above, was actually carved in stone. Indeed, some radical differences can be found between the visual presentation of the *Eulogy* and that of conventional epitaphs. First, compared to contemporary epitaphs, the *Eulogy* inscription (approximately 235 × 204 cm) is much larger (about four times larger than Xiao Rong's epitaph at 60 × 60 cm). Second, the characters of the *Eulogy* are arranged in an informal manner not found among contemporary epitaphs, where neat characters are executed in regular grids. Finally, the material was not a piece of quarried, polished stone like that on which most medieval epitaphs were carved but a wall of rock displayed in a public space. Unlike entombed epitaphs, which address the invisible spirit world, such an object was clearly intended to attract the attention of readers in the real world, who, being aware of the literary expressions in the text, would have also recognized the paradox in the visual presentation of the "epitaph."

What, then, was the purpose of this "epitaph"? If the meaning of an epitaph cannot be separated from its configuration within a tomb, the interpretation of the *Eulogy* must take into account its location within a particular landscape setting. While the physical form of the inscription is indeed appropriate for an epitaph, it must also be considered in the context of another tradition of stone inscription that was not unfamiliar to sixth-century audiences: *moya*, or inscriptions carved on natural cliffs.

Inscribing the Mountains

Inscribed on cliffs or rocks, early *moya* inscriptions—most date to the Eastern Han and are found in western China—initially functioned as monuments to celebrate the completion of massive road- and tunnel-building campaigns and to eulogize the officials in charge of these projects.[72] As a special genre of inscription, *moya* achieve their monumental effect by displaying super-large writings in spectacular mountain settings. Few *moya* inscriptions were carved after the fall of the Han, but in the sixth century, the practice of carving words on natural stone surfaces was revived in several areas of China.[73] As Robert E. Harrist argues in his study of the visual spectacles of *moya*, inheriting the legacy of Han precursors, these new *moya* inscriptions, often driven by religious purposes, took advantage of the topography and transformed their environment into a kind of mind landscape.[74]

The most striking examples, and most pertinent to the *Eulogy*, are the Daoist *moya* inscriptions carved on Cloud Peak Mountain (Yunfengshan) and on nearby peaks in the coastal area of Shandong, composed or supervised by Zheng Daozhao (ca. 455–516), a Daoist adherent and high official of the area.[75] At the base of the mountain, Zheng had an epitaph carved for his late father, who was in fact buried far away. Higher up the mountain, Zheng inscribed the names of imaginary paradises and immortals, as well as poems evoking sightings of supernatural beings. The inscription illustrated in figure 1.6, for example, reads, "Prince Jin pilots a phoenix and rests on Mt. Taishi."[76] The effect of these inscriptions was to transform the granite mass of Cloud Peak Mountain into a representation of a mountain paradise in which, it was hoped, the soul of Zheng's father would dwell.[77]

This efficacy of large *moya* writing may also have been inspired by the Daoist belief in mysterious writings that reveal themselves in the heavenly domains.[78] One early Daoist sutra describes vividly how "natural writing" emerges in the sky:

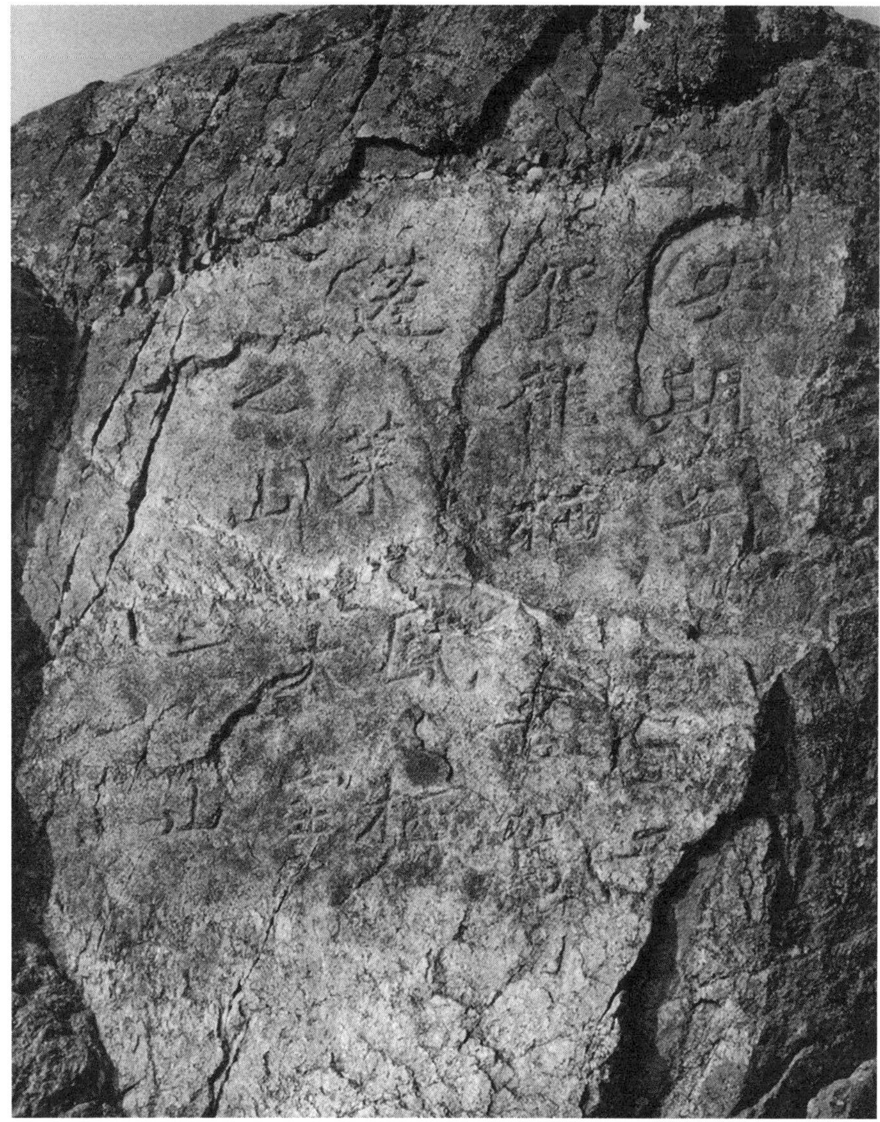

FIGURE 1.6. Inscriptions at Cloud Peak Mountain, Laizhou, Shandong. Courtesy of Lai Fei.

> The eight flying mysterious and natural characters are each as large as one *zhang* [about 2.5 m at the time]. The shining pattern and color are illuminating through the eight directions.[79] (1M)

On some occasions, these radiant characters are said to appear on windows, pillars, and other architectural parts of celestial buildings;[80] in others, the mysterious characters are believed to be carved on Daoist mythic mountains:

> After seven thousand years, [the heavenly writings] were inscribed on the chambers of Mt. Kunlun and the source of the Northern Caves. The size of

each character is one *zhang*. The pattern is flourishing and shining, radiating the light to four directions. Rising from the void in the mist they are looming and disappearing. The shimmering light and purple pneuma [*qi*] clean up the dust, and the golden essence and cold refinement polish the text. Over the multiple kalpas [*jie*], the form of the writing is still bright and illuminating.[81] (1N)

It is worth noting that these scenes are not just literary imaginings. The monumental placement and presence of the writings are supposed to be seen in the mind's eye during the practice of *cunsi*, the Daoist adherent's visualization of his or her spiritual journey to the cosmic world.[82] The imagined spectacles of heavenly writings at Mt. Kunlun may have inspired the sixth-century revival of the *moya* inscriptions, although the texts themselves are not sacred. It is believed in the Daoist tradition, however, that initially, the heavenly writings were illegible to human eyes and needed to be translated into certain forms of human writing.[83] Tao Hongjing, for example, mentioned that the celestial "script of the three origins and eight connections" (*sanyuan bahui zhi shu*) was translated into legible script by early masters of the Shangqing sect.[84] As modern scholars have suggested, such a translation process may have stimulated the aesthetic sensitivity and given birth to a calligraphic innovation in the Six Dynasties.[85] The Daoist *moya* of Cloud Peak Mountain thus may have originated in similar logic: the large inscriptions were meant to materialize and translate heavenly writing in front of a human witness.

Although no other comparable examples are found, the Daoist practice of inscribing text on a natural landscape must have been practiced elsewhere at the time.[86] We do know that Tao Hongjing, the alleged author of the *Eulogy*, once planned to have a series of his poems, "Eulogy on Huayang" (Huayang song), carved on rocks.[87] Had it materialized, the project would have resembled the one on Cloud Peak Mountain. Viewed from this context, *Eulogy for Burying a Crane*, enlarged and inscribed at the base of Jiaoshan, may also be the manifestation of the same Daoist vision. If the inscriptions at Cloud Peak Mountain were meant to create a virtual paradise, the *Eulogy* may have been intended to transform this mountainous island into a monument of a very particular kind—a virtual tomb mound.

To a sixth-century viewer, tombs and mountains were closely associated sites. Back in the Han dynasty, some royal tombs had been cut into the sides of mountains.[88] The custom was carried on later, though not in the same exact fashion. Royal tombs of the Southern Qi dynasty (479–502), for example, were often located on mountainsides.[89] These tombs took advantage of the topography and made the natural mountains resemble artificially raised mounds over burial sites—an ancient form of mortuary monument invented in the Eastern Zhou (770–225 BCE).[90] The author of the *Eulogy* must have been well aware of mountain-burial traditions. The tumulus-like form of Jiaoshan would have inspired its choice as a burial site. Furthermore, two huge rocks in the water, named Song and Liao—only one is still standing in the river today, but both can be seen on the left side of a eighteenth-century

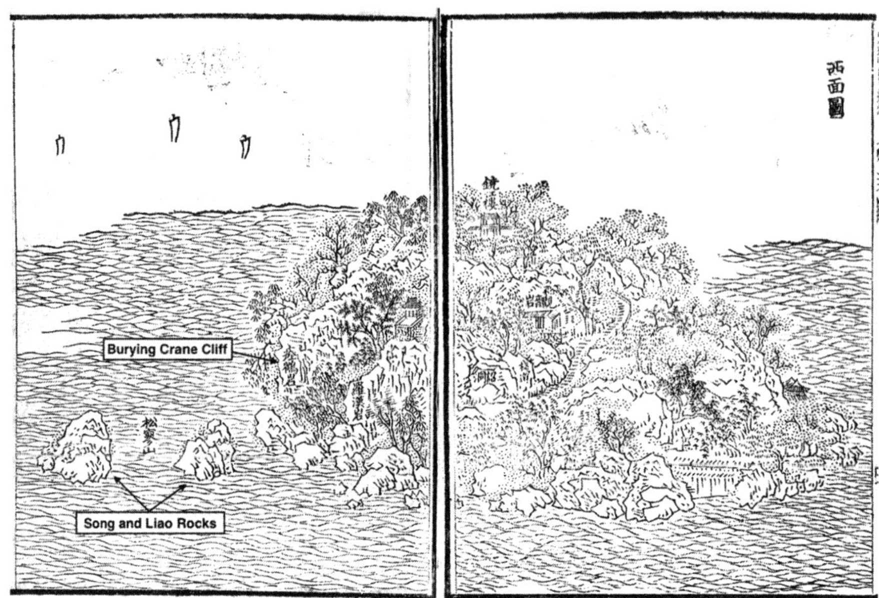

FIGURE 1.7. West view of Jiaoshan. Woodblock print. From Wu Yun, *Tongzhi Jiaoshan zhi* (1865).

woodblock print (figure 1.7)—resemble the pair of *que* towers that mark cemeteries in the Later Han dynasty.[91] This natural setting echoes the description about "quiet and peaceful" land in the text (lines 27–34), which demonstrates a great attention to the auspicious geomancy of the site. Thus, the inscribed *Eulogy* transforms real topography into a symbolic landscape, now a representation of a colossal tumulus.

Revisiting the Eulogy's Authorship

To summarize our observation and speculation so far, the *Eulogy* seems to resemble real mortuary monuments in many aspects—textual, physical, and visual—but at the same time distinguishes itself from such monuments by the metaphorical language of the writing, the paradox in its textual and material form, and its power to transform the physical landscape. Running throughout the "epitaph" and the virtual tomb it marks is the symbolic representation of human misfortunes and suffering that we discerned in the literary imagery of the crane. Thus, *Eulogy for Burying a Crane* should not be read as a literal epitaph for a dead bird, if there was one, but as a much more complex monument erected as an expression of discontent and sorrow.

If my interpretation is correct, who, then, was in a position to conceive the sophisticated design and have the inscription carved in Jiaoshan? As the Japanese scholar Toyama Gunji has correctly pointed out in his discussion of Zheng Daozhao's project, "It is not difficult for us to imagine the scale of the project, which could only have been patronized by very few powerful families such as Zheng's. Such a project must have

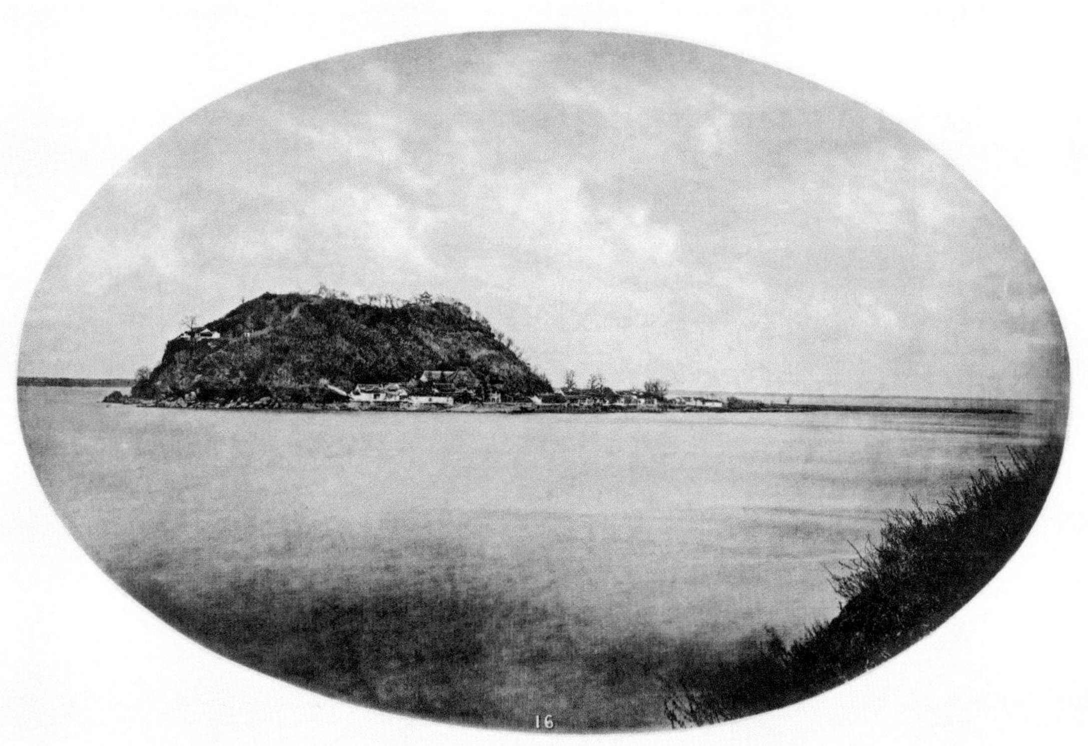

PLATE 1. View of Jiaoshan in the 1870s. From John Thompson, *Illustrations of China and Its People* 3, vol. 3, plate 16. Photo by John Thompson.

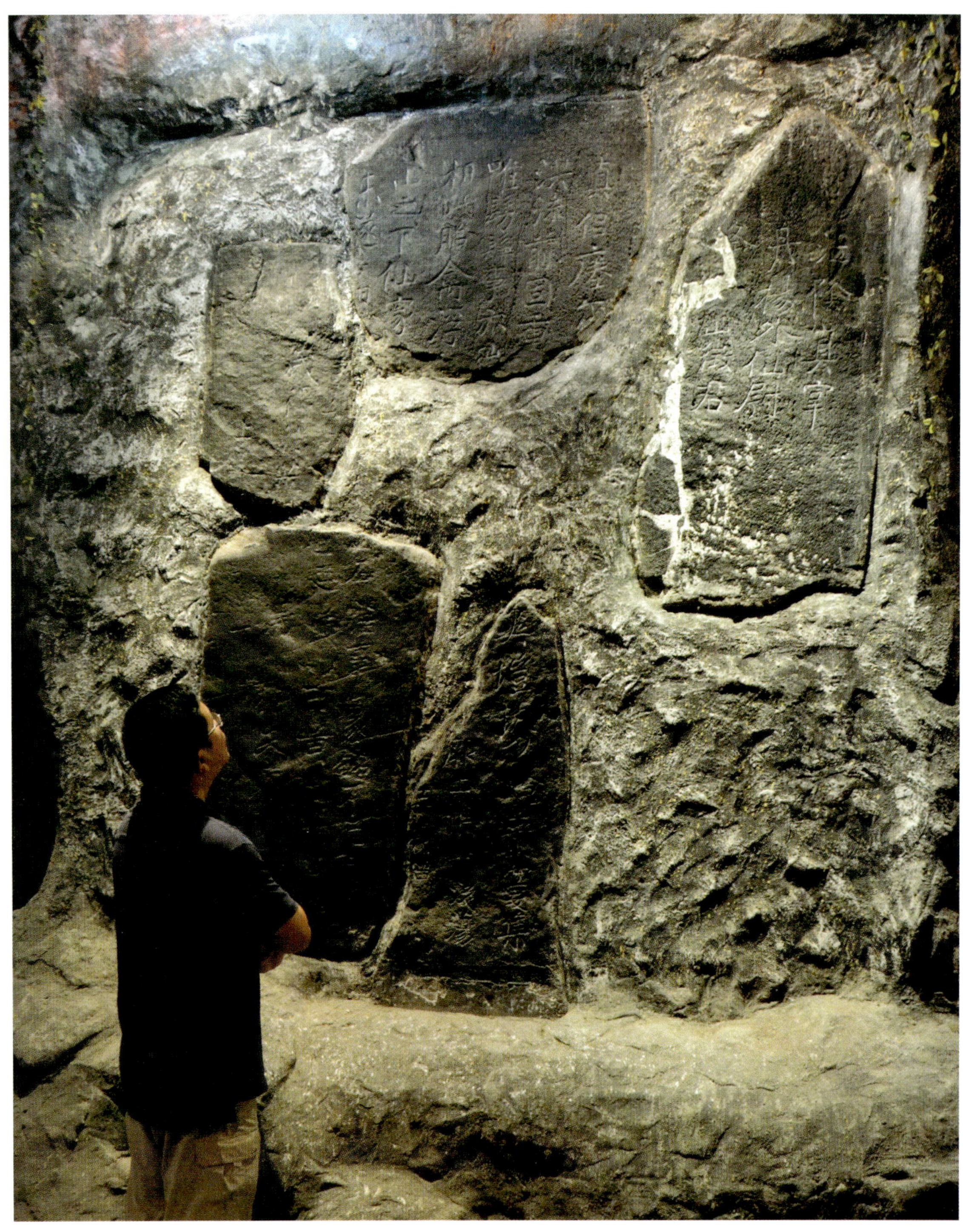

PLATE 2. *Eulogy for Burying a Crane*. Jiaoshan Stone Inscription Museum, Zhenjiang, Jiangsu. Author's photo, 2011.

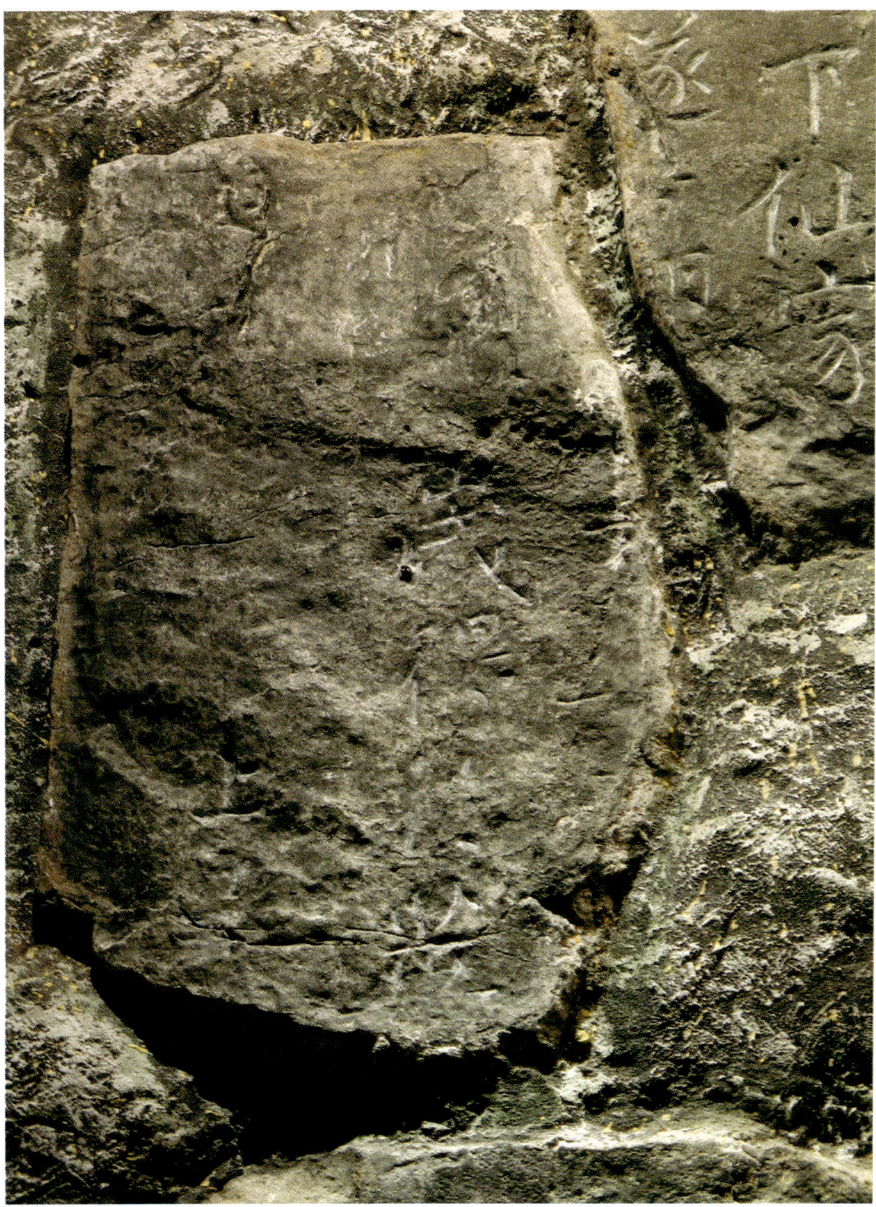

PLATE 3. Fragment no. 1 of *Eulogy for Burying a Crane*. Jiaoshan Stone Inscription Museum. Author's photo, 2011.

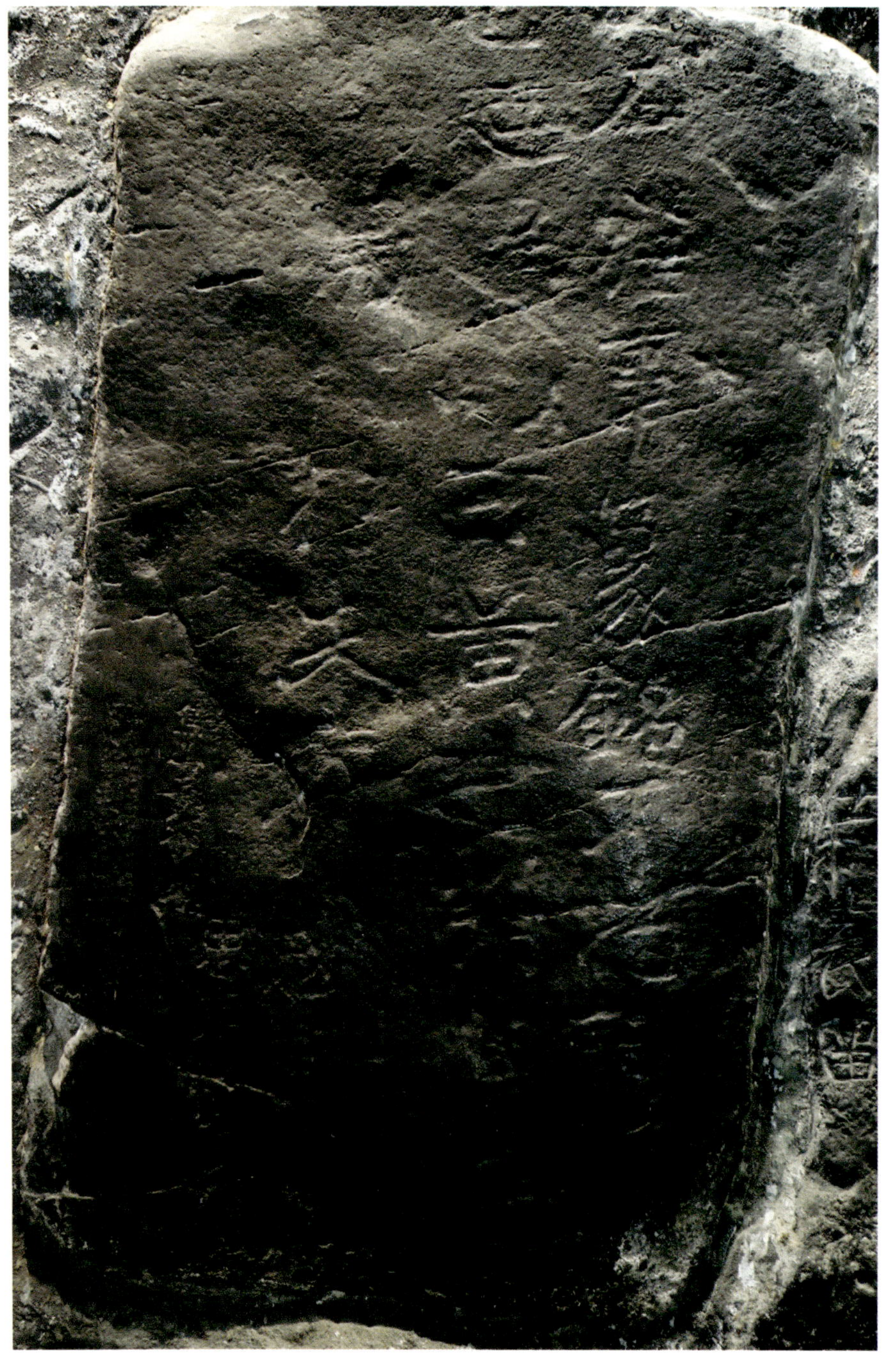

PLATE 4. Fragment no. 2 of *Eulogy for Burying a Crane*. Jiaoshan Stone Inscription Museum. Author's photo, 2011.

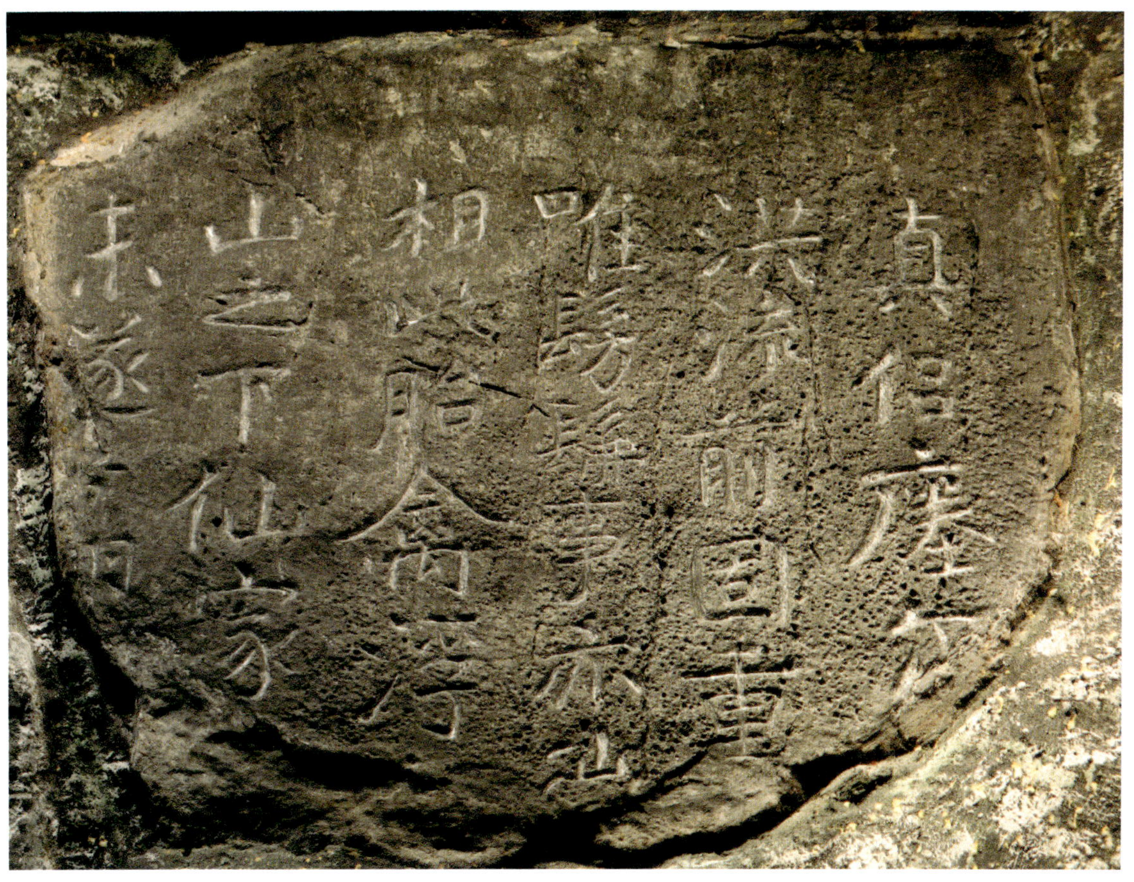

PLATE 5. Fragment no. 3 of *Eulogy for Burying a Crane*. Jiaoshan Stone Inscription Museum. Author's photo, 2011.

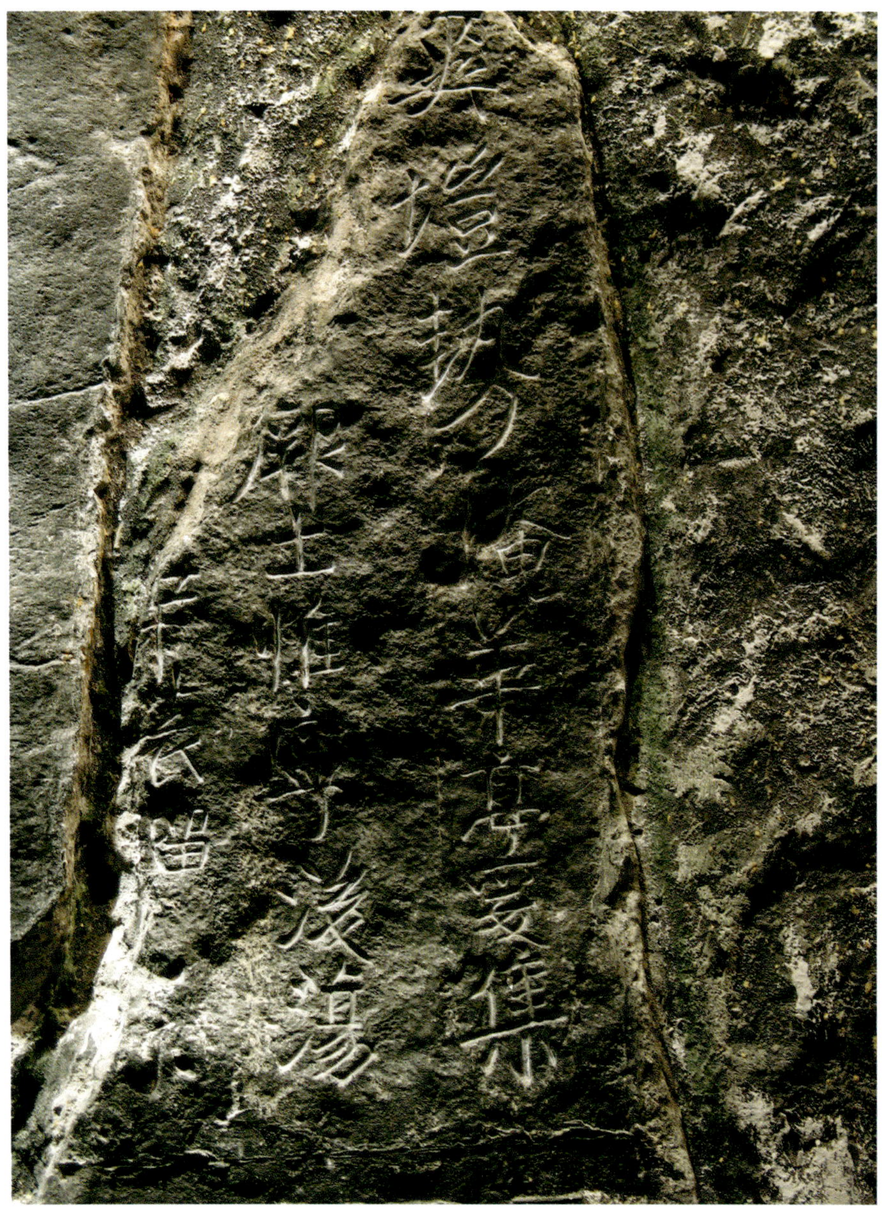

PLATE 6. Fragment no. 4 of *Eulogy for Burying a Crane*. Jiaoshan Stone Inscription Museum. Author's photo, 2011.

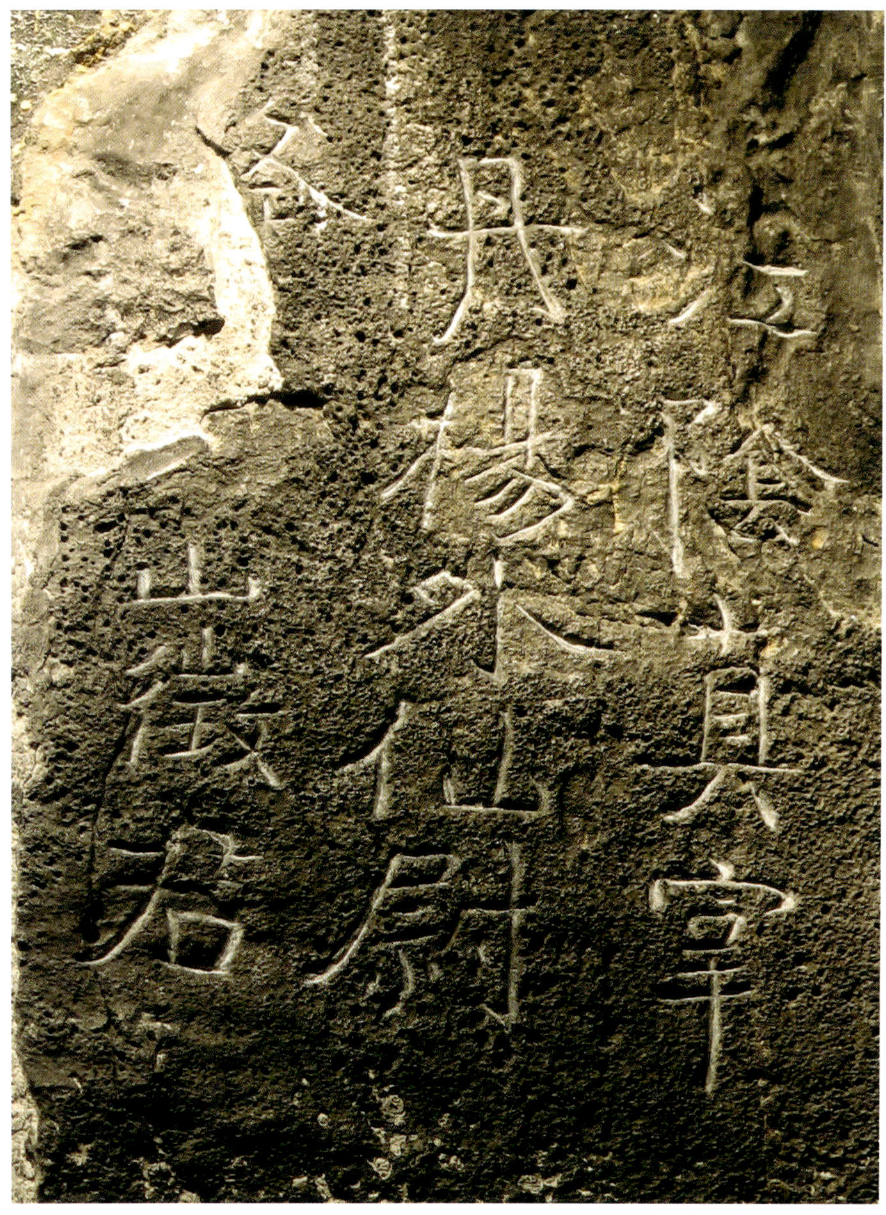

PLATE 7. Fragment no. 5 of *Eulogy for Burying a Crane*. Jiaoshan Stone Inscription Museum. Author's photo, 2011.

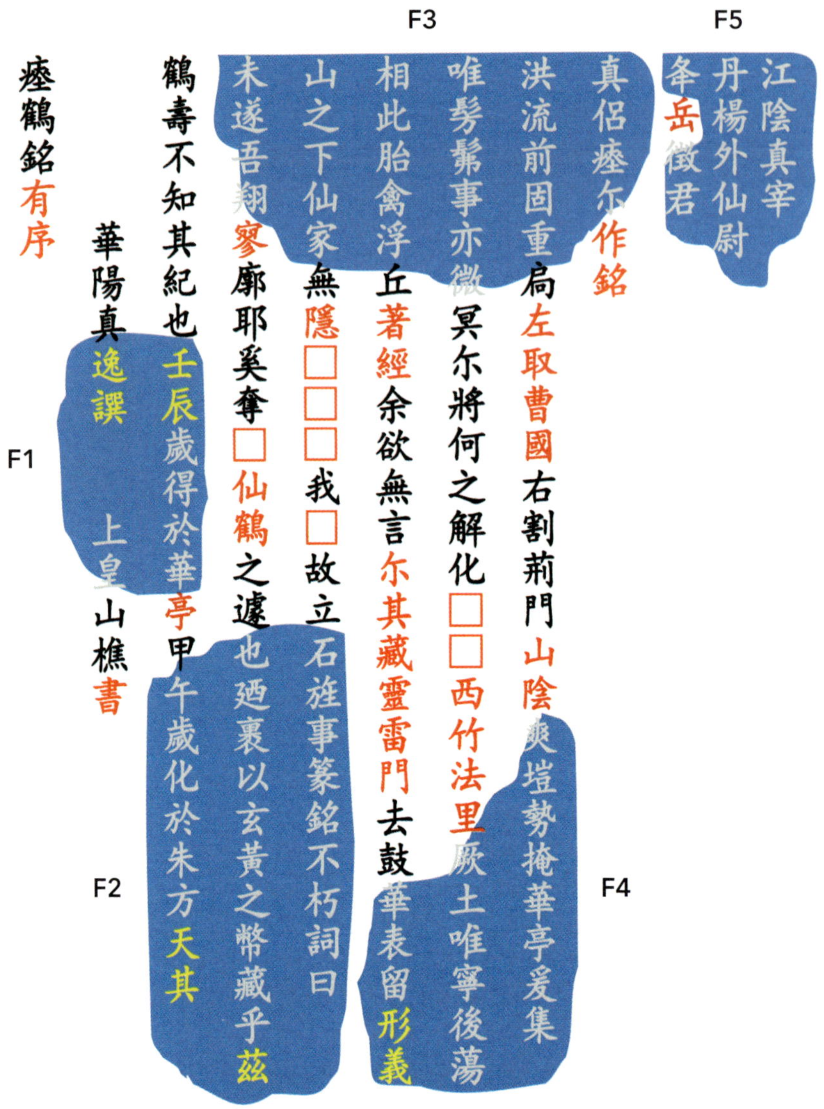

F3 F5

江陰真宰
丹楊外仙尉
夆岳徵君
真侶瘞尓作銘
洪流前固重扃左取曹國右割荊門山陰爽塏勢掩華亭爰集
唯髣髴事亦微冥尓將何之解化□□西竹法里厥土唯寧後蕩
相此胎禽浮丘著經余欲無言尓其藏靈雷門去鼓華表留形義
山之下仙家無隱□□□我□故立石旌事篆銘不朽詞曰
未遂吾翔寥廓耶奚奪□仙鶴之遽也迺裹以玄黃之幣藏乎茲
鶴壽不知其紀也壬辰歲得於華亭甲午歲化於朱方天其
華陽真逸譔　上皇山樵書
瘞鶴銘有序

F1 F2 F4

PLATE 8. Text of *Eulogy for Burying a Crane*, based on Wang Shihong's reconstruction, including the extant characters (in gray) on the fragments F1–F5 (in the blue area). The characters in yellow are worn out today. Other characters are either from early transcriptions (in black) or were made according to Wang's speculation (in red). The empty squares represent long missing characters that are not able to be reconstructed.

benefited from his wealth and political power. With this support, Zheng was able to realize his artistic dream and thus leave us a great number of *moya*."[92] This insight can be applied to the present case as well. The most fundamental one concerns the size of the inscription; this was a big monument, and its production was radically different from that of a text brushed on bamboo, silk, or paper or carved on a piece of quarried stone. Carving the text on the cliff at Jiaoshan involved meticulous planning and considerable expense, as well as a certain degree of authority over the landscape of this island. The composition of the text, moreover, demanded full knowledge of elite literature and culture. In other words, certain political and cultural elites with wealth and power must have been behind the production of the monument.

The authorship of Tao Hongjing may still be debatable. But even for skeptics, it is hard to overlook the connection between the *Eulogy* and the members of the Shangqing (highest clarity) school of Daoism, of which Tao was a leading master, headquartered at Maoshan (see map 1 at beginning of book), which had become the dominant school of Daoism in southern China by the late fifth century.[93] The school originated in southern China and was remarkable for the lyrical language of its teachings and its focus on the interiorization of religious practice, which was highly popular among the southern aristocracy.[94] The Shangqing Daoists also tended to live together, much in the manner of Buddhists living in monasteries. It is reported that major priests built their own residential halls (*daoguan*) on Maoshan, where they and their disciples formed a large community.[95] According to a later compiler of a Maoshan gazetteer, more than fifty *daoguan* were built under the Qi and Liang dynasties, and the community enjoyed continuous imperial sponsorship.[96] Tao Hongjing was certainly among the most distinguished masters in this community.

The connection between *Eulogy for Burying a Crane* and the Shangqing Daoists may be found in the crane imagery itself. While the crane had a universal role in Daoist beliefs, it had special meaning for the Maoshan sect. It is believed that the founding masters of the sect, the three Mao brothers, arrived at the mountain on white cranes. By no later than the fifth century, a temple to the cranes was built on top of the mountain.[97] One subpeak of Maoshan is named Mt. Dinggong and was the site where Ding Lingwei, the mythical Daoist, transformed into a crane (see the *Eulogy* text, note for line 21).[98] For Tao Hongjing and his contemporary Maoshan Daoists, the crane was a part not only of ancient myth but also of daily reality. It was reported that around 495, Zhang Yuanzhi (fl. late fifth century), one of the headmasters at Maoshan, built a structure at his residence called the Crane Platform (Hetai) to commemorate the place where "cranes often come to visit."[99] Thus, while there is no direct mention of cranes in the surviving writings of or about Tao Hongjing, he was certainly familiar with the company of cranes in his environment.

These close connections between Maoshan and cranes only provide a general background for our reading of the "epitaph," however. If, as we read above, the *Eulogy* text did draw on a literary tradition of using crane imagery to express human sorrow, and if the inscription was designed as a virtual monument and was sponsored by powerful men, the inscription had to be associated with specific people and historical events. Assuming that the author was indeed Tao Hongjing or one of his associates from Maoshan, is it possible to discover a connection between the lament voiced in the text and the circumstances of their lives? Was there occasion for Tao or his fellow Shangqing adepts to turn to the symbolism of cranes in a literary response to misfortunes visited upon the Maoshan community?

Tao Hongjing's Discontents

These questions prompt me to reexamine a murky episode in the history of early sixth-century Daoism: a proscription decreed by Liang Wudi, or Emperor Wu, founder of the Liang dynasty (r. 502–549). The emperor was reportedly born to a family with a Daoist background, but he turned to Buddhism soon after ascending the throne.[100] His decision seems to have contributed to a rise in existing religious tension. In early 504, the emperor held a debate on religious topics at his court, perhaps in response to the escalating conflict between Buddhism and Daoism.[101] A source found in a Buddhist document indicates that the result of this debate was that the emperor formally declared his conversion to Buddhism, issued an edict denouncing Daoism as a "delusive way" (*xiefa*) and commanded all ministers, officials, and imperial family members to abandon their Daoist beliefs.[102] It is unknown how much the account exaggerates the situation because of its Buddhist stance. But fragmentary information gathered from various sources, including Tao's hagiography in the *Daoist Canon* (Daozang), suggests that Tao Hongjing and the Maoshan community indeed faced serious trouble under Liang Wudi's reign, very likely a consequence of religious proscription.

Born into a family of scholars, Tao Hongjing was known for having an exceptional literary talent at an early age. He served in the office of Xiao Daocheng (427–482), who would go on to found the Qi dynasty in 479. In the Qi period, he seemed to have had a successful career and gained fame as an expert on alchemy, calligraphy, and the connoisseurship of swords. When he retired from official duties and departed for Maoshan in 492, according to his biography in the *Southern History* (Nan shi), Tao was granted a generous imperial honor:

> [The emperor] bestowed silks, and ministers set a farewell banquet in the Conquering Barbarian Pavilion. The meal was luxurious; chariots and horses filled the road. All said nothing like it had been seen in the Song and Qi dynasties. People from the court and the countryside all honored him.[103] (1O)

And after the founding of the Liang dynasty, the biography continues,

> whenever the state faced auspicious or inauspicious affairs and matters of military policy, [Liang Wudi] would ask for advice. There were often several

> correspondences in a single month. At the time, Tao was called the "Prime Minister [Retreating] in the Mountains." The emperor and the crown prince, as well as other aristocrats, sent their regards to him constantly. Their gifts never stopped.[104] (1P)

The biography, compiled at a later time (the early seventh century), says nothing about the proscription against Daoism, leading some historians to doubt whether it was even a true account.[105] However, a more complicated image of Tao Hongjing and his fellow Daoists emerges when one reads closely more "internal" sources preserved by the Maoshan sect, in particular the "Internal Biography for Tao the Hermit at Huayang" (Huayang Tao Yinju neizhuan) by a Tang dynasty Maoshan Daoist named Jia Song (dates unknown).[106]

In the court debates held in 504, Tao Hongjing was firmly on the side of the Daoists, of course, but it does not appear that he was punished for his stand.[107] His problems arose, however, from the emperor's constant demands for elixirs. The dark side of Tao's career was long ignored until it was revealed in a recent study.[108] Although Liang Wudi had become an ardent Buddhist, he was reportedly interested in alchemy and, like many of his predecessors, eager to achieve longevity or immortality through magical potions. He likely funded Tao and his Shangqing associates in their alchemical research, but they were apparently unsuccessful.[109] Around 506 CE, after several failures, Tao asked the emperor for a leave of absence to search for a better location for producing the desired elixir—a request the emperor denied, perhaps recognizing it as an excuse to escape royal control.[110] Two years later, and after a few more failures, Tao's concern for his own safety seems to have grown. The "Internal Biography" records that on one occasion, he told his disciples:

> It is not impossible for me to release in the form of a pillow and staff. But it is a lesser way that only can benefit myself. Abandon you and depart like this—that would not serve a good example for our teaching.[111] (1Q)

In this context, the Daoist "release" (line 25 of the *Eulogy* text) may be read as referring to Tao's consideration of suicide. Tao rejected the idea, however. The same biography relates that one night in the fourth month of 508 CE, without the emperor's permission, Tao Hongjing fled from Maoshan under the cover of an assumed name and in the company of two disciples.[112] They remained in the coastal region around today's Wenzhou until the emperor sent an emissary in 512 CE to find them. There seems to be no indication that Tao was punished. Instead, the emperor ordered that a new residential hall be built for him at Maoshan in 516. The emperor's demand—an elixir of immortality—remained in force, however, and Tao may have had no choice but to return to work. Around 519, he claimed success and decided to try the elixir himself, but when a deity appeared to him in a dream and said, "Do not try it," he gave up on the experiment.[113] The elixir project then seemed to go nowhere.

What is not mentioned in the "Internal Biography" is the curious move that Tao took on his way back to Maoshan in 512: he visited the Asoka stupa in Maoxian (modern Ningbo, Zhejiang) and took the Five Precepts, the formal ritual of commitment to the Buddhist path.[114] Furthermore, a mortuary stele for Tao Hongjing, composed by Prince Xiao Lun (507–551), son of Liang Wudi, recalls that when Tao returned to Maoshan, he began to "set up Buddhist icons, write sutras, and build stupas."[115] And perhaps not without a little exaggeration, a seventh-century Buddhist account reports, "At Maoshan, [Tao] built two halls for Buddhism and Daoism and worshipped at them on every other day. The Buddhist hall has an icon; the Daoist hall does not."[116] This seemingly impossible development is found in Tao's own writings as well. In *Stele for the Old Studio and Altar* (Jiu guan tan bei, dated 518), which still survived at Maoshan in the sixteenth century, Tao depicts a memorial site at Maoshan that had just received a renovation:

> [This site] follows the imperial standard and explicates the general law. On the east seating the green altar; on the west standing the white pagoda. Between the altar and the pagoda is the foundation site [of the old buildings].[117] (1R)

The "green altar," or *qingtan*, is where a Daoist ritual is performed;[118] the "white pagoda" is evidently a Buddhist structure.[119] This strange blending of two religions continued until his death in 536; according to his biography in *Southern History*, Tao left a will instructing that his body be dressed in Daoist clothes but covered with a *kāṣāya*, the robe of an ordained monk.[120]

Some scholars interpret Tao's embrace of Buddhism as an expression of religious syncretism common in many periods of Chinese history, but the reality was probably more complex. Although it was not unusual for Buddhist elements to be adopted into Daoist theology,[121] Tao Hongjing's assumption of dual religious identities at Maoshan, in particular its materialization in architectural form, may be better explained in relation to Liang Wudi's suppression of Daoism. Under great political pressure, Tao's conversion may have been an expedient device to both please the emperor and win protection for the Maoshan community. We do not find anywhere in his writings a defense or explanation of his conversion, but his intentions were perhaps an open secret and can be inferred from his comparison between himself and Zhang Liang (ca. 250–186 BCE), a Han dynasty minister who successfully avoided conflict with the emperor by withdrawing from the political scene. "No worthy person in history can match him [Zhang]," said Tao Hongjing.[122] Tao and his Daoist fellows at Maoshan may have been rewarded for their adoption of Buddhism, sincerely or not. It is reported that the emperor promulgated a harsher edict in 517, closing all Daoist temples and commanding Daoists to return to secular life, but the Maoshan monasteries appear to have been exempt and survived to Daoism's next golden age under the Tang dynasty.[123]

This relatively secure environment did not mean that Tao was able to live in peace, however. Instead, Tao's compromise may have been regarded by some as a betrayal of his original faith. This can be discerned in accounts of disappointment and dissent among his followers at Maoshan. One of Tao's disciples, Huan Kai (fl. early sixth century), was probably among the malcontents. In an account of meeting a "perfected immortal" (*zhenren*), he delivers the latter's message: despite being a highly intelligent person who has made a great contribution to the sect, Tao Hongjing will not be able to achieve immortality because he was "not consistent in searching for the truth."[124] No direct evidence shows how Tao Hongjing responded to such criticism. There is, however, a corresponding record dated 515 CE by Tao himself: one night, he dreamed a deity came to announce that his appointment to an immortal official position was suspended—a dream that caused him considerable unease.[125] Furthermore, right before his death—his "release"—Tao was told that he would be assigned the immortal official title Supervisor to the Water of Penglai (Penglaidu Shuijian), a quite low, if not downright insulting, rank in the Daoist pantheon that in no way matches Tao's influence and status in life.[126]

The experiences of Tao and his Maoshan fellows would have made the allegorical imagery of *Eulogy for Burying a Crane* suitable for the literary expression of their misfortunes. The traditional date of the inscription, 514, was right after Tao's return to Maoshan and his conversion to Buddhism and before the uneasy dream caused by mounting criticism of his betrayal. In this atmosphere, the imagery associated with the death of a crane would have been a perfect vehicle for conveying the discontent that Liang Wudi's policies and demands had caused. The literary and visual devices that disguised the inscription as an epitaph would have been carefully chosen to express Tao's frustration while avoiding a direct confrontation with the emperor.

Revisiting the Island

To proceed with my assumption, why, then, did Tao Hongjing choose Jiaoshan as the location? A simple explanation might be that whereas carving the inscription anywhere at Maoshan would have revealed the Daoists' intentions, a place such as Jiaoshan seemed a safer location for the project. And the topographic resemblance to a tomb mound, discussed above, may partly account for the choice. Nevertheless, a more direct connection between the island and Daoist belief, and in particular that of the Shangqing sect, can be found in its historical association with Daoism and the mental landscape it evokes.

Today, the island is near the southern bank of the Yangzi River and a long distance from the ocean.[127] In the early sixth century, however, the coastline was much closer and the river wider.[128] Jiaoshan, along with the adjacent rocks, Song and Liao, was called Ocean Gate (Haimen), implying a structure leading directly to the Pacific.[129]

This topography made Jiaoshan resemble an imaginary island of the immortals. Upon visiting Jiaoshan, the Eastern Jin general Xun Xian (322–359) vividly described what he saw:

> Although I am not able to see the Three Mountains, [this scene] makes me want to soar up to the clouds. If the emperors of the Qin and Han [were to see this], they would surely "lift up their skirts" and get their feet wet [to cross over the water to the mountains].[130]

"Three Mountains" refers to the belief that at the eastern extremity of the Chinese world, immortals lived on fantastic mountains floating offshore. It was their longing to find these island-dwelling immortals and to achieve immortality themselves that lured the First Emperor of the Qin and Emperor Wu of the Han dynasty (156–87 BCE) to the seacoast of Shandong, where they gazed across the waves, hoping for a glimpse of the mist-shrouded mountains and their deathless inhabitants.[131]

Viewed from the shore through the mist of the river, Jiaoshan readily evokes the appearance of immortal islands. Aside from the comment by Xun Xian, few records survive from the sixth century or earlier indicating how people appreciated the scene. A little later, however, the great Tang poet Li Bai (Li Bo, 701–762), also known as a Daoist adherent, visited the site and left the poem "Standing on Jiaoshan and Overlooking the Song and Liao Mounts" (Jiaoshan wang Song Liao shan):

> Viewed from the cliff, the Song and Liao
> look as if amidst the blue clouds.
> Where can I find the five-color rainbow
> and make it into a long bridge crossing over the sky?
> If the immortal favors me,
> he will raise his hand in welcome.[132]
> (1S)

Judging from the location of Song and Liao rocks (figure 1.7), Li Bai's position was only a few yards from the *Eulogy*. Unfortunately, the poet did not leave any writing about the inscription, if indeed he saw it. What Li Bai depicts vividly in his poem is not just a generic literary imagination. He may have been attracted to the island by its particular Daoist association.

The name of the island is derived from Jiao Guang (dates unknown), an Eastern Han dynasty hermit who is said to have retreated to the mountain and finally become immortal there.[133] By the early sixth century, Jiaoshan was known as a place to achieve immortality—at least to the Maoshan Daoists. Two such cases are reported in *Declarations of the Perfected* (Zhen gao), a collection of early Shangqing texts compiled by none other than Tao Hongjing:

> In the past there was a Master Fu. He pursued Daoism at a young age and retreated to a stone chamber on Jiaoshan. After seven years, the Old Lord of the Great Ultimate [Taiji laojun][134] visited him and gave him a wooden drill to drill a five-*chi*-thick stone disk. [The Old Lord] said, "Once you drill it through, you will achieve immortality!" The man then drilled day and night. After forty-seven years, when the drill had completely worn out, the stone disk was drilled through. The man then acquired the divine elixirs and ascended to the Upper Clarity to become the Perfected Man of the Southern Peak [Nanyue Zhenren].[135] (1T)

The next paragraph in the same collection records another man, Huang Guanzi, who also entered Jiaoshan and, after passing the tests, became an immortal.[136] We do not know the dates for Master Fu and Huang Guanzi, or indeed whether there were such persons. And Master Fu's stone chamber left no traces in today's Jiaoshan. But the strong Daoist tradition might be part of the reason for inscribing the *Eulogy* at the foot of the island.

The landscape of the monument becomes even more inspiring when it is viewed from a distance, especially from Mount Beigu, a famous and historic hill on the bank of the Yangtze River, less than two miles to the west of Jiaoshan (see map 2 at beginning of book). Numerous people have no doubt climbed the hill to view Jiaoshan from this vantage point. Among them was the emperor Liang Wudi, who is known to have visited here at least once, in the spring of 544 CE, and left a poem describing the epic view of the Yangzi River.[137] Today, the lower water level of the Yangzi and the modern apartment complexes along its bank have changed the landscape forever, but one can still imagine the spectacle in the sixth century: the silhouette of Jiaoshan looming in the mist over the expanse of water, evoking the image of the immortal mountains in the sea. Gazing at their monument in the distance, Tao and his fellows may have recited the text of the "epitaph" they had carved on the cliff and mourned the faith and freedom lost in the imperial proscription against their religion.

Coda

This chapter has sought to demystify the origin of *Eulogy for Burying a Crane*. While the poem is unique, its literary form follows patterns similar to the parody tradition of medieval literature, its physical form appropriates that of contemporary stone epitaphs, and its spectacular appearance and the surrounding environment manifests the cultural tradition of *moya* inscriptions that was revived in the sixth century. These features merit consideration in relation to the significance of medium and space for understanding calligraphy or, more broadly, the visual culture of writing.

The physical presence of the *Eulogy* has prompted us to reconsider it as a monument far more significant than a literal tombstone for a bird. That the monument might have been erected by Tao Hongjing and his fellow Maoshan Daoists as a way to silently mourn Liang Wudi's proscription against Daoism in the early sixth century may never be proved with hard evidence. This explanation at least rescues the *Eulogy* from a generalized discussion of its symbolic meaning.

CHAPTER 2

Discovering the Past

Liang Wudi tragically starved to death in 549 CE in a military rebellion against him.[1] A few years later, the Liang dynasty collapsed. In the ensuing years, *Eulogy for Burying a Crane* and the island of Jiaoshan witnessed the rise and fall of the great Tang dynasty and the short but culturally brilliant Southern Tang (937–975) during the Five Dynasties and Ten Kingdoms period, which eventually yielded to the rule of the Song dynasty in 975 CE. Nothing about the *Eulogy* is mentioned in writings surviving from these centuries, however. The earliest report of the inscription emerged in the early eleventh century. It was perhaps from this moment that the Wang Xizhi story that we read at the opening of the book began to circulate.

In the fall of 1046, Qian Yanyuan (994–1050), a high official in the court of Emperor Renzong of the Song (r. 1022–1063), was appointed prefect of Runzhou, today's Zhenjiang.[2] Qian was known mainly as a statesman but also had great interest in cultural activities. Sometime during his two-year tenure in Runzhou, he had a structure built at the foot of Jiaoshan housing four ancient inscribed stones, including *Eulogy for Burying a Crane*. He named the building Treasured Ink Pavilion (Baomoting).[3] To celebrate the event, Qian Yanyuan asked his scholar friends to compose essays and poems. Su Shunqin (1008–1048), a noted poet and the most important calligrapher at the time, sent him this work:

> In Shanyin, no longer is found the [*Yellow Court*] *Sutra* in exchange for geese,[4]
> but *Eulogy for Burying a Crane* still survives in Jingkou [Zhenjiang] nowadays.
> For this inscription, the untrammeled scholar of the Jixian Academy composed an essay,[5]

and the dashing prefect [Qian Yanyuan] built the [Treasured Ink]
 Pavilion.
The dust has been just washed from the two pieces of "Poems on Jade
 Blossoms;"[6]
the moss remains green in the silver-hook strokes of the characters in
 four script types.
Having studied calligraphy for a long time yet with little progress,
I wish that, by observing the brush method [left in the inscriptions],
 I could break through my obstacles.[7]
(2A)

In comparing the *Eulogy* to the *Yellow Court Sutra,* another piece attributed to Wang Xizhi, Su Shunqin echoed the local belief that the inscription was written by the calligraphy sage. One important point that Su failed to mention in this poem was that the *Eulogy* stone in the Treasured Ink Pavilion was only a fragment of the original inscription. More details were revealed in another poem by Su Song (1020–1101), then a young scholar-official living in Zhenjiang, who must have visited the site in person:

From ancient temples [Qian Yanyuan] found and purchased the
 surviving inscriptions,
in the new pavilion he placed into the alcove the extraordinary broken
 pieces of jade.
They will be copied and circulated like the calligraphy of the *Yellow
 Court Sutra,*
and shall not be buried and lost like the Stone Drums.[8]
(2B)

The reference to "broken jade" suggests that all of the inscriptions placed in the pavilion were fragments. It is unclear when the cliff wall on which *Eulogy for Burying a Crane* was carved began to collapse, though it is unlikely that this happened all at once (as an old story of the inscription being struck by lightning would suggest). Instead, the destruction of the inscription may have extended over several centuries.[9] When the pavilion was built, the collapse may still have been at an early stage, though no authors mention the inscription on the nearby cliff or how the fragment was collected and what characters it bore. There are no traces of the pavilion in today's Jiaoshan, and the fragment is long lost. Examining a later reconstructed text (see figure 1.4), however, we may deduce that the fragment was very likely from somewhere in the center section, between the extant stone fragments F3 and F4 in figure 1.1.

Around the same time, Ouyang Xiu (1007–1072), the most influential scholar of his day and a pioneer of the epigraphic study, became aware of the *Eulogy,* perhaps through the above authors, whom he must have known in person.[10] He managed to obtain a rubbing from the *Eulogy* and included it in his monumental *Collection of Antiquities* (Jigu lu), a catalog of his extensive collection of rubbings of ancient inscriptions. The entry on the *Eulogy* reads:

> [The *Eulogy*] is carved at the foot of Jiaoshan. It is often immersed in the water of the river. Those who were interested [*haoshizhe*] in it waited until the water level fell in order to make rubbings, usually getting no more than the few characters, which reads "*he shou bu zhi qi ji* 鶴壽不知其幾" and ends there. It was regarded as precious because of the difficult access. Only [the rubbing] I acquired has as many as six hundred [characters]. Although *Illustrated Records of Runzhou* [Runzhou tujing] attributes it to Wang Xizhi, its calligraphic style, despite being extraordinary and unrestrained, is not in accordance with the brush method of Wang Xizhi; instead, it is like that of Yan the duke of Lu [Yan Zhenqing]. I do not know who wrote this. Someone said that "Huayang Zhenyi" is a Daoist title for Gu Kuang [ca. 725–ca. 814] and the inscription was written by him.[11] (2C)

Ouyang Xiu's scholarly approach will be analyzed later in this chapter. It is sufficient for now to note the difference in tone between the two Sus' poems and Ouyang's remark. If the two poems seem aligned with the fantasized version of the *Eulogy*'s association with Wang Xizhi, Ouyang Xiu's comment reflects a more complicated view. On the one hand, he indeed shares the excitement of "those who were interested," boasting about his rare acquisition; on the other hand, his analytical tone and historical inquiry into the origin of the inscription mark the emerging intellectual trend of *kaozheng*, or evidential research in epigraphy and history. This persistent cultural fascination with the ancient past and growing scholarly interest in evidential research are two distinctive but intertwined themes in Northern Song intellectual discourses. Both attitudes complicated the reception of the *Eulogy* and other ancient inscriptions and, more generally, the material remains of the past.

The new intellectual trend in history and epigraphy affected calligraphy at the time. Whereas the Northern Song dynasty witnessed a consistent and far-reaching imperial codification of the calligraphy canon, it was in Ouyang Xiu's generation that many scholars began to challenge the canon and the received historical knowledge about calligraphy. Norms and values of calligraphy profoundly reshaped both their discourses and their practices. It was in this context that the *Eulogy* was transformed into a calligraphy model for the first time.

Myth of the Past

Upon the rediscovery of the stone in the early Song, one may wonder why—if the *Eulogy* was indeed erected in 514 CE and Jiaoshan was for a long time a favored destination for visitors—the inscription was not mentioned by Tang writers, such as the great poet Li Bai, who certainly had been to the place and left the poem we read in chapter 1. This question, first raised by Northern Song antiquarian scholars, has been echoed in many modern studies.[12] One simple explanation is to attribute the loss of countless texts to the disorder and fall of the Tang dynasty; the existing writings of Tang and earlier authors were but a tiny portion of those produced.[13]

A more complex reason for the absence of Tang accounts may be rooted in a different intellectual paradigm, however. As many have noted, during the Tang dynasty, scholars concentrated on a textual exegesis known as *zhushu*, or "commentarial study," which was mainly concerned with providing supplements to ancient commentaries on the Confucian classics.[14] For most cultural elites, interpretation of the classics was a matter of accumulating ever finer explications of ancient texts, and instead of undertaking historical inquiries into artifacts, scholars of the Tang period devoted their talents largely to literary exegesis.[15]

This is not to say that there was no interest in old inscriptions during the Tang. On the contrary, obsession with ancient writings and material culture reached a peak in the middle Tang period, when the *guwen* (archaic-style essay) revival movement dominated literary production.[16] But the attitudes of Tang scholars toward stone inscriptions differed from those of antiquarians in later periods. This is apparent in early writings about the Stone Drums, mentioned in Su Song's poem. These inscribed granite monoliths (figure 2.1), still surviving today in the Palace Museum, Beijing, were discovered in the early Tang and were immediately recognized as important relics from the ancient Zhou dynasty.[17] Interest in them and in the fragmentary tetrasyllabic verses they bore was expressed in poems and essays, the best known of which is "Song of the Stone Drums" (Shigu ge) by Han Yu (768–824), a leading literary figure and Confucius scholar.[18] After having been shown a rubbing taken from the stone, Han Yu praises both the calligraphic style and poetic content of the inscriptions:

> But severe in expression, obscure in meaning, hard to understand,
> And the script type of calligraphy neither "official" nor "tadpole"—
> Of such antiquity, how could it escape disfigurement?
> The strokes like living dragons, hewn with a keen sword.
> Like phoenix flying and argus wheeling, a crowd of immortals
> descending,
> Sea coral and jade trees with branches firmly entwined,
> Or golden cords and iron wires strongly twisted and locked,
> Like ancient tripods skipping into water or shuttles soaring like dragons.
> Ignorant scholars collecting poems forgot to include these,
> The two *Books of Solemn Songs* were too narrow, lacked scope.
> Confucius traveling westward did not reach Qin State—
> He gathered a constellation of stars but missed the sun and moon.[19]

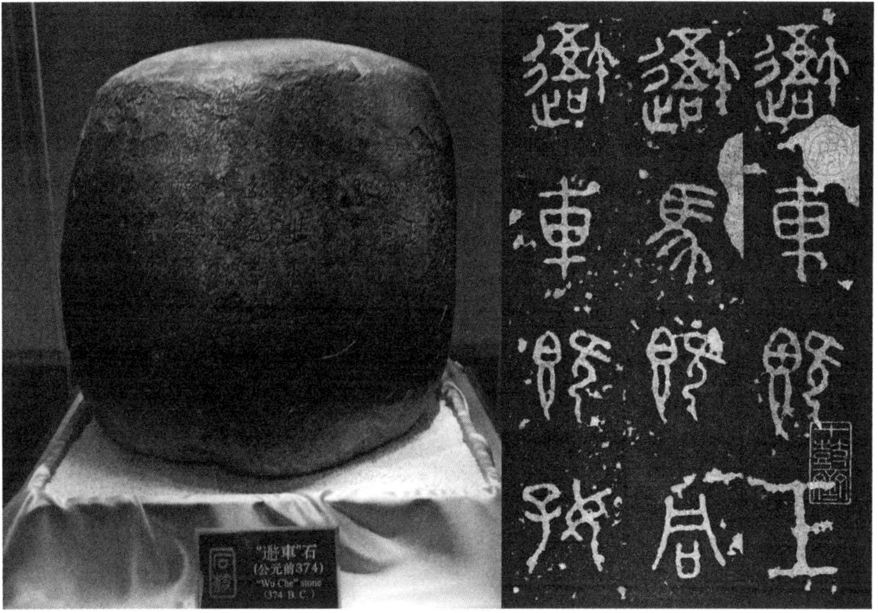

FIGURE 2.1. One of the Stone Drums with an ink rubbing. Palace Museum, Beijing. Author's photo, 2004. Ink rubbing, from *Zhonggou meishu quanji: shufa zhuanke bian*, 1:33.

Han Yu's account of the history of the Stone Drums, however, exhibits more imagination and literary rhetoric than historical investigation. What he stresses is the symbolic value of the Stone Drums, which he saw as embodiments of the cultural and literary glory of *shanggu* (or "high antiquity," defined as the time before the fall of the Han dynasty in 220 CE) that he and his like-minded Tang scholars promoted during the ninth century. For these men, on the other hand, more recent inscriptions and artifacts, such as those of the Northern and Southern Dynasties period, were inferior products of a decadent era and thus unworthy of appreciation.[20] This attitude explains, at least in part, why so few pre-Tang inscriptions, especially those with Buddhist and Daoist content, are mentioned in records from the Tang period.[21] Within this intellectual context, *Eulogy for Burying a Crane*, an anonymous text unrelated to high antiquity, was unlikely to attract much attention even if it were exposed to scholars like Han Yu.

Although they were largely ignored in the writings of Tang literati, steles and other inscriptions were documented in geographical books and local gazetteers. The tradition of compiling records of this kind can be traced back to the sixth century, when the geographer and writer Li Daoyuan (466–527) noted more than one hundred steles in his geographical and cultural survey, *Commentary on the Classic of Waterways* (Shuijing zhu).[22] In the Tang dynasty, gazetteers called *tujing*, or "illustrated records," played a particularly important role in preserving knowledge of local cultural history and myth.[23] Also during the Tang period, the central government required an updating of local geographical records every three or five years. This requirement continued under the Song dynasty and can be illustrated by the large project of gazetteer revision, under the general title *Illustrated Records of the Xiangfu Era* (Xiangfu tujing), undertaken during the Xiangfu reign (1008–1016) in the early Song.[24] It was likely at this time that the *Illustrated Records of Runzhou*, which Ouyang Xiu cited, was revised as part of the Xiangfu project and reached a wide range of scholars.[25] These illustrated gazetteers are by no means plain records of local geographic features. Associating famous names with sites of historic or scenic interest was a common strategy used by the authors of local gazetteers, who were expected to promote the prestige of the regions they covered and shape the collective cultural identity. Attributing the *Eulogy* to Wang Xizhi may be one of the many myths created during the compilation of gazetteers. And the Treasured Ink Pavilion that the prefect Qian Yanyuan built, in this light, may be seen as a symbolic landmark inserted into the landscape of Jiaoshan and materializing the associated local cultural pride.

Evidence of the Past

In contrast to the "commentarial study" tradition of Tang scholarship and the early Song myth making, as many modern scholars have pointed out, Ouyang Xiu and his neo-Confucian fellow writers developed a passionate interest in antiquarian research, known as *jinshixue*, "the study of bronze and stone," which seeks historical knowledge by a new methodology of combining textual and visual evidence.[26] The scholarly trend may be best illustrated in Ouyang Xiu's entry on the *Eulogy*; his assessment of the *Eulogy* was based on concrete visual material and historical sources, and his speculation about the date and authorship introduced the critical method that paved the way for research on the *Eulogy*.[27]

Despite his evidential approach to the study of the *Eulogy*, Ouyang Xiu's account of the actual condition of the stones is vague. For example, he gives no indication that the inscription was already in a fragmentary state. It is also unclear from his account that the stone from which he knew the rubbing was taken—a stone "often immersed in the water of the river"—was probably a fragment rather than a stone with the complete inscription; the rubbing he saw consists of only sixty or so characters. Ouyang is not known to have visited Jiaoshan to conduct an on-site investigation—it is perhaps unrealistic to expect him to have visited every ancient inscription that he wrote about in *Collection of Antiquities*.

Ouyang Xiu may not have had a chance to mention, if indeed he knew, contemporary on-site investigations into the inscription, including a new discovery about the *Eulogy* stone in 1070, which was undertaken by Zhang Yu (d. 1105), a scholar from the nearby town of Changzhou.[28] Zhang's investigation and reconstruction of the text (figure 2.2) survives in a later quotation by Dong You (d. 1129), the prolific Northern Song antiquarian scholar.[29]

> [The above text] includes all surviving characters of *Eulogy for Burying a Crane* on [the cliff of] Jiaoshan and those on the [fragment] in the Treasured Ink Pavilion. There are more than one hundred and thirty characters in total, to count all the characters and phrases that are still legible or with surviving strokes. About fifty characters are missing. The complete inscription should be in nine columns and each has twenty-five characters. This does not include the beginning and the end of the text. In the spring of the third year of the Xining era [1070], Guo Fengyuan, whose name is Gongyu, of Fenyang, Zhang Yi, whose name is Ziwei, of Fanyang, and I searched for the remaining fragments on the north side of Jiaoshan. We found twelve characters by accident among the wild rocks. Only ten characters, including *biao* 表, *liu* 留, *wei* 惟, and *ning* 寧, remained intact. The other two characters were damaged. The [space between] the rocks was so narrow that only by lying down could one read these characters under them. That is why no one had seen them before, and these characters had never been known in the world.[30] (2D)

The earliest and most important in situ report on the *Eulogy* inscription, Zhang Yu's account describes the actual condition of the stones at the time of his visit. From the first line of this passage, we learn that part of the inscription still remained on the cliff; we learn also that the fragment found by Qian Yanyuan was still in the Treasured Ink Pavilion by this time. Furthermore, in arranging the reconstructed text according to the extant stone, we realize that the twelve characters Zhang Yu found were on the lower part of the inscription (the shaded area in figure 2.2). The fragment Zhang discovered can be identified as the stone F4 (plate 6).

Zhang Yu was not the only scholar attracted to the remaining inscription. When Dong You cited the above research, he mentioned that a similar investigation and reconstruction of the text was made a little earlier by Shao Kang (1014–1075), a renowned scholar and calligrapher and a native of Zhenjiang.[31] This early on-site research and reconstruction eventually made the *Eulogy* an object of the ongoing "study of bronze and stone" by contemporary scholars. In another entry about the *Eulogy*, Dong You quoted a more recent study by his colleague at the Palace Library, Huang Bosi (1079–1118), one of the most noted calligraphy connoisseurs.[32] It is the latter who first proposed that the inscription was composed and written by Tao Hongjing.

Huang's speculation began with two terms, *renchen* and *jiawu* (the dates in the sexagenary cycle calendar), in the reconstructed text of the *Eulogy*. Without a reign title, they could be any two years in another sixty-year cycle, of course. However, after a close study of the career of Tao Hongjing, Huang Bosi believed that the two dates fit Tao's timeline of activities: in the year of *renchen* (512 CE), Tao was traveling to the east coast (see chapter 1) and had a chance to pass by Huating and obtain the crane there; in the year *jiawu* (514 CE) he was at Maoshan, close enough to Jiaoshan, and

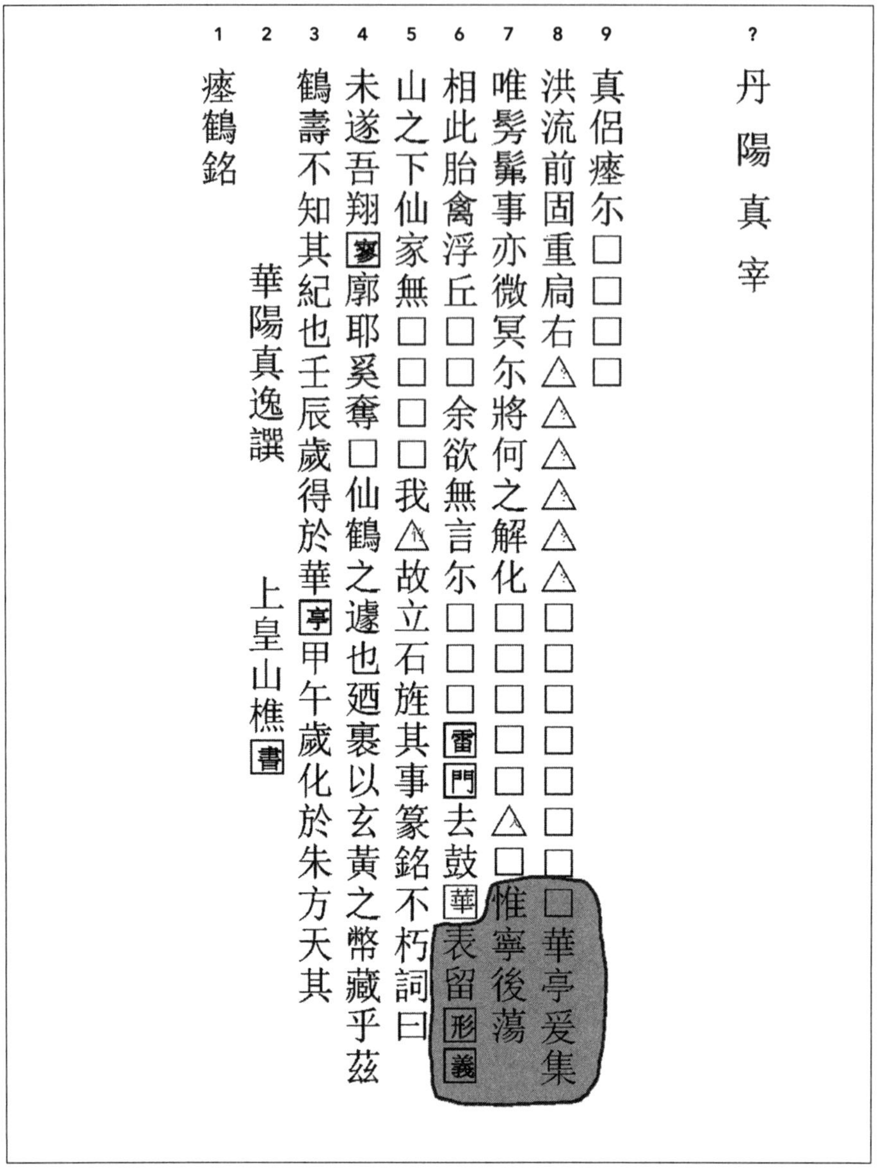

? 丹陽真宰

9 真侶瘗尔□□□□

8 洪流前固重扃右△△△△△△□□□□□□□□華亭爰集

7 唯髣髴事亦微冥尔將何之解化□□□□□△□惟寧後蕩

6 相此胎禽浮丘□□余欲無言尔□□□雷門去鼓華表留形義

5 山之下仙家無□□□□我△故立石旌其事篆銘不朽詞曰

4 未遂吾翔寥廓耶奚奪□仙鶴之遽也廼裹以玄黃之幣藏乎兹

3 鶴壽不知其紀也壬辰歲得於華亭甲午歲化於朱方天其

2 華陽真逸譔　上皇山樵書

1 瘗鶴銘

FIGURE 2.2. Zhang Yu's reconstruction of *Eulogy for Burying a Crane* text. Squares: missing characters; triangles: damaged characters. The shaded area indicates the new discovery made by Zhang Yu.

thus had the opportunity to bury the dead crane.[33] Huang also found that the reign title for sexagenary dates in Tao Hongjing's other writings was frequently absent—a seemly sign of the latter's personal habit. The calligraphic style, too, "quite resembles that of Tao Hongjing," added Huang Bosi, though he offered no further discussion, not even a stylistic comparison.[34] Despite the lack of direct evidence, Huang's discussion of the dates and speculation on authorship has been accepted by most later scholars and has directed them, including this author, to the close relationship between the inscription and the Daoist community at Maoshan (see chapter 1).

Huang Bosi's evidence may appear weak to modern readers who are used to easy access to vast library sources. At the time, however, it indicated a paradigm shift of knowledge inquiry, as we found in Ouyang Xiu's short remark on the *Eulogy*. The reasoning in Huang Bosi's comment on the *Eulogy*, found elsewhere in his writing, also reflects the rigorously evidential study of ancient artifacts. This approach to the *Eulogy* would be resumed in the eighteenth century and at a greater scale and depth.

Controversy over the Calligraphy Model

Although Ouyang Xiu called the calligraphy of the *Eulogy* "extraordinary and free [*qifang*]," he seemed to show little interest in taking it as a model for his own calligraphy.[35] Indeed, it may be a modern projection. Antiquarian scholars in the nineteenth century would often adopt ancient styles, creating so-called stele-study calligraphy that we will examine in the concluding chapter. Their Northern Song predecessors, however, rarely did so. Ouyang's calligraphy can be illustrated by the surviving entries of the original manuscript of *Collection of Antiquities*.[36] One of them discusses the content and historical significance of the *Stele of the Temple for Mount Hua* (Xiyue Huashan miao bei, dated 165 CE).[37] Although the stele's calligraphy would become a highly sought model in the nineteenth century, it did not draw the attention of Ouyang Xiu and his contemporary calligraphers.[38] The blocky and austere appearance of Ouyang Xiu's calligraphy instead demonstrates the Yan Zhenqing style that prevailed among scholars, to which we will return soon.

On the other hand, for most scholars and connoisseurs of calligraphy, the charm of *Eulogy for Burying a Crane* resides in its mysterious origin and the viewer's imagination. Its badly damaged status, often only found in blurred and creased rubbings, hardly provides any model for practicing calligraphy. Most viewers, including today's visitors, may agree with Huang Bosi's remarks that follow his historical study of the *Eulogy*:

> The stone was hard to carve and has been eroded by water. Therefore, the characters barely have sharp strokes, as if they were all written with a worn brush. Those who blindly follow and imitate [its style] are quite ludicrous.[39] (2E)

Huang never specified at whom his criticism was directed. But contemporary and later readers may have immediately recognized that it must have been Huang Tingjian, a generation older than Huang Bosi and the most influential poet and calligrapher at the time. Huang Tingjian had written ardently about the *Eulogy*'s calligraphy and named it one of the superior historical models. One of his writings tells us about his revelation upon first encountering the legendary inscription:

> Recently in Jingkou, on the broken cliff I saw the large calligraphy *Eulogy for Burying a Crane* by Youjun [Wang Xizhi]. Its superiority is impossible to describe in words . . . *Eulogy for Burying a Crane* has been attributed to Youjun—nothing makes one doubt [it]. The calligraphy by [Tang masters] Ou[yang Xun], Xue [Ji, 649–713], Yan [Zhenqing], and Liu [Gongquan] are all upright and vigorous. However, they only get part of the way toward the excellence of *Eulogy for Burying a Crane*. Only the duke of Lu's [Yan Zhenqing] *Stele for Song Kaifu*, which is vigorous, slim, pure, and upright, was able to achieve half [of the excellence of *Eulogy*].[40] (2F)

His full acceptance of the dubious attribution to Wang Xizhi would be put aside by all other serious scholars of his generation. And few would agree with him that the worn-out inscription surpassed the Tang masters. In comparison with Huang Bosi's cool-headed assessment of the eroded stone, Huang Tingjian's views seem radical, if not downright delusional. One may attribute this extreme rhetoric to contemporary Chan Buddhist teaching that often informed Huang's writings.[41] And his new vision also fits well into the historical account of his contemporaries' emphasis on personal self-expression as a challenge to *fa*, or technical "methods," of Tang calligraphy.[42] The complexity of the historical context of Huang's vision and calligraphy practice at the turning point of the calligraphy history may require a closer look.

Departing from the Brush Method

The centuries-old calligraphy tradition of the Two Wangs focuses on the concept of *bifa*, or "brush method," a term that refers to (secret) techniques of writing, including modulated strokes, carefully balanced composition, subtle changes of ink tonality, and a fluent and swift flow, stroke by stroke. All the subtleties are learned through intimate hands-on instruction, guidance, and correction, with the tutor providing his own writings as the model. The brush method was thus transmitted from generation to generation, from master to student. It was the exclusive knowledge of the imperial court or prestigious clans (like that of Yan Zhenqing's) and was sustained and reinforced by the hereditary society (like the Tang).[43]

The private transmission of the brush method became elusive and mystified after the fall of the Tang and the old aristocratic clans. In the meantime, *fatie*, or model letters—that is, rubbing reproductions of ink-written or tracing copies (see the introduction for the term and the technical process)—emerged as the major source of learning calligraphy. Whereas rubbings from monumental steles, usually written by prominent calligraphers, were definitely made and circulated in the Tang period, model letters were designed to reproduce calligraphy and took it to a totally different level of application.[44] The latter's impact on the practice and perception of calligraphy cannot be overestimated.

The *Model Letters in the Imperial Archives in the Chunhua Era* (Chunhua bige fatie, *Chunhua Model Letters* hereafter) was the pioneer of this game-changing production.[45] Compiled at the order of Emperor Taizong of the Song (r. 976–997) in 992 CE, it reproduced selected ancient works of calligraphy in the imperial collection. The project was originally conceived as a limited publication, and copies were granted only to royal family members and high officials. By the time of Huang Tingjian, however, copies of the *Chunhua Model Letters* were available in the market, and replicated editions or other similar titles had been extensively published.[46] The boom of model letters must have been due partly to the increasing demands of the expanding scholar class and the burgeoning print culture in the later eleventh century, which, as recent studies have demonstrated, profoundly changed the mode of knowledge and literary production.[47] The parallel role of the newly published model letters in this cultural transformation still awaits further study. On the one hand, official and commercial publications, such as the *Chunhua Model Letters*, helped consolidate the classical tradition and became the major visual sources for numerous would-be calligraphers. On the other hand, however, these works may have stirred an unexpected aversion among the new generation of scholars.

Unlike their noble predecessors of the Tang dynasty, most scholar-officials in the Song dynasty were from more humble families and never had the luxury of receiving private instruction in the "brush method." As a child born to a poor family, for example, Ouyang Xiu is known to have learned to write by applying a reed stick to the ground.[48] When he turned to the art of calligraphy at an older age, he had to admit that his hand was too "unskillful" to produce fine calligraphy—less a self-deprecating comment than a candid confession, considering his quite rigid calligraphy style.[49] Some talented peasant-born scholars like Cai Xiang (1012–1067), from whom Ouyang Xiu never withheld his admiration, eventually mastered the nuances of brush techniques when they gained access to fine art.[50] But a more common reaction among scholars when they were finally shown a work of fine calligraphy was perhaps the frustration that they had wasted too much time on model letters; the black-and-white rubbing images hardly capture the subtle twists and turns, not to mention the rich tonality and brushwork, of the ink-written works.

In a widely spread lament on the lost "ancient methods," the younger generation of scholar-officials began to seek an alternative to the elusive methods. Their new attitude was signaled by their mounting criticism of the long-revered *Chunhua Model Letters*.[51] In addition, the *Preface to the Holy Teaching of Tripitaka of the Great Tang* (Da Tang sanzang shengjiao xu, dated 672, figure 2.3), perhaps the most well-known and studied model of Wang Xizhi's elegant running-script calligraphy, was now dismissed by the scholars as in an "academic style" (*yuanti*) only suitable for neat yet mechanical scribal writings.[52] Instead, many scholars turned to the robust, and sometime awkward, Yan Zhenqing style, which had become the antithesis of the elegant calligraphy of the Two Wangs.[53]

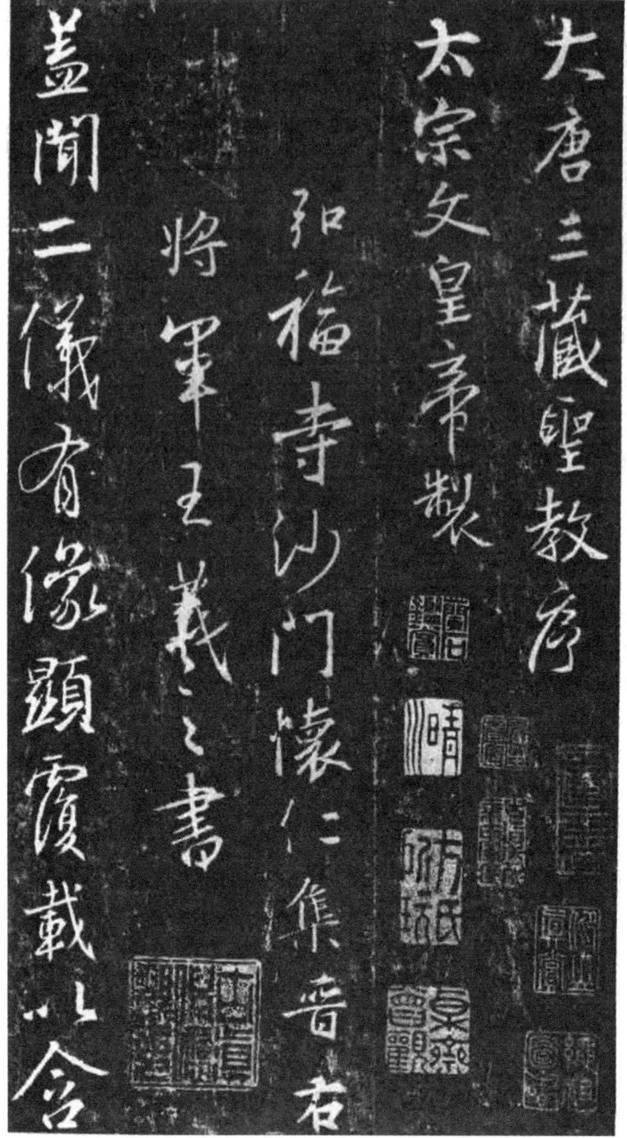

FIGURE 2.3. *Preface to the Holy Teaching of Tripitaka of the Great Tang* (Da Tang sanzang shengjiao xu). Detail. Dated 672. Ink rubbing. From Liu Zhengcheng, *Zhonggou shufa quanji* 18:212.

On the other hand, scholars began to "rediscover" ancient works within the Two Wangs tradition to justify their new aesthetics. It was in this context that *Essay on Yue Yi* (Yue Yi lun) and the even more famous *Preface of Gathering of the Orchid Pavilion* (Lanting ji xu), both traditionally attributed to Wang Xizhi, resurfaced as the subject of scholarly debate.[54] The "Dingwu version" of the latter, which would be accepted widely as authentic, was first recognized and advocated by none other than Huang Tingjian.[55] This version, which only exists in rubbing form (figure 2.4), shows a much less dynamic and intricate composition of characters than one can find in *Preface to the Holy Teaching*. This hitherto unfamiliar plain and blunt "Wang Xizhi style" has deeply affected the later perception of the classical canon.

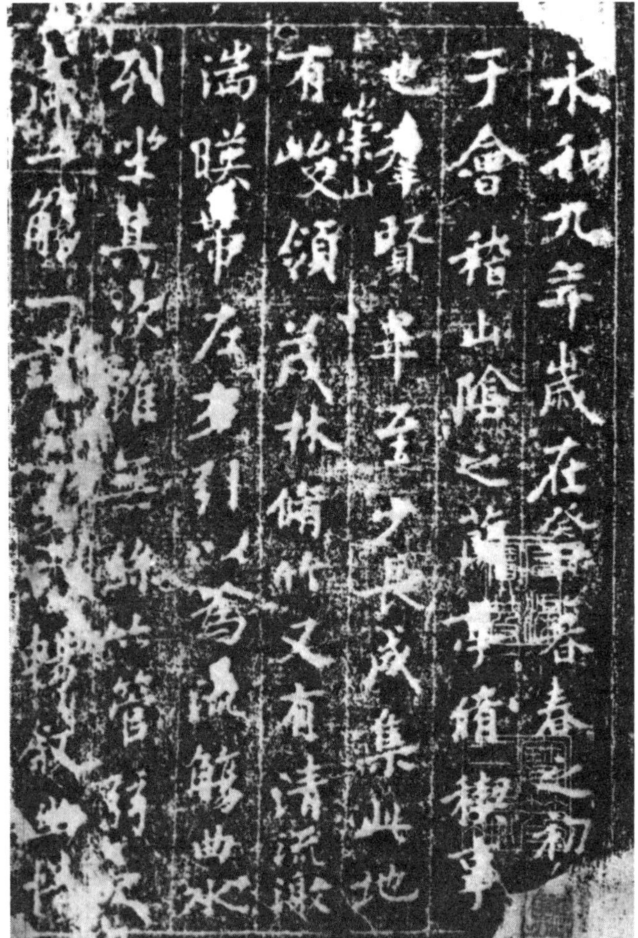

FIGURE 2.4. Wang Xizhi, *Preface to the Orchid Pavilion Gathering* (Lanting ji xu; Dingwu version). Dated 353. Ink rubbing. From *Zhongguo meishu quanji: Shufa zhuanke bian*, 2: plate 55.

At the same time, ambitious scholars developed various theories to promote a self-expressive nature of calligraphy—which would lead to the "literati art" that permanently changed the value and practice of calligraphy and historical writings about the art form.[56] Su Shi (1037–1101), the most eloquent literati writer, famously advanced the theory of *yi*, or "idea," as the central value of his calligraphy.[57] Another major calligrapher and connoisseur, Mi Fu (1052–1107), dedicated himself to the exploration of *ziran* (naturalness) in calligraphy, which he believed was the essence of the classical tradition that had been lost in rubbings and recovered by himself.[58] The theories of Huang Tingjian were perhaps the most radical of all. He challenged the very idea of copying itself. Rather than carefully reproducing earlier works through stroke-by-stroke copying, he advocated the concept of *guan*, or observation, which he once explained to a student in the following terms:

> The old masters did not study calligraphy only through copying. If one hung the calligraphy of old masters on the wall and observed [*guan*] it in complete

absorption, then when lowering his brush, he naturally realized their intentions.[59] (2G)

Guan was not a new concept in Chinese visual culture. Derived from the Buddhist/Daoist notion of visualization, the term has been widely used in the language of connoisseurship.[60] Huang Tingjian's view, though, perhaps refers to a more specific meaning in the Chan Buddhism that he practiced. According to Chan teachings, everyone has an inner gift, called "dharma eye," with which to discover the ultimate truth hidden within physical existence. One must practice meditation in order to remove the mental obstacles that cloud this clear vision.[61] In his writings on calligraphy, Huang used this analogy to demonstrate how calligraphy should not be mechanically copied but assimilated visually and somatically through intuition.[62] This new discourse, to Huang, was meant to save the calligrapher from desperate adherence to the model letters and free him from the burden of attempting to retrieve the brush method of earlier masters.

His take on the Stone Drums provides such an example of his unconventional views. Ouyang Xiu and Huang Bosi discussed the textual and historical value of the Stone Drums, but they showed little interest in the calligraphic style of these artifacts.[63] In contrast, Huang Tingjian wrote of the Stone Drums, "Observing [*guan*] the calligraphy closely, one can understand the principle of standard and cursive-running calligraphy."[64] Huang saw in the battered seal-script characters of the Stone Drums manifestations of aesthetic principles that were the foundation of modern forms of writing—an assessment that appears paradoxical. It was not a coincidence that Huang selected the *Eulogy* as his model; whereas other viewers were troubled by its indeterminate visual forms caused by natural damage, Huang found it to be a perfect example that demands one use the dharma eye to see through the ruinous status and ambiguous forms and discover its excellence.[65]

This more or less metaphysical interpretation should be considered in a more specific historical context, including the issue of calligraphy which seemed urgent to Huang and his contemporaries: to apply the new self-expressive aesthetics to large-size calligraphy. Huang's unusual attention to the *Eulogy* may be understood as his personal solution to the problem.

Large-Size Calligraphy

It is unclear when and how Huang Tingjian encountered the *Eulogy* for the first time. The earliest evidence is found in his poem dated 1080, when he was a promising young scholar at the age of thirty-five:

> Small-character calligraphy should not be composed like a flock of rigid
> frozen flies,

Essay on Yue Yi is superior to the *Sutra of Buddha's Bequeathed Teaching.*[66]
Large-character calligraphy is towered over by *Eulogy for Burying a Crane,*
cursive calligraphy created by Guannu [Wang Xianzhi] outdoes that of
Boying [Zhang Zhi].[67]
[Nevertheless,] by following others all the time, one will always be left
behind;
only in becoming oneself can one reach the truth.[68]
(2H)

From this poem, we know that the significance of the *Eulogy* for Huang Tingjian lay in its unusual size. This view was repeated in his other writings. In a colophon to his friend's collection of rubbings, he again stressed the large size of the inscription and called it "the patriarch of large-character calligraphy," using the Chan term that refers to the sect's founding masters.[69] It is true that compared with other models of calligraphy commonly studied in the Northern Song, the characters in the *Eulogy* are dramatically larger; the size of each character in *Preface to the Holy Teaching* is roughly an inch tall, for example, and the largest characters in the *Chunhua Model Letters* do not exceed one-fourth the size of the characters of the *Eulogy.*

Huang's interest in the issue of the scale of the writing may have been sparked by Su Shi, his close friend and mentor.[70] In a colophon to Su Shi's calligraphy, he remarks,

Dongpo [Su Shi] said, "The challenge of composing large characters is being compact and without any loose space; the challenge of composing small characters is being spacious and relaxed." This is definitely true. I have expanded on his theory and said, "'Compact and without any loose space,' that is epitomized by *Eulogy for Burying a Crane*; 'spacious and relaxed,' by the *Orchid Pavilion.*" To explain this with examples in seal script: large-character calligraphy is exemplified by Li Si's Yishan stele, and in the case of small-character calligraphy, by the "tadpole inscriptions" on the pre-Qin ancient bronze vessels.[71] (2I)

In another similar comment, perhaps written around the same time, he added to his models for large calligraphy *Hymn to the Revival of the Great Tang Dynasty* (Da Tang zhongxing song), Yan Zhenqing's great *moya* inscription dated 771.[72] To understand Huang and other Song scholars' unusual interest in the size of calligraphy, we may need to review what "large calligraphy" meant up to their time.

Writing large-size characters had been considered a specialized calligraphic skill since at least the Eastern Han dynasty. Shi Yiguan (fl. second half of the second century), the noted Eastern Han court calligrapher, was known for his ability to write characters larger than one *zhang.* A little later, another calligrapher, Liang Hu (d. after 220 CE), was admired as a master of the large-character format.[73] This special skill of writing seemed important for practical reasons: prominent calligraphers sometimes were called on to write extra-large characters for wooden plaques displayed on buildings. A well-known anecdote mentions that the eminent courtier and calligrapher Wei Dan (179–253) was asked to write calligraphy directly on such a large plaque. He hung from a rope over the plaque to complete the dangerous task. Back from the scene, he was so horrified—and perhaps humiliated—that he warned his sons "to never do this themselves."[74] Another anecdote recounts that Wang Xianzhi refused to write such calligraphy on a large plaque.[75] Wei Dan's admonition and Wang's rejection, which may rather reflect later storytellers' attitudes toward the large character, at least show that writing this type of calligraphy was once considered part of the duty of court calligraphers. And the rejection may suggest the changing value of calligraphy in the Southern Dynasties. The extremely refined sensibility developed in the letter writings was indeed an antithesis of those required for plaque calligraphy: bold and straightforward brushwork, robust composition in the large space, and an eye-catching effect even when viewed from the distance.

The emergence of the new aristocratic taste, however, did not mean the decline of large calligraphy. To the contrary, in the following centuries, large calligraphy adorned many public and semi-public spaces. Walls and screens were the favored media for displaying such calligraphy in diverse script types.[76] Fancy decorative scripts, sometimes even adorned with a bird's feather, were among the most popular in screens, and one can still find examples in eighth-century Japanese imitations, now preserved in Shosoin, the imperial collection in Nara.[77] Another type of large character that enjoyed a long life was *feibai*, or "flying white" script, illustrated by the well-known *Stele of the Prince Who Ascended to the Immortal* (Shengxian Taizi bei, dated 699, figure 2.5), which was reportedly written by Wu Zetian, the first and only female emperor in Chinese history (r. 690–705), and dedicated to none other than Wangzi Qiao, the crane-riding immortal discussed in chapter 1.[78] The interplay between the ink and void space also offered the potential for spreading the brush lines across a large area and adding such embellishments as bird shapes in the characters. In addition to the tradition of the decorative scripts screen, a new fashion that spread in unprecedented scale in the mid-eighth century was the cursive calligraphy screen, thanks to the phenomenal calligrapher Huaisu (725–785), whose calligraphy, according to the famous poem "Ballad for Cursive Calligraphy" (Caoshu gexing) by Li Bai, showcases characters that are each "as big as a bucket" and, in his home region of Hunan, "every household has screens with his calligraphy."[79]

The fashion of large-character calligraphy was carried into the Song dynasty. Emperor Taizong, who ordered the compilation of the *Chunhua Model Letters*, was known to have devoted himself to writing "flying white" calligraphy and often wrote on plaques of various buildings in the palace.[80] Screens and walls decorated by large cursive calligraphy can be found in contemporary paintings, though no actual examples survive to today.[81]

Despite the long tradition of large-character calligraphy, the reason for Huang Tingjian's and other contemporary scholars' pursuit of large calligraphy must have

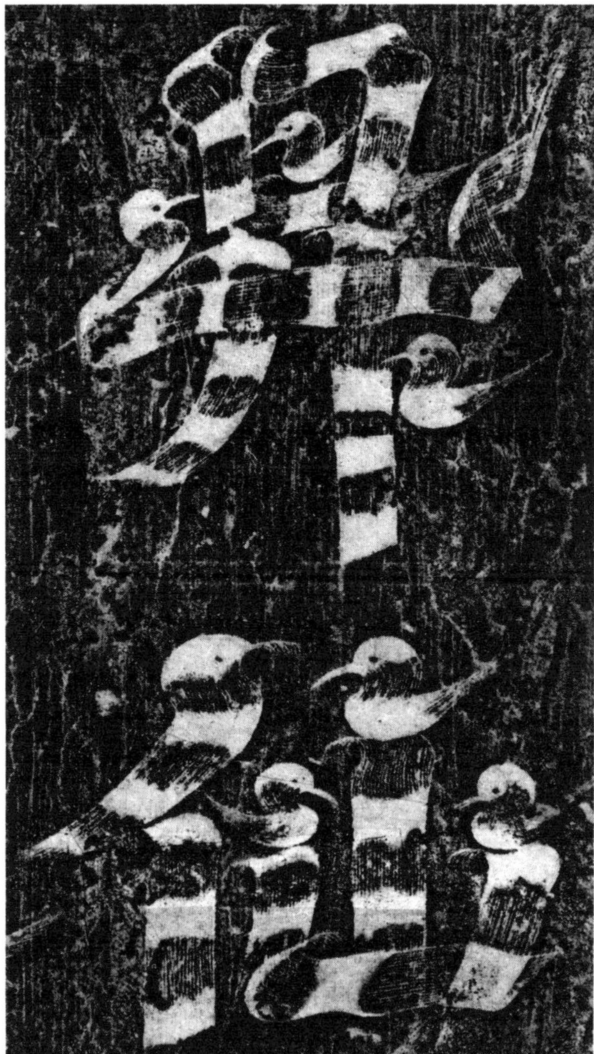

FIGURE 2.5. Wu Zetian, *Stele of the Prince Who Ascended to the Immortal* (Shengxian Taizi bei). Dated ca. 699. Detail of title heading. Ink rubbing. Courtesy of Mr. Fu Chunxi.

originated elsewhere. Whereas the above calligraphy examples are more or less decorative and adorn exterior or interior spaces, the three ancient monuments that Huang singles out as his models for large calligraphy, the *Eulogy*, the Yishan stele, and Yan Zhenqing's *Hymn*, are all self-contained monuments and not subordinate to architectural space. It is perhaps in this sense that Huang compares them to the *Orchid Pavilion*—its calligraphy naturally flows with the literary content but does not address any external adornment. To Huang Tingjian, they may represent a candid way of writing.[82] Furthermore, it might not be coincidental that the three ancient works Huang lists are all found in the natural environment—a possible evocation of the origin of script as a response to natural traces. Huang Tingjian's interest was in line with his peer Northern Song scholars, yet his approach to the ancient inscriptions was unique.

Transforming "Worn-Brush Writing"

Among Huang Tingjian's three models, the most direct connection to Huang's own calligraphy is *Eulogy for Burying a Crane*. Carved into a limestone cliff, the layout of the *Eulogy* was adapted to the irregular surface of the stone; both the sizes of the characters and the spaces between them vary dramatically. The irregular size and spacing of characters and the constant shifts in the axis of individual characters and columns in these works find a similar visual effect in Huang's own work. It may be sufficient here, following a detailed stylistic analysis by modern calligrapher and art historian Fu Shen, to consider a few examples from *Scroll for Zhang Datong* (Zeng Zhang Datong juan bawei, dated 1100; figure 2.6a and b), a long colophon to a now-lost transcription of an essay by Han Yu that Huang Tingjian did for Zhang, his nephew.[83] The number of characters per line ranges from three to five; some are aligned vertically, but there is little sense of horizontal rows. Several characters, such as *zhi* 之, *liu* 六, and *wushi* 五十 in figure 2.6b, are squeezed into narrow spaces. These visually dense passages contrast with others in which large characters, such as *nian* 年, extend into the space surrounding them.

Huang's visual reinterpretation of the ancient inscription also seems apparent in his elongated strokes and sharp ends, as well as in the subtle twists and turns in the middle of strokes—a kind of calligraphic vibrato called *chanbi*, or "trembling brushwork."[84] For instance, in the character *she* 舍 (figure 2.7), the left diagonal stroke maintains a regular shape but the right one is twisted in the middle and ends with a sharp tip. These opposing movements create a visual tension, which may illustrate Huang's term for good brushwork, *qinzong*, or "constrain and release."[85] This effect, if we agree on Fu Shen's observation, could also be meant to approximate the appearance of the eroded carved characters as they appear in ink rubbings. Furthermore, some characters in the *Scroll for Zhang Datong*, such as *tong* 同, *jing* 徑, and *po* 頗, at the left end of the section in figure 2.6a, are written with blunt and rounded strokes—an effect that places the characters outside the Wang Xizhi tradition that stresses fluent movement and elegant shapes by quick shifts of the pressure and angle of the brush.[86] Huang's unique brushwork indeed resembles many characters in the *Eulogy*, which are "as if written with a worn brush," as his critic Huang Bosi observed—though the inscription in stone was rather the result of natural erosion. Still, Huang Tingjian insisted that they were remnants of ancient seal-script brushwork.

Huang's attention to seal-script writing is evident in his inclusion of the Yishan stele in his large-calligraphy models. The ancient stele was erected by the First Emperor in his inspection of the eastern part of his empire in 219 BCE. In the time of Huang Tingjian, however, it was only known as a recent copy (figure 2.8), which still stands in the Beilin Museum in Xi'an.[87] Its relationship to the original was questioned early on by Ouyang Xiu in his *Collection of Antiquities*.[88] Huang Tingjian was unlikely to have been impressed by the formal and mechanical look of the modern copy. To him, however, the unmistakably large size may have served as a convenient example to stress the value of seal-script brushwork in a work of large calligraphy.

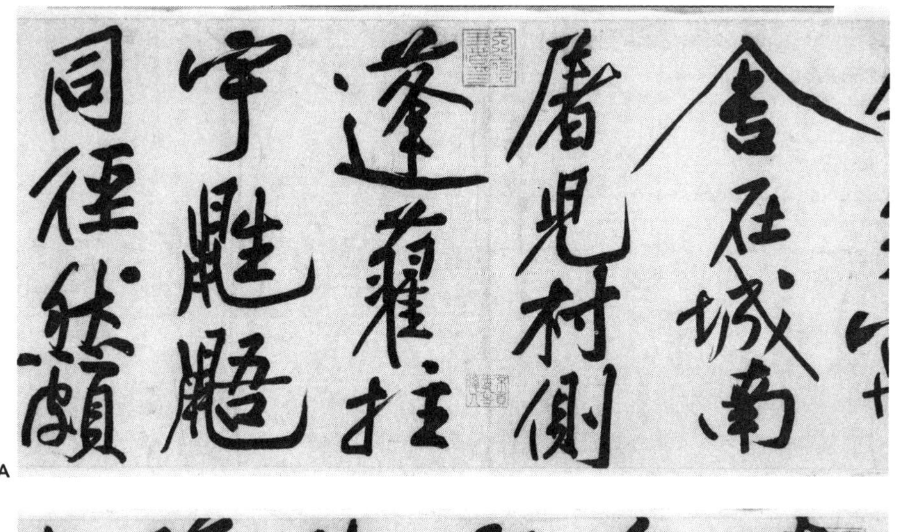

A

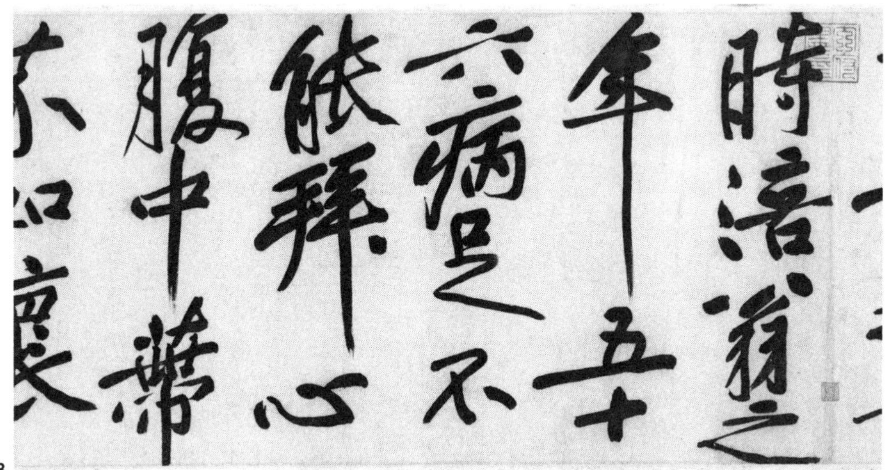

B

FIGURE 2.6. (A AND B) Detail from Huang Tingjian, *Scroll for Zhang Datong*. Dated 1100. Handscroll, ink on paper, 34.1 × 552.9 cm. Princeton University Art Museum, Princeton. Gift of John B. Elliott. Photo by Bruce M. White.

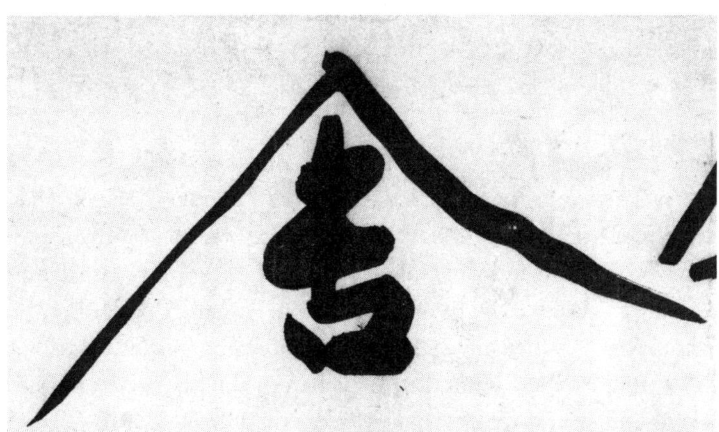

FIGURE 2.7. Detail of figure 2.6a.

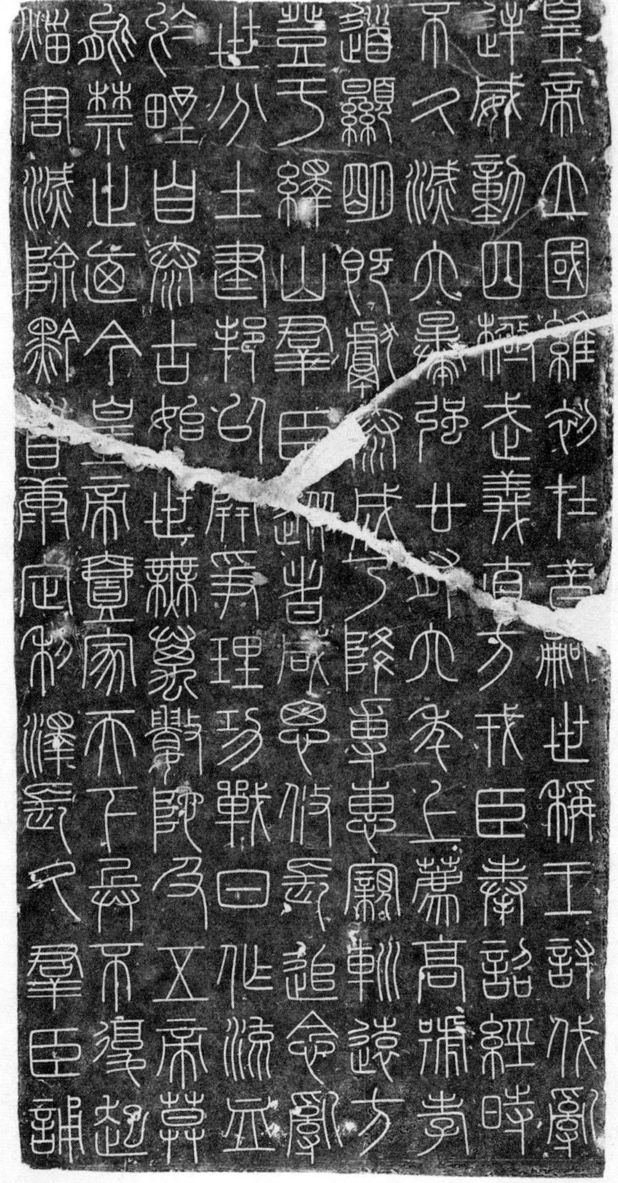

FIGURE 2.8. Li Si (attributed), *Yishan Stele*. A Song dynasty copy by Xu Xuan. Ink rubbing, 218 cm (height). Courtesy of the Metropolitan Museum of Art. Seymour and Rogers Funds, 1977.

It might have been the same concern that led him to Yan Zhenqing's *Hymn to the Revival of the Great Tang Dynasty*, a large *moya* inscription more than fourteen feet tall, which still survives (most likely as a result of numerous recarving campaigns) on the cliff overlooking the Wuxi River in today's Qiyang, Hunan Province (figure 2.9). The text was composed by the eminent official and poet Yuan Jie (723–772) to celebrate the recovery of the dynasty after the An Lushan Rebellion (755–63). Yuan asked Yan, his close friend, to transcribe it in the latter's distinctive style, featuring four-square character compositions and bold, simplified brushwork (figure 2.10).[89]

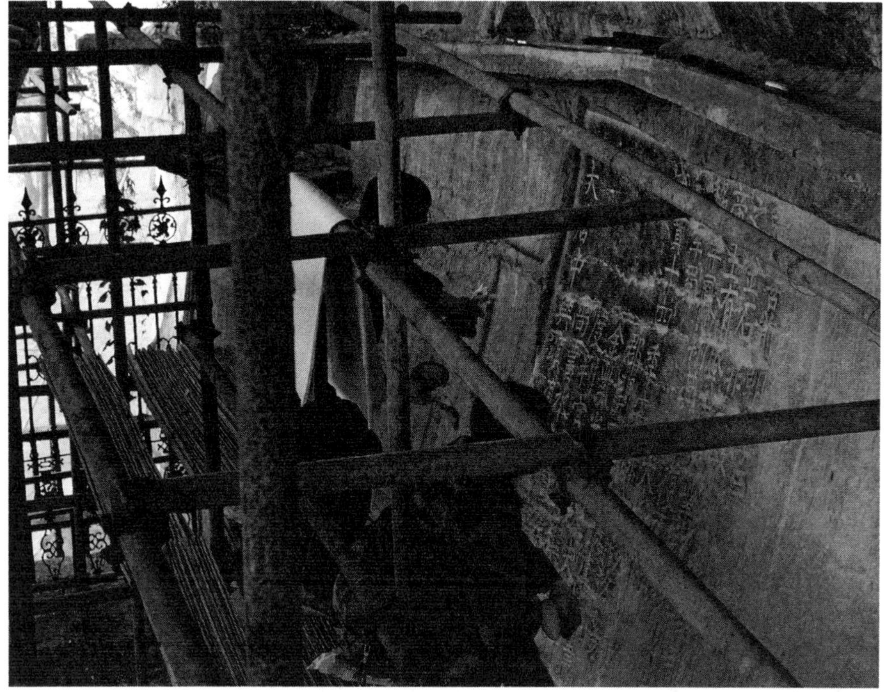

(*above*) **FIGURE 2.9.** Making rubbing at the site of *Hymn to the Revival of the Great Tang Dynasty* (Da Tang zhongxing song), Wuxi, Hunan. Author's photo, 2017.

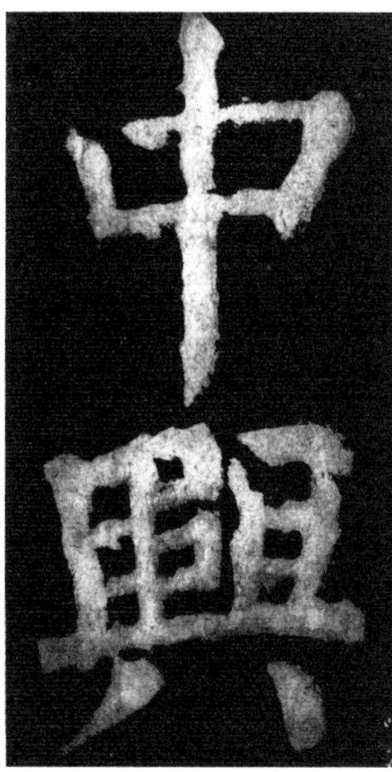

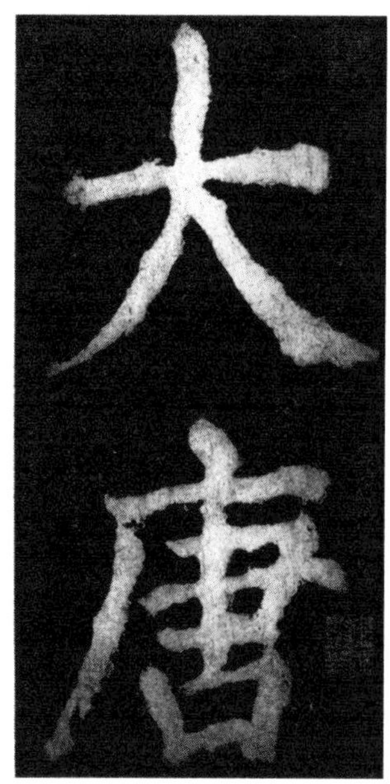

(*right*) **FIGURE 2.10.** Yan Zhenqing, *Hymn to the Revival of the Great Tang Dynasty*. Dated 771. Detail. Ink rubbing. From *Zhongguo meishu quanji: Shufa zhuanke bian* 4:149.

Thanks to the great influence of Yan calligraphy in the Northern Song, rubbings of *Hymn* became so sought-after that even silk versions were reportedly made from it and mounted on screens—an old-fashioned way to display large calligraphy.[90] Unlike his peer scholars, including Su Shi, and despite his constant praise of Yan's calligraphy, Huang Tingjian demonstrated less interest in incorporating the prevailing

"Yan style" in his own calligraphy.[91] Perhaps what interested him was the heavy and blunt engraved strokes that evoke seal-script calligraphy. Indeed, surprising similarities can be found between the *Hymn* and the *Eulogy*: both were carved on cliffs overlooking water, the sizes of the characters in the two inscriptions are roughly the same, and both texts read from left to right, a format unusual in early Chinese writing.[92] But an intrinsic connection between the two, and to the Yishan stele, was the seal-script brushwork that Huang eventually turned into his original creation.

One aspect of Huang's interpretation of the *Eulogy* requires further explanation: his insistence on the authorship of Wang Xizhi, which had been dismissed by all his peer antiquarian scholars. In a colophon to a rubbing of the *Eulogy*, Huang specified that the "energetic force" of its calligraphy illustrates *longzhuashu*, or "dragon-claw writing," a legendary script type said to have been invented by Wang Xizhi and known only through hearsay.[93] This rhetorical ploy was consistent with other seemingly incongruous interpretations of the history of calligraphy found in Huang's writings. Consider his statements about the style of Yan Zhenqing. Whereas Huang Tingjian argues that Yan was among the few calligraphers who were true artistic heirs of the Two Wangs, he singles out Yan's monumental stone inscriptions—those works that were least like the transmitted models by Wang Xizhi—as the greatest examples.[94] He attempts to explain this discrepancy by asserting that "all of them [Yan's works] are in accord with the brush method of Youjun, father and son [Wang Xianzhi]."[95] Huang identifies his approach as a "roundabout" (*quzhe qiuzhi*) way of understanding Yan's calligraphy, but his reasoning is not duplicitous or self-serving.[96] His analysis attempts to reconcile a larger paradox between the allegiance to tradition and the quest for originality in the discourse of Northern Song literati calligraphers and critics. And within the larger context, it can be seen as the collective effort of Northern Song scholars to reestablish a connection to history—associating the *Eulogy* with the elusive dragon-claw style thus legitimated Huang's own innovative project of inventing a personal style of monumental calligraphy.

Nevertheless, Huang Tingjian's interpretation of the *Eulogy* was by no means revelatory to his contemporaries. Despite the epigraphic studies, adopting pre-Tang inscriptions as models was an unusual choice for calligraphers of Huang's generation. Although these calligraphers had new knowledge of ancient writing thanks to the research of epigraphic scholars, they did not necessarily consider these carved texts to be suitable artistic models.[97] In fact, Huang's advocacy of the *Eulogy* may have received no support at all. For example, his most like-minded friend, Su Shi, wrote extensively about calligraphy but left no direct commentary on the controversy over the *Eulogy*, at least in his extant works—a curious omission considering his broad intellectual interests and intensive exchange with Huang. Mi Fu, the long-term resident of Zhenjiang, who must have known the *Eulogy* well (we shall see his inscription left at Jiaoshan soon), demonstrated great interest in large calligraphy, but he left not one word about its calligraphy in his extant writings.[98] It is an unusual gesture given his notorious outspoken criticism. Their silence, if not due to neglect, may be read as a polite disagreement with Huang Tingjian. Furthermore, none of the immediate followers of Huang Tingjian's bold large-character calligraphy are known to have demonstrated interest in the *Eulogy*. His aesthetic theories and vision of the *Eulogy* would resurface in later times and become unexpectedly influential in different cultural milieus, which we will examine in the following chapters.

Tagging Names

It may be fair to say that the heated scholarly debates on the date and authorship of the *Eulogy* and the revolutionary change in calligraphic aesthetics discussed above were limited to a narrow elite circle. What did not change was the continuing popular fascination with the legendary stone—clearly, it was still the name Wang Xizhi that attracted a broad range of visitors. As Jiaoshan became a destination for a growing numbers of tourists in the eleventh century, seeking out the "Wang Xizhi stele" became a sort of cultural pilgrimage. These visits were sometimes documented in the inscriptions left on the island.[99]

One of the earliest inscriptions documents a visit in 1068 by a certain Liu Guinian (dates unknown). It is carved on the standing rock known as the Lightning Striking Stone (figure 2.11; see its location in figure I.4, h):

> Liu Tangnian, [*zi*] Junzuo [polite name, same below], and his younger brothers Yannian, [*zi*] Ziyong, Guinian, [*zi*] Renfu, and Pengnian, [*zi*] Yuanlao climbed here to visit Youjun's [Wang Xizhi] stele. The twentieth day of the third month, the first year of the Xining era [1068]. Inscribed by Guinian. We were accompanied by the monk Jingzong. (2J)

Nothing else is known about the Liu brothers. Reading through the inscription, one can envision an outing to Jiaoshan that would be repeated by countless later visitors: on a beautiful spring day, guided by a monk from a local temple, a group of visitors wanders over rocks and through weeds on the wild bank of the river to search for the traces of the legendary "Wang Xizhi stele." Although some among them, like Shao Kang and Zhang Yu (whom we introduced earlier), took their trips as serious research, in most cases visitors simply enjoyed the pilgrimage-like trip itself, paying tribute to the relics from the ancient sage and, more importantly, leaving an inscription of their own—indeed it might be the only trace they left to the world. And perhaps the Lightning Striking Stone was chosen for its resemblance to a stele monument.

These inscriptions left by tourists at Jiaoshan belong to the category of epigraphy known in Chinese as *timing*, or "tagging names," that, though arguably originating in the mid-Tang period, began to proliferate in many places in the late eleventh century.[100] Unlike modern graffiti found in almost any tourist destination around the world,

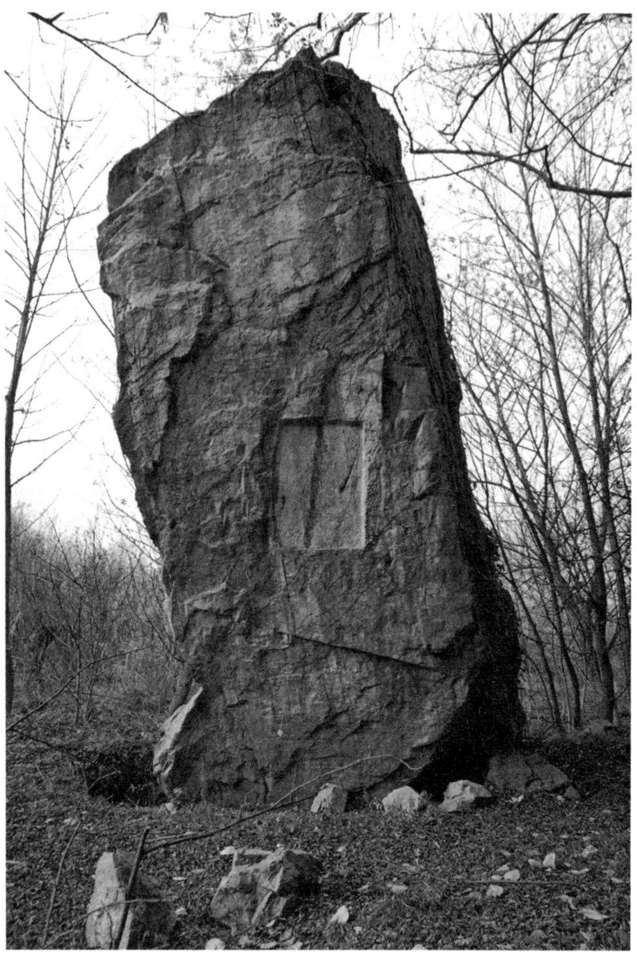

FIGURE 2.11. Lightning Striking Stone (Leihongshi) at Jiaoshan. Author's photo, 2007.

timing should be seen as carefully planned cultural products that entail institutional authorization and support. At places like Jiaoshan, it was often the local Buddhist temples that took charge of the business. Depending on the social status of visitors, or perhaps the amount of their donations to the temple on the island, their writings would be carved into rocks around the sites they had visited. These inscriptions could be produced in one of two ways: calligraphers brushed characters in cinnabar directly on stone surfaces, to be carved later; or inscriptions on paper were traced and transferred to stone for carving. Monks at the temple on Jiaoshan or in the nearby area, as we found in the above inscription, probably played a key role in arranging to have inscriptions carved, selecting both texts and sites for permanent display.

A vivid example of *timing* from the following century is preserved in a brush-written work by the noted calligrapher Wu Ju (fl. late twelfth century), now in the National Palace Museum, Taipei (figure 2.12). This inscription records that Wu and two friends visited Jiaoshan in 1192. This sheet may have been given to a Jiaoshan monk in the expectation that it would be carved on the cliff, though the inscription

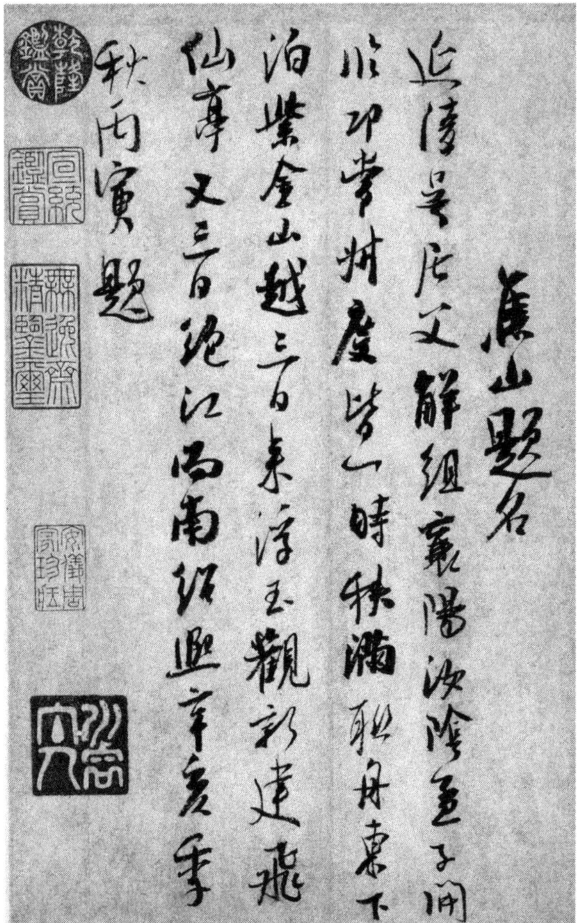

FIGURE 2.12. Wu Ju, *Timing inscription at Jiaoshan*. Dated 1192. Ink on paper, 32.8 × 44.9 cm. National Palace Museum, Taipei.

does not survive today, or perhaps it never did, for some reason. Another work by Wu Ju, dated 1184 and with a more elaborate poetic form, was indeed carved into stone and is still visible today at Jiaoshan (figure 2.13; see its location in figure I.4c). The poem records Wu's visit to the *Eulogy* and ends with a sentiment resonant with the sixth-century inscription:

> The Crane of Huating has returned [to its home];
> the Yangzi River is running to the east.
> A solitary mind transcends a thousand years;
> in the sunset rise the mist and fog.
> (2K)

For Wu Ju, it was a great opportunity to integrate his literary immortality into the historical site, identifying himself with a luminous cultural tradition in which Tao Hongjing (or Wang Xizhi, if he chose to believe) was a towering figure.[101] From the

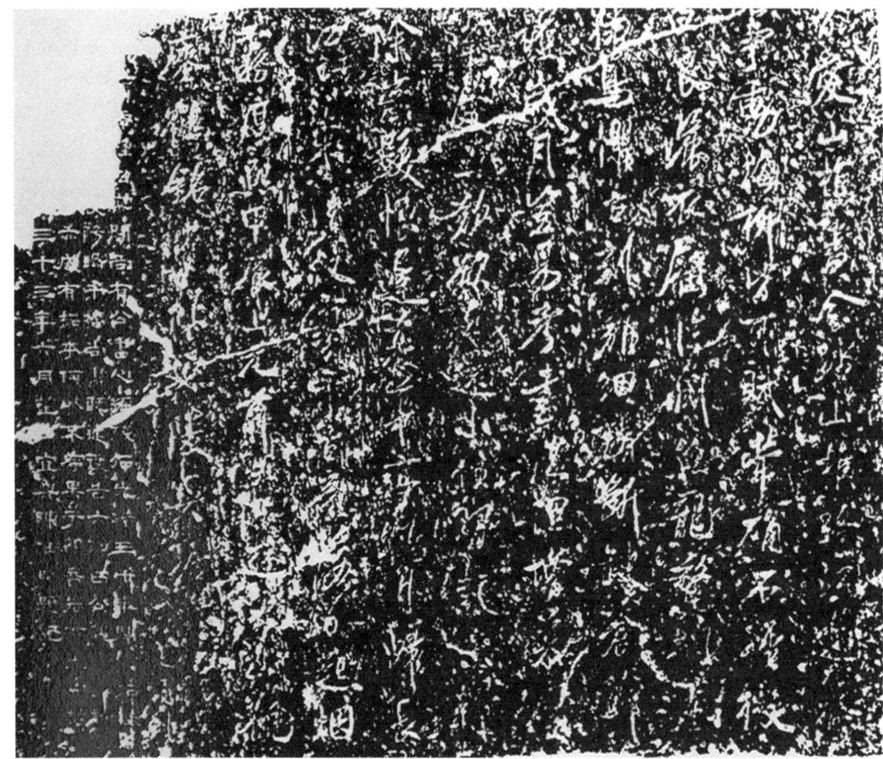

FIGURE 2.13. Wu Ju, stone inscription at Jiaoshan. Dated 1184. Ink rubbing, 125 × 122 cm. Courtesy of Jiaoshan Stone Inscription Museum.

temple's perspective, inscriptions from cultural celebrities like Wu Ju promoted the fame of Jiaoshan and the prestige of the temple, and they might well have encouraged visitors to return and make further donations.

Sometimes an inscription tells us more than generic literary sentiments. In 1164, Lu You (1125–1210) visited Jiaoshan with a group of friends after he had been assigned to an official post in Zhenjiang. The patriotic poet then left the most prominent inscription (figure 2.14; see its location in figure I.4f) of those carved at Jiaoshan. The text reads:

> Lu Wuguan [Lu You], He Deqi, Zhang Yuzhong, and Han Wujiu trod on snow to visit *Eulogy for Burying a Crane* on the twenty-ninth day of the eleventh month of the *jiashen* year of the Longxing era [1164]. We prepared wine on the top of the cliff. The beacon fire had not yet died out. Looking at the full sails of the battleships in the mist [over the river], we all sighed and got drunk. In the dusk, by boat we went back from the Ganlu Temple. The next year, on the *renwu* day of the second month, the Chan master Yuan inscribed this on the cliff. Written by Wuguan.[102] (2L)

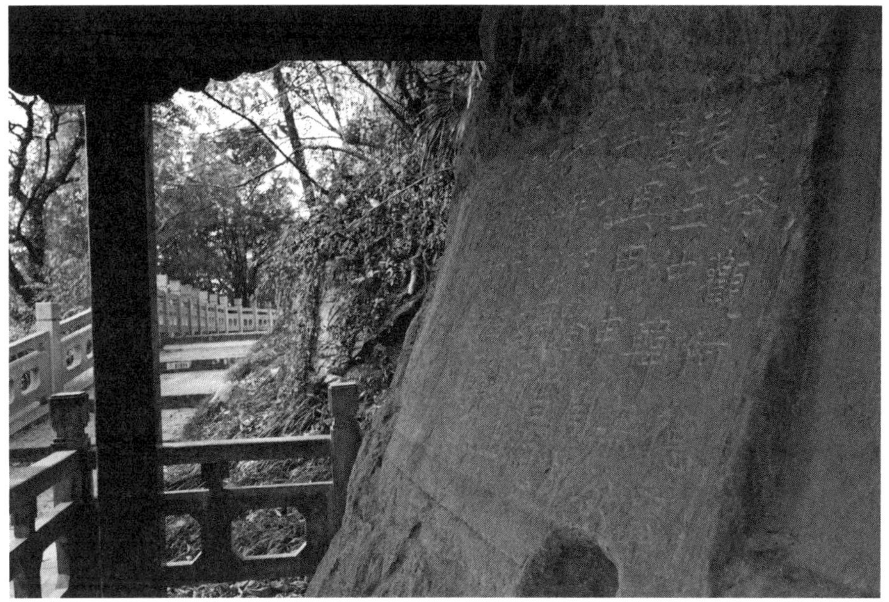

FIGURE 2.14. Lu You, stone inscription at Jiaoshan. Dated 1165. Author's photo, 2017.

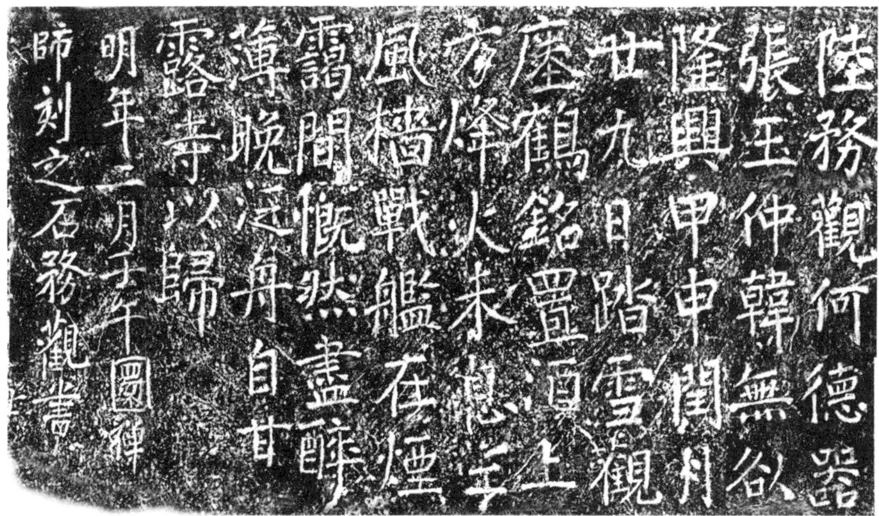

FIGURE 2.15. Lu You, stone inscription at Jiaoshan. Dated 1165. Ink rubbing, 106 × 198 cm. Courtesy of Jiaoshan Stone Inscription Museum.

The large inscription (about 106 × 198 cm) is clearly in the Yan Zhenqing style (figure 2.15) and would have immediately reminded viewers of *The Hymn to the Revival of the Great Tang*. It is unknown how faithfully this inscription represents the original handwriting of Lu You, which otherwise survives only in small pieces in cursive or running scripts.[103] In any case, the message conveyed in the text is unmistakable: the beacon fire and the battle ships signify the Southern Song's failed military campaign to recover its northern territories that were taken by the Jurchen Jin

(1115–1234) two decades before. Right at the time of Lu You's visit in 1164, a peace agreement was reached, which must have greatly frustrated patriots like Lu You, who had high hopes for the campaign.[104] In this context, Lu You's tribute to the *Eulogy*, a remnant from another historical period of division, can be understood as an expression of his patriotic sentiments. His imitation of Yan Zhenqing's *Hymn* was meant to evoke the latter's historical message of dynastic revival. In this way, his *timing* inscription added more layers to the historical meaning of the monument and contributed to the transformation of Jiaoshan into a type of cultural shrine.

Discovery and Replication

Neither Lu You nor Wu Ju provides a detailed description of the *Eulogy* in their own inscriptions. It is from other sources that we know severe damage to the *Eulogy* occurred, perhaps not long before their visits:

> *Eulogy for Burying a Crane* is in the river of today's Zhenjiang prefecture, at the bottom of the backside of Jiaoshan. Only in winter months and in lower water, putting a mat and lying on the back, was one able to make rubbings. In the middle of the Shaoxing era [1131–1162], [the emperor] was seeking old copies [of rubbings?]. A messenger stopped by, commanding workers to cut the inscriptions off from the rock. The rock was too hard to cut through. He got only ten characters or so. And because [the fragments] were too heavy to carry, he took away only one or two characters and left the rest, which are now in the east hall of the controller general's office.[105] (2M)

The author, Zhao Yanwei (ca. 1140–ca. 1210), a local official and an antiquarian scholar, may have seen the fragments in person.[106] The event perhaps refers to an imperial project of recovering calligraphic models by Emperor Gaozong (r. 1127–1162), who was known as an admirer of Huang Tingjian's calligraphy and perhaps was guided by the latter's words to Jiaoshan.[107] The search for the *Eulogy* ironically led to more damage to the inscription. Fortunately, according to Zhao, most characters were still intact. Comparing the Northern Song reconstruction (see figure 2.2) and an investigative report in 1667 (see figure C.1), we can speculate that what was destroyed might have been the long-lost beginning part of the inscription, including the title.

A much later local gazetteer tells us that during the Xianchun era (1265–74), the Treasured Ink Pavilion was demolished and the fragment it housed was lost forever.[108] Despite the continuing enthusiasm of tourists, no reliable reports on the fate of that stone were written since then. There was, however, an unexpected result of the flourishing tourism at Jiaoshan—namely, the production of replicas of the stone in various forms.

Recarving (*chongke*) old inscriptions, such as that of the Yishan stele in the early Song, was not a new phenomenon. The making of replicas served multiple purposes. In some cases, they were intended to protect the original or preserve historical information when the originals were lost. Or, since the original inscription had collapsed and was difficult to view, replicas satisfied curious visitors and helped maintain the prestige of the site. Other replicas—called *fanke* by rubbing specialists—of stone inscriptions were the products of tricksters; as the demand for rubbings from the stone grew and the supply was limited by lack of access to the original stones, replicas provided handier and faster sources for rubbings.[109]

One early *chongke* replica of *Eulogy*, known as *Alternative Carving at the Grand View Pavilion* (Zhuangguanting bieke; figure 2.16), still partly survives on the cliff of Floating Jade Rock (see its location in figure I.4e) at Jiaoshan. In spite of the replica's name, there are no traces left at the site of the pavilion structure, presumably built in the Song. Only thirty characters remain, as the lower part was cut away and the stone surface was polished to receive a new inscription.[110] All are the same as those on the original stones and obviously were based on rubbings from them. The replica appears to have been carved after the time of Zhang Yu and Shao Kang, as neither mentioned it in accounts of their investigations in the 1070s. It might already have been in place by 1091, as Mi Fu left his *timing* inscription under the lower right corner (see a rubbing in figure 2.17; location is marked in figure I.4d). It reads:

> Zhongxuan, Fazhi, and Mi Fu viewed the calligraphy of [Shanghuang] Shanqiao in the fourth month of the *xinwei* year of the Yuanyou era [1091]. (2N)

It is known that the first two persons named were monks from a temple at Mount Jin, another nearby famous historical site (see map 2 at beginning of book). The location of the inscription suggests that what Mi Fu saw when he visited Jiaoshan might have been the replica, not the original stones in the river, which would have been submerged during his late spring visit. Following the Mi Fu inscription, carved near the replica are names of more Song visitors (see appendix 1, nos. 7, 8, 10, 14, and 15.). The location of their inscriptions suggests that most of them took the replica as the original.

Toward the end of the twelfth century, more replicas were reported. According to Ma Ziyan (*jinshi* 1175), a noted poet who served as a local official in Zhenjiang:

> In the *jiyou* year of the Chunxi era [1189], I held the position of director of education of Danyang Prefecture. On a free day I visited Jiaoshan and looked for the inscription of [*Eulogy for Burying a Crane*]. At first, in front of the offering table [in the temple], I saw a stone fragment that bears twenty characters or so. They are the beginning section [of the *Eulogy*]. A monk said, "This piece fell from the cliff some years ago in an earthquake [a landslide?]." I was not convinced. Then I took a boat to the cliff for a thorough examination. Beginning

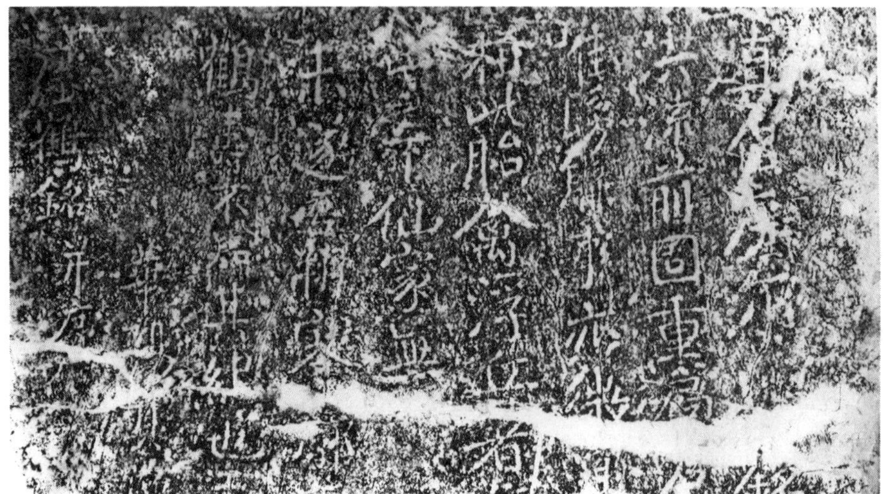

FIGURE 2.16. *Alternative Carving at the Grand View Pavilion*. Ink rubbing, 70 × 120 cm. Courtesy of Jiaoshan Stone Inscription Museum.

> with "*zi shan zhi xia*" 茲山之下, there are more than twenty characters left. In the water there was a rock standing askew. The boatman said, "This is a fragment of the [*Eulogy*] stele, and one can make a rubbing when the water level is lower." I then pleaded with the prefect [of Zhenjiang], the acting scholar of the Longtu Pavilion Zhang Ziyan [fl. late twelfth century], to send soldiers to pull it out. [There were] more than twenty characters [on the stone], beginning with "*jia wu sui*" 甲午歲. A soldier recalled, "Below this rock there lay a smaller one; when touching it with fingers I felt there were engraved strokes." I then had the stone pulled out too. The inscription on the stone is exactly the same as what I had seen in front of the offering table. I compared them side by side. [On the newly found stone] only two characters were missing but the force of the brushwork differed apparently. Then I realized that the one I had seen was forged by the monks of the temple.[111] (2O)

Comparing the description with the reconstructed text (see figure 1.4), we can deduce that a top portion of the inscription, corresponding to today's F3 stone (plate 5), still survived on the cliff at that time. Furthermore, the first rock pulled out from the water appeared to be today's F2 (plate 4), and the second, which was replicated in the temple, was a fragment corresponding to today's F1. It would be dangerous, however, to draw such a direct connection. As we will see in chapter 3, today's F2 was reported as a late replica and thus may not be the same one as Ma discovered. And it is impossible to track the origin of F1, too. Ma Ziyan does not tell us how he and other officials dealt with the fragments and the replica, which are not mentioned in other contemporary sources.

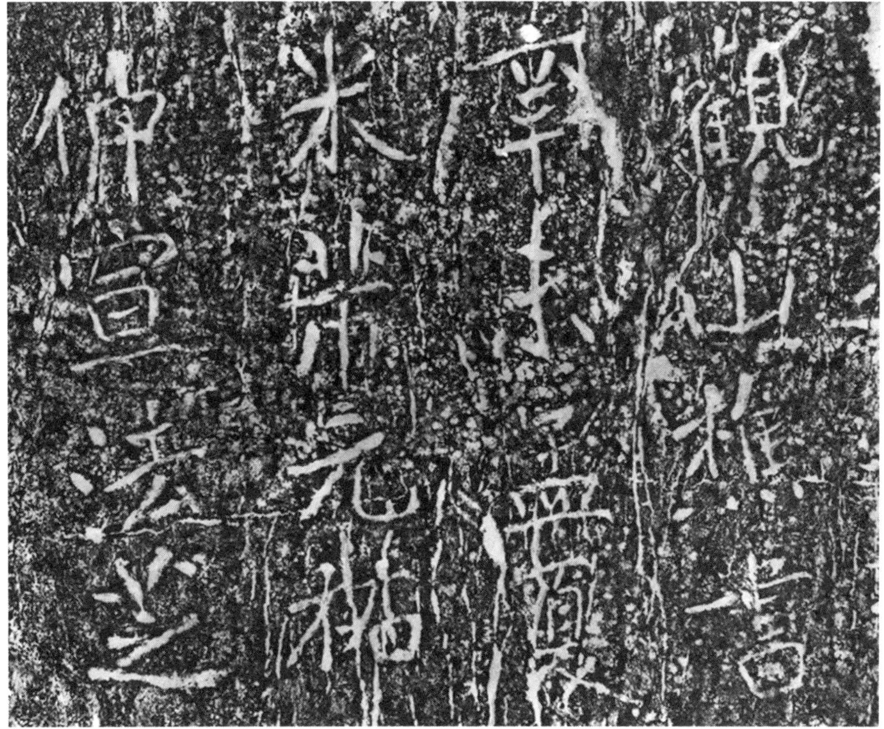

FIGURE 2.17. Mi Fu, inscription at Jiaoshan. Dated 1091. Ink rubbing, 65 × 77 cm. Courtesy of Jiaoshan Stone Inscription Museum.

A *fanke* replica that would have circulated widely was called *Alternative Carving at Zhenjiang Prefectural Hall* (Zhenjiang fuzhi bieke), which was reported to have been displayed in the prefectural hall of Zhenjiang at least since the early thirteenth century.[112] The stone is long gone but the text was recorded by a scholar named Liu Changshi (*jinshi* 1205).[113] The preface section is almost identical to the reconstructed text. The *ming* section, however, shows many variations, as italicized below:

> *The immortals want to* set up a stone to honor his virtues.
> The eulogy reads,
> To judge the physiognomy of the "viviparous bird,"
> [The immortal] Master Fuqiu wrote the Crane Classic.
> *Then we trace past records,*
> *which were derived from the upper perfected.*
> I do not wish to say anything more,
> *except recording the year of [your birth and death].*
> At the Thunder Gate you departed the drum;
> on the huabiao pillars you left behind your *sound.*
> *My words* are obscure and subtle;

Your life are elusive and mysterious.
Where is it that you will go?
Released and transformed *in the peaceful land*
Behind flows the raging torrent;
in front stand firmly the double-layered gates.
[*Missing character here*] fenced with a thorny gate.
You have not yet descended to Huating.
Therefore, I have gathered my "Perfected Companions,"
buried you here, and written this eulogy.
Calligraphy by the Woodcutter of Mount Shanghuang, *Yishao*
Stone erected by the Recluse of Mount Jiang, the Outer Immortal Commandant of Danyang, and the Perfected Steward of Jiangyin. (2P)

Liu compares this text with Shao Kang's reconstruction and concludes that this replica was based on sources from two origins: the fragmentary original inscription and earlier transcriptions. He argues that such additional characters as "then we trace past records" (*nai zheng qian shi* 乃徵前事) in this so-called early transcription were very likely pastiches assembled from elements of existing characters from the stones themselves or from rubbings.[114] Furthermore, the inscription adds Wang Xizhi's polite name, Yishao 逸少, at the end of the signature line. This fabricated signature, transforming the attribution of Wang Xizhi from an oral legend to a visual fact, demonstrates the longevity of the myth.

Ironically, a replica would become the main source for knowledge of the *Eulogy* when it was reproduced in a seventeenth-century calligraphic model-letters compendium. And the newly forged Wang Xizhi signature finally materialized visitors' fantasies about the legendary stone. The concept of authenticity became tenuous, but the multiplication of replicas, as well as the dissemination of rubbings taken from them, increased the cultural value of the inscription, even as the original stones faded away from historical records.

CHAPTER 3

Remaking the Model

It was a misty day when I first visited Jiaoshan in 2004. The foot of the island was covered with overgrown bushes and strewn with rocks. Walking down to the muddy shore and searching for the rock cliff on which *Eulogy for Burying a Crane* had been carved, I spotted a fishing boat on the river that seemed to be out of a lyrical Song painting. The landscape around Jiaoshan, like everywhere else during the last decade in China, has changed dramatically thanks to the skyrocketing construction since my first visit. Large apartment complexes have risen along the banks of the Yangzi River. Brand-new temple buildings and park facilities crowd the island.

What has not changed is the experience of walking along the winding mountain path, looking at and touching the inscriptions on the cliff (figure 3.1). They define the site, which is saturated with layers of cultural memory. In his classic essay on Suzhou, a famous nearby historical city, the historian Frederick W. Mote discerned a very different sense of the past in Chinese versus Western culture. He explained that in a place like Suzhou, instead of ancient ruins (which a Western traveler might expect to see in an old city), "the past was a past of words, not of stones."[1] By "stones," Mote meant the remnants of monumental architecture. In Jiaoshan, which is undergoing great physical change, the words of the past were not only recorded in books but also carved in stone—in this case, the natural rocks. In this way, we may say, the past is secured in both textual and material forms.

Departing from the large Lu You inscription (see figure 2.14) that marks the starting point of the "calligraphy path" today and continuing to read through the other remaining inscriptions on the cliff, one may find some historical patterns: the early inscriptions are dated up to the end of the Southern Song, and no inscriptions survive from between 1272 and 1425 (see appendix 1). This may suggest that visits to the crane's epitaph decreased dramatically as a result of the invasion of the Mongols and

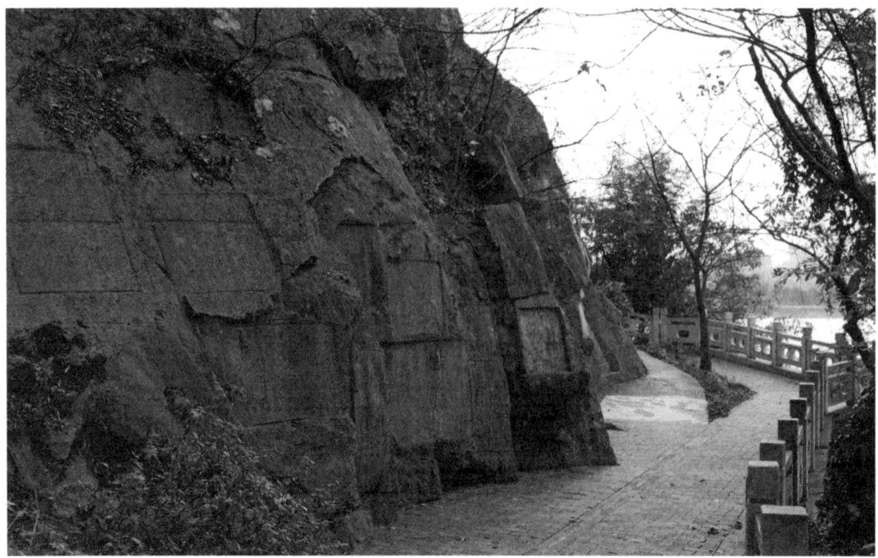

FIGURE 3.1. *Moya* inscriptions at Floating Jade Rock (Fuyuyan), Jiaoshan. Author's photo, 2017.

their rule until 1367, or at least that visitors were no longer enthusiastic about leaving *timing* inscriptions, a cultural fashion that waned with the fall of the Song dynasty.[2]

A few inscriptions on the island date to the fifteenth century—the early Ming dynasty— but it was not until the middle of the sixteenth century that there was a resurgence of visitors' inscriptions. The locations of these carved texts, near the *Alternative Carving at the Grand View Pavilion* (see figure I.4e), suggests that they all refer to the Song replica of the *Eulogy* rather than the original inscription that had fallen at the foot of the island. Despite sporadic accounts about the *Eulogy* and its rubbings, knowledge of the stones seems to have become obscure. This oblivion is illustrated by an anecdote concerning the famous antiquarian collector Du Mu (1459–1525), who owned a large collection of rubbings but once complained that he could not find a single rubbing of the *Eulogy*, even though it was not far from his hometown of Suzhou. When he had a chance to visit Jiaoshan in 1504, he was disappointed to hear from local monks that the inscription had been completely destroyed.[3] However, during another trip, when he stopped by Zhenjiang in the winter of 1517, a local scholar told him that the inscription still survived. Excited by the news, he immediately set off for Jiaoshan with the informant:

> After climbing up to the mountain and treading through the snow to search for it, we indeed found it on the stone cliff. Only twenty characters were legible. Therefore, I made a rubbing [from the inscription] and returned. About several dozen steps before reaching the inscription is the inscribed name of Lu Fangweng [Lu You] from the second year of the Jiaxi era [1238],[4] which reads, "treading on the snow we viewed *Eulogy for Burying a Crane*." Then I

realized that people of the past were in favor of the strange [*hao qi*] before I came along.[5] (3A)

Judging by the description of the location, we know that Du Mu, like many Song visitors, mistook the *Grand View Pavilion* replica for the original inscription. The rubbing he finally acquired, therefore, was from the replica, which is "about several dozen steps" away from Lu You's inscription (see figure I.4f). Obviously, Du was not alone; around the time of his two visits, *timing* inscriptions were carved into the cliff, all near the location of the replica, and some of them still survive (see appendix 1, nos. 23 and 34).

One year after Du's visit, his student Gu Yuanqing (1482–1565), a prolific writer who perhaps visited Jiaoshan with his mentor, published the first monograph on the *Eulogy*. Titled *An Evidential Study of Eulogy for Burying a Crane* (Yi he ming kao, preface dated 1518), it is a collection of previous writings on the subject, the first of its kind.[6] This "evidential study," though so titled, has been dismissed by many later scholars for including neither substantial research nor original discovery.[7] For instance, although Gu acknowledged the writings by Song scholars Zhang Yu and Shao Kang, he simply ignored their on-site findings and reconstructed texts. Instead, he published the less reliable text of the *Alternative Carving at Zhenjiang Prefectural Hall* that we discussed at the end of the last chapter, disregarding the manifold problems of this source. This "negligence" in the monograph, in many respects in contrast to the evidential research by Song scholars, was shared by other contemporary writings on history and artifacts.[8] As we shall soon see, the interests of the late Ming scholars—and that of the calligraphers as well—rested elsewhere.

The "Strange Thing" and the "Marvelous View"

Not long after Du Mu and Gu Yuanqing's visit, the fallen original stones began to garner more attention. *Timing* inscriptions on the Lightning Striking Stone (appendix 1, nos. 35 and 39) indicate that from the 1520s onward, some visitors followed the eleventh-century pioneers and began to search through the bushes and mud for the so-called Wang Xizhi stele. By the late sixteenth century, the location of the original stone in the water must have been exposed to the public. Visitors left more inscriptions (see appendix 1, nos. 40, 41, and 43), and rubbings made from the original inscription emerged as well. When such a rubbing was brought to the influential writer and calligrapher Wang Shizhen (1526–1590) by his friend Ye Boyin (fl. mid-sixteenth century), Wang carefully compared it with an old rubbing in his possession. He concluded that the new rubbing, though consisting of much fewer characters, was from the original stones, a fact of which he had been unaware.[9] Ye also told Wang about his regrettable visit to the site: the stone was submerged in water and it had been impossible to make a rubbing. All he could do was "walk into the water to touch the inscription and finger it for a long time."[10] The story must have fascinated Wang Shizhen. On another occasion, when Wang heard about the same account from another friend, he could not help but exclaim excitedly, "Touching *Eulogy for Burying a Crane* underwater and reading it—what a strange thing [*qishi*]!"[11]

On the twenty-fifth day of the sixth month of 1570, perhaps not long after he wrote the foregoing reflections, Wang Shizhen visited Jiaoshan and stayed overnight on the island.[12] It was his second time visiting the island but possibly the first time that he went down to the river, finally "touching the *Eulogy for Burying a Crane* and reading it [with fingers]."[13] This tactile experience, perhaps even more than the pleasure of viewing, must have excited the visitors. It was aligned with the well-known late Ming cultural phenomenon of the flavor of "the strange" (or "the marvelous," used hereafter as an interchangeable translation of *qi*, depending on the context), which we have already read about in Du Mu's account of his visit.[14]

The view Wang Shizhen and his friends saw at Jiaoshan may be not much different from the scene in a panoramic handscroll by the famous Suzhou painter Wen Jia (1501–1583), *Landscape of Jinshan and Jiaoshan* (Jin Jiao shan tu), dated 1563 (figure 3.2). The detail reproduced here shows the southern view of Jiaoshan. Temple structures and trees dot on the island. In the front, two tiny figures, recognizable by their dress as a scholar and a monk, are pointing to two huge boulders at the left corner of the island. They resemble the ones bearing the fragments of the *Eulogy* that we visited (see figure I.2). The two figures are therefore probably talking about the location of the *Eulogy*.

The fantasy about *qi*, "the strange," continued to thrive, as the remaining inscriptions at Jiaoshan suggest. One large inscription (figure 3.3; see also I.4g) on the Lightning Striking Stone, dated 1590, deserves special attention:

> In the autumn, the seventh month of the *gengyin* year of the Wanli era [1590], Wang Zongni from Zhangjun took the lady Ma Fengsheng to visit Jiaoshan. Shortly after, Chen Yangchan [1551–1610], Cheng Yingqu [fl. late sixteenth century], and Mao Zhen [fl. late sixteenth century] arrived one after another. Crossing the wild grasses and striding in the mud together, we searched for the ancient inscription *Burying a Crane*. Leaning on the rock, we drank steadily. Each of us then composed a poem. And we inscribed them on the rock wall before leaving.[15] (3B)

Following this text are five poems, including one by Ma Fengsheng (fl. late sixteenth century), self-identified as a courtesan of Qinhuai, the famous pleasure quarter in Nanjing. Armed with a good supply of wine and accompanied by a courtesan, the men completed their visit to Jiaoshan by savoring what they took to be traces of writing by Wang Xizhi. This combination of sensual enjoyment and appreciation of high culture was characteristic of the late Ming period, when seeking

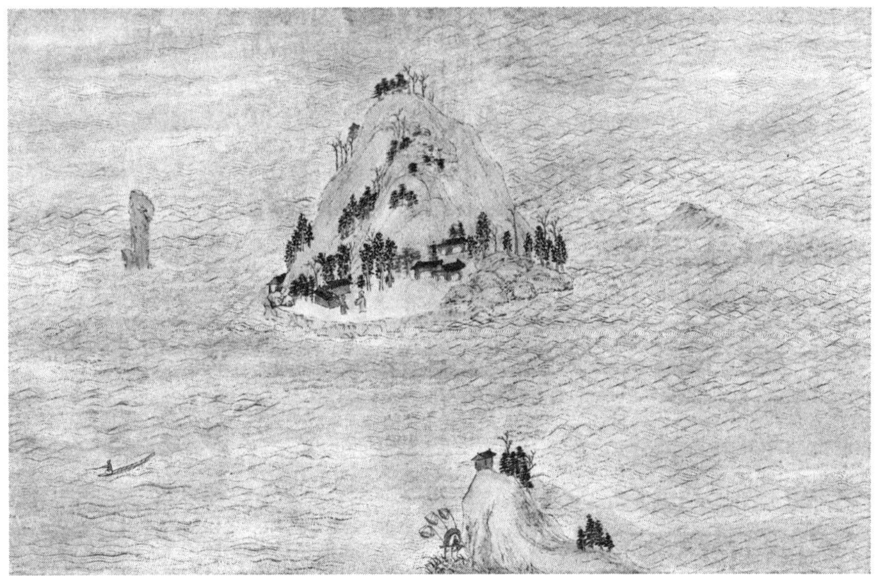

FIGURE 3.2. Wen Jia, *Landscape of Jinshan and Jiaoshan*. Dated 1563. Detail. Handscroll, ink and color on paper, 28.6 × 313.6 cm. Courtesy of Yale University Art Gallery, New Haven. Gift of Wango H. C. Weng.

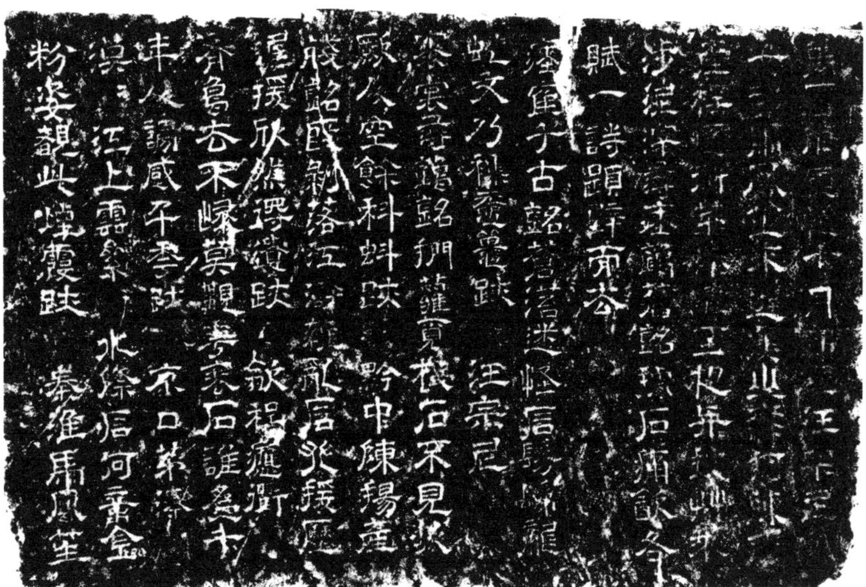

FIGURE 3.3. Wang Zongni et al., stone inscriptions at Jiaoshan. Dated 1590. Ink rubbing, 42 × 68 cm. Courtesy of Jiaoshan Stone Inscription Museum.

pleasure became a central value of both the elite and middle classes.[16] The inscription is written in clerical script, which, despite its archaic origin, was revived at the time as a rather fanciful decoration that appears in contemporary luxury objects and architectural elements.

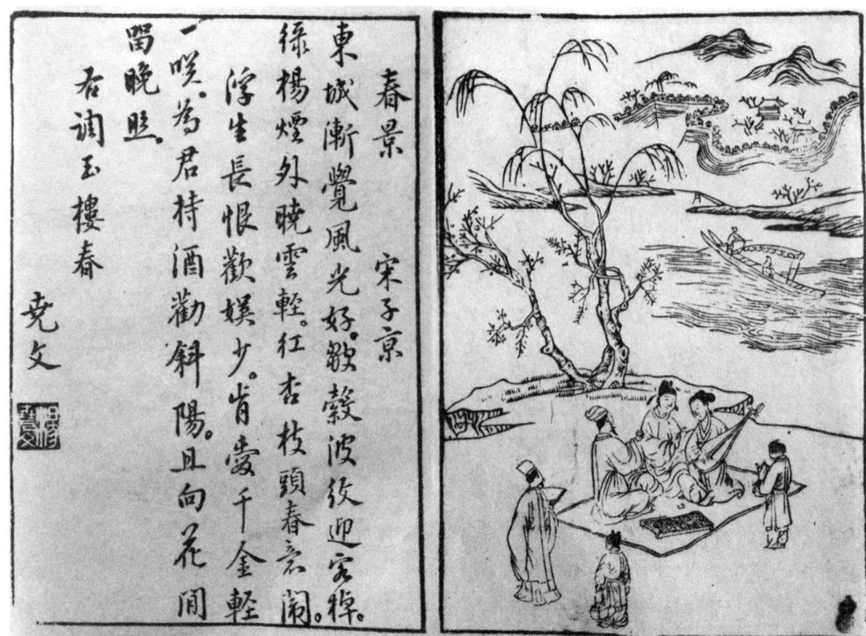

FIGURE 3.4. Pages from *Painting Manual of the Remnants of Poems* (Shiyu huapu). From Zheng Zhenduo, *Zhongguo banhua shi tulu* 20:367–68.

Although their drinking party was similar to that enjoyed by Lu You, the symbolic meaning changed within this new sociocultural context. The site had become one of countless destinations for quasi-literati tourists in the Jiangnan region intent on deriving pleasure from cultural outings, unencumbered by too much concern for historical or antiquarian investigation.[17] The cohort would return at another time to enjoy viewing their own inscriptions carved into the stone, now permanently accompanying the ancient inscription. It is worth noting that the execution of the inscription may have required the paid services of the local temple. The inscription thus indicates a revival of the *timing* economics that we saw in the Song dynasty.

A leisure literary party like Wang Zongni's is vividly recast in a page from a contemporary woodblock, *Painting Manual of Remnants of Poems* (Shiyu huapu, preface 1612; figure 3.4), though the imagined scene is supposed to illustrate a *ci* lyrical poem by the Song poet Song Qi (998–1061).[18] Three scholars, accompanied by a courtesan who is holding a *pipa* lute, are having a drinking party on the bank of a river or lake. To the side are two boy servants carrying wines and food. In the water, another person on a boat may be traveling to join the party. The city walls and buildings emerging from the background mist seem to imply the urban identity of the participants. An informed viewer would recognize the boat and the lute player as references to the famous poem "Ballad of the Pipa" (Pipa xing) by Bai Juyi (772–846).[19] But the lamenting tone of the "Ballad" was replaced by an unmistakable pleasure-seeking one, as the accompanying poem reads:

> In the floating life I only regret not having enough pleasure;
> why do you treasure a thousand pieces of gold and not a smiling face?
> I hold a wine cup for you to ask the sunset
> to leave the late glow lingering among the flowers.
> (3C)

The entire volume of *Remnants of Poems*—full of pictures and poems about beautiful women, wine drinking, seasonal sentiments, and melancholy landscapes—reflects the contemporary lifestyle of the new urbanists, such as Wang Zongni's party at Jiaoshan.

If Wang Shizhen's writing, Wen Jia's painting, and Wang Zongni's inscription can be seen as products of literati culture, in the next decades, the "strange" artifact would be advertised to a much wider audience through popular travel guidebooks, such as *Newly Engraved Marvelous Views within the Seas* (Xinjuan Hainei qiguan), published in 1609.[20] Its collection of "wonders of the world" includes a picture-map of Jiaoshan with a clear label, "Yi he ming," marking the location of the *Eulogy* stone (figure 3.5). The accompanying text explains: "*Eulogy for Burying a Crane*, written by Youjun [Wang Xizhi], was struck by lightning and fell on the shore. One needs to sprawl under the rock to observe it."[21] It goes on to describe the surrounding view that we may imagine through the printed picture:

> The endless wave of the river exhausts one's eyesight. Full sails and trees in cloud are looming near and far. It is indeed a marvelous view [*qiguan*].[22] (3D)

Note that the picture does not fail to hint at the flourishing urban culture—city walls are seen at the top and bottom of the scene. Curiously, the two standing rocks, representing Song and Liao, which should be in the north (correctly placed in another picture in figure 1.7), have been moved to the east side of the island in the print. And compared to their more accurate rendition in figure 1.7, the rocks are depicted in a much larger size and with grotesque shapes, which may be derived from popular images of the immortal peaks that are exemplified in contemporary paintings.[23] Furthermore, Mount Beigu, which is about two miles away from Jiaoshan (see map 2 at beginning of book), now has been inserted into the lower left corner of the picture, right across the river. The exaggerated representation and collapsed space may have been meant to enhance the "marvelous view" for the curious reader.

The cultural turn in the late Ming, epitomized by these printed pictures, is not unfamiliar to scholars of Chinese literature and art. The Jiangnan region's economic growth and urbanization led to the rapid rise of popular culture and the consumption of art among the new middle class.[24] Calligraphy, like other image-making domains, became a field negotiating the boundary between elite taste and popular interest. It was in this context that knowledge of *Eulogy for Burying a Crane*, as both a "strange"

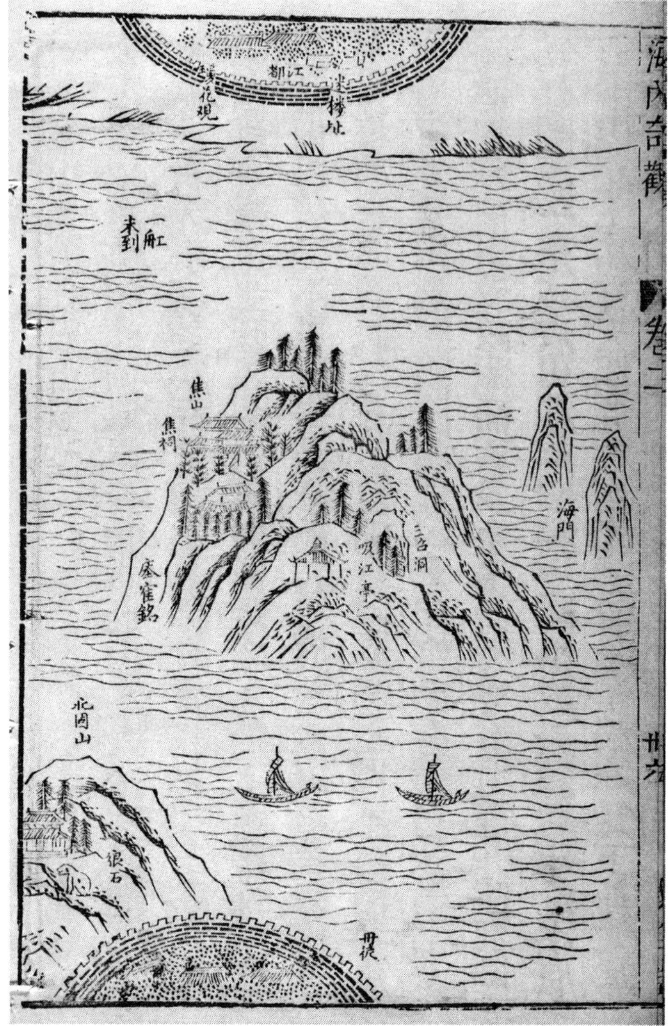

FIGURE 3.5. View of Jiaoshan, in *Newly Engraved Marvelous Views within the Seas* (Xinjuan Hainei qiguan), 2.36a. Woodblock print. Courtesy of Harvard-Yenching Library, T3042 4218.

object and legendary calligraphy, would be disseminated through mass-reproduced texts and images with great speed and on an unprecedented scale, and the *Eulogy* would reach its canonical status through an unexpected medium.

Printed Calligraphy

The proliferation of visual knowledge via woodblock-printed images, as well as the consumption of pictures brought about by the booming publishing industry in the late Ming, has been a rigorous field of study.[25] Much less attention has been paid, however, to the role of calligraphy in this profound cultural shift, partly because the latter falls into an awkward zone between image and text.[26] Recently, art historian Wang Cheng-hua has noted the circulation of calligraphy knowledge in *leishu*, or vernacular encyclopedias, such as *Collected Illustrations of the Three Realms* (Sancai tuhui, first published in 1609), which includes the basic writing techniques of standard script, illustrated guides to other script types, a lineage of historical calligraphers, a "curriculum" for studying calligraphy, and a recommended list of the calligraphic model letters.[27] As Wang suggests, these popular publications were not meant to train serious calligraphers but rather to provide a language for talking about the "art"—a social skill that was becoming important in a local society with more ambiguous social boundaries.[28]

The incorporation of calligraphy in painting manuals such as *Remnants of Poems* may point to a subtle but significant change in the perception of calligraphy in contemporary consumer culture. The collection includes ninety-seven pairs of paintings and poems, put together by a publisher who reveals only his last name, Wang, and native town, Wanling (today's Xuancheng, Anhui Province), then the center for woodblock prints. By no means the first publication of its type, it was undoubtedly inspired by the famous *Painting Manual of the Gu Family* (Gushi huapu, 1603), published nine years earlier, and even "borrowed" many pictures from it. The focus of *Remnants of Poems* differed, however. Whereas the earlier *Manual* was designed as an illustrated textbook of the history of painting, accompanying pictures with art historical comments, the *Remnants* was instead intended to provide a multimedia experience of leisure reading, a cheaper version of the literati calligraphy-painting album, combining picture, poem, and calligraphy (though in the volume, the pairs of calligraphy/picture are awkwardly placed on the two sides of a page back-to-back, since the sheet of paper on which a pair is printed had to be folded to be assembled in book format).[29]

Although the pictures in the album may have been drawn by only a few hands, the calligraphy pages, which demonstrate a great diversity of styles, give the impression that they were produced by many different calligraphers. In some instances, the poet's personal calligraphic style is applied; a Huang Tingjian poem, for example, is rendered in the distinctive Huang style with "trembling brushwork" in elongated *heng* strokes.[30] Other pieces show more random choices of styles; to embellish a poem of Su Shi, for example, an archaic clerical style is employed, not unlike that of the Wang Zongni inscription at Jiaoshan.[31]

According to the colophon of *Remnants of Poems*, written by Huang Mianzhong (fl. early seventeenth century), an obscure scholar, the publisher Gentleman Wang (again, no first name is revealed) "hired noted people to paint the pictures. All pieces imitate ancient brushwork, as each character is genuine handwriting of the noted worthies."[32] The claim of authenticity is questionable, though, at least for two "Dong Qichang" pieces, in which the weak brushwork and mechanical layout was unlikely to have been from Dong's hand.[33] At any rate, the claim by the publisher that he recruited so many "worthies" to work together on this commercial project sounds too good to be true. More plausibly, the publisher may have hired a few local calligraphers (or even only one person) to create a diversity of styles, in some cases based on actual works.[34] The calligraphy in *Marvelous Views within the Seas,* published two years earlier than *Remnants of Poems* and arranged in a similar layout, suggests the existence of such anonymous professional calligraphers. Some volumes include sections titled "inscribed poems" (*tiyong*) and juxtaposing views with calligraphy in various styles—though in *Marvelous Views,* the ghost calligrapher(s) left no signature or seal—perhaps intentionally concealing their identities.[35]

Nevertheless, the issue of authenticity is perhaps irrelevant in these new kinds of publications; just like the picture in the album, which cannot be seen as a forged "painting," printed images of calligraphy or a seal were hardly considered to be counterfeit works. Indeed, if any calligrapher bothered to complain, the publisher would simply defend the printed calligraphy as nothing but the "illustration," like the "paintings" published in the same album. How could one mistake a reproduced image for a real object of calligraphy?

More late-Ming publishers would grab this opportunity. Huang Fengchi (fl. first half of the seventeenth century), who also hailed from the same region of Anhui, produced an even larger number of woodblock-printed albums in the 1620s, including the bestsellers *Painting Manual of Tang Poems* (Tangshi huapu) and *Painting Manual of Tang Liuru* (Tang Liuru huapu), besides six other titles.[36] The latter was published in the name of Tang Yin (1470–1524), one of the best-known Ming painters, whose studio name is Liuru. In this album, the publisher became so bold in promoting his products that he managed to have the painter Tang Yin, who had been dead for about a century, "write" the preface, printed in his personal calligraphic style.[37] Such a publication, as Craig Clunas notes, was part of the "commodification of knowledge" in late Ming, which, in turn, exerted a great impact on the way of looking.[38]

Knowledge of calligraphy was certainly the most desired cultural capital that held monetary value. Like images in the vernacular encyclopedia, the woodblock-printed pages of calligraphy are meant to deliver a casual knowledge of calligraphy, in particular the "must-know" popular calligraphic styles. The small size of the printed calligraphy and the monotone images hardly allowed students to see subtle brushwork and rich ink tonality or use them as models for copying. It is also unlikely that the albums were useful as buying guides for serious collectors. The image of calligraphy was intended to be reproduced as a self-sufficient product that gave the pleasure of looking at and owning (albeit printed images of) artworks to a mass audience that otherwise would not be able to afford any works by Dong Qichang or others. In other words, calligraphy now joined text and pictures in celebrating an "age of woodblock reproduction."[39]

If the difference between woodblock-printed calligraphy and the handwritten work was still evident to viewers, it was in model letters, now also undergoing a subtle but profound shift toward commodification, that the boundary between the copy and the original began to blur. It was at this moment that *Eulogy for Burying a Crane* was transformed from a "strange" object into a widely received calligraphy model.

The Publication of the *Eulogy*

Imagine that it is a sunny spring day in 1613. You live in Nanjing, then called Jinling, the prosperous "southern capital city" of Ming China. Thanks to your well-to-do family, you have received a good education and are living a decent life, although you are frustrated by several unsuccessful attempts at the increasingly competitive civil service examinations.[40] Now imagine that you are in the painting in figure 3.6, walking out of the little bookstore (in the lower left corner), where you have just enjoyed leafing through a newly published *Remnants of Poems*.[41] You have heard about the contemporary writers featured in it but have never been introduced into their circle nor viewed their collection of fine paintings and calligraphy. The volume is not cheap, considering your monthly allowance, but it may still be worth it. People at tea parties and banquets talk about art more than ever. Yesterday, your friend brought over a handscroll painting that he had just purchased for one *tael* from a *huayu*, or "painting studio," right next to the bookstore you have just visited.[42] You do not want to appear ignorant at these social occasions, and the *Remnants* seems to provide a shortcut to otherwise esoteric knowledge about calligraphy and painting. With these thoughts, imagine squeezing yourself through the busy crowd and camels (!) in the painting, crossing the wooden bridge over the Qinhuai River, turning left, and following the parade row. Before reaching the puppet show stage, near the turn of the street, you see a large sign: "Model Letters of the Past and Present."

It was in just such a place that our fictitious character and the real residents of Nanjing in 1613 found their sources for calligraphy models. At the time, the best-selling title of model letters in a store like this was perhaps *Model Letters of the Frolicking Geese Hall* (Xihongtang fashu), compiled in 1603 by Dong Qichang, the most prestigious calligrapher and connoisseur at the time. But another publication that would soon sweep the market was *Model Letters of the Jade Smoke Hall* (Yuyantang fatie), published in 1612 by the noted Chen clan of Haining, Zhejiang. The preface to the new model letters was written by none other than Dong Qichang, who seemed unperturbed by the potential competition:

> Spanning a thousand years but selected with critical discernment, . . . when this compendium comes out, students of calligraphy will have a comprehensive collection [of models].[43] (3E)

Indeed, in twenty-four volumes, the *Jade Smoke* begins with a Han dynasty piece of calligraphy and ends with the work of Yuan dynasty master Zhao Mengfu (1254–1322).[44] The size is double that of the *Chunhua Model Letters* and its imitators, not to mention other earlier "private model letters" that we shall discuss soon.

The most distinctive content in *Jade Smoke* is perhaps *Eulogy for Burying a Crane* (figure 3.7), which occupies the entire sixth volume. Its large characters were

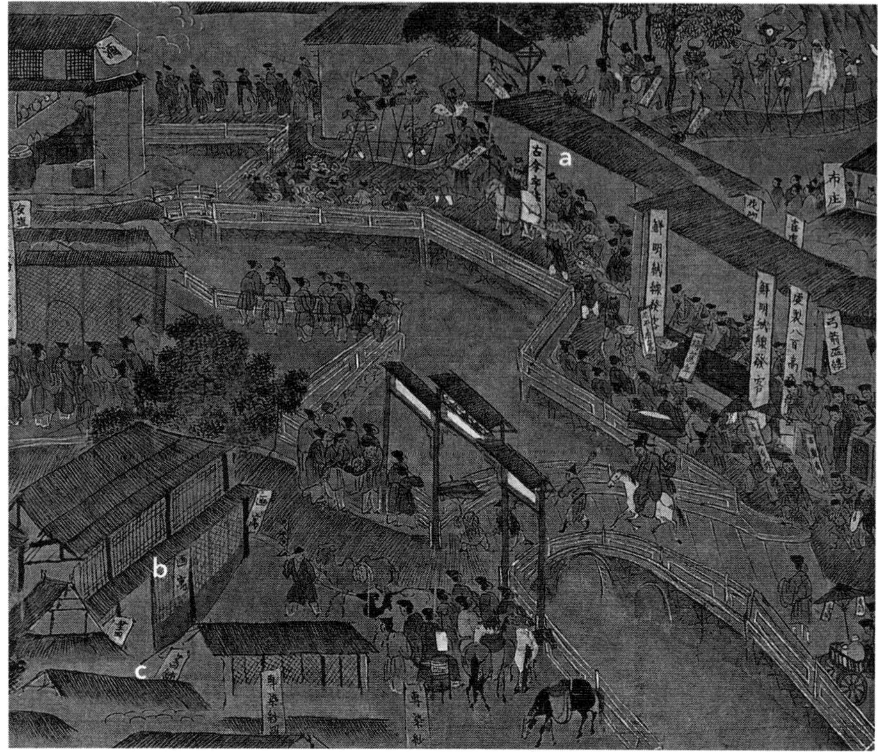

FIGURE 3.6. Qiu Ying (attributed), *Prosperous Scenes of the South Capital City* (Nandu fanhui tu). Late sixteenth century. Detail of a handscroll, ink and color on silk, 44 × 350 cm. National Museum of China, Beijing. The signs read (a) Model Letters from the Past and the Present (Gujin zitie), (b) Painting Studio (Huayu), (c) Bookshop (Shupu).

reproduced two per page, taking up the largest amount of space in this collection. (The only another comparable example of large-character calligraphy is Huang Tingjian's *Chant on Seven Buddhas* [Qi fo jie], which takes up half of its own volume.) Obviously, the publisher took great pains to maintain the original large size of the characters, the source of its visual spectacle. This also marks the debut of the *Eulogy* in any model-letters compendium. Although the compiler provides no specific reasons, its inclusion may be partly explained by the ongoing myth about the legendary large writing of "Wang Xizhi." The *Eulogy*'s large characters were intended to satisfy the rapidly growing public interest in large hanging scrolls, a format of calligraphy in vogue at the time but not represented in any previous model letters.[45]

Nevertheless, the copy of the *Eulogy* in the *Jade Smoke* was evidently not derived from the original inscription, which was still under water at the time. The clean appearance does not resemble any rubbings taken from the eroded stone surface (see figures 1.1 and 1.3). The variations in the text suggest that it is most likely related to the earlier half-forged *Zhenjiang Alternative Carving* (see figure 2.16), although there are no extant rubbings of the latter to enable a comparison. Characters like *yishao* 逸少, as we saw at the end of last chapter, were added later to the *Zhenjiang*

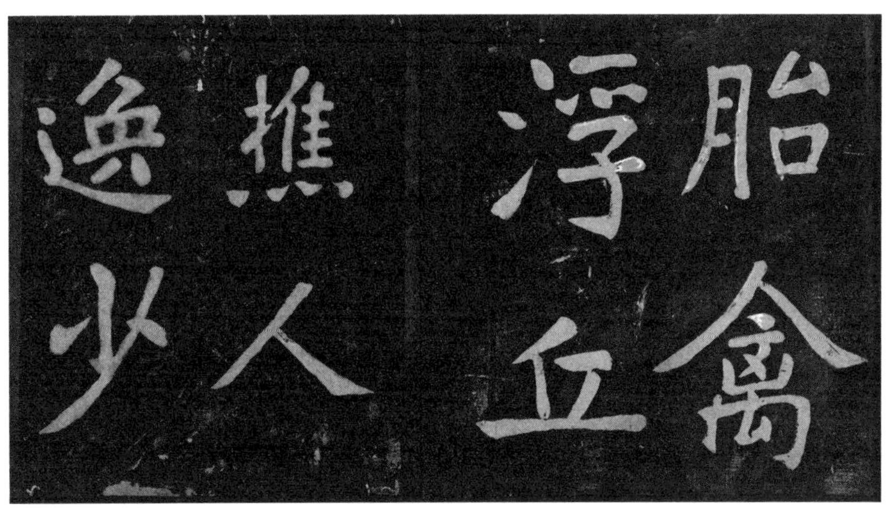

FIGURE 3.7. Details of *Eulogy for Burying a Crane*, in *Model Letters of the Jade Smoke Hall* (Yuyantang fatie). Courtesy of Harvard-Yenching Library, Cambridge, Massachusetts. TP0004.

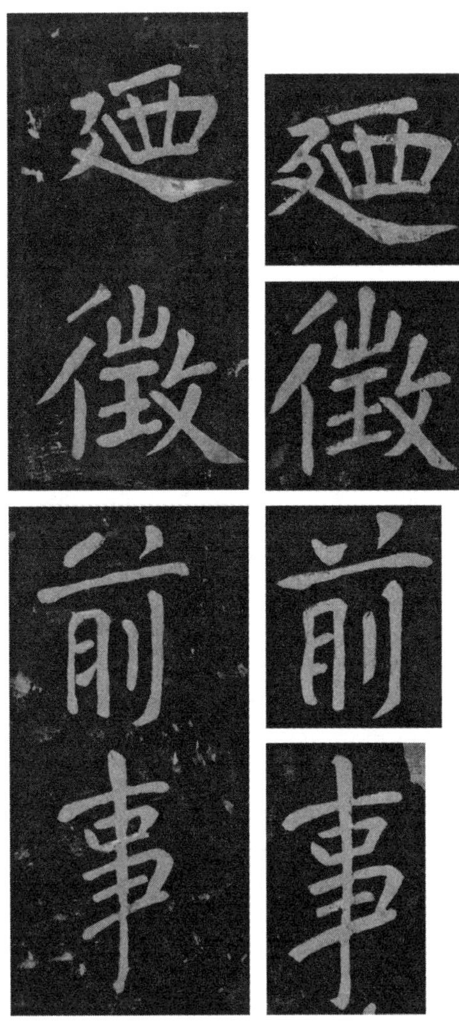

FIGURE 3.8. Comparison of characters in the Jade Smoke version of *Eulogy for Burying a Crane*.

Alternative Carving to justify the alleged attribution to Wang Xizhi. Now they appear in the *Jade Smoke* version (figure 3.7).

A close examination of individual characters reveals traces of forgery. As an example, take the line *nai zheng qian shi* 廼徵前事 (figure 3.8, column A) in the *Jade Smoke* copy. Comparing the characters with those in column B in figure 3.8, which are taken from elsewhere in the same rubbing, one can easily recognize that they share almost identical forms. This pastiche approach is not unusual in the forgery of rubbings; a new line is made by copying and pasting existing characters. In other places, new characters could be generated by adding or removing a radical from an existing graph. Through this cunning method, forgers were able to avoid the risk of composing new characters that would be visually inconsistent in the rubbing. The purpose was to create a more "complete" and valuable object.

The *Jade Smoke* version, therefore, was anything but a rubbing from the original inscription. Yet it became the major source for the wide circulation of the *Eulogy*. This ironic outcome cannot be easily understood without an inquiry into the peculiar market and cultural demands on model letters in later Ming China, to which we now turn.

Model Letters for Sale

For a long time, "model letters" referred only to replicas derived from the *Chunhua Model Letters*, discussed in chapter 2. This tradition was expanded and revitalized in the sixteenth century, when entrepreneurial scholars and collectors went into business, compiling and publishing volumes called "private letters" (*sitie*) to distinguish them from earlier "official letters" (*guantie*) issued by government agencies.[46] This was a new phenomenon in the materially prosperous and culturally rich Jiangnan region, where works of art were collected and patronized by rich merchants and scholar-officials in an unprecedent scale.[47]

The first known private model letters in the Ming were all reproduced from original works collected by the compilers themselves. The most famous examples include *Model Letters of the True Appreciation Studio* (Zhenshangzhai tie, 1522), *Model Letters of the Halting Clouds Studio* (Tingyunguan tie, 1537–1560), and *Model Letters of the Remaining Purity Studio* (Yuqingzhai tie, 1598). They were initially conceived to share rubbings of precious works with an exclusive group of like-minded scholars and connoisseurs. For instance, as the first product of its kind, *True Appreciation* includes only a few works in three volumes—all were selected from the collection of the compiler.[48] Also reproduced in the rubbing version were the long comments on issues of connoisseurship by later collectors or scholars on original scrolls.[49] Replicated from the original and preserving the complete information of the object, the rubbing of *True Appreciation* was intended for a serious scholar and collector and simultaneously served as a token of the family's prestige.[50]

Production of this type of private calligraphic compendium continued to flourish in subsequent centuries and deserves its own close study. What we will focus on here is the long-overlooked commercial turn of model-letters production that would fundamentally change the reproduction and consumption of calligraphy, similar to what happened with printed books and painting manuals. Although model books and other rubbings had long been available in the market, they had been treated mostly as antiques or "artworks."[51] For example, it is said that the first ten copies of *True Appreciation* were made with extremely expensive antique paper and became highly sought-after objects in their own right.[52] Nevertheless, the mass-market publication of model books, beginning in the late sixteenth century, aimed at a very different audience—the growing reading public who began to look for more "advanced" calligraphic knowledge that was once the privilege of elite scholars and collectors.

Scholars of book culture have often been limited by the scarcity of direct records on book publishing. Even less is known about details of the model-letters business. The store sign "Model Letters of the Past and Present" that we saw in figure 3.6 suggests the existence of such specialized stores selling both newly published copies (perhaps even pirated copies) and antique rare editions. By the late Ming, cheap pirated editions of the time-honored *Chunhua Model Letters* flooded these stores. Gu Congyi (1523–1588), a collector and publisher, complained that the quality of these pirated copies had deteriorated greatly by his time. Rushing to produce more copies ever more quickly, some publishers, he observed, even put layers of paper on the recut woodblocks to produce multiple copies simultaneously.[53] Gu's criticisms were probably made to promote his own recent replication of the *Chunhua Model Letters*, among many other similar publications now aimed at the new reading public. Soon, many "private letters" would be produced for the lucrative market.

A collection such as *True Appreciation* may not have easily met this new demand of the mass market, not simply because it was originally designed as a luxury object but also because its connoisseur-oriented content may have intimidated a general audience and beginners at calligraphy. Other compendia appeared to have more success in adapting to the new audience. The history of *Model Letters of the Halting Clouds Studio* illustrates this commercial turn of private model letters.[54] Inscriptions in the volumes of the compendium, ranging in date from 1537 to 1560, indicate that the project may have been reissued over time. It is said that the first four volumes were personally compiled by the eminent literati painter and calligrapher Wen Zhengming (1470–1559), hand copied by his two sons, Wen Peng (1498–1573) and Wen Jia (the painter of the Jiaoshan scroll we just visited), and engraved by Zhang Jianfu (1491–1572), the master carver who also executed *True Appreciation*.[55] It thus might have first been conceived as an exclusive art object, like *True Appreciation*. Also like the latter, it is believed that the earliest edition was carved on woodblocks, which suggests it was produced as a limited edition, as the wood would have been worn down in the rubbing-making process.

All extant copies of *Halting Clouds*, however, appear to be rubbings from stone—a more durable material to produce a greater number of rubbings—which in turn suggests an audience much larger than the exclusive literati circle assumed before.[56] The extant copies also consist of an additional eight volumes, bringing the total to twelve volumes. Little is known, however, about how and when more volumes were added, but the largely expanded and mixed content may suggest an interest in appealing to the mass market; whereas some rubbings seem to have been copied from original works of art, often bearing long colophons written by Wen Zhengming or Wen Jia, others simply reproduced works from preexisting official compendia from various sources. In 1583, Wen Yuanshan (1554–1589), son of Wen Jia and the heir to the *Halting Clouds* legacy, had to publish a note to help the reader distinguish the authentic copies from pirated ones.[57] Whereas this note may have been intended to claim proprietary ownership, it also reveals the commercial purpose of the production of *Halting Clouds* at the time.

Although recent scholars have noted the Wen family's other economic activities, few historical records enable us to explore how the *Halting Clouds* business was actually run.[58] We do know, however, that in 1614, when Wen Yuanshan's daughter, the talented painter Wen Chu (1595–1634), married Zhao Jun (1591–1640) of the local scholar family, *Halting Clouds* was listed among objects in the dowry.[59] It is unclear why this family treasure was given away and whether the entry referred to the physical stone set or just the permission to make recarvings. At any rate, Zhao Yiguang (1559–1625), a noted antiquarian scholar and calligrapher and now the father-in-law of Wen Chu, took over its publication. In one statement, perhaps attached to the rubbing copies, he boasts about the rarity and superb quality of his product. At the end, he adds a price list, which suggests that *Halting Clouds* was in fact quite affordable: a set of unmounted copy alone ranges from a half to one *tael*, depending on the type of paper and ink.[60] Ironically, mounting cost more than the rubbings alone; a deluxe mounted version, with a crafted wooden box, was priced up to five *taels*.[61] The publication, therefore, was certainly designed for the mass market, competing with other popular products such as *Model Letters of the Frolicking Geese Hall*, to which we shall soon return.

Although model letters and painting manuals appeared in the same market, sold within the same price range of printed books and painting manuals (a copy of *Painting Manual of Remnants of Poems* was priced at 0.8 *tael*) and targeting the same audience, publishing model letters required a specific privilege.[62] The authority of model letters derived from the assumption early on that the publishers owned the original calligraphic works or at least had access to them, a cultural (and potentially monetary) capital enjoyed only by prestigious clans such as the Wen family. In contrast, to my knowledge, there were no model letters published by contemporary book publishers. This special status of model-letters publication remains rooted in the myth of rubbing the medium.

Rubbing: From Primal Object to Printed Image

In an insightful comparison between rubbing and photography, the art historian Wu Hung observes that a rubbing "minimizes the physical distance between an object and its image; it is akin to a manufactured skin peeled off the object."[63] Unlike a printed image, digital photograph, or other product of modern mechanical reproduction, a rubbing maintains its own materiality and objecthood through the physical contact between the original and the copy and thus preserves a certain degree of "presence of time and space," in Walter Benjamin's words.[64]

The legitimacy of a rubbing is derived from the authenticity (*zhen*) that can be transmitted only through the complicated process that we have outlined in the introduction. One may observe that although each step of the copying process moves away from the original and perhaps adds more alterations, physical contact is constantly maintained during the transfer from one medium to another, creating a symbolic "material linkage."[65] If the original was viewed as the traces of contact left by the calligrapher's hand gesture, such a connection to the personal presence of the artist is preserved and passed down through the series of physical contacts inherent in the process. The tactile impression of the slightly sunken characters on the rubbing may well demonstrate the material link and the physical connection with the original and cannot be replicated in the printed calligraphy images in painting manuals, not to mention digital photographs, such as those reproduced in this book.

This symbolic connection to the calligrapher's presence has become the source of the aura and authenticity of rubbings—including model letters. The first edition of rubbings is always highly appreciated, not only for its sharper and more accurate images but also for its presumably maximum degree of aura and authenticity. On the other hand, even the worst copies, such as those pirated *Chunhua Model Letters* that Gu Congyi dismissed, still maintain, like DNA, a physical connection to the traces of ancient masters, however slight. Any rubbing can therefore be seen as a primal object in this sense.

Nevertheless, this traditional attachment to material and physical traces changed quietly in the mass-produced model letters of the late Ming, perhaps best illustrated by Dong Qichang's *Model Letters of the Frolicking Geese Hall*. Unlike the private model letters we have seen, Dong's new publication did not reflect his personal collection. Instead, most of the works were copied from elsewhere. A striking allegation regarding the making process comes from Wang Kentang (1552–1638), Dong's close friend and a publisher of model letters. Most of the works in *Frolicking Geese*, according to him, were not original ancient works but "freehand copies made by Dong himself."[66] Han Fengxi (1576–ca.1665), another contemporary collector, recalled that Dong (or more likely his agents) once came to borrow a work from his family collection. Instead of lending the original, Han hastily made a freehand copy and gave it away. To his surprise, Dong seemed unconcerned and went on to publish the fresh copy in *Frolicking Geese*.[67]

It is difficult for us to judge how much exaggeration is found in these accounts, given that the surviving copies of the compendia may have been heavily edited and recompiled later. However, some rubbings in the volume seems to support the charge.[68] A comparison of the details between Su Shi's famous *Poems on Cold Food Festival in Huangzhou* (Huangzhou hanshi shi, datable to 1082; figure 3.9) and a copy that Dong proudly included in his *Frolicking Geese* (figure 3.10) reveals that the latter was unlikely to have been a direct tracing copy of the original; the differences in brushwork, found in the middle *shu* stroke and the shortest horizontal *dian* stroke of the character *nian* 年 (figure 3.11), for instance, are hardly explained by a careless tracing copy or a mistake of the carver. They are more likely derived from a freehand brushed copy—perhaps Dong's own. It should be noted that the original Su Shi scroll was in the collection of Han Shineng (1528–1598), father of Han Fengxi mentioned in the above anecdote and a mentor of Dong Qichang. Dong must have studied the scroll closely and made numerous freehand copies of it.[69] Nevertheless, it might not have been realistic for Dong to borrow the fragile antique piece from the cautious collector in order to make a tracing copy, which would not only have involved laborious work but also would have risked damaging the original. Instead, it is not inconceivable that Dong or his agent would have taken a freehand copy he had already made and had it carved into stone.

The use of freehand copies (or *lin*, in calligraphy terms) in making rubbings presents a problem of authenticity. Indeed, it is often difficult to tell the difference between the results of the two approaches. A good freehand copy is perhaps even closer to the original than a badly altered tracing copy, and modification to a certain degree is always needed for carving and recarving. When *True Appreciation* was executed, it is said that the master carver Zhang Jianfu put the original and the stone side by side and made adjustments to the carving.[70] The result was even more accurate than the preparatory ink tracing copy. Nevertheless, this sort of modification or alteration does not change the physical connection to the original and thus still keeps a certain amount of aura in the rubbing. A freehand copy, however, fundamentally breaks the "material link" that a rubbing traditionally sustains. When the physical connection with the traces of ancient masters is lost, the authenticity of the rubbing is at stake and the nature of the reproduced calligraphy image is called into question. Let us return to the freehand rendition of Su Shi in *Frolicking Geese*. We may ask, Are we looking at an altered copy of the original? A copy of a forged Su Shi? Or, as we have encountered in the painting manuals, a caricature of what is perceived to be the essential characteristics?

Numerous criticisms of *Frolicking Geese* appeared after its publication. Many have correctly pointed out the failed judgment in its selection, while others have complained about the poorly made rubbings.[71] Dong's defenders have posited that someone else in his family was actually in charge of the manufacture after he left for an official position in Hubei in 1605.[72] Indeed, the long signature line in front of each volume says that the publication is "reviewed and approved" (*shending*) by Dong—a term vague enough to exclude his substantial role in the manufacture

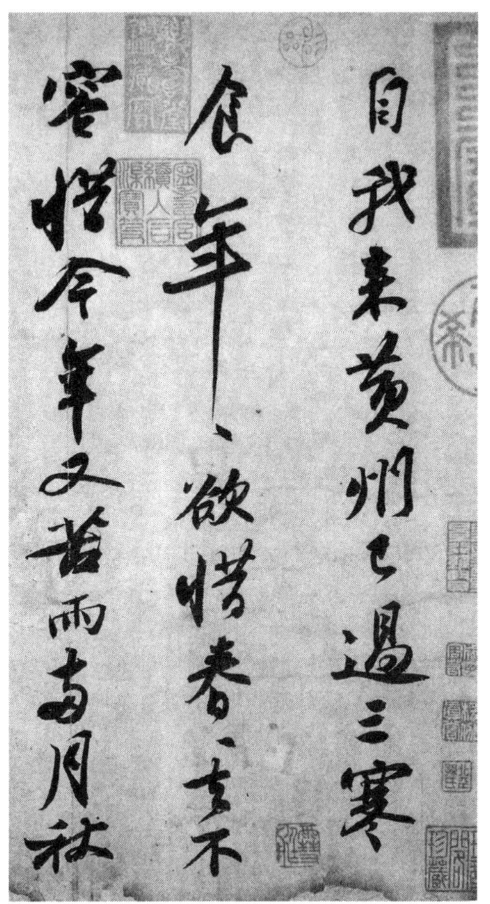

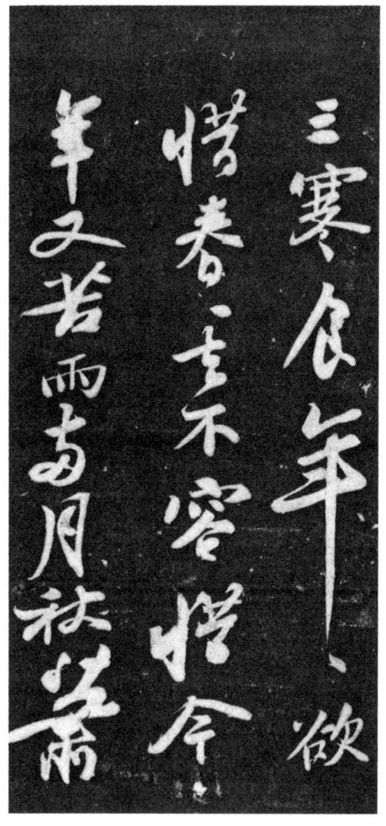

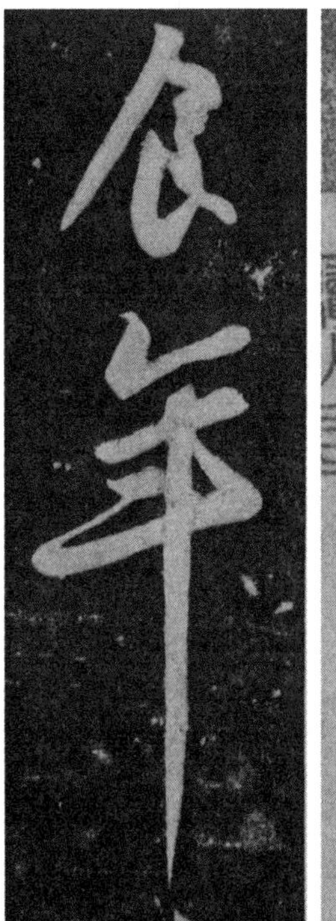

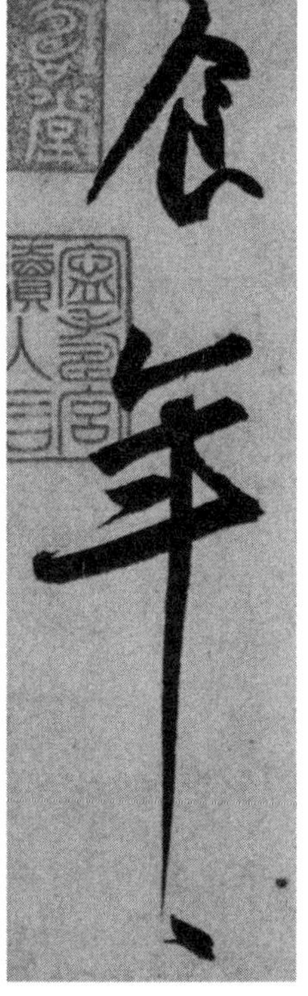

(*above, left*) **FIGURE 3.9.** Su Shi, *Poems on Cold Food Festival in Huangzhou* (Huangzhou hanshi shi tie). National Palace Museum, Taipei.

(*above, right*) **FIGURE 3.10.** Copy of Su Shi's *Poems on Cold Food Festival in Huangzhou* in *Model Letters of the Frolicking Geese Hall* (Xihongtang fashu). Courtesy of Harvard-Yenching Library, TP0002.

(*left*) **FIGURE 3.11.** Comparison of details from figures 3.9 and 3.10.

and publication. Ironically, Dong himself also seemed confused, unable to defend the "defects" of his product. It appears he never responded to any criticism of this sort; on the contrary, he sometimes even concurred with his critics, disparaging the sloppy carving and rubbing making.[73]

Whereas all the critics deserve credit for their serious scholarly concerns, the problem of *Frolicking Geese* is worth a second look in its own context—namely, that of the popular visual culture of the late Ming. Rather than the elite's sensibility to the tactile traces of the brush method and the material linkage, the public interest in calligraphy lay in what we may call a "visual linkage" provided by the printed images and an encyclopedic knowledge of calligraphy.[74] The rubbing of a freehand copy may not have been considered legitimate according to the conventions of rubbing making and appreciation, but it would have been sufficiently aligned with the popular consumption of mass-produced texts and printed pictures at the time.

From another perspective, the controversy over *Frolicking Geese* might be read as one symptom of the elite's widespread anxiety over the blurred social boundaries at the time, as the appreciation of calligraphic compendia, once the exclusive privilege of the literati scholars, was now opened to popular consumption. As soon as the market-oriented publication was normalized, a new boundary formed. The scholarly criticism of the inferior quality of *Frolicking Geese* thus may be interpreted as a powerful discourse that reasserted the elite's impeccable taste and social status.[75] In the meantime, old-style model letters based on family collections continued to be made and circulated within elite circles on an even larger scale.[76]

Living in a rapidly changing society, even the eloquent writer Dong Qichang might never have been able to explicate the status of his model letters publication and its relationship to social distinction as analyzed above. But he was certainly aware of the commercial aspect of his production. In a letter addressed to an unidentified recipient, perhaps a model-letters dealer, Dong explains:

> The unmounted edition of *Model Letters of the Frolicking Geese Hall* is priced at one and a half *taels*. This is the firm price. Only you got a discount. Please do not let others know. I will be having people clear up the transaction.[77] (3F)

This letter gives us a rare glimpse of another facet of Dong's life besides that of an eminent scholar-official and artist. Before long, copies of *Frolicking Geese* would be available at the store in Nanjing, along with other new products, such as the expanded *Halting Clouds*, awaiting their buyers—individuals like our fictional character. What was negotiated for these compendia was not only the wholesale price but also the elite taste and the cultural capital they provided their readers.

Revisiting *Jade Smoke*

Explicitly aimed at mass consumption and the psychology of the new audience—the clientele of the urban middle class, degree candidates, and would-be literati of

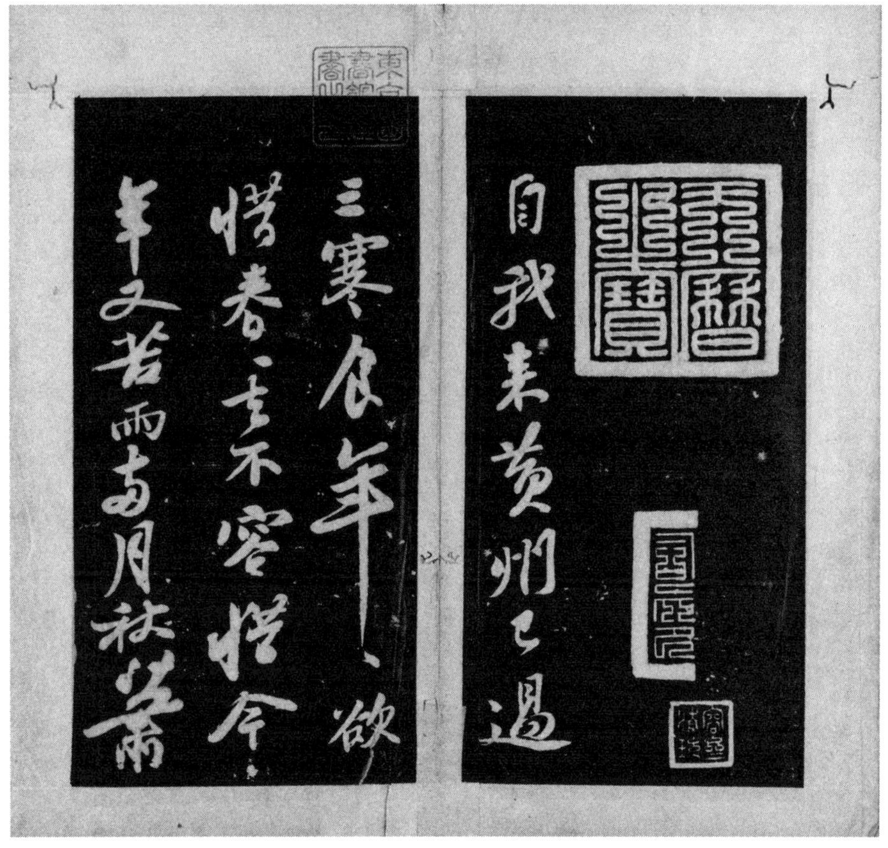

FIGURE 3.12. Copy of Su Shi's *Poems on Cold Food Festival in Huangzhou* in *Model Letters of the Jade Smoke Hall*. Courtesy of National Diet Library, Tokyo.

modest means—the publication of *Model Letters of the Jade Smoke Hall*, including its spurious copy of *Eulogy for Burying a Crane*, took the commercial publication of model letters to the next level. The compiler, Chen Huan (1565–1626), was born into a prestigious family. His father, Chen Yujiao (1544–1610), was an active collector and calligrapher.[78] Chen Huan himself was also known as a calligrapher, and he maintained a close relationship with Dong Qichang.[79]

Despite Chen's rich family collection, *Jade Smoke* included surprisingly few reproductions from original calligraphic works. Chen Huan never clarified the sources for his model letters, which range from copies of dubious ancient works to extant writing specimens in contemporary collections. It seems, however, that most of the works were copied from earlier publications of model letters, including the familiar *Chunhua Model Letters* and more modern ones—and certainly Dong Qichang's *Frolicking Geese*.[80] It also includes a copy of Su Shi's *Poems on Cold Food Festival* (figure 3.12), which points to a curious connection with the *Frolicking Geese* version (see figure 3.10) versus the original. The identical edited layout and details in brushwork, as well as the traces of dents on stone, suggest that the two rubbings were made from the exact same stone. Given the close relationship between the Chen family and Dong Qichang, it is not impossible that some sources were shared by them. And

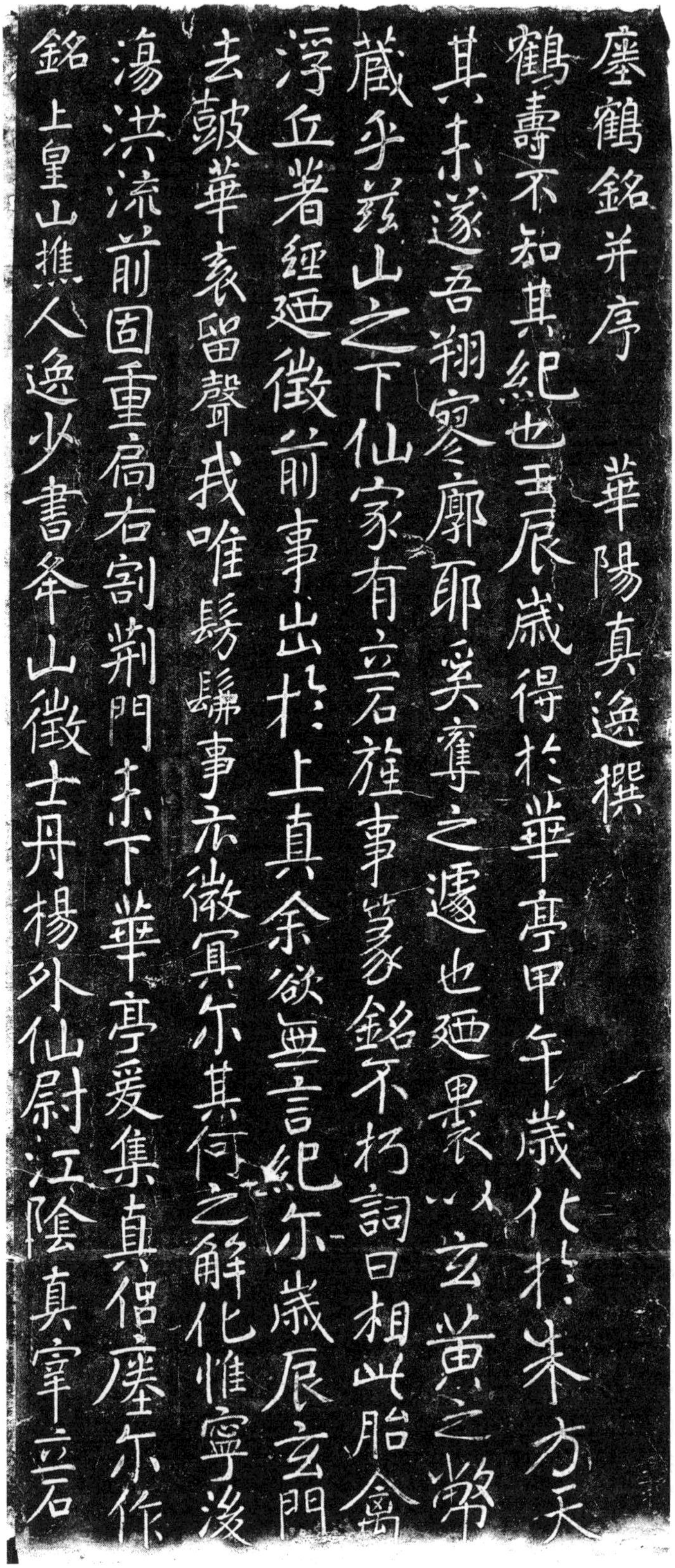

FIGURE 3.13. Emperor Qianlong (attributed), copy of the Jade Smoke version of *Eulogy for Burying a Crane*. Ink rubbing. Courtesy of Jiaoshan Stone Inscription Museum.

Dong may have played a much bigger role than merely writing the preface in the publication of the *Jade Smoke*.

The problematic copy of the *Eulogy*, in this light, was by no means intended to satisfy antiquarian scholars or rubbing connoisseurs. The fresh clarity of the image, however, made the *Eulogy* a legible and lucid model that could easily be incorporated into the "must-know" pool of calligraphy for the general public. Repackaged in the encyclopedia-like publication and sold in the mass market, *Eulogy for Burying a Crane* was no longer as elusive and indeterminate as it had been when it was known only through older rubbings or legends—it had been transformed into an iconic work of calligraphy in the era of popular consumption of knowledge.

The *Jade Smoke* version soon became the most well-known image of the *Eulogy* inscription. It was known to have even been carved back to stone in 1661 and, ironically, placed in Jiaoshan to serve as a substitute for the original stone.[81] The copy is not found in the Jiaoshan Stone Inscription Museum's inventory. But I suspect that it is very likely an inscription now labeled "the Qianlong Emperor's freehand copy," found in the museum's covered gallery (figure 3.13). A close examination reveals that instead of "freehand" rendition, the characters are almost identical to those of the *Jade Smoke* version, though they have been rearranged in the vertical stele's layout. Rubbings from this and other replica stones must have been constantly made and circulated, becoming the major sources for the students of the *Eulogy* and for later publishers. More remote replications would be made in the following centuries, even in Japan, as commercial model letters and the *Eulogy* found new audiences there.[82]

Deconstructing the Model

When we categorize *Jade Smoke* as commercial publication, we do not intend to assume a clear-cut social identity for its audiences. In reality, consumption of this and other model letters must have been shared by people from various social classes. Whereas a member of the "low-brow" reading public would purchase a copy of *Jade Smoke* to gain some knowledge of calligraphy, Dong Qichang—the most revered calligrapher—is actually known to have used *Jade Smoke* for his everyday practice of calligraphy.[83] It is also interesting to note that despite having the same problematic content, unlike Dong's *Frolicking Geese*, *Jade Smoke* has received much less harsh criticism, if any. The critics' tolerance may signal the elite's changing attitude toward the popular compendia, recognizing them as a legitimate mirror of cultural taste.

This shifting attitude toward the calligraphy of the *Eulogy* in the late Ming period is particularly interesting in this light. Back in the middle of the sixteenth century, Wang Shizhen, despite his fascination with the broken inscription in the water, was disdainful of what he considered overenthusiasm for its calligraphy, writing this about a rubbing from the *Eulogy*:

> Archaic and plain, marvelous and distinctive, magnificent and great, free and untrammeled, this inscription deserves to be called a monumental work of calligraphy. However, the composition of its characters often appears loose, [which shows that] the hand was not able to follow the intent. Youjun [Wang Xizhi] would not have done that. As for the worn and broken brush tip, it may not fully demonstrate the calligraphy's original quality [*benzhi*]—this may be due to the fact that the stone is hard to carve, or due to natural erosion by the water. Luzhi [Huang Tingjian] praised this work to the skies and extremely adored it. Was [his comment as superficial] as the "neighbor lady covering her heart with hands?"[84] (3G)

Wang Shizhen may simply have been honest about what he observed. But a more profound reason for his remark may lie in the culture of calligraphy, which had been continuously dominated by the aesthetic authority of the Two Wangs and revitalized from time to time by talented calligraphers such as Zhao Mengfu. The latter's elegant calligraphy was among the most popular models and deeply shaped the value of calligraphy in the Ming dynasty.[85] Although the *Eulogy* was admired as a cultural relic and rubbings from it were continuously collected, few students of calligraphy—as if heeding the warning of the Song scholar Huang Bosi, who conducted a pioneering study on the *Eulogy* but dismissed its calligraphy—devoted time to studying the calligraphy of the damaged inscription. Nor did Huang Tingjian's theory and experiments in calligraphy, as analyzed in the previous chapter, change the common practice of learning calligraphy through close copying of model letters and the appropriate structure and brushwork they exemplified.

The Two Wangs tradition of studying model calligraphy was only reinforced during Wang Shizhen's own lifetime, when archaism and the emulation of orthodox models were key aesthetic issues in literature and the visual arts.[86] Wang's major criterion for calligraphy, *guya*, "archaic and elegant," perfectly demonstrates such an aesthetic.[87] By this standard, an eccentric work like the *Eulogy* may be called "archaic," but it is certainly anything but "elegant."

A generation younger than Wang Shizhen, Dong Qichang took a different view of the *Eulogy*. It is not known whether he visited Jiaoshan in person and enjoyed "touching" the inscription underwater like his predecessors. His interest may have lain less in the "strange thing" than in the size of calligraphy that was derived from Huang Tingjian. In 1623, after a freehand copy of the *Eulogy* that he made, Dong Qichang referred to Huang Tingjian's poem we read in the previous chapter:

> Huang Fuweng [Tingjian] once said, "For large-character calligraphy nothing matches *Eulogy for Burying a Crane*, for small-character calligraphy nothing surpasses *Sutra of Buddha's Bequeathed Teaching*."[88] The extant copy of *Bequeathed Teaching* was from the hands of Tang sutra scribes. *Eulogy* is Tao the Hermit's [Tao Hongjing] handwriting—Shangu [Huang Tingjian] studied it. I had thought of reducing it into the small-regular script calligraphy but lost the

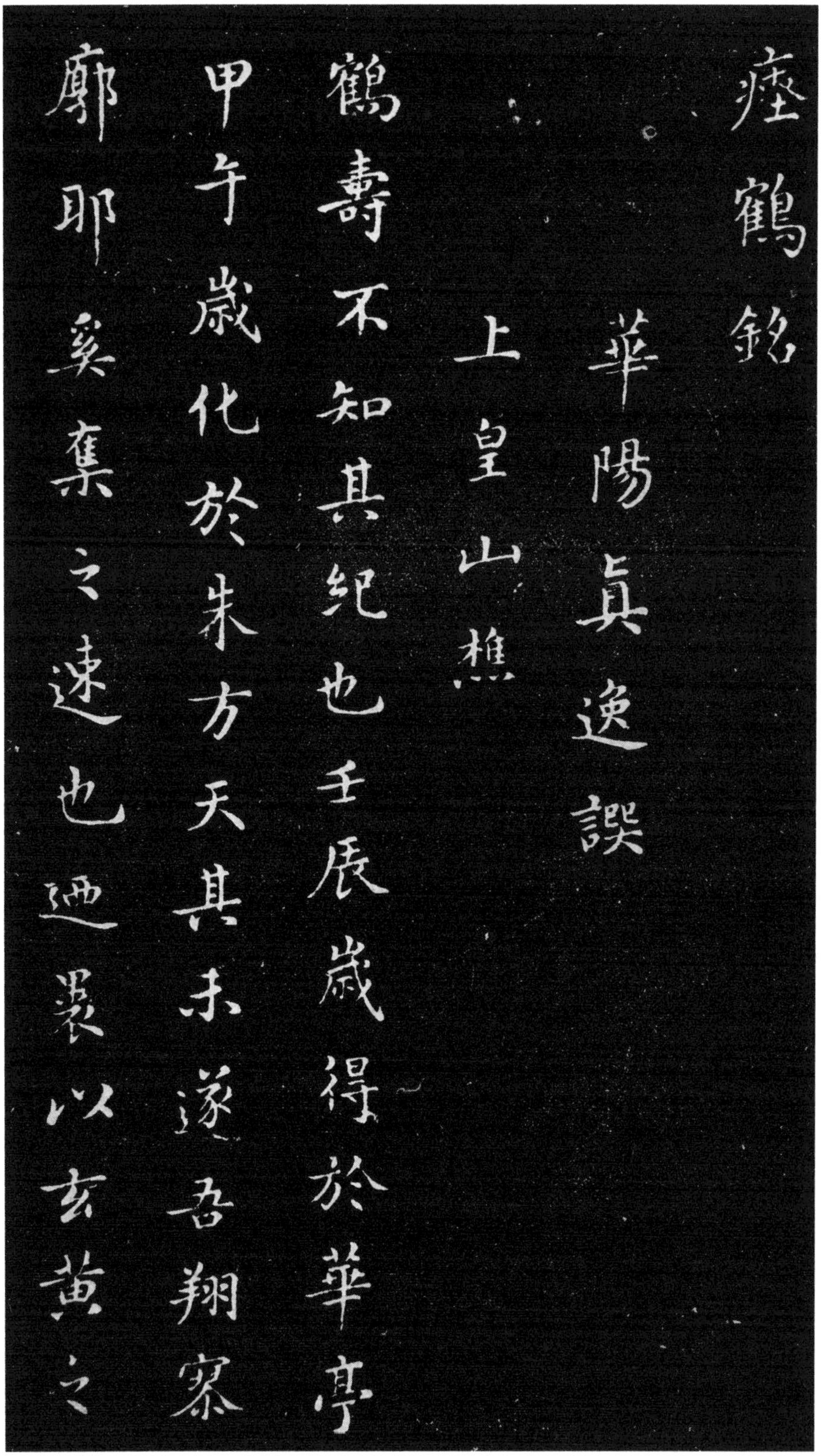

瘞鶴銘

華陽真逸譔

上皇山樵

鶴壽不知其紀也壬辰歲得於華亭

甲午歲化於朱方天其未遂吾翔寥

廓耶奚奪之遽也迺裹以玄黃之

FIGURE 3.14. Dong Qichang, "Copy" of *Eulogy for Burying a Crane*, in *Model Letters of the Treasuring Tripod Studio* (Baodingzhai fashu). From Lu Jiaming *Rong Geng cangtie* 14, no. 102.

rubbing by accident [before the project had been realized]. So I wrote this with the brush method of *Yellow Court Sutra*.[89] (3H)

The reduced-size copy, with the above colophon, survives in *Model Letters of the Treasured Tripod Studio* (Baodingzhai fashu), a rubbing collection of Dong's own calligraphy published in 1609 (figure 3.14).[90] The calligraphic style of the "copy," as Dong announces in above text, shows no connection to the *Eulogy*. Rather, it was written in an elegant Two Wangs style for small standard calligraphy.

The expression "copying X's calligraphy using the brushwork of Y," in the above case, paradoxical as it appears, is not unusual in Dong Qichang's critical commentary and practice of calligraphy and painting. He claimed to make a copy of Mi Fu in Zhong You's (151–230) style, of Huaisu in Wang Xianzhi's style, and so on.[91] All these hybrid works demonstrate striking differences from the original.[92] Sometimes, aside from the text, no similarity at all can be observed between his copies and the originals. He even deliberately omitted the actual stylistic sources, leaving his work as an art historical ID quiz for the viewer. In doing so, in his own words, he intended to "escape" (*li*) from the rigid study of the model letters and, in the meantime, to "unify" (*he*) himself with the great tradition.[93]

A compelling example of Dong's unique approach, and of particular interest for our purpose, is his *Copy of the Eulogy for the Biography of Ni Kuan* (Ni Kuan zhuan zan, figure 3.15), datable between 1612 and 1616, around the time when *Jade Smoke* was published.[94] The original work that Dong saw is believed to have been written by Chu Suiliang (596–658), the Tang master of calligraphy, and still survives.[95] Dong's "copy," however, has little to do with Chu's style, as we found in his other hybrid copies. In the colophon to the scroll, he claims that it was written "using the brushwork of Yan Zhenqing." The reader of this book, however, may instead recognize the resemblance between this large scroll and the *Jade Smoke* version of *Eulogy for Burying a Crane*, though Dong does not mention the connection at all.

A comparison of characters (figure 3.16) selected from both eulogies (perhaps not a coincidence) suggests that Dong may well have studied the *Jade Smoke* rubbing and incorporated it into his "copy." Taking the third character, *yi* 亦, as an example, Dong seems to purposely preserve the loose structure and the coarse and blunt strokes of the character on the rubbing. The *heng* stroke starts with a direct and blunt downward dot, subtly changes direction in the middle part, and ends abruptly with a hook toward the beginning of the next stroke. These unexpected twists and turns in the dramatic execution of each stroke echo the visual effect that one finds on the *Jade Smoke* rubbing. The result is a solemn yet awkward look. Unlike Huang Tingjian's dazzling *Scroll for Zhang Datong* (see figure 2.6), which is intended to create dynamic flow throughout the writing, Dong's experiments with large-character calligraphy seem to focus on the internal structure of individual characters, an intriguing hybrid of Yan Zhenqing's robustness and the *Eulogy*'s looseness.

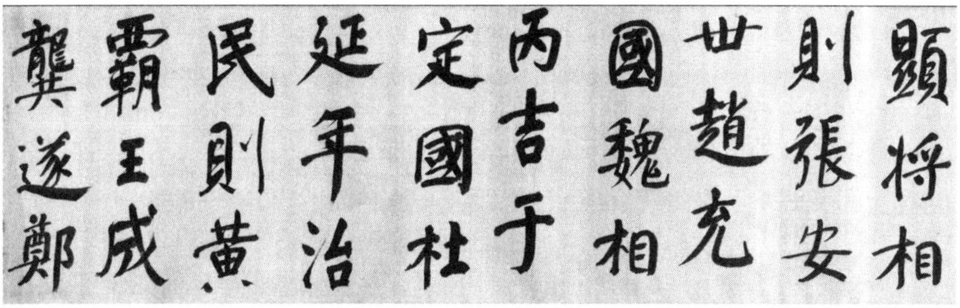

FIGURE 3.15. Dong Qichang, *Eulogy for Ni Kuan's Biography*, ca. 1612–16. Detail. Ink on silk, 36.8 × 1,588 cm. The Palace Museum, Beijing.

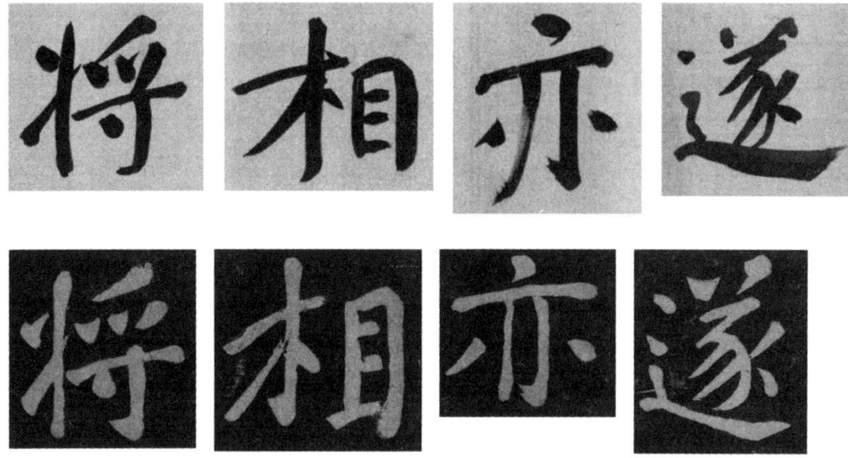

FIGURE 3.16. Characters from Dong Qichang, *Eulogy for Ni Kuan's Biography* (upper) and *Jade Smoke* version of *Eulogy for Burying a Crane* (lower).

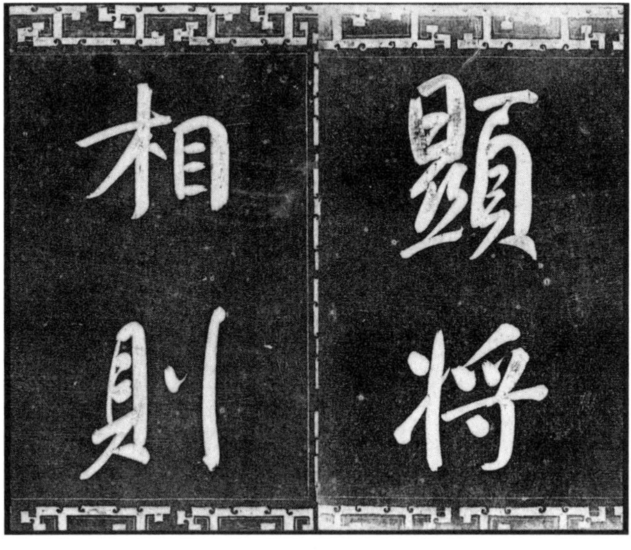

FIGURE 3.17. Dong Qichang, *Eulogy for Ni Kuan's Biography*, in *Model Letters of the Three Rarities Hall* (Sanxitang fatie), 1747. Ink rubbing. Courtesy of Harvard-Yenching Library, TP0001.

A century later, Dong's *Copy of Eulogy for the Biography of Ni Kuan* would be carved and published as part of *Model Letters of the Three Rarities Hall* (Sanxitang fatie, 1747), the monumental calligraphy collection that were reproduced by the order of the Qianlong Emperor, to whom we will return in the next chapter.[96] This work occupies two whole volumes, easily the largest space for a single work among more than three hundred pieces of calligraphy in the vast thirty-two volumes and the singular model for large-character calligraphy. The characters were rearranged in a layout that allows only two characters per page (figure 3.17).[97] The new appearance closely resembles that of the *Jade Smoke* copy of the *Eulogy* and was perhaps intended to pay tribute to the first "encyclopedia" of calligraphy. Furthermore, the position of the monumental work, at the very end of *Three Rarities*, also suggests the imperial endorsement of Dong's status as the last master of calligraphy in the classical tradition.

Coda

Dong's unorthodox approaches in both calligraphy and painting have been the subject of numerous studies, impossible to summarize in full here. Modern scholars have related his new approach in both calligraphy and painting to a fundamental intellectual change led by critics and theorists such as Li Zhi (1527–1602) and the Yuan brothers (Yuan Zongdao, 1560–1600; Yuan Hongdao, 1568–1610; and Yuan Zhongdao, 1575–1630), who advocated free creation and the attainment of a "child-like mind" rather than faithful imitation of the past in literary composition.[98] On the other hand, Dong's open attitudes toward the calligraphic canon, as art historian and calligrapher Bai Qianshen suggests, may well have aligned with his interest in contemporary vernacular novels and dramas, in which parodies and appropriations of classical texts were common, not unlike his own free transformation of the ancient models.[99]

Dong's revolutionary vision of calligraphy may also reflect the contemporary popular visual culture discussed in this chapter. Despite his own aesthetic and intellectual pursuits, Dong would have been sensitive to the shifting paradigm in the public perception of calligraphy from material objects to mass-reproduced images. Once the goal of preserving authenticity was no longer regarded as essential in calligraphy, the calligrapher was freed from the frustration of the absence of the primal object and the futile search for the lost "brush method." What might be termed Dong Qichang's deconstructivist view of the authority of the Two Wangs tradition marks a turning point in the history of Chinese calligraphy.[100] It paved the way for later calligraphers, especially those who would, ironically, reject Dong's style and the classical tradition it represents.

As an object, the *Eulogy* was also undergoing great transformation during the century we have portrayed in this chapter. Its changing fortunes—discarded into oblivion and rediscovered as a "strange thing"—as well as its multiplication in the form of stone replicas and rubbings reflect the flux of cultural and intellectual trends that have mixed popular fantasy, literati sentiments, scholarly pursuits, and commercial interests. These different visions would find their development in the centuries to follow.

Conclusion

On the eighteenth day of the tenth month of 1667, Zhang Chao, a Zhenjiang scholar, made his way to the muddy shore of Jiaoshan and found the long-forgotten fallen inscription. Shortly thereafter, he published his discovery in a monograph, *Discussion on Eulogy for Burying a Crane* (Yi he ming bian), starting with a vivid account of his visit with a boy servant:

> We first visited the two replicas [of *Eulogy for Burying a Crane*] and then went to the right of the Grand View Pavilion, from where I looked over the scattered broken rocks in the wild. I tightened my robe, and we went down [to the shore]. I found a rock lying on its back in the front, while another was face down behind it. The inscription was on the bottom of the stone, only a *chi* away from the sandy ground. Only by lying on the ground and looking up could I see the traces of the inscription. There is another rock standing on one side that has been severely eroded. The remaining characters on these rocks vary in number. I let the servant make a rubbing from each of them. At this moment, the sun was going down and the wind was cold. We could not stay longer. Then we took [a] boat and went back to the temple at Mount Yin where we lodged [see map 2 at beginning of book]. [At night] I examined [the rubbings] in the lamplight but was not able to see many [legible characters]. At bedtime I kept thinking of it and did not fall asleep all night. The next day I again went to make rubbings, just like meeting an old friend. Under the downward-facing rock, it was difficult to make rubbings by facing upward. With only his own hands, the servant could not handle the tools. Taking red and purple leaves nearby and spreading them on the ground, I lay on my back to help him. The ink dripped and stained our faces, but we did not care. Before we completed the work and

came back by boat, I had spent three busy days among the rocks. Our hands and feet had never taken a rest and our clothes were worn out. Finally I got four sheets of rubbings from each [rock].[1] (4A)

This is the most detailed premodern account of the physical condition of the fragments of the *Eulogy* inscription. Comparing the reconstruction by Zhang Chao (figure C.1) with today's fragments (see figure 1.2), we know that the stone he found face-up was F3 and the one face down was F4. The standing stone was F1. A small piece of stone with the three names, F5, is on the same sheet of paper as the text of F4.

Zhang's notes read:

> A: In the title only the character *he* 鶴 survives. The characters *hua yang zhen yi* 華陽真逸 are still perceivable but hard to make rubbing. I heard that a few years before the two characters *ji ye* 紀也 were still extant. Now they have gone.
>
> B: This is the standing stone. Only eight characters exist but not clear.
>
> C: These are the three lines, thirty-three characters, recarved by Song people. They are on the back of the facing-down rock.
>
> D: This is the facing-up stone. There are thirty characters in six lines.
>
> E: This section in the center has been lost for a long time.
>
> F: This is the facing-down stone. The characters are on the bottom. There are nineteen characters in three lines of inscription, plus one damaged character, which, if completed, looks like the character *zai* 宰. On the top [of the facing-down stone] lies a stone in the shape of a pillow, which attaches to the three lines, twelve characters, of the signature section. There is also a damaged character, which only a radical *jiang* 夅 on its upper right. The left and low section are illegible.

An important detail is that, as Zhang Chao found, the inscription on today's F2 stone was carved on the back of the downward-facing stone, that is, F4. Zhang suspected that the three lines on F2, consisting of thirty-four characters, were recarved by Song people and the original was long gone.[2] As we knew from Ma Ziyan's account, the F2 stone was reported to have been taken out of the river in 1189, but it later disappeared. Ma also tells us that the beginning section of the inscription had more than twenty characters, yet in 1667, only eight of them remained, according to Zhang Chao, and six survive on today's F1.[3] Zhang also announced a new discovery of eight characters on F4 and F5, as he marked with small circles in his reconstruction, which had never been recorded by any earlier visitors.

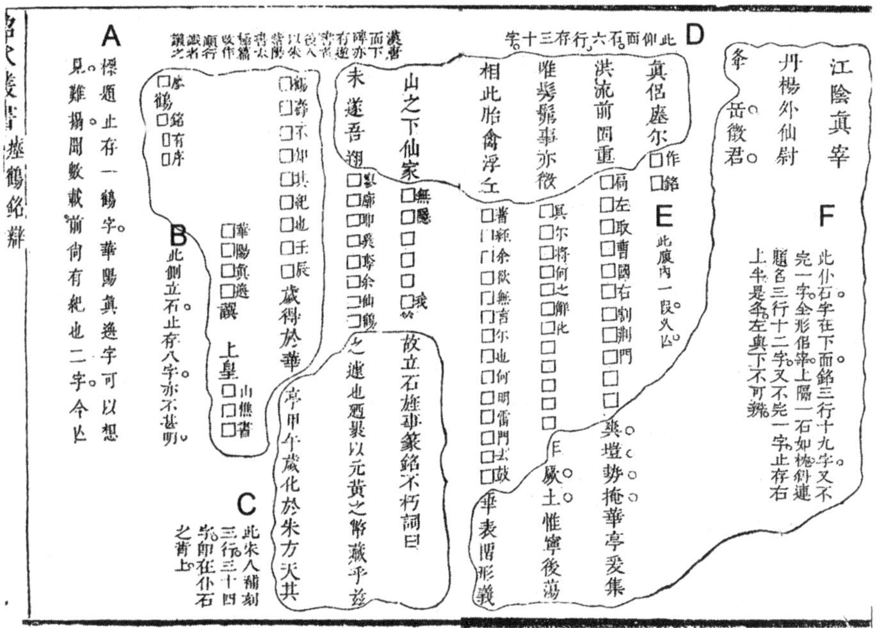

FIGURE C.1. Zhang Chao's reconstruction of *Eulogy* text in *Yihe ming bian*. Letter labels A–F mark Zhang's notes, translated in the text.

With the evidence from the original stone, Zhang continued to juxtapose the popular *Jade Smoke* version and point out its numerous problems, including altered and forged characters, line by line. He then proposed his own reconstruction, which we read in chapter 1. In this manner, his project resumed the evidential approach initiated by Zhang Yu and Shao Kang in their studies of the stones during the Northern Song. His project was part of the "study of bronze and stone" that was resurgent in the late seventeenth century, when many antiquarian scholars, notably Zhang Chao's close friend Gu Yanwu (1613–1682), engaged in searching for ancient inscriptions for *kaozheng*, or evidential study, a new scholarly trend that sought substantial historical knowledge through extensive research on textual evidence.[4] This paradigm shift in scholarship would lead to another dramatic change in the perception of calligraphy and its related fields.[5]

In the final section of his monograph, Zhang Chao anticipated a plan to restore the damaged stones. "If someday the stone is really restored," he dreamed, "from far away, one can see the auspicious cloud and know that this precious thing is under there."[6] Unfortunately, Zhang Chao did not live to see the realization of his plan, which occurred in 1713, twenty years after his death. The large project was under the supervision of Chen Pengnian (1663–1723), the former prefect of Suzhou, who was temporarily living in Zhenjiang at the time. In an inscription for a stele that still stands in Jiaoshan, Chen celebrated the project he oversaw:

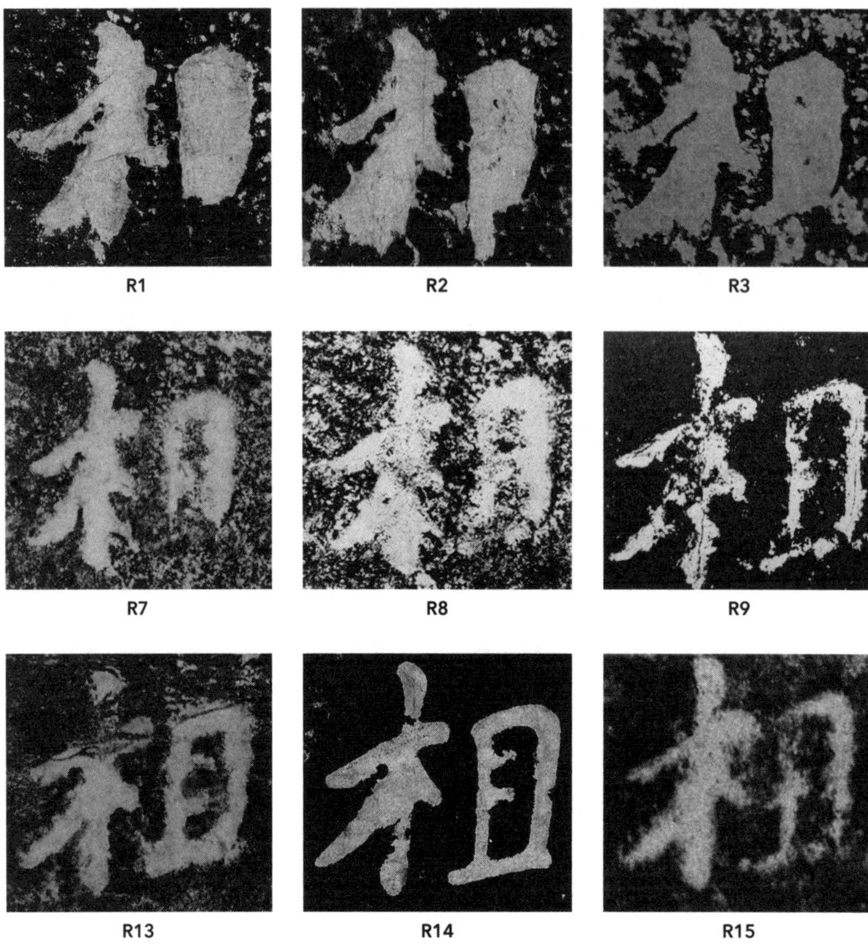

FIGURE C.2. Comparison of character *xiang* from major extant rubbings of *Eulogy for Burying a Crane*. The R numbers refer to the rubbings in appendix 1.

> It happened that there was scarcely any rain and snow [that year]. The water level dropped and the stones emerged much more than usual. Therefore, I had workmen choose [the right locations] and hew [the rock]. [The rocks] were as large as one *xun* [around 2.8 m] or *zhang* [around 3.3 m] and hard to haul the whole piece. [The workmen] exhausted their efforts to cut and to chisel, in order to bring the remaining inscription out of the deep water and move it up to the higher land. Finally, we got seventy characters or so. . . . From the winter through the spring, [the project] took three months to complete. It was the sixteenth day of the second month of the *guisi* year [1713].[7] (4B)

The five fragments (including the suspicious F2) cut from the rocks by Chen Pengnian's workmen were placed into a newly built pavilion on Jiaoshan. Originally, Chen's stele may have been erected next to it. Although the process sounds quite

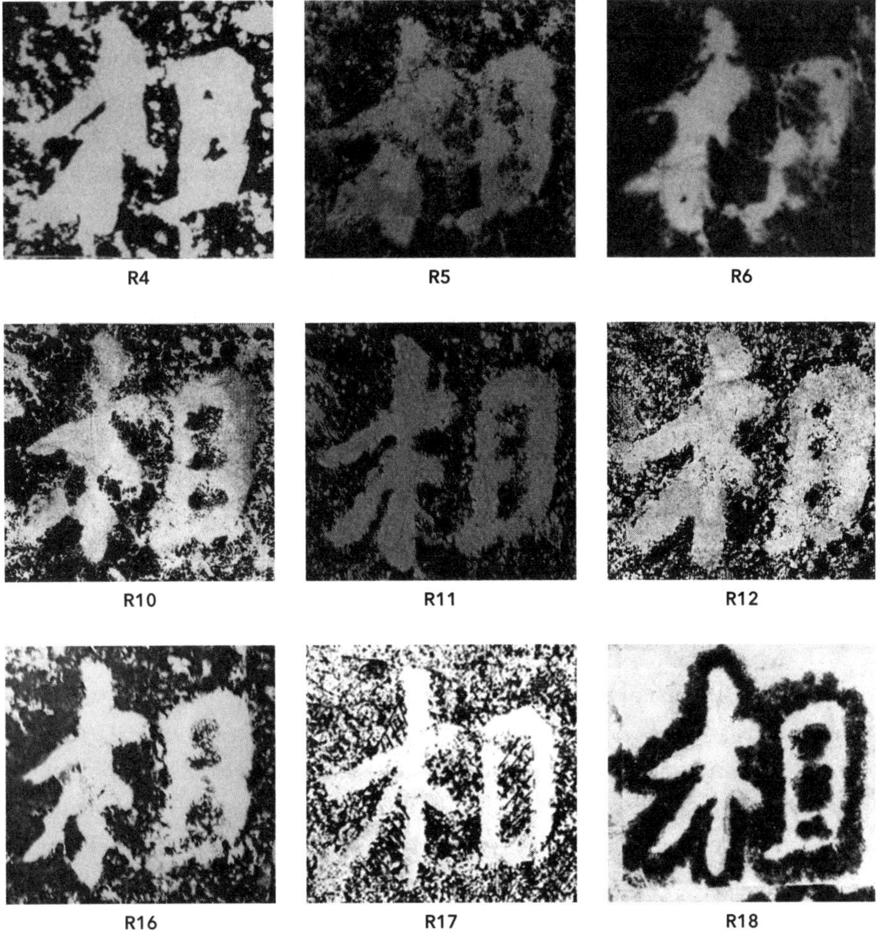

violent, the result seemed successful—all of the inscriptions reported by Zhang Chao survived. Following this excavation, a monograph was published in 1714 by the contemporary scholar and calligrapher Wang Shihong. Most of the volume consists of previous writings on the stone, including Zhang Chao's work. Wang added his own meticulous research on the newly available stones, with illustrations of the position of the fragments and the characters each stone bore. Despite some minor errors, the book was the most accurate account of the *Eulogy* ever written up to Wang's time, and it remains an important source for studies of the inscription, including this one.

Somewhat surprisingly, instead of celebrating the recovery of the stones from the river, Wang Shihong worried about their fate:

> Nevertheless, since [the inscription of *Eulogy*] has been moved out of the river, it is now easy for people to have access. They will vie to make rubbings. I am afraid that after a while, [the inscription] will be obliterated, no different from shattered stones along the riverbank.[8] (4C)

It was perhaps out of the same concerns that Chen Pengnian had a replica stele carved and erected in front of the original stone.[9] The substitute inscription, however, was soon discarded and the original stones were exposed to extensive pounding and scrubbing. In the following decades, the carved characters had become so worn that it was said to be almost impossible to make an acceptable rubbing.[10] These human activities, as Wang Shihong predicted, damaged the inscription and distorted the characters more than the natural erosion that had already partially effaced them.

The course of physical changes to the stone can be demonstrated by the extant rubbings taken at different times, though it is impossible to give the individual rubbings a precise chronological order. Figure C.2 illustrates the same character, *xiang* 相, taken from the extant rubbings listed in appendix 2. On rubbings R1 to R7, which are believed to be earlier versions, often called *shuiqian ben* (the edition before [the stone coming out of] water), the right *mu* 目 radical is nearly illegible, and spaces between the short *heng* strokes with which this radical is normally written are hard to see, reduced to a small dot in R2–R4.[11] In R5 and R6, the right radical looks different: a short *heng* stroke in the middle makes the radical look like the character *ri* 日 instead of *mu* 目. The character in R7 looks similar to those in R5 and R6, but evidence of restoration is visible in the well-defined outline of the *mu* 木 radical. In contrast, from R8 on, the shape of the right radical changes: it becomes more elongated and its bottom *heng* stroke is extended. In R10–R14 and R18, this same radical becomes more legible, and the strokes are thicker and bolder, perhaps caused by constant rechiseling. Another discernible change in this character is a small spot attached to the bottom *heng* stroke, clearly seen in R2–R4, blurred in R5–R6, and absent in R7–R14. R15 and R16 may represent a "transitional" status.

It should be noted that a skillful rubbing maker can easily manipulate the way of applying ink and take liberties in order to create more "legible" characters. R17 and R18 may demonstrate such skillful tactics; despite their later date, the characters are even sharper. The result presents a paradox in connoisseurship to art historians: whereas the "makeup" approach certainly betrays the rubbing's commitment to the authenticity (see the discussion in chapter 3), these rubbings cannot be called fakes—they were indeed from the original inscription, not a *chongke*, *fanke*, or *weike*.

The Continuing Impact of the *Jade Smoke* Version

Ironically, after the fragments of the *Eulogy* were restored from the water and put on display, their dilapidated status must have disappointed many students of calligraphy, especially those who had long admired the mysterious inscription. Wang Shu (1668–1743), a noted antiquarian scholar, echoed the long tradition of critical doubt and mixed feeling to which Huang Bosi, Wang Shizhen, and many other scholars contributed when he remarked:

> The inscription has been eroded, but the calligraphy was relaxed and detached [*xiaoshu danyuan*], indeed like the traces of immortals. Tuigu's [Wang Shihong] comments—"the relaxed composition showing the ancient clerical style; the brushwork, though worn out, radiates the spiritual light"—might be a fair judgment. Some over-evaluated it and said that the wonderful brushwork tops all calligraphy. That is an overstatement.[12] (4D)

On the other hand, the influence of *Model Letters of the Jade Smoke Hall* on calligraphers was still so strong that even after the original stones were recovered in 1713 and the version reproduced in *Jade Smoke* was exposed as a partial forgery, its status as the standard embodiment of the inscription did not change. This mixture of scholarly inquiry and public knowledge may be illustrated by Wang Shihong's calligraphy. In 1714, the same year in which he completed his monograph on the stone, he made a copy of the *Eulogy* (figure C.3). Although he may well have known about the inaccuracy of the *Jade Smoke* version, in his copy, Wang followed the calligraphic style and the text of the forged replica! The line "*nai zheng qian shi*," for example, was after the *Jade Smoke*'s forged characters, as we saw in figure 3.8. Wang must have been aware of the problem but may have felt it more appropriate to follow the public perception in this social occasion; as Wang's own colophon indicates, the copy was made upon a request from a friend who showed him a rubbing, most likely the *Jade Smoke* version. At any rate, his copy reveals a close study of the *Jade Smoke* version, which, thanks to Dong Qichang's promotion, had been widely accepted as the best-known model for writing large-character calligraphy.

The contrast between the dilapidated stone and the calligraphy model found a dramatic example in a series of calligraphy projects by the Qianlong Emperor during his famous six inspection tours of southern China to reinforce the Manchu emperor's omnipresent political and cultural power over the Chinese subjects.[13] He visited Jiaoshan on each trip and even had a temporary residence built there for the island's scenic view and cultural legacy, and also for its natural security.[14] At every notable site on the island, the emperor composed poems and wrote calligraphy, which were carved on steles by local officials as an honor. One of them was a copy of the *Eulogy* that the Qianlong Emperor made in his own hand in 1757 during another stay at Jiaoshan. In a long colophon that he added to the copy, the emperor explained that his goal in producing a replica of his own was to protect the original stones by substituting his copy for them.[15] The emperor also ordered the original stones moved and mounted on the wall of the Dinghui Temple on the island, where they would remain until the early twentieth century.

The emperor's stele was lost at some point, but the imperial "copy" may survive in a miniature version carved in a jade desk screen, perhaps for the emperor's enjoyment back at his court in Beijing.[16] The carved inscription (see a rubbing in figure C.4) is filled in with gold and framed with refined incised lines and patterns.

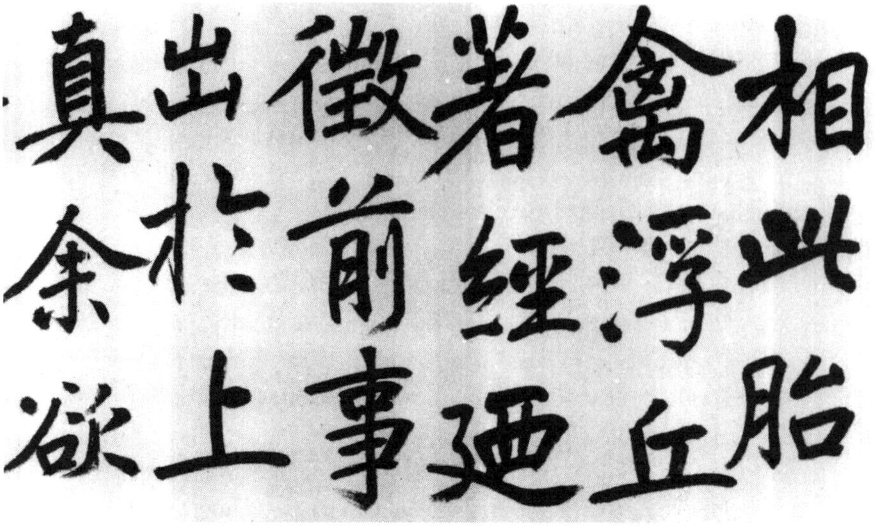

FIGURE C.3. Wang Shihong, *Copy of Eulogy for Burying a Crane*. Dated 1714. Detail. Ink on paper, 30.5 × 540 cm. Guangdong Provincial Museum, Guangzhou. From *Zhongguo meishu quanji: Shufa zhuanke bian* 6: plate 67.

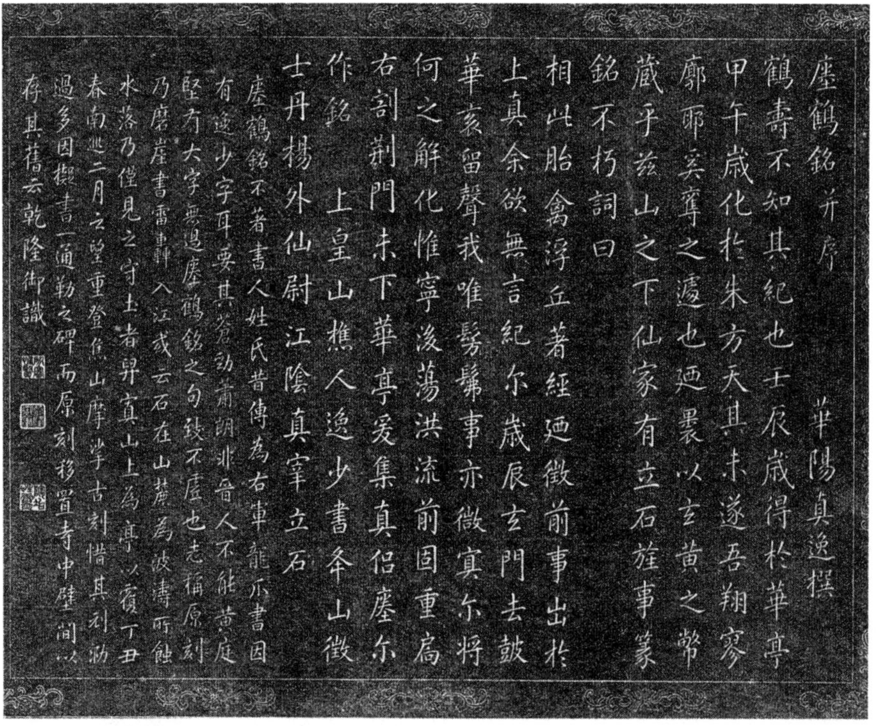

FIGURE C.4. Rubbing taken from the front side of a jade desk screen inscribed with Qianlong's copy of *Eulogy for Burying a Crane*. 28 × 23 cm. Private collection. Poly Autumn Auction, December 5, 2010, lot 4662, Beijing.

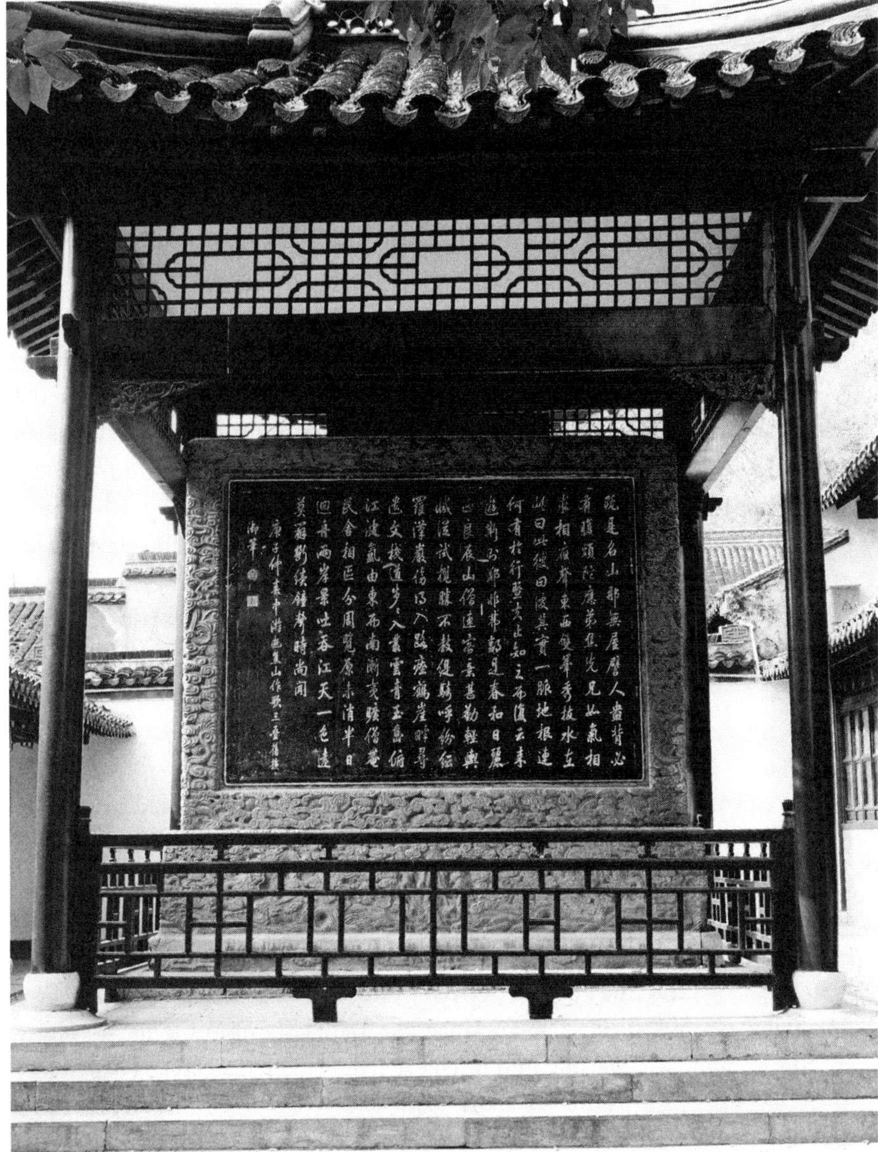

FIGURE C.5. The Qianlong emperor's inscription at Jiaoshan. Author's photo, 2017.

The other side of the jade screen depicts the landscape of Jiaoshan. The original stone stele was perhaps not unlike another one carrying the imperial writing that still stands at Jiaoshan (figure C.5). What is intriguing about the emperor's copy, if the jade inscription is indeed an exact miniature copy, is that instead of trying to imitate the *Eulogy*'s style, Qianlong transcribed the text in his clean and monotonous personal style. The text runs from right to left, the opposite of the original inscription. Furthermore, the text turns out to be a transcription of the *Jade Smoke* version, though the copy was made after viewing the original stone. The emperor may have never bothered to "study" the barely legible inscription, nor did he pay attention to the epigraphic scholarship, such as Wang Shihong's. The imperial goal, though unstated, was surely to leave his traces on the historical site and to "collect" the ancient artifact, in the miniature replica, thereby identifying himself with the immortal cultural tradition that the *Eulogy* had come to signify.

The Re-Vision of Calligraphy

What scholars, calligraphers, and the emperor shared was frustration at the diminished status of the *Eulogy* inscription; its legendary calligraphy existed only in the imagination, for the dilapidated fragments out of the water hardly served as an actual model. This vision, however, would be dramatically changed in the following century. The earliest sign of the shifting attitudes among scholar-calligraphers may be found in the writing of Weng Fanggang (1733–1818), who became the most ardent (and influential) student of the *Eulogy* since Huang Tingjian. Weng composed a series of essays on the subject. One of them, written around 1775, expresses his unreserved enthusiasm about the *Eulogy*:

> Now examine the calligraphy of the inscriptions closely. Characters such as *shanghuang* 上皇, *xian* 仙, *shan* 山, *xiang* 相, *shi* 石, and *zhenlü* 真侶 refer to the style of *Yellow Court Sutra* and *Stele of the Huadu Temple* [dated 631 CE, by Tang calligrapher Ouyang Xun]; *Wei* 未, *wei* 唯, *hong* 洪, and *gu* 固 are fully robust like the style of Pingyuan [Yan Zhenqing]; *Jiangyin zhenzai* 江陰真宰, *zhu* 朱, *hua* 化, and *taiqin* 胎禽 are ethereal and lofty like the style of Yongxing's [Yu Shinan]. *Weining* 惟寧 and *houdang* 後蕩 are like through Chu [Suiliang] and Xue [Ji] and derived from Yang [Xin] and Bo [Shaozhi]. *Huating* 華亭, and *yuanji* 爰集 are squat like Taifu [Zhong You]; *Jing* 旌, *jue* 厥, *zhi* 之, and *fu* 浮 are slim and intensive like Han clerical style. *Fang* 方, *zhuan* 篆, *tu* 土, and *shi* 勢 are archaic and strange like the Stone Drums in seal script. These dozens of surviving characters demonstrate the calligraphy through thousands of years. . . . This work gained much from the seal script. How is it enough to only call it as spacious as clerical-script calligraphy? That is why I closely examined the inscription's connection to the broader issues on calligraphy. It demonstrates the spirits of all the Six Dynasties masters and synthesizes them.[17] (4E)

Despite the specific examples given in the essay, those who are familiar with the history of calligraphy may find that the visual connections between the *Eulogy* and other works that Weng Fanggang points out seem random and arbitrary, if not utterly confusing. The tone is reminiscent of that in Huang Tingjian's writing seven centuries before. And his perception of the seal-script brushwork in the *Eulogy* is clearly derived from Huang's, as we read in chapter 2. Weng's renewed interest in the calligraphy, however, must be understood in the context of the new intellectual and artistic environment, as epigraphic research, antiquarian interest, and the trend of calligraphic practice converged in one of the most distinctive phenomena in the history of calligraphy, the so-called *beixue*, or "stele study [calligraphy]," presumably a combination of learning and art.

Collecting rubbings of steles and studying ancient inscriptions attracted renewed interest in the seventeenth century, and calligraphers such as Fu Shan (1607–1684) and Zheng Fu (1622–1693) began experimenting with calligraphic styles based on ancient inscriptions.[18] It was during the last decades of the eighteenth century, however, that many more scholars began to engage themselves in these experiments.[19] Weng Fang-gang's comment on the *Eulogy*'s calligraphy may be seen as a product of this change. Unlike earlier and contemporary antiquarian scholars, who paid attention to the historical or philological content of ancient inscriptions and often saw calligraphy as a secondary subject, Weng argued for the significance of the latter as a scholarly field. On one occasion he commented, "It would be hypocritical to say studying bronze and stone [inscriptions] is *not* for their calligraphy."[20] This statement is a great departure from the traditional attitude of "study of bronze and stone" and marks the turning point of the discourse and practice of stele-study calligraphy.[21] Weng's comments on the *Eulogy* and attention to the formal traits were meant to establish an alternative historical narrative on calligraphy that compromises the Two Wangs classical tradition and the long-ignored calligraphy of anonymous ancient inscriptions. As we shall see, his theory would become the keystone of the later reception of the *Eulogy*.

This new trend of stele-study calligraphy would be further theorized by the prominent official and antiquarian scholar Ruan Yuan (1764–1849) in his two essays published around 1811: "On the Northern and Southern Schools of Calligraphy" (Nan bei shupai lun) and "On Northern Steles and Southern Letters" (Beibei nantie lun).[22] In these two essays—what may be considered a manifesto of stele-study calligraphy—Ruan argued that after the collapse of the Han dynasty, the "ancient methods" (*gufa*), which refer to the brushwork of seal script and clerical script, were preserved only in north China, as the Southern Dynasties witnessed the rise of the Two Wangs "southern school" that lacked the proper "methods." Whereas the "northern school" remained influential after the reunification of the south and north under the Tang, Ruan continued, the invention of model letters in the Song dynasty led to the domination of the "southern school" in calligraphy practice and the complete loss of "ancient methods." Now, Ruan declared, it was time to save the degenerated art of writing by turning to the ancient monuments for the ancient methods.[23] Ruan's interpretation of the historical development was meant to challenge the received knowledge about calligraphy of his time. His persuasive narrative, though overly reductive and selective, was fueled by a revolutionary historical view and methodology, which would lead to a paradigm shift in the study of calligraphy that still influences many writings this day.[24]

It was within this theoretical framework that Ruan Yuan wrote about *Eulogy for Burying a Crane*:

> Due to the official ban on carving steles in the Southern Dynasties, steles were rare. Only the model letters were appreciated. So all writings were turned into standard, running, or cursive scripts, and there was no returning to the ideas of the ancient styles. Compared with Zheng Daozhao's *Mountain Gate* inscription in Laizhou, *Eulogy for Burying a Crane* on Jiaoshan shows a similar style but demonstrates [a] more beautiful appearance [*yantai*] and less of the ancient methods.[25] (4F)

Ruan Yuan was one of the first epigraphers to investigate the inscriptions of Cloud Peak Mountain (see figure 1.6) and make them widely known in his influential writing. This comparison between Zheng's calligraphy and that of the *Eulogy*, initiated here by Ruan, has been revisited by many later scholars.[26] Ironically, his reserved attitude toward the *Eulogy* would be gradually twisted by his later followers who continued to advocate for stele-study calligraphy. It was the similarity between the calligraphic style of Zheng Daozhao and that of the *Eulogy* that became the focus of mainstream discourse on the ruined inscription. This view is represented in the calligrapher and critic Bao Shichen's (1775–1855) *Paired Oars for the Boat of Art* (Yizhou shuangji), another important treatise of the increasingly popular stele-study calligraphy. Among the advocates of the new trend of calligraphy, Bao went furthest by arguing that even Tang dynasty calligraphy was inferior for its mechanical, print-like look and only the calligraphy in the Northern Dynasties was the descendant of the true "ancient method."[27] The exception found in the south, though, Bao argued, was none other than *Eulogy for Burying a Crane*, for its "relaxed and detached" qualities (*xiaosan junyi*).[28] And it is also in Bao's writing that we find a renewed version of Huang Tingjian's theory on large-character calligraphy:

> Writing large-character calligraphy should [be] like writing small-character calligraphy—this means the writing should appear composed and dignified, not intimidated by the vast environment. . . . The free execution in *Eulogy for Burying a Crane* and the relaxed maneuver in Sutra Stone Valley [Jingshiyu]—these two works well deserve [regard].[29] (4G)

The "Sutra Stone Valley" refers to the sixth-century monumental inscription of the *Diamond Sutra* at Mount Tai. Carved on a vast, raw surface of rock, each character of the sutra inscription is larger than 1.5 feet, creating a spectacle in the natural environment.[30] In drawing a comparison between the *Eulogy* and the sixth-century carved sutra on Mount Tai, Bao enters a new aesthetic discourse of calligraphy that pits free composition and brushwork against the rigid specimens in model letters. Furthermore, the attention to the relationship between calligraphy and its physical space

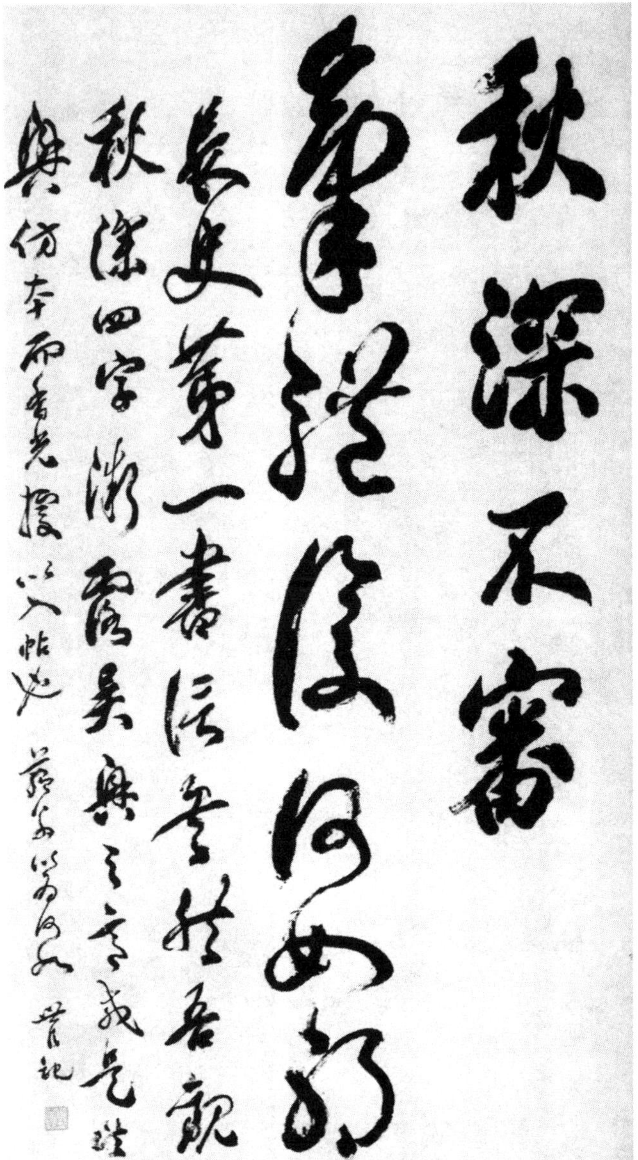

FIGURE C.6. Bao Shichen, *Copy after Zhang Xu's Letter of "Qiushen."* Ink on paper, 167.5 × 89.5 cm. Yangzhou Museum. From *Zhongguo meishu quanji: Shufa zhuanke bian* 6: plate 67.

reflects a fresh visual interest in stele-study calligraphy: its favorite formats, such as large hanging scrolls and couplets, demand a careful consideration of the spatial environment.

Despite their persuasive discourses, none of the above pioneering advocates of stele-study calligraphy applied their theory to their own calligraphy. Weng Fang-gang and Ruan Yuan are both known for their quintessential model-letters styles. Although Bao Shichen wrote extensively about the stele inscriptions, we rarely find seal or clerical scripts—the favorite types of stele-study calligraphy—in his extant works.[31] Later critics note that Bao's calligraphic style never departed from the

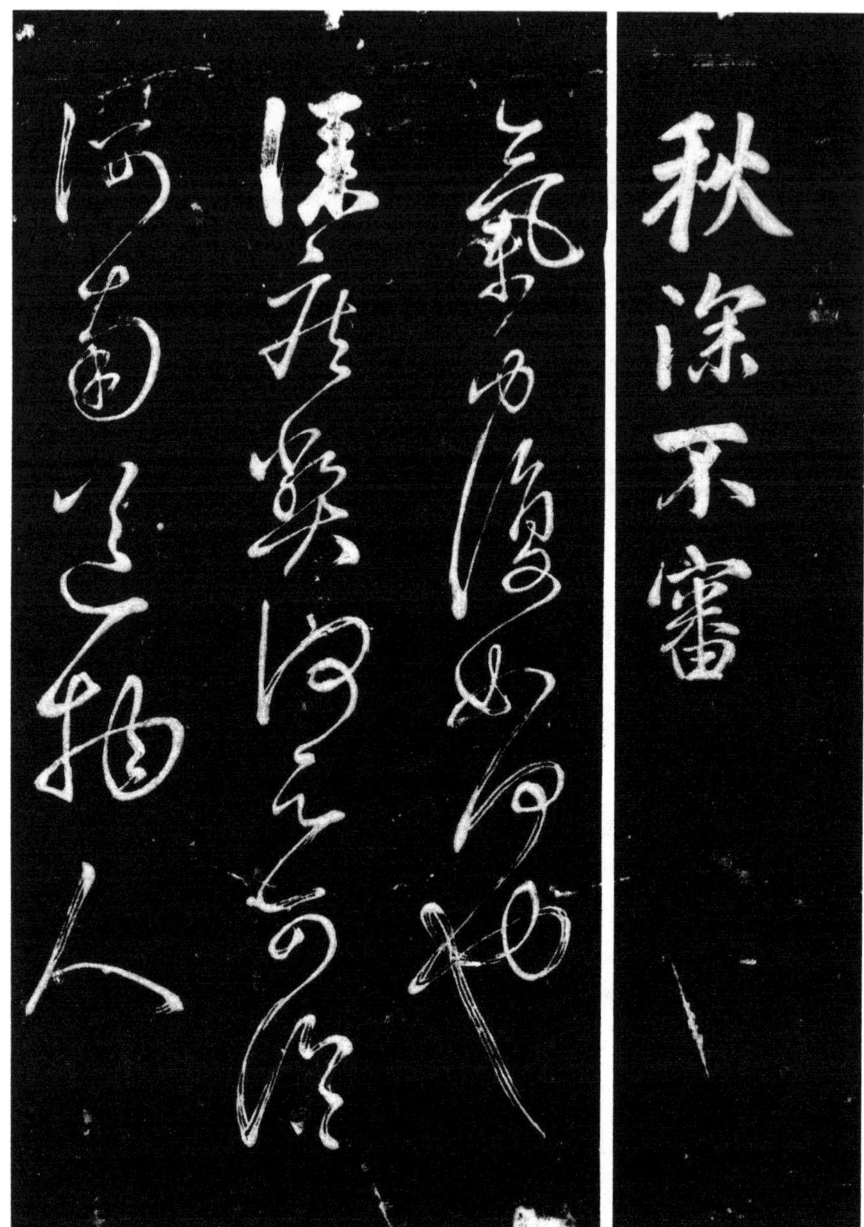

FIGURE C.7. Zhang Xu (attributed), *Letter of "Qiushen,"* in *Model Letters of the Frolicking Geese Hall*. Courtesy of Harvard-Yenching Library, TP0002.

traditional Two Wangs model.[32] An exception may be found in the large calligraphy illustrated in figure C.6. At first glance, it seems to be a traditional study; the model for Bao was a piece attributed to the Tang calligrapher Zhang Xu (ca. 675–ca.750) in Dong Qichang's *Model Letters of the Frolicking Geese Hall* (figure C.7). Bao's work is, however, a freehand copy, and even the text varies from the original. The slow and awkward turns in the longest column may demonstrate the effort to recast the seal-script brushwork of ancient steles, though Bao never explicated his intention. Bao's subtle approach is not comparable to the bold and direct application of ancient works, including the *Eulogy*, by the calligraphers of the next generation, who would turn stele-study calligraphy into a phenomenal scene.

Appropriating the *Eulogy*

The most distinguished calligrapher among Ruan Yuan's disciples was He Shaoji (1799–1873), who was also an ardent epigrapher and collector of early rubbings. On one occasion, He named the four most inspiring works of calligraphy in history, echoing Ruan Yuan and Weng Fanggang's views:

> [The historical works that] have synthesized the northern and southern schools and enlightened [later] calligraphers include only these: *Yellow Court Sutra* at the earlier time, and [*Stele of*] *the Huadu* [*Temple*][33] at the later time. In the middle are Zhenbai's [Tao Hongjing's] *Eulogy for Burying a Crane* and Zhiyong's *A Thousand-Character Text*.[34] (4H)

Unlike Weng and his other predecessors, He actually applied his admiration for the *Eulogy* to his own practice of calligraphy. And his approach was straightforward to the viewer, as illustrated by the couplet he wrote in 1862 (figure C.8):

> Leaving the inscribed words to be carved on the mountain rock;
> With the immortal companions gathering in the river pavilion.
> (4I)

The text was pieced together with the characters from the *Eulogy* in a favorite form of stele-study calligraphy, *jizi lian*, or "collated-text couplet," which flourished in the late Qing period.[35] Producing such a literary exercise challenges the ability and knowledge of the calligrapher. On the one hand, the text and the style of the couplet must be from appropriate sources, usually ancient inscriptions. On the other hand, unlike the direct textual transcription as we have seen in other copies of earlier work, the finished work must convey a relevant but new verbal meaning and visual appearance.

The literary-calligraphic game often fulfilled the requirements from various social occasions. He Shaoji produced the couplet when he visited a close friend, Yang Han (1812–1879), also a noted antiquarian scholar and calligrapher, who at the time was serving as the prefect of Yongzhou, Hunan (which happened to be He's native town). One of the many cultural projects Prefect Yang conducted was a renovation of Chaoyang Cliff, a scenic site known for a noted literary piece, "Inscription on Chaoyang Cliff" (Chaoyangyan ming), by the Tang poet Yuan Jie (the author of

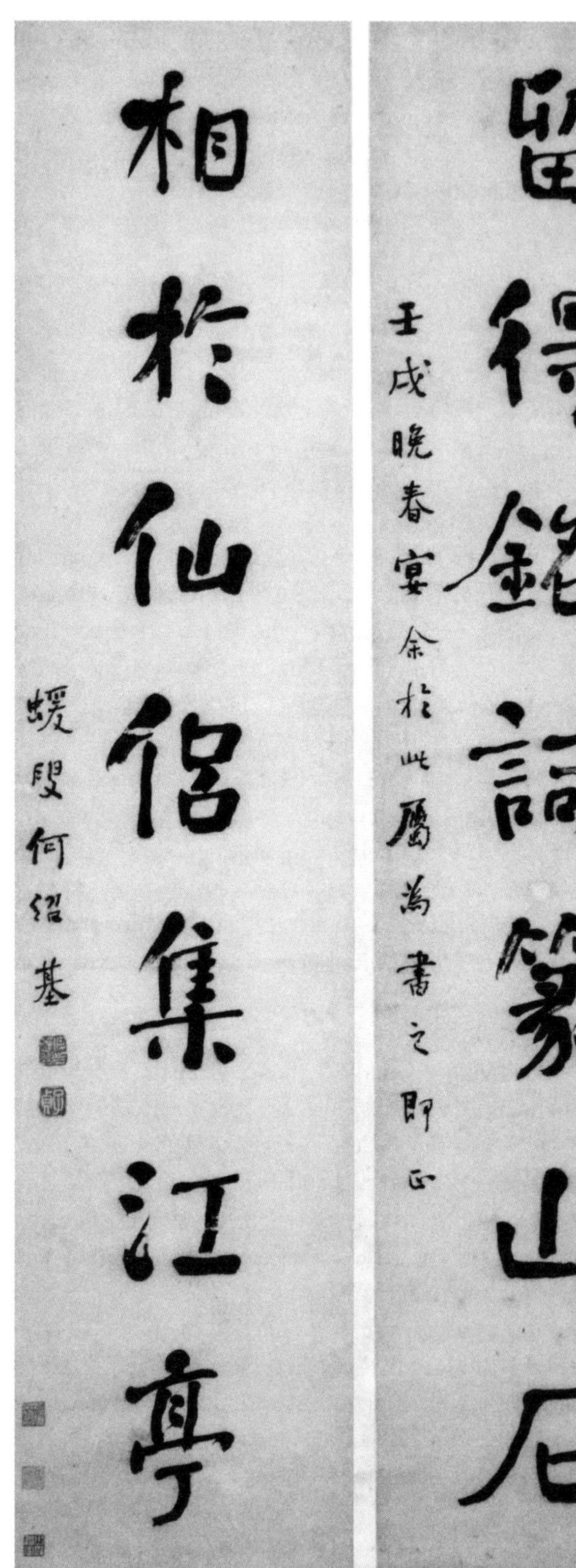

FIGURE C.8. He Shaoji, *Seven-Character Couplet for Yang Han*. Dated 1862. Ink on paper, 136.8 × 30.5 cm. Sichuan Provincial Museum, Chengdu. From *Zhongguo meishu quanji: Shufa zhuanke bian*, 6: plate 178.

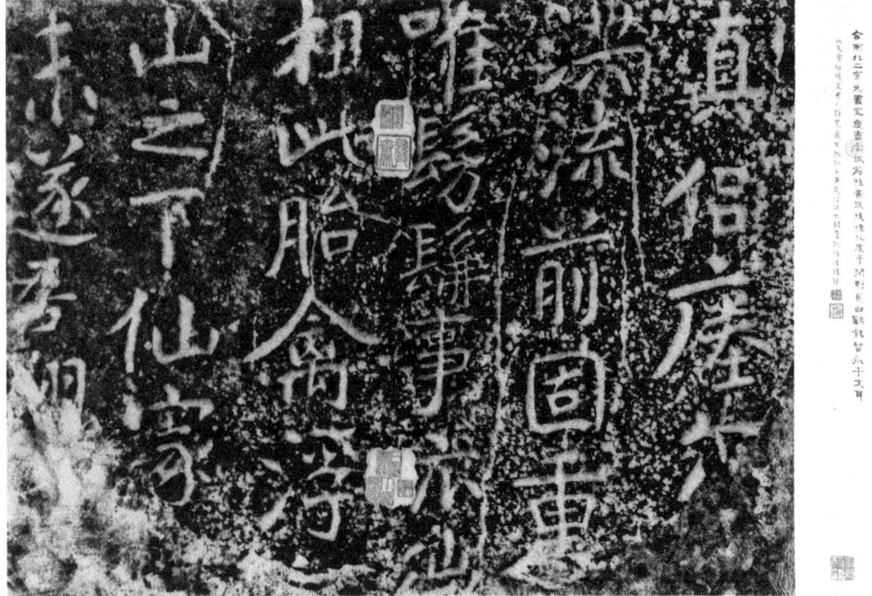

FIGURE C.9. Rubbing of *Eulogy for Burying a Crane*. Formerly in He Shaoji's collection. The Palace Museum, Beijing. From *Zhongguo meishu quanji: Shufa zhuanke bian* 2:142.

Hymn to the Revival of the Great Tang; see chapter 2), which comprised more than a hundred *moya* inscriptions added over later centuries, making it another famous site of tagging-name inscriptions.[36] Yang managed to renovate the place as a virtual gallery of calligraphy. Since the legendary Yuan Jie's inscription was long gone by this time (or perhaps had never really been carved into stone), Yang Han invited the contemporary calligrapher Deng Shouzhi (1795–1870), son of Deng Shiru, to write a new transcription in seal-script, which he then had carved on the rock. A pavilion, named Inscribed Stone (Zhuanshiting), was built on top of the newly made "ancient" inscription.

He Shaoji's couplet may have been carved on wood boards and placed on the pillar of the building, though no traces are found today. The choice of *Eulogy for Burying a Crane* as the source for the project might not have been a coincidence. Although the *Eulogy* is nearly a thousand miles away from Chaoyang Cliff, its presence through the couplet transcends the geographic and historical distance, evoking universal antiquarian sentiments and a collective cultural memory at this and many other newly constructed historical sites.

Unlike all the works after the *Eulogy* discussed earlier, He Shaoji's calligraphy was directly based on rubbings from the original stones, perhaps none other than the extant rubbings illustrated in figure C.9 and C.10, which, bearing He Shaoji's seals and colophons, were both in his own collection. Juxtaposing He's copy with the characters from the rubbings, one can observe how he rearranged the characters by adjusting the composition and brush strokes deliberately to approximate the appearance of the carving. The ink blots at the beginning of strokes in characters such

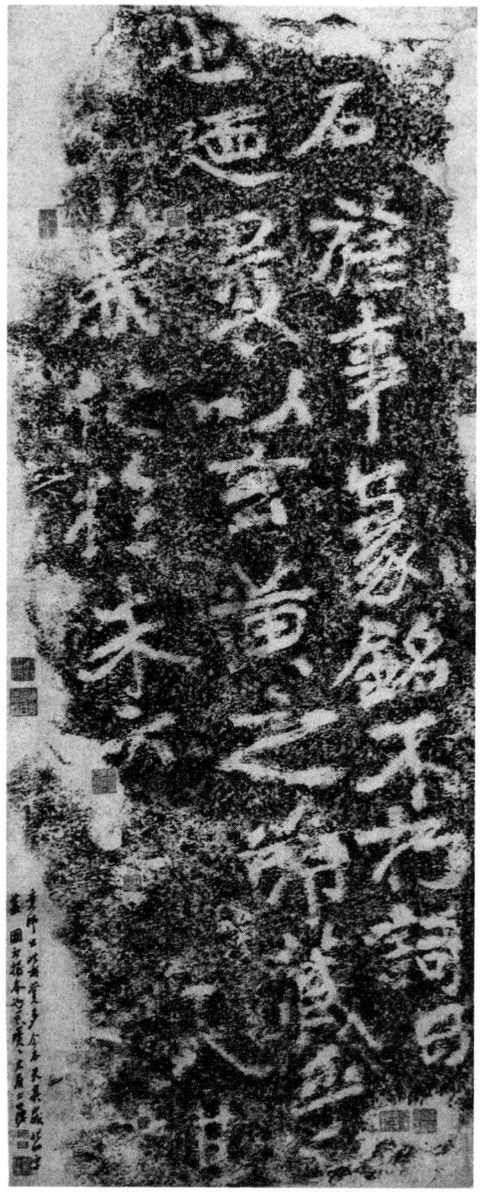

FIGURE C.10. Rubbing of *Eulogy for Burying a Crane*. Formerly in He Shaoji's collection. The Palace Museum, Beijing. From *Zhongguo meishu quanji: Shufa zhuanke bian* 2:143.

as *xiang* 相, *yu* 於, and *xian* 仙 in the couplet, as well as the "flying-white" effect in many characters, are intended to resemble the erosion on the original inscription. To achieve the distinctive visual effect, He might have experimented with "gibbon's arm," a special gesture of writing that he famously invented.[37] Bending the wrist and holding the brush from a higher position, He must have forced himself to break the traditional rules of writing. The result is an unusual tension between awkward strokes and subtly balanced structure, which echoes the visual appeal of the worn surface of the stone.

Just as striking as the similarities between He Shaoji's calligraphy in the couplet and the characters on the rubbing is his departure from this model. Characters such

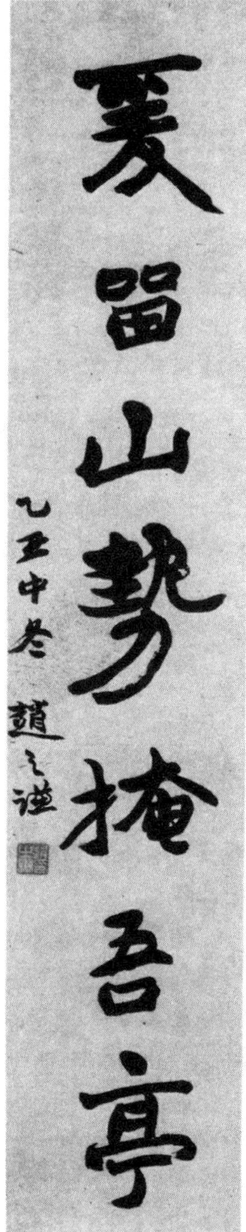

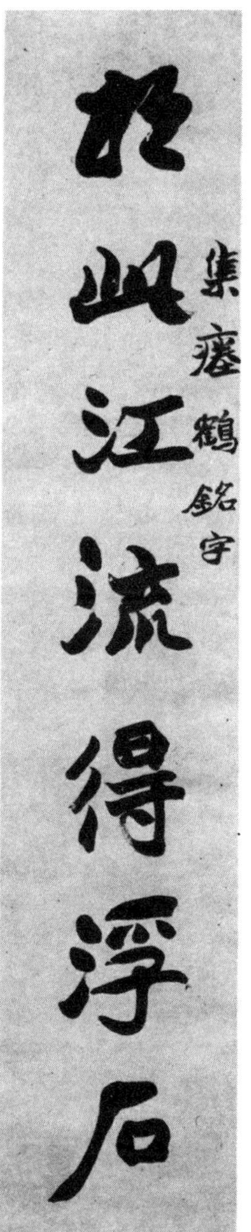

FIGURE C.11. Zhao Zhiqian, *Couplet in Characters from Eulogy for Burying a Crane*. Dated 1865. Ink on paper. Unknown collection.

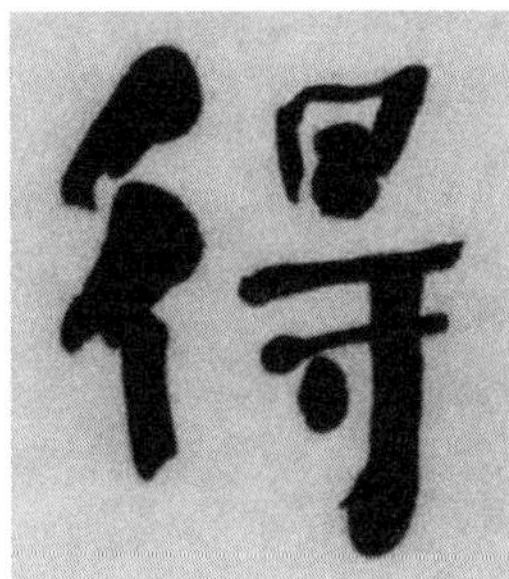

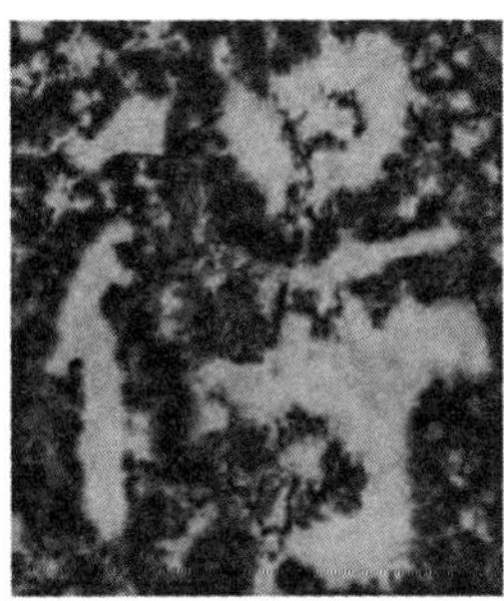

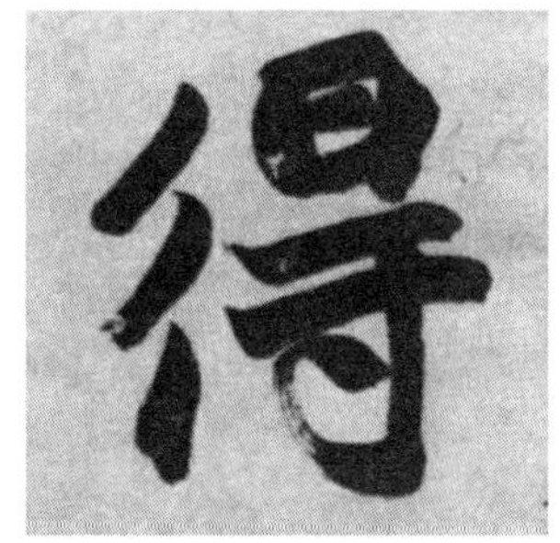

FIGURE C.12. Comparison of the character *de* from figure C.8 and figure C.11.

as *liu* 留 and *ting* 亭 are elongated vertically, while others, such as the character *shan* 山, are compressed, as if squeezed in from the sides. For other characters, though He preserves the brushwork and structure of the *Eulogy*, he adapts their compositions according to his own creative impulses. The character *ci* 詞 in He's couplet, for instance, is based on the corresponding character on the rubbing, but in the left radical, the three short *heng* strokes are reduced in size to produce a better sense of visual balance. Another detail worth noting is the character *shi* 石; He's handwritten version is executed in rounded strokes typical of seal script, while in the rubbing, the character is clearly in standard script. He's new invention may have been meant to materialize Huang Tingjian's and Weng Fanggang's visions about the seal-script brushwork of the *Eulogy*'s calligraphy.

Overall, He's approach departs greatly from what we have seen in the works of Huang Tingjian and Dong Qichang, which were self-contained—one does not need to know the *Eulogy* to appreciate them. Their reference to the *Eulogy* is not visible without our elaborate (and perhaps teleological) art historical analysis. In contrast, He's take on the *Eulogy* may be defined as appropriation that—not unlike what has been commonly found in contemporary art—reuses and reconfigures old artworks in a new intertextual and intermedia complex.[38] The context was completely different, of course. Whereas appropriation in contemporary art has been read as the postmodern challenge to the received notion of art, appropriation in stele-study calligraphy, as He Shaoji's couplet shows, should be seen as a visualization of antiquarian inquiry and taste, an attempt to reengage the "ancient method" of calligraphy.

Another "collated-text couplet" (figure C.11), by Zhao Zhiqian (1829–1884), another major figure of stele-study calligraphy, illustrates a quite different mode of appropriation. The characters are all taken from the *Eulogy* text too, though it seems that only in the left line can one discern the resemblance to the original; the distorted forms of the characters *yuan* 爰, *liu* 留, *shi* 勢, and *yan* 掩 may be attributed to the eroded inscription. Unlike He Shaoji, however, Zhao demonstrated little interest in recreating the physical appearance of the original inscription. Rather, he translated the forms into his personal brush writing, known to later critics as "square-brush" (*fangbi*), which emulated the result of chisel carving on sixth-century stone inscriptions. The different approaches of the two calligraphers is illustrated by a comparison of the way they write the character *de* 得 (figure C.12). Both recall the appearance of this character in stone carving, but whereas He retains and even exaggerates the coarse and fragmented appearance of the inscription, Zhao assimilates the character into his powerful angular brushstrokes.

The incorporation of the *Eulogy* must not have been a random choice for Zhao Zhiqian. It is known that Zhao, a follower of Bao Shichen's calligraphic theory, had long been an admirer of the inscription. It may, however, have taken him a while to figure out how to transcend the problem of the dilapidated stone. A copy of the *Eulogy* (figure C.13) made a few years before the couplet may suggest such a transition.[39] The small piece was written for Wei Xizeng (1828–1881), also an antiquarian scholar and ardent collector of rubbings. The work is more like a study: there is no

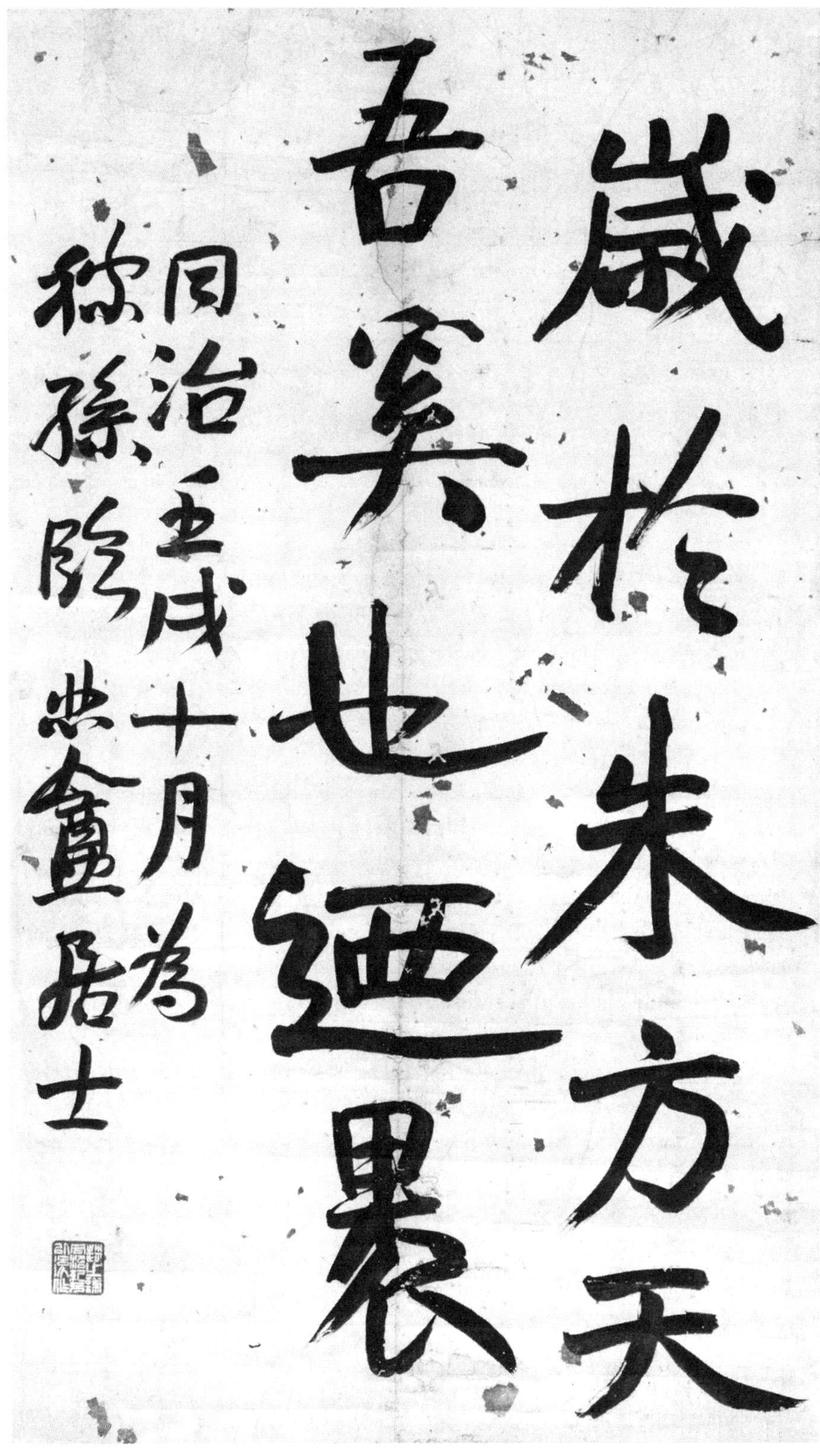

FIGURE C.13. Zhao Zhiqian, *Copy of Eulogy for Burying a Crane*. Dated 1862. Ink on paper, 73 × 41 cm. From Liu Zhengcheng *Zhongguo shufa quanji* 71:50.

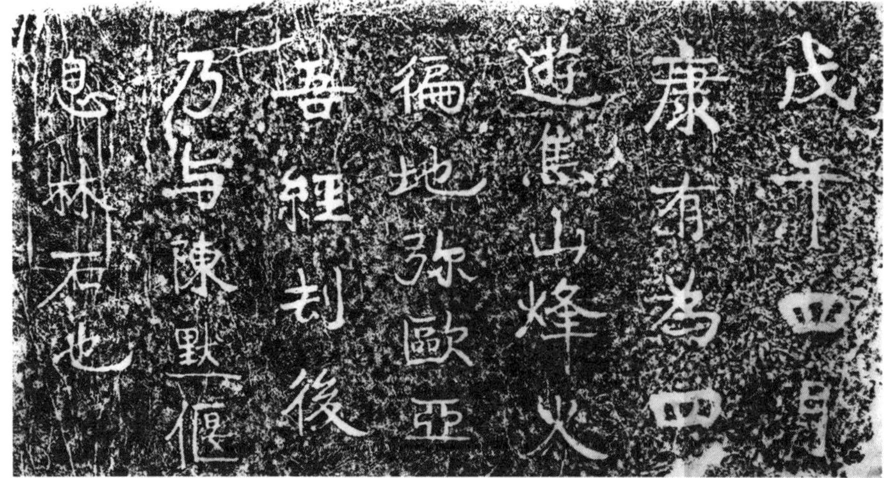

FIGURE C.14. Kang Youwei, stone inscription at Jiaoshan. Dated 1918. Ink rubbing, 70 × 135 cm. Courtesy of Jiaoshan Stone Inscription Museum.

semantic meaning—Zhao made copies only of selected legible characters from the *Eulogy,* and the forms of characters do not follow the original ones exactly. It may reflect Zhao's early experimentation with transforming the eroded carving into a Yan Zhenqing style that he was studying at the time.[40] The oddly stretched strokes largely disappear in the couplet and are only discernable in some places, like the elongated *na* stroke of the character *yuan* 爰 and the distorted character *shi* 勢.

Zhao Zhiqian famously distanced himself from He Shaoji, the most sought-after calligrapher of the generation before him. After a meeting between the two around 1870, Zhao recalled, "If not discussing calligraphy, we liked each other very much. Whenever we went to this topic, we ended up with bitter debates."[41] No details of these debates were revealed, though. Despite their different approaches, both calligraphers transformed the *Eulogy* into a quintessential example of stele-study calligraphy.

By the end of the nineteenth century, stele-study calligraphy had formed its own tradition and canons, marked by the publication of Kang Youwei's (1858–1927) *Extended Paired Oars for the Boat of Art* (Guang Yizhou shuangji) in 1889, literally an expanded version of Bao Shichen's title. Kang regards stone inscriptions of the Northern and Southern Dynasties as the highest models for calligraphy.[42] In the section called "Ranking Steles," he places the *Eulogy* in the second top category of *miaopin,* "wonderful rank," which also includes the inscriptions at Cloud Peak Mountain and a few other fifth- and sixth-century works.[43] Helped by the popularity of Kang's book, and also thanks to the recently introduced technology of photographic reproduction, the *Eulogy* became one of the most sought-after calligraphic models. Four different versions of the *Eulogy* were published in collotype in 1915 by Youzheng Shuju, the largest publisher of calligraphy in Shanghai.[44]

The sensational reception of Kang's unorthodox calligraphy theory, as well as modern stele-study calligraphers' collective mentality, may be read, as Lothar

Ledderose argues, as a response to a national crisis at a pivotal historical moment. China's identity was "badly needed in a period when all institutions of the empire were questioned, and even China's survival as a political entity was in doubt."[45] Kang's theory of stele-study calligraphy was thus meant to reinvent a unified "Chinese calligraphy" as part of the formation of a modern national identity.

Kang himself visited Jiaoshan and the crane's epitaph several times. He left a "tagging-name" inscription on a rock in the spring of 1918, in his distinctive stele-study style (figure C.14, see location in figure I.4, b):

> In the fourth month of the *wuwu* year [1918], Kang Youwei visited Jiaoshan for the fourth time. Beacon fires are everywhere, spreading in Europe and Asia. I just barely survived the holocaust. Now I only want to rest in the forest and rocks with Chen Mo [perhaps Chen Moan (fl. early twentieth century), Kang's disciple]. (4J)

No topics on calligraphy—including the *Eulogy*—are mentioned in this inscription. Instead, Kang's mood seems to echo that of the Lu You inscription (see figure 2.14), even though it arises during a totally different historical moment. The island and the inscription bore witness to the political chaos that Kang had just experienced in China and the ongoing Great War in Europe.[46] In the previous decades, the landscape of Jiaoshan had changed greatly. In 1851, the Taiping Rebel troops devasted the island and destroyed many artifacts there.[47] A decade later, right after the second Opium War, the British consular office was temporarily located at the island, when Zhenjiang was one of the treaty ports forced to open to Western merchants. The crisis of national identity after the collapse of dynastic rule was now added to the sheer cultural layers of Jiaoshan that had been visualized in the inscriptions accumulated over centuries. It was perhaps this unique environment that attracted Kang to the island.

The *Eulogy* in Modern Shanghai

Entering the modern era, *Eulogy for Burying a Crane* continued to receive attention among calligraphers, but in an unexpected place: Shanghai, the center of a rising art market in China. The copies of the *Eulogy* in figures C.15 and C.16 are among numerous similar works created, respectively, by Li Ruiqing (1867–1920) and Zeng Xi (1861–1930), the two most successful calligraphers, culturally and commercially, in early twentieth-century Shanghai.[48] Both copies are written in large format, whereas Li's work consists of four large hanging scrolls. In the colophon to his scrolls, Li Ruiqing states that he had spent two days and two nights studying the *Eulogy* at Jiaoshan. When he was making the copy, he "still feels the wind from the Yangzi River." Zeng Xi also added a critical comment in the colophon:

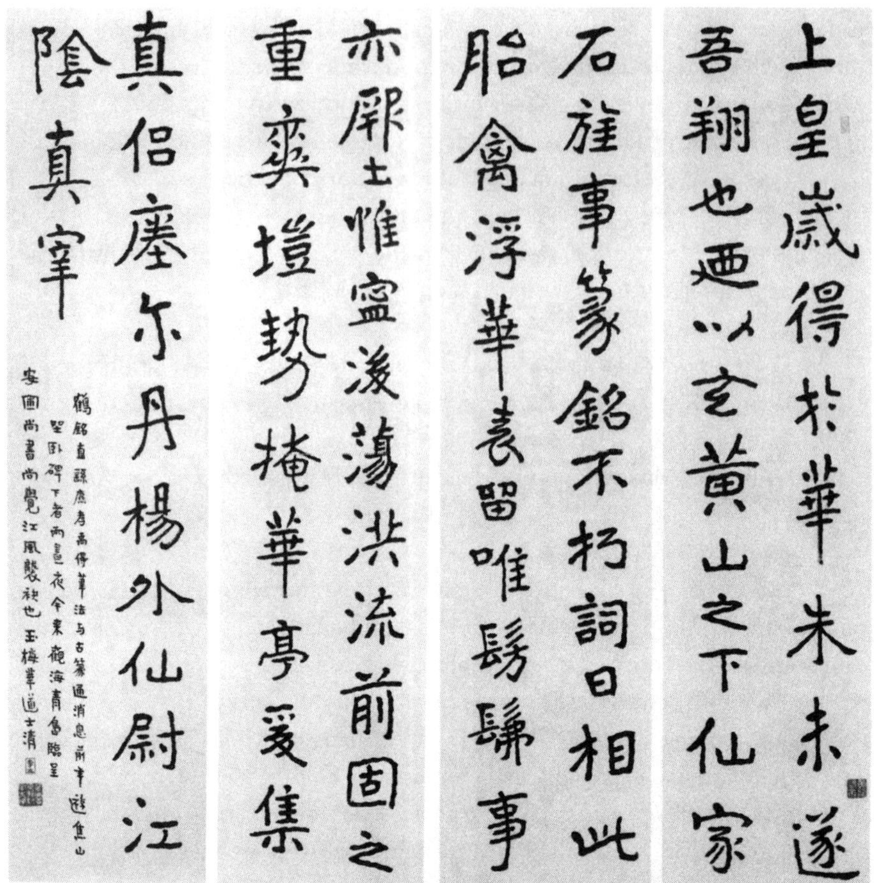

FIGURE C.15. Li Ruiqing, *Copy of Eulogy for Burying a Crane*. Undated. Ink on paper. From Zeng Yingsan, *Zeng Xi, Li Ruiqing, Zhang Daqian Yihe ming yaji*, 202–3.

> This [copy] was made from a rubbing "before [the stone coming out of] water" that I acquired when I lived in the capital city. The characters [of the rubbing] are disarranged. But their spirit (*shenli*) indeed exceeds [that of the rubbing] owned by Taozhai. Zeng Xi. (4K)

Taozhai is the studio name of Duanfang (1861–1911), an eminent Manchu official and ardent collector of rubbings and ancient bronzes.[49] In both works, the emphasis on the original stones and rubbings demonstrates the stele-study orientation; the calligraphers are trying to evoke authentic forms through the study of reliable rubbings. Indeed, unlike their predecessors in stele-study calligraphy, who often adapted the original characters to their new creation, both Li and Zeng strived to maintain the form of the original characters as is.

The two works also suggest an unprecedent direction in calligraphy: although presented as finished works of calligraphy, their contents are actually fragmentary and illegible and thus appear to contradict the core concept of calligraphy as a form

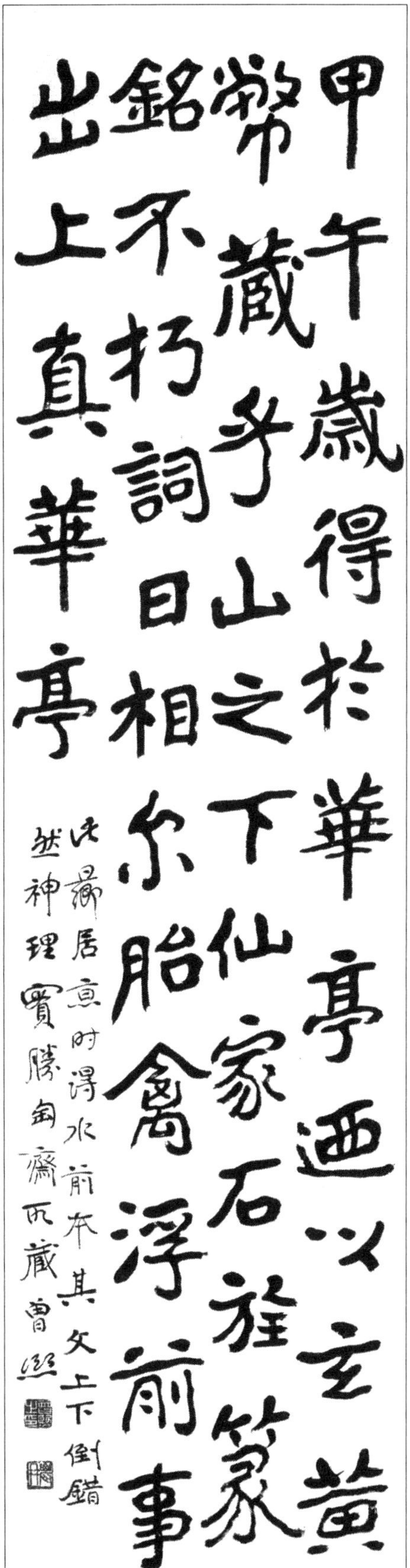

FIGURE C.16. Zeng Xi, *Copy of Eulogy for Burying a Crane*. Undated. Ink on paper. From Zeng Yingsan, *Zeng Xi, Li Ruiqing, Zhang Daqian Yihe ming yaji*, 194.

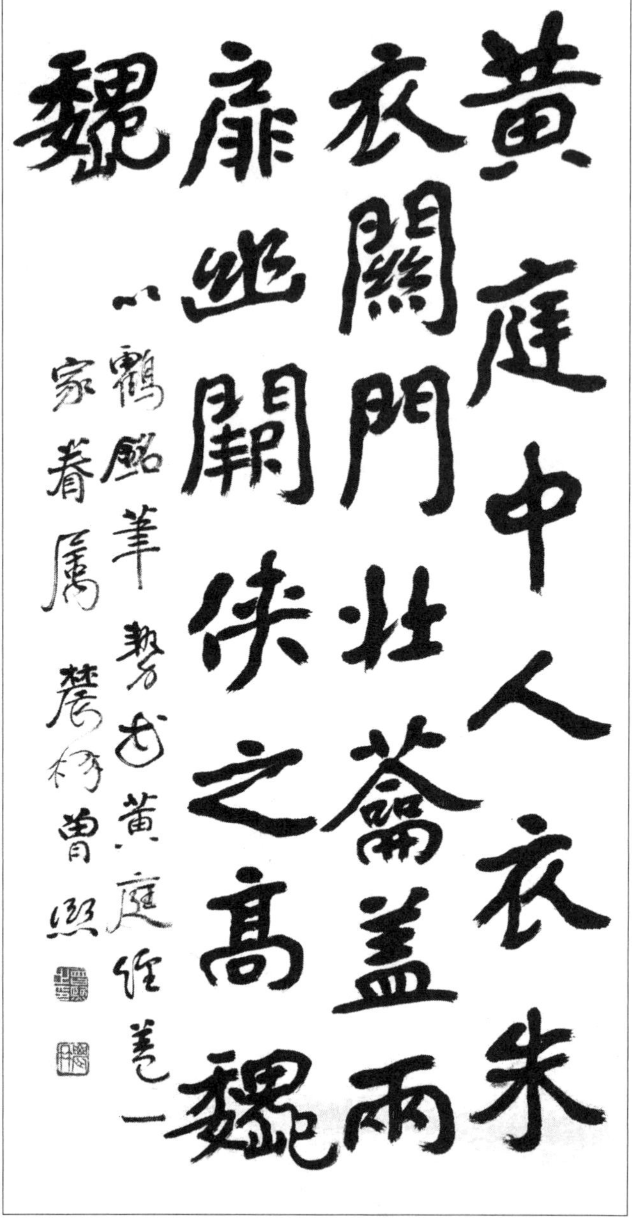

FIGURE C.17. Zeng Xi, *Calligraphy in the Style of Eulogy for Burying a Crane*. Undated. Ink on paper. From Zeng Yingsan, *Zeng Xi, Li Ruiqing, Zhang Daqian Yihe ming yaji*, 196.

of writing. Indeed, an informed reader would be able to fill in the missing words from the *Eulogy*, and this fragmentariness is an essential part of stele-study calligraphy. The apparent lack of semantic coherence in these calligraphy scrolls may be striking to most contemporary audiences. Instead of being "read," these works may rather have been intended to recreate on paper the visual spectacle of the deteriorated stone inscription in its natural setting.[50] And perhaps not least important to the Shanghai artists, the bold brushwork would be an eye-catching trademark, ready to be purchased to adorn the living room of a modern apartment.

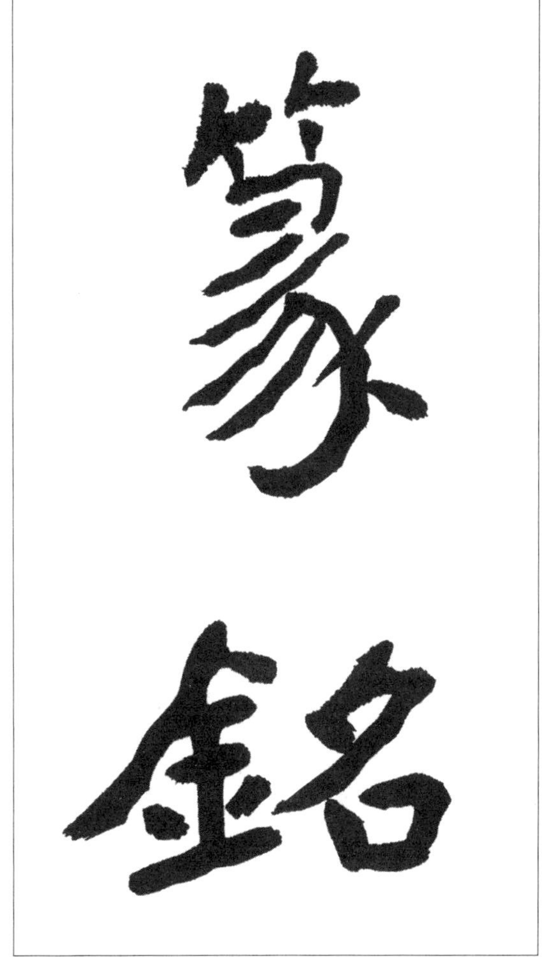

(*above*) **FIGURE C.18.** Zhang Daqian, *Copy of Eulogy for Burying a Crane*. Dated 1931. Ink on paper. From Zeng Yingsan, *Zeng Xi, Li Ruiqing, Zhang Daqian Yihe ming yaji*, 212.

(*left*) **FIGURE C.19.** Zhang Daqian, *Copy of Eulogy for Burying a Crane*. Dated 1958. Album leaf, Ink on paper. Private collection. From Zeng Yingsan, *Zeng Xi, Li Ruiqian, Zhang Daqian Yihe ming yaji*, 167.

Zeng Xi would take his study of the *Eulogy* to another level. In another work (figure C.17), he seems to reverse what Dong Qichang had done centuries before (see figure 3.14); whereas Dong made his "copy" of the *Eulogy* in in style of *Yellow Court Sutra*, now Zeng applied the composition and brushwork that he had absorbed from the *Eulogy* to a transcription of *Yellow Court Sutra*, transforming the classical work of small-standard calligraphy into a bold large hanging scroll. In this and many other works by Zeng Xi, something we may call the "*Eulogy* style" was invented, providing easily understood formulas for viewers and students of calligraphy.[51] In this way, the ancient inscription was no longer intangible and ambiguous. It had been converted into a schematized calligraphic model like that in *Model Letters of the Jade Smoke Hall*, ready to be studied. Ironically, however, this time it was seen as a fountainhead of stele-study calligraphy.

The effect of the reinvented "*Eulogy* style" can be illustrated by two calligraphy works of Zhang Daqian (1899–1983), the most celebrated modern Chinese painter, who once studied calligraphy with Zeng Xi and Li Ruiqing.[52] The long hanging scroll (figure C.18) was written in 1931, near the beginning of his artistic career, and the album version (figure C.19) was dated early 1959, when Zhang Daqian was at the peak of his fame in the world of Chinese art. Comparing the two works separated by twenty-eight years, one is surprised by their resemblance. The characters *zhuan* 篆 and *ming* 銘 in both works, for instance, are almost identical in composition and in the subtle turns of the brushstrokes. Furthermore, the album illustrated here was one of many copies that Zhang made in the same month at his residence in Mogi das Cruzes, Brazil.[53] In the colophon, Zhang Daqian states that his copy is the result of *beilin*, "back-to-back copying," or copying from memory.[54] At first glance, one may attribute the resemblance between the two works to Zhang Daqian's precise visual memory and accurate draftsmanship. From another perspective, however, we may say that to Zhang Daqian, the *Eulogy* was no longer the decayed and blurred inscription that once stirred many scholarly debates and inspired artistic imagination. Instead, what Zhang meticulously rendered in all these copies was actually the version that had been schematized by his teachers. Making copies of the *Eulogy* may have become a ritualized rehearsal to remind himself of the origin of his art and perhaps also to express his homesickness during his years overseas.

The Immortal Crane

Returning to the Ming critic Wang Shizhen's comment on the "original quality," or *benzhi*—the irretrievable original appearance of the inscription—we may ask the following question: If the stones had never fallen from the cliff on Jiaoshan and had never been exposed to the eroding waters of the Yangzi River, would *Eulogy for Burying a Crane* have played the same role in the history of calligraphy? The question is partly answered by the modern calligrapher and scholar Qi Gong in his witty poem on *Eulogy* rubbings:

> The *Eulogy* rubbings made in the water of the river;
> The mass-market wooden carving versions of *Yellow Court Sutra*,
> For what reason did Weng [Fanggang] and He [Shaoji] extoll them
> repeatedly?
> It may be because both works are too blurred to see![55] (4L)

The enchantment of the calligraphy, therefore, lies in the freedom to interpret the ambiguous and intangible forms in accordance with the viewer's own taste and vision of the history of calligraphy, which are in turn dependent largely on the cultural contexts, social milieus, and aesthetic aspirations of the particular historical moments that we have discussed.

The present study has attempted to bring to light facts about the context in which *Eulogy for Burying a Crane* was created and to trace with new clarity its transmission and interpretation. However, the stones remain enigmatic likenesses of their former state, and the identity of the author and calligrapher remain speculative. The quest to understand the inscription will no doubt continue for generations to come.

As the origins of the inscription were forgotten over the centuries, few readers considered the possibility that the inscription was not what it appeared to be—a burial text for a dead bird. Like the broken stones themselves, the context in which the inscription was composed, written, and made was lost or misplaced. With this loss of memory, layers of signification detectable in the monument were overlooked. My interpretation, which treats the inscription as a monumental expression of suffering and discontent among the Maoshan Daoists of the early sixth century, is speculative, but the cultural and historical context I have reconstructed can serve as a starting point for further exploration of this and other inscriptions as a text, an object, and a historical monument.

The canonization of the *Eulogy* as a masterpiece of Chinese calligraphy was not a self-evident process but the product of shifting discourses concerning the role of authenticity and copying in art and the sources of creativity. The problem can be traced all the way back to the creation of the *Eulogy*, as the formation of a calligraphic canon has often been conditioned by contemporary social-cultural-political agendas. The history of the reception of the calligraphy of the *Eulogy* was constantly shaped by changing attitudes toward cultural relics and how they should be studied.

The striking contrast between obscurity of the inscription in the Tang dynasty and the passionate interest in it that emerged during the Northern Song reflects more than the discovery of the stones at Jiaoshan. What might be termed "*Eulogy* fever" broke out as part of a widespread desire to investigate the traces of antiquity, reflected in the early flourishing of the "study of bronze and stone." Behind the antiquarian enthusiasm of Song scholars was a deep anxiety over the culture of their own day and a longing to revive ancient cultural models in art and politics. Huang Tingjian's response was his personal solution to a particular aesthetic crisis of his time. In a challenge to traditional brush methods and the authority of model letters, he used the *Eulogy* as a model to create self-expressive large-character calligraphy.

Confusion over the location of the original stones in the later times can be read as a cultural symptom as well; the enjoyment of leisure and tourism drew members—or would-be members—of elite classes to Jiaoshan. Their eligibility to be considered elites was demonstrated by their participation in such outings to enjoy traces of ancient monuments and scenic areas. Ironically (but not surprisingly), it was because of its inclusion in popular publications that the *Eulogy* entered the canon of calligraphy in the late Ming and was widely copied and studied. In the eighteenth and nineteenth centuries, the recovery and restoration of the stones and the formation of a new stylistic ideal of calligraphy based on epigraphy led to a marriage of archaeological investigation and artistic innovation. Finally, stele-study calligraphers appropriated the ancient inscription and transformed it into a modern expression. The reception history of *Eulogy for Burying a Crane* cannot be separated from the work's cultural history; in tandem, they shaped the cultural memory of the inscription and created the folklore of the monument and its calligraphy.

Coda

The story of the stone inspires a fundamental question, one that I raise even as I confess my inability to provide an adequate answer: Why *was* the idea of antiquity so central to Chinese culture?[56] This question is not irrelevant to contemporary life in China. Although the terms on which antiquity could be admired and studied in the twentieth century were shaped and disrupted by political upheaval, since the late 1980s, after decades of politically mandated rejection of many aspects of traditional culture, obsession with the past has reemerged in Chinese society on a scale that would amaze even the most ardent antiquarians of earlier times.[57] In the public sphere, renewed interest in antiques, for both their cultural and market values, have grabbed the new rich and the middle class alike. The state-sponsored media, now enjoying more freedom alongside its duty as the ruling party's mouthpiece, have helped to drive the scene to an unprecedented level. Since 2003, a popular weekend show, *Appraising the Treasure* (Jianbao), invites audiences to bring their "treasures"—usually an old ceramic pot inherited from a grandmother or purchased in one of the antique markets now proliferating across in China—to the television studio for an on-site appraisal by a row of specialists. The most exciting moment—or the most heartbreaking, if you happen to be the owner—occurs when the specialists decide that the object is not valuable. After the specialists shake their heads, the host grabs a hammer and smashes the pot—a gesture of violence unsettlingly reminiscent of the cultural vandalism of the past century, especially during the Cultural Revolution.

In the fall of 2008, a television program titled *Exploring the Secrets of Eulogy for Burying a Crane* (Tanmi Yi he ming) was broadcast on CCTV, China's national network. This program, a mixture of documentary and costume drama, not only rendered the story of Wang Xizhi at Jiaoshan but also followed the progress of an archaeological excavation at the island in search of new information about the *Eulogy*.[58] The program was part of the local government's plan to renovate Jiaoshan as a major tourist destination and the city's "cultural business card" (*wenhua mingpian*). The most ambitious part of the plan was realized in June of 2010, when the local government managed to hire a giant salvage ship to haul the rocks from the water. After a few tests, on June 4, 2010, at around 1:00 p.m., the final attempt was made. The large boulders that we visited (see figure I.2), seven hundred tons in total, were extracted and moved to a platform built on the riverbank. The process was broadcast live across the country.[59]

The project continued the centuries-long tradition of combining the veneration of antiquity, literati musings, scholarly fieldwork, and sheer fantasy in the quest to understand ancient works—a quest that had now passed into the hands of China's booming mass media and entertainment industry. This promotion of local cultural pride was complicated by various political agendas; creating the "cultural business card" has become an important index for assessing local administrations, and the renewed interest in "cultural relics" like the *Eulogy* has become inseparable from nationalistic propaganda, which has resurged in recent years.

Considering the high profile and cost, the result of the recent excavation was a little disappointing, if not controversial.[60] When I visited the island and the *Eulogy* inscription the following summer, Yang Yuanhui, an old friend on the staff of the Jiaoshan Stone Inscription Museum, led me to the exhibition hall for the stones located during the recent excavation. It had taken him and his colleagues several months to clean the stones found among the detritus pulled from the river. There was not much to see except for some scratches. "Some people believe there is a character," Yang said as he pointed to a rock displayed at the center of the room. Lingering in the space for some time, I also seemed to see the character emanating from the random scratches—that is, *hua* 化, meaning "transformation."

We left the exhibition hall and walked to the site of *moya* inscriptions. The once muddy shore has now been covered by a wooden walkway. At the end of the walkway is the platform where the large boulder rests (figure C.20, which shows Lightning Striking Stone on the far right). The renovation, which seems very successful, has transformed the historical site into a modern park, complete with young couples enjoying taking photos in front of the rocks. In fact, Jiaoshan is no longer an island; a new road on its east side connects it to the river bank, and visitors can now conveniently drive all the way to the new gate of the park. The ferry that has been used for over a thousand years may be abandoned soon.

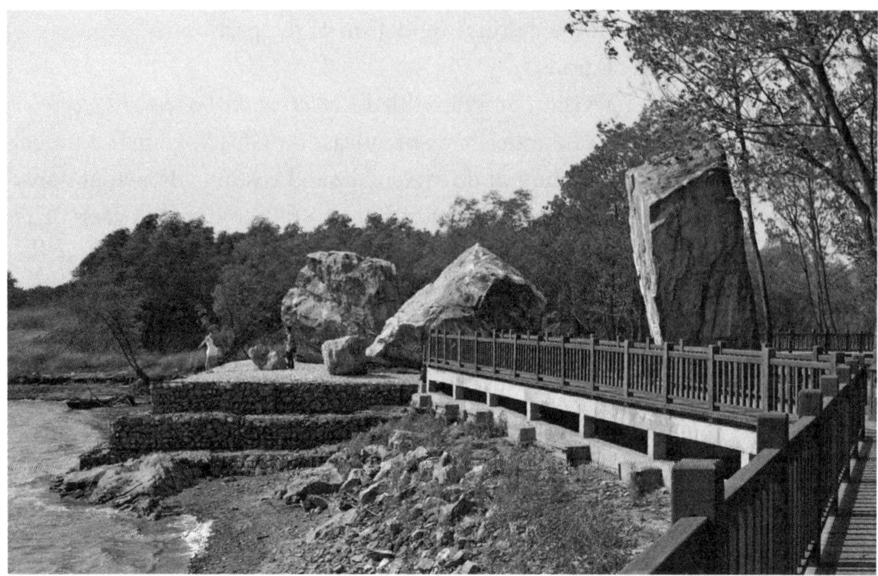

FIGURE C.20. Rocks after the 2010 excavation at Jiaoshan (with the Lightning Striking Stone on the far right). Author's photo, 2011.

This is only the latest chapter, but surely not the last, of the long story of writing about the epitaph for a crane carved long ago on Jiaoshan. For now, I would like to conclude our journey through the centuries by finishing the story cited at the very beginning of this book:

> Many years after Wang Xizhi wrote the epitaph, on the night of a thunderstorm, the inscription was struck by lightning and collapsed into the water. For a long time, only in winter when the water fell did the stones appear. However, most of the inscription had been worn away. To express their regret, visitors called the stone "Stele without Characters." Since then, many years have passed. On another stormy night, a flock of cranes descended on the stone, dancing and crying. The next day, people were surprised to find that the inscribed characters had reappeared with fresh and vivid strokes. It was the cranes that transformed themselves into the characters.[61]

The story might be read as an allegory about both the reception history of *Eulogy for Burying a Crane* and the formation of Chinese calligraphy. The antiquarian scholars, calligraphers, emperors, tourists, and dealers who responded to the inscription over the centuries created a folklore of their own. Embodied in treatises and works of art, it frames our ongoing efforts to understand this remarkable monument and its place in the history of Chinese literary and visual culture, defining and redefining the art of calligraphy, telling and retelling its history.

Appendix 1

Dated *Moya* Inscriptions at Jiaoshan

No	Date (Y.M.D)*	Visitors	Location
1	993.11.20	Wang Zuoshi 王作師 et al.	Floating Jade Rock
2	1064.2.18	Pei Yu 裴煜 et al.	Floating Jade Rock
3	1068.3.9	Chen Pu 陳朴 et al.	Lightning Striking Stone
4	1068.3.20	Liu Guinian 劉龜年 et al.	Lightning Striking Stone
5	1081.11.4	Zhang Kechong 張克從 et al.	Unknown
6	1091.4	Mi Fu 米芾 et al.	Floating Jade Rock
7	1096.3.23	Chen Anmin 陳安民	Floating Jade Rock
8	1101	He Zhu 賀鑄 et al.	Floating Jade Rock
9	1101	Mi Fu 米芾 et al.	Luohan Rock
10	1102.3.9	Hu Shiwen 胡師文 et al.	Floating Jade Rock
11	1109.3.7	Chen Kuo 陳廓 et al.	Luohan Rock
12	1164.1.29	Lu You 陸游 et al.	Floating Jade Rock
13	1184.1.12	Wu Ju 吳琚	Luohan Rock
14	1194.1.10	Li Gui 李珪	Floating Jade Rock
15	1199.9.7	Li Gui 李珪	Floating Jade Rock
16	1234	Xie Yixiu 謝奕修 et al.	Unknown
17	1238.11.30	Wang Rui 王濬 et al.	Floating Jade Rock
18	1239	He Zishao 何子韶	Floating Jade Rock
19	1272.9.28	Zhao Jin 趙溍 et al.	Luohan Rock
20	1273 summer	He Zhongzi 何仲子	Floating Jade Rock
21	1425.2. 29	Zhao Mingshu 趙明叔 et al.	Floating Jade Rock

No	Date (Y.M.D)*	Visitors	Location
22	1430.3.15	Yang Shen 楊紳	Floating Jade Rock
23	1435.6	Huang Huai 黄淮	Floating Jade Rock
24	1464.5	Xu Youzhen 徐有貞 et al.	Floating Jade Rock
25	1505.7.9	Zheng Yang 鄭陽 et al.	Floating Jade Rock
26	1509.10.22	Yuan Xuan 原軒 et al.	Floating Jade Rock
27	1511.4.10	Qiao Yu 喬宇	Floating Jade Rock
28	1511.4.22	Xie Chen 謝琛 et al.	Floating Jade Rock
29	1511.10.28	Feng Lan 馮蘭	Floating Jade Rock
30	1514.8.4	Liu Qian 劉乾 et al.	Floating Jade Rock
31	1515.4.9	Zhang Yu 張羽 et al.	Floating Jade Rock
32	1518.8.2	Zhu Yan 朱衮	Floating Jade Rock
33	1519.7.16	Cong Lan 叢蘭 et al.	Floating Jade Rock
34	1519.10.19	Fang Hao 方豪	Floating Jade Rock
35	1521.12.2	Xu Dai 徐岱 et al.	Lightning Striking Stone
36	1521.10.13	Shao Tianhe 邵天和 et al.	Floating Jade Rock
37	1524.10.9	Zhu Baochang 朱寶昌 et al.	Stone Screen
38	1533.2.29	Pan Zhen 潘珍 et al.	Floating Jade Rock
39	1536.9.5	Quanya shanren 泉崖山人 et al.	Lightning Striking Stone
40	1583 Autumn	Li Zhu 李柷 et al.	Lightning Striking Stone
41	1583.8.15	Zhu Zhenji 朱貞吉 et al.	Lightning Striking Stone
42	1586.8.1	Wang Daokun 汪道昆	Floating Jade Rock
43	1590.7	Wang Zongni 汪宗尼 et al.	Lightning Striking Rock
44	1609 Summer	Fang Chengyu 方承郁	Unknown
45	1802.6.12	Hong Liangji 洪亮吉	Jugong Cliff
46	1803.10	Ji Daokun 嵇導崑	Stone Screen
47	1805	Qin Ying 秦瀛	Unknown
48	1808.4.2	Elhebu 額勒布 et al.	Jugong Cliff
49	1813.8	Zhang Wentao 張問陶 et al.	Jugong Cliff
50	1822.6.6	Ruan Yuan 阮元, et al	Unknown

No	Date (Y.M.D)*	Visitors	Location
51	1829.11	Tao Shu 陶澍	Floating Jade Rock
52	1830.3	Tao Shu 陶澍	Jugong Cliff
53	1831.2.2	Tao Shu 陶澍	Luohan Rock
54	1831.3.6	Zhao Guanglu 趙光祿 et al.	Floating Jade Rock
55	1833.4.1	Yan Lang 嚴烺 et al.	Floating Jade Rock
56	1838	Monk from Wumen 吳門僧	Floating Jade Rock
57	1849.3	Zhou Mengbo 周孟博	Floating Jade Rock
58	1852.11	Huang Wenhan 黃文涵	Floating Jade Rock
59	1862.2.18	Zhuang Yu 莊棫	Lightning Striking Stone
60	1871.9.13	Yao Zhengyong 姚正鏞	Jugong Cliff
61	1873.4	Lin Shaonian 林紹年	Floating Jade Rock
62	1873.8.1	Chen Renyang 陳任暘	Floating Jade Rock
63	1886	Zhang Shiheng 張士珩	Floating Jade Rock
64	1890.8	Wu Dacheng 吳大澂 et al.	Floating Jade Rock
65	1890.9	Liang Dingfen 梁鼎芬	Jugong Cliff
66	1890	Liang Fu 梁敷	Jugong Cliff
67	1895.6	Zhao Shuqiao 趙舒翹	Floating Jade Rock
68	1897.8	Jin Tao 金燾	Jugong Cliff
69	1903.5	Dou Diangao 竇甸膏	Floating Jade Rock
70	1918.4	Kang Youwei 康有爲	Luohan Rock

Sources: Wu Yun, *Tongzhi Jiaoshan zhi*; Chen Renyang, *Jiaoshan xuzhi*; Yuan Daojun, *Jiaoshan shike yanjiu*.
*Y.M.D. = Year.Month.Day. The month and day refer to those in the Chinese lunar calendar.

Appendix 2

Major Extant Early Rubbings of *Eulogy for Burying a Crane*

No.	Title	Format	Current Provenance
R1	潘寧舊藏本 Formerly Pan Ning Collection edition.	album	Palace Museum, Beijing
R2	何紹基舊藏本 Formerly He Shaoji Collection edition.	album	National Library, Beijing
R3	楊澥（龍石）舊藏汪士鋐本 Formerly Yang Longshi Collection edition.	album	Palace Museum, Beijing
R4	楊賓（大瓢）舊藏水拓本 Formerly Yang Bin Collection edition.	album	
R5	徐用錫跋本 Xu Yongxi Colophon edition.	album	Private
R6	顏光敏舊藏本 Formerly Yan Guangmin Collection edition.	whole piece	Private
R7	曾熙舊藏出水本 Formerly Zeng Xi Collection edition.	album	
R8	端方舊藏本 Formerly Duanfang Collection edition.	album	Shodo Museum, Tokyo

Number of Characters	Corresponding Fragment No.	Publication
30	F3	*Zhongguo meishu quanji: Shufa zhuangke bian* 2. *Ming bei shi pin*. Hong Kong: Shangwu Yinshuguan, 2007.
29	F3	*Zhongguo guojia tushuguan beitie jinghua*. Beijing: Beijing Tushuguan Chubanshe, 2001.
53	F1, F3, F4	*Zhongguo meishu quanji: Shufa zhuangke bian* 2. *Shufa congkan* (2004), no. 6 *Yi he ming*. Bowentang, 1913 *Bokuhi* 246, no. 12 (1974).
78	All	*Yi he ming*. Luo Zhenyu, 1918 *Yi he ming*, Youzheng Shuju, 1912.
56	F3, F4	*Yi he ming moya shike*. Beijing: Wenwu Chubanshe, 2010.
30	F3	*Shupu* no. 3 (1979).
89	All	*Yi he ming*. Chengdu: Sichuan Meishu Chubanshe, 1987
84	All	*Bokuhi* 246, no. 12 (1974).

(*continued*)

No.	Title	Format	Current Provenance
R9	王效曾藏本 Formerly Wang Xiaozeng Collection edition.	album	
R10	俞復藏水前本 Formerly Yu Fu Collection edition.	album	
R11	俞復藏水後本 Formerly Yu Fu Collection edition. B	album	
R12	李瑞清舊藏本 Formerly Li Ruiqing Collection edition.	album	Mitsui Bunko, Tokyo
R13	沈均初舊藏本 Formerly Shen Junchu Collection edition.	album	Shanghai Library
R14	梁啟超舊藏鶴洲本 Formerly Liang Qichao Collection edition.	album	National Library, Beijing
R15	何紹基舊藏翁方綱題簽本 Formerly He Shaoji Collection (with Label by Weng Fanggang) edition.	hanging scrolls	Palace Museum, Beijing
R16	北京文物商店藏本 Beijing Wenwu Shangdian edition.	album	Beijing wenwu shangdian
R17	勞長齡舊藏本 Formerly Lao Changling Collection edition.	album	
R18	李國松舊藏本 Formerly Li Guosong Collection edition.	album	Shanghai Library

Number of Characters	Corresponding Fragment No.	Publication
89	All	*Yi he ming.* Tianjin: Tianjin Guji Shudian, 1988.
91	All	*Yi he ming.* Shanghai: Shanghai Shuhua Chubanshe, 2001. *Yi he ming.* Nanjing: Jiangsu Meishu Chubanshe, 1989.
93	All	*Yi he ming.* Shanghai: Shanghai Shuhua Chubanshe, 2001. *Yi he ming.* Nanjing: Jiangsu Meishu Chubanshe, 1989.
92	All	*Shoseki meihin shokan.* Tokyo: Nigensha, 1959–1970.
91	All	*Hanmo huanbao.* Shanghai: Shanghai Guji Chubanshe, 2005.
89	All	*Yi he ming.* Hangzhou: Zhejiang Guji Chubanshe, 2006.
68	F2, F3, F5	*Zhongguo meishu quanji: Shufa zhuangke bian 2.*
92	All	*Yi he ming.* Shijiazhuang: Hebei Meishu Chubanshe, 1986.
92	All	*Yi he ming,* Shenzhou Guoguangshe, 1949. *Shupu* no. 3–4 (1979).
42	F3, F4	*Hanmo huanbao.* Shanghai: Shanghai Guji Chubanshe, 2005.

Appendix 3

Chinese Texts

CHAPTER 1

1A

瘞鶴銘[有序]

華陽真逸譔 上皇山樵[書]

鶴壽不知其紀也。壬辰歲得於華[亭]，甲午歲化於朱方。天其未遂吾翔[寥]廓耶？奚奪[口仙鶴]之遽也？廼裹以玄黃之幣，藏乎茲山之下。仙家無[隱]，口口口我口。故立石旌事，篆銘不朽。詞曰：

相此胎禽，浮丘[著經]。余欲無言，[爾其藏靈]。[雷門]去鼓，華表留形。義惟髣髴，事亦微冥。爾將何之？解化口口。[西竹法里]，厥土惟寧。後當洪流，前固重扃。[左取曹國]，右割荊門。[山陰]爽塏，勢掩華亭。爰集真侶，瘞爾[作銘]。

絳嶽徵君

丹楊外仙尉

江陰真宰

1B

果乘白鶴駐山頭，望之，不得到，舉手謝時人。數日而去。

1C

傷本規之違忤，悵離羣而獨處，恒竄伏以窮栖，獨哀鳴而戢羽。

1D

冀大網之解結，得奮翅而遠遊。

1E

余以玄冬脩夜，忽聞階前有孤鶴鳴，遡寒風而清叫，感淒氣而增悲。屬聽未終，余有感焉，乃為文以弔之。

1F

惟海隅之奇鳥，資秀氣以誕生。擬鸞皇而比翼，超羽族而獨靈。濯冰霜之素質，颺九皐之奇聲。啄荒庭之遺粒，漱絶澗之餘清。望雲舒而息翮，仰朝霞而晨征。

1G

輟王子之靈轡，縶虞人之長纓。辞丹穴之神友，與雞鶩而同庭。軒天衢而奔想，顧樊籠而心驚。獨中宵而增思，負清霜而夜鳴。資冲天之儁翮，曾不殊於鳥雀。禀櫺壽之修期，忽同彫於秋薄。匪茲物之足悲，傷有理而横落書。

1H

王春秋卅，永元三年十二月十二日奄從門禍。中興二年追贈給事黄門侍郎。皇上神武撥亂，大造生民，冤恥既雪，哀榮甫備。

1I

天監元年太歳壬午十一月乙卯一日，窆於弋辟山。禮也。懼金石有朽，陵谷不居。敢撰遺行，式銘泉室。梁故散騎常侍、撫軍大將軍、桂陽王融、謚簡王墓誌。長兼尚書吏部郎中臣任昉奉勅撰。

1J

龕黎在運，業茂姬昌。蟬聯寫丹，清越而長。顯允初筮，邁道宣哲。藝單湪書，學窮縑税。友于惟孝，閒言無際。

1K

歳次攝提，星居鶉首，梁故觀寧侯蕭永卒。嗚呼哀哉！人之滅也，既非金石所移；士之悲也，寧有春秋之異。高臺已傾，稷下有聞琴之泣；壯士一去，燕南有擊筑之悲。項羽之晨起帳中，陵之徘徊歧路，韓王孫之質趙，楚公子之留秦，無假窮秋，于時悲矣。

1L

山陽相送，惟餘故人。孀機嫠緯，獨鶴孤鸞。閨深夜靜，風月俱寒。生平已矣，懷故何期。匣中弦斷，鄰人笛悲。昔爲幕府，今成繐帷。

1M

其八字飛玄自然之書，字方一丈，文彩焕曜，洞明八方。

1N

積七千年後，題崑崙之室北洞之源。字方一丈，文蔚焕爛，四合垂芒，虚生菴藹，若存若亡，流光紫炁拂其穢，金精冷鍊瑩其文，遂經累劫，字體鮮明。

1O

賜以束帛。公卿祖之于征虜亭，供帳甚盛，車馬填咽，咸云宋齊以來，未有斯事，朝野榮之。

1P

國家每有吉兇征討大事，無不前以咨詢。月中常有數信，時人謂為山中宰相。二宮及公王貴要參候相繼，贈遺未嘗脫時。

1Q

吾若委形枕杖，非不可為，是獨濟小道。若脫爾便逝，不可以為教跡。

1R

既仰祇帝制，兼闡大猷。東位青壇，西表素塔，壇塔之間，通是基址。

1S

石壁望松寥，宛然在碧霄。安得五彩虹，架天作長橋。仙人如愛我，舉手來相招。

1T

昔有傅先生，其少好道，入焦山石室中，積七年而太極老君詣之。與之木鑽，使穿一石盤厚五尺許，云："穿此盤便當得道。"其人乃晝夜穿之，積四十七年，鑽盡石穿，遂得神丹，乃升太清，為南嶽真人。

CHAPTER 2

2A

山陰不見換鵝經，京口今存瘞鶴銘。瀟灑集仙來作記，風流太守為開亭。兩篇玉蕊塵初滌，四體銀鉤蘚尚青。我久臨池無所得，願觀遺法快沉冥。

2B

古寺購尋遺刻在，新亭龕置斷珉奇。模傳遂比黃庭字，埋沒非同石鼓碑。

2C

[瘞鶴銘]石在焦山之足，常為江水所沒。好事者伺水落時，摸而傳之，往往秖得數字，云"鶴壽不知其幾"而止。世以其難得，尤以爲奇。惟余所得，獨若此之多也。《潤州圖經》以爲王羲之書。字亦奇放，然不類羲之筆法，而類顏魯公。不知何人書也。或云華陽真逸是顧況道號，銘其所作也。

2D

瘞鶴銘今存於焦山及寶墨亭者蓋盡於此。凡文字句語，讀之可識、及點畫之僅存者，百三十餘言。而所亡失幾五十字。計其完書畫，蓋九行之全者，率二十五字。而首尾不預焉。熙寧三年春，予與汾陽郭逢原公域、范陽張褘子偉索其逸遺於焦山之陰，偶得十二字於亂石閒。"表留惟寧"十字完，餘二字訛缺。石甚迫隘，偃臥其下然後可讀，故昔人未之見，而世不傳。

2E

石頑難刊，且為水泐，故字無鋒穎，若掘筆書，昧者從而學之，深可一笑。

2F

頃見京口斷崖中瘞鶴銘大字，右軍書。其勝處乃不可名貌。...瘞鶴銘斷為右軍書，端使人不疑。如歐、薛、顏、柳諸公書最為端勁，然才得瘞鶴銘彷彿爾。唯魯公宋開府碑勁瘦清拔，在四五間。

2G

古人學書不盡臨摹。張古人書於壁閒觀之入神，則下筆時隨人意。

2H

小字莫作痴凍蠅， 樂毅論勝遺教經。大字無過瘞鶴銘，官奴作草欺伯英。隨人作計終後人，自成一家始逼真。

2I

東坡云：大字難於結密而無間，小字難於寬綽而有餘，此確論也。余嘗申之曰：結密而無間，瘞鶴銘近之；寬綽而有餘，蘭亭近之。若以篆文說之，大字如李斯嶧山碑，小字如先秦古器科斗文字。

2J

劉唐年君佐，弟延年子永，龜年仁父，彭年元老，因訪右軍碑，躋攀至此。熙寧元年季春廿日，龜年謹題。釋景宗同遊。

2K

華亭鶴自歸，長江只東注。寂寥千古意，落日起煙霧。

2L

陸務觀、何德器、張玉仲、韓無咎隆興甲申閏月廿九日踏雪觀瘞鶴銘，置酒上方。烽火未熄，望風檣戰艦在煙靄閒，慨然盡醉。薄晚泛舟自甘露寺以歸。明年二月壬午，圜禪師刻之石。務觀書。

2M

瘞鶴銘在今鎮江府大江中，焦山後巉下。冬月水落，布席仰卧，乃可摹印。紹興中訪舊本，有使者過，命工鑿取之。石頑重不可取，衹得十許字。又以重不能攜，但攜一兩字去，棄其餘，今通判東廳者是也。

2N

仲宣、法芝、米芾元祐辛未孟夏觀山樵書。

2O

余淳熙己酉歲為丹楊郡文學，暇日游焦山，訪此石刻。初於佛榻前見斷石，乃其篇首二十餘字。有僧云：往年於崖閒震而墜者。余不信然，遂挐舟再歷觀崖閒，尚餘“兹山之下”二十餘字。波閒片石傾倒。舟人云：“此斷碑，水落時亦可摩搨。”今因請於州將龍圖閣直學士張子顏發卒挽出之，則“甲午歲”以下二十餘字。偶一卒曰：“此石下枕一小石，亦覺隱指如是刻畫。”遂並出之。其文與佛榻前所見者同。持以校之，第闕二字，而筆力頓異。乃知前所見者為寺僧所紿耳。

2P

相此胎禽，浮丘著經。乃徵前事，出於上真。余欲無言，紀爾歲辰。雷門去鼓，華表留聲。我唯彷彿，爾亦微冥。爾其何之，解化惟寧。後湯洪流，前固重扃。（此闕一字）割荊門，未下華亭。爰及真侶，瘞爾作銘。

上皇樵人逸少書

夆山徵士、丹楊外仙尉、江陰真宰 立石

CHAPTER 3

3A

登山踏雪尋之，果得於石壁之上。可讀者僅二十字。因搨以歸。未至銘數十步，崖上有宋嘉熙二年陸放翁題字云“踏雪觀瘞鶴銘”，乃知昔人好奇，已先於予。

3B

萬曆庚寅秋七月，鄣郡汪宗尼載女郎馬鳳笙來游焦山。無何，陳揚產、程應衢、茅溱繼至。相與披草萊涉泥滓，尋瘞鶴蒼銘，據石痛飲，各賦一詩，題壁而去。

3C

浮生長恨歡娛少，肯愛千金輕一笑。為君持酒勸斜陽，且向花間留晚照。

3D

江波浩渺，極目無際。風帆雲樹，隱映遐邇，誠奇觀也。

3E

雖網羅千載而鑒裁特精，...此帖出而臨池之家有所總萃矣。

3F

鴻堂帖未裱者壹兩半。此畫一之价，惟兄所損，然勿得會他人知也。即令人清理之。弟其昌頓首。

3G

此銘古拙奇峭，雄伟飞逸，固書家之雄。而結體閒涉疏慢者，手不隨意，恐右軍不得爾。至於鋒秃穎露，非盡其本質，亦以石頑水泐之故。而魯直極推之，又極愛之，得無作捧心鄰女耶。

3H

黃涪翁云，大字無過瘞鶴銘，小字無過遺教經。今世所傳遺教，直唐經生手耳。瘞鶴則陶隱居書，山谷學之。余欲縮為小楷，偶失此帖，遂以黃庭筆法書之。

CONCLUSION

4A

先觀重刻二石，次至壯觀亭址右，俯瞰破石叢雜。攝衣下尋，見一石仰臥於前，一石仆於後。字在石下、去泥沙咫尺。臥地仰觀，始見字跡。又一石側立，剝甚。各存字多寡不一。命僕各搨一紙。時落日風寒，不能久立，遂乘片帆回所寓之銀山蘭若。挑燈審視，未得其詳，及就寢，則又念此不置，竟夜無眠。次日復往搨之，遂有如晤故人之意。第仆石之下，仰搨為難。僕之兩手又不能兼理搨具。予乃取其旁之紅紫落葉，敷藉於地，親仰臥以助之。墨水反落污面不顧也。及挐舟而返，予之周旋於石隙者已三日矣。手足不寧、衣履皆穿，始各得四紙。

4B

適雨雪稀少，水落石露，異乎常時。乃命工人是相是伐，巉巗尋丈，力難全舁，是割是剔，不遺餘力。以求遺文出之重淵，躋之崇岡。乃得七十餘字。...自冬徂春，凡三閱月，闕功乃成。是為癸巳二月既望。

4C

然既出於江，則人得之易，競相傳拓，恐日月逾遠，將與江邊腐石同其湮沉。

4D

書法雖已剝蝕，然蕭疏淡遠，固是神仙之跡。退谷所謂“字體寬綽具古隸，鋒棱雖刓精光瑩”者，分兩正得。或者推許太過，意謂筆法之妙可為書家冠冕，殆過也。

4E

今以銘書審之，若“上皇、仙、山、相、石、真侶”，則《黃庭》、《化度》之蹲注也。“未、唯、洪、固”，平原之圓健也。“江陰真宰、朱、化、胎禽”，永興之超舉也。“惟寧、後蕩”，由褚薛溯羊薄之筋脈也。“華亭、爰集”，太傅之扁闊也。“旌、厥、之、浮”，漢隸之瘦掣也。“方、篆、土、勢”，籀鼓之奇古也。寥寥乎數十字之僅存，而兼賅上下數千年之字學。...是銘得於篆者為多也。而豈僅寬綽之隸之足云乎。愚故詳審是銘有關於書道之大者，而六朝諸家之神氣，悉舉而淹貫之。

4F

且以南朝敕禁刻碑之事，是以碑碣絕少（見《昭明文選》），唯帖是尚，字全變為真行草書，無復隸古遺意。即以焦山《瘞鶴銘》與萊州鄭道昭《山門》字相較，體似相近，然妍態多而古法少矣。

4G

大字如小字，以形容其雍容俯仰，不爲空濶所震懾耳。...唯鶴銘之如意指揮，經石峪之頓挫安詳，斯足當之。

4H

合南北二宗，為書家度盡金針，前唯黃庭，後唯化度，中間則貞白鶴銘、智永千文耳。

4I

留得銘詞篆山石，相於仙侶集江亭

4J

戊午四月，康有為四遊焦山。烽火遍地彌歐亞。吾經劫后，乃與陳默偃息林石也。

4K

此鼒居京時得水前本，其文上下倒錯，然神理實勝匋齋所藏。曾熙。

4L

江心水拓瘞鶴銘，坊間木刻黃庭經。翁何遮讃緣何故，一樣模糊看不清。

Glossary of Chinese Characters

aice 哀冊
An Lushan 安祿山

Bai Juyi 白居易
"Baihe fu" 白鶴賦
Baisha 白沙
Bao Shichen 包世臣
Bao Zhao 鮑照
Baodingzhai shu 寶鼎齋法書
Baodingzhai tie 寶鼎齋帖
Baojinzhai fatie 寶晉齋法帖
Baomo Pavilion 寶墨亭
bei 碑
"Beibei nantie lun" 北碑南帖論
bei'e 碑額
Beigushan 北固山
beilin 背臨
beixue 碑學
bifa 筆法

Cai Xiang 蔡襄
Cai You 蔡攸
Cao Cao 曹操
Cao Pi 曹丕
Cao Zhi 曹植
caoshu 草書
"Caoshu gexing" 草書歌行
chanbi 顫筆
Chaoyangyan 朝陽巖
"Chaoyangyan ming" 朝陽巖銘
Chen Anmin 陳安民
Chen Huan 陳瓛
Chen Jiru 陳繼儒
Chen Moan 陳默庵
Chen Pengnian 陳鵬年
Chen Si 陳思
Chen Yangchan 陳揚産
Chen Yujiao 陳與郊
Cheng Kangzhuang 程康莊
Cheng Yingqu 程應衢
Chengqingtang tie 澄清堂帖
chongke 重刻
Chongyuangong bei 崇元宮碑
Chu Suiliang 褚遂良
Chunhua bige fatie 淳化秘閣法帖
chushui ben 出水本
ci 詞
Cui Wenzi 崔文子
cunsi 存思

Da Tang sanzang shengjiao xu 大唐三藏聖教序
Da Tang zhongxing song 大唐中興頌
dahuang zhi ting 大荒之庭
Daji jing 大集經
Damo yan 達摩眼
danding he 丹頂鶴
Danyang 丹陽
daoguan 道館
Daoxuan 道宣
Daozang 道藏
Deng Shiru 鄧石如
Deng Shouzhi 鄧守之
Deng Yu 鄧郁

dian 點
diao 弔
"Diao he wen" 弔鶴文
Diao Yue 刁約
"Diaochong lun" 雕蟲論
diaowen 弔文
Ding Lingwei 丁令威
Dinggongshan 丁公山
Dinghui (Temple) 定慧(寺)
Dingwu 定武
Dong Qichang 董其昌
Dong You 董逌
Dongshutang tie 東書堂帖
Du Mu 都穆
Duanfang 端方
duti zi 獨體字

fa 法
fang 仿
fangbi 方筆
fangkuai zi 方塊字
fangshi 方士
fanke 翻刻
Falin 法琳
Fashu yaolu 法書要錄
fatie 法帖
feibai 飛白
Feitian 飛天
fenggu 風骨
fu 賦
Fu Shan 傅山
Fu Xiansheng (Master Fu) 傅先生
Fuqiu Gong (Master Fuqiu) 浮丘公
Fuyuyan 浮玉岩

Ganlu tie 甘露帖
ganzhi 干支
gou 鉤
goumo 鉤摹
Goushishan 緱氏山
gu 古
Gu Chen 顧宸
Gu Congyi 顧從義
Gu Kuang 顧況
Gu Yanwu 顧炎武
Gu Yuanqing 顧元慶
guan 觀
Guang Yizhou shuangji 廣藝舟雙楫
guantie 官帖
gufa 古法
Gui Fu 桂馥
Guiyang 桂陽
Gujin wenzi 古今文字
Gushi huapu 顧氏畫譜
guwen 古文
guya 古雅
guyi 古意

Haimen 海門
Han Shineng 韓世能
Han Fengxi 韓逢禧
Han Yu 韓愈
Handan Chun 邯鄲淳
hao 號
He Shaoji 何紹基
He Weiran 何偉然
"He zan" 鶴讚
He Zhu 賀鑄
heng 橫
hetai 鶴臺
Hezhou 鶴洲
hu 壺
Hu Sanxing 胡三省
Hu Shiwen 胡師文
Hua Xia 華夏
Huachanshi 畫禪室
Huayang 華陽
Huayang Shanren 華陽山人
"Huayang song" 華陽頌
"Huayang Tao Yinju neizhuan" 華陽陶隱居內傳
Huayang Zhenyi 華陽真逸
Huaisu 懷素
Huainan bagong 淮南八公
Huan Kai 桓闓
Huang Bosi 黃伯思

Huang Fengchi 黃鳳池
Huang Guanzi 黃觀子
Huang Mianzhong 黄冕仲
Huang Tingjian 黃庭堅
huangting 荒庭
Huangting neijing jing 黃庭內景經
Huangting jing 黃庭經
Huangzhou hanshi tie 黄州寒食帖
huayu 畫寓
Huqiao 胡橋

Ji Chang 姬昌
Ji Han 嵇含
Ji'an 集安
Jia Song 賈嵩
Jia Yi 賈誼
Jianbao 鑑寶
Jiankang 建康
Jiao Guang 焦光
Jiao Xian 焦先
Jiaoshan 焦山
"Jiaoshan wang Song Liao shan" 焦山望松寥山
Jingang jing 金剛經
Jingde 景德
Jingshiyu 經石峪
Jingwang shenmiao bei 荆王神廟碑
Jinling 金陵
Jinshan 金山
jinshi 進士
jinshixue 金石學
Jiu guan tan bei 舊館壇碑
jiwen 祭文
Jixianyuan 集賢院
jizi lian 集字聯
Juqushan 句曲山
juebi shu 掘筆書
juemiao 絕妙

kaishu 楷書
Kaiyuan 開元
Kang Youwei 康有為
kaozheng 考證
Kong Zhigui 孔稚圭
Kunlun 崑崙
kuotian 廓填

Lanting ji xu 蘭亭集序
lei 誄
Leihongshi 雷轟石
leishu 類書
li 離
Li Bai (Bo) 李白
Li Chuo 李綽
Li Daoyuan 酈道元
Li Deyu 李德裕
Li Fangjun 李方君
Li Gonglin 李公麟
Li Ling 李陵
Li Ruiqing 李瑞清
"Li sao" 離騷
Li Shan 李善
Li Si 李斯
Li Zhi 李贄
Li Zong'e 李宗諤
Liang Hu 梁鵠
Liang Qichao 梁啟超
Liang Wudi 梁武帝
Liao (Rock) 寥
Liexian zhuan 列仙傳
Liezi 列子
lin 臨
Lin Qizhong 林企忠
lingu 臨古
Linji 臨濟
lishu 隸書
Liu Changshi 劉昌詩
Liu Gongquan 柳公權
Liu Guinian 劉龜年
Liu Na 劉那
Liu Sheng 劉勝
Liu Xiang 劉向
Liu Xiaobiao 劉孝標
Liu Xie 劉勰
Liu Xizai 劉熙載
Liu Yuxi 劉禹錫

Longyindong 龍隱洞
longzhuashu 龍爪書
Lu Ji 陸機
Lu Jingyou 陸敬游
Lu You 陸游
Luohanyan 羅漢岩

Ma Ziyan 馬子嚴
Ma Zonghuo 馬宗霍
Mancheng 滿城
Mangshan 邙山
Mao Jin 毛晉
Mao Zhen 茅溱
Maoshan 茅山
Maoxian 鄮縣
Mi Fu 米芾
Mi Heng 禰衡
miaopin 妙品
ming 銘
Mo Youzhi 莫友芝
moya 摩崖
Mochi bian 墨池編
muzhi 墓志
muzhiming 墓志銘

na 捺
"Nan bei shupai lun" 南北書派論
Nan shi 南史
Ni Fan 倪璠
Ni Kuan zhuan zan 倪寬傳贊
nigushi 擬古詩
Ningbo 寧波

Ouyang Xiu 歐陽修

paixie 俳諧
Pan Ni 潘尼
Pan Ning 潘寧
Pan Xu 潘勖
Penglai Shuijian 蓬萊水監
Pi Rixiu 皮日休
pianpang 偏旁
pie 撇

"Pipa xing" 琵琶行

qi 奇
Qi fo jie 七佛偈
Qian Sheng 錢升
Qian Yanyuan 錢彥遠
Qian zi wen 千字文
Qianlong 乾隆
qiguan 奇觀
qifang 奇放
Qin Shihuandi 秦始皇帝
Qingshantang fatie 晴山堂法帖
qingtan 青壇
Qinhuai 秦淮
"Qinzhou Tianshui Jun Maijiya fokan ming" 秦州天水郡麥積崖佛龕銘
qinzong 禽縱
qishi 奇事
Qiyang 祁陽
Qu Yuan 屈原
que 闕
quzhe qiuzhi 曲折求之

Ren Fang 任昉
Rong Geng 容庚
Ruan Yuan 阮元
Ruan Zhuo 阮卓
Runzhou tujing 潤州圖經
Rushan tie 入山帖
Ruyu 如玉
Ryōkan (Japanese) 良寬

Sancai tuhui 三才圖會
sanqu 散曲
Sanxitang fatie 三希堂法帖
sanyuan bahui zhi shu 三元八會之書
Shan hai jing 山海經
shanben 善本
shanggu 上古
Shangqing 上清
Shanhuang Shanjiao 上皇山樵

shangshi 上石
Shao Kang 邵亢
Shazhou dudufu tujing 沙州都督府圖經
Shen Dacheng 沈大成
Shen Yue 沈約
Shen Zhou 沈周
shending 審定
Shengyuanguan 昇元觀
Shengxian Taizi bei 昇仙太子碑
shenli 神理
shensi 神似
Shi Yiguan 師宜官
"Shigu ge" 石鼓歌
shigu 石鼓
Shilin guangji 事林廣記
Shimen ming 石門銘
Shishuo xinyu 世說新語
Shiyu huapu 詩餘畫譜
Shizishan 獅子山
Shosoin (Japanese) 正倉院
shu 豎
Shu duan 書斷
"Shuang he" 雙鶴
shuanggou 雙鉤
shufa 書法
shuiqian ben 水前本
shushu 署書
"Si jiu fu" 思舊賦
"Si jiu ming" 思舊銘
sikong 司空
Sima Qian 司馬遷
sishen 四神
sitie 私帖
Song (Rock) 松
Song ben 宋本
Song Jing 宋璟
Songfengge shi 松風閣詩
Songjiang 松江
su 俗
Su Shi 蘇軾
Su Shunqin 蘇舜欽
Su Song 蘇頌
Su Yijian 蘇易簡
suli 俗隸
Sun Chuxuan 孫處玄
Sun En 孫恩
Sun Shen 孫詵
Sun Wentao 孫文韜

ta 塔
taben 拓本
Taihu 太湖
Taishan 泰山
tan 壇
Tang Liuru huapu 唐六如畫譜
Tangshi huapu 唐詩畫譜
Tangshi pinhui 唐詩品彙
Tangsong badajia fashu 唐宋八大家法書
Tanmi Yi he ming 探秘瘞鶴銘
Tao Hongjing 陶弘景
Tao Qian 陶潛
Tao Yi 陶翊
Tao Zongyi 陶宗儀
ti 提
Tianbao 天寶
Tianjian 天監
Tianyige 天一閣
tianzhu 填硃
tie 帖
Tieshan 鐵山
tiexue 帖學
timing 題名
Tingyunguan tie 停雲館帖
tiyong 題詠
Tonggou 通溝
tongpan 通判
tuizao 推鑿
tujing 圖經

wan 彎
Wanling 宛陵
Wanxiangtang fatie 晚香堂法帖
Wang Houzhi 王厚之
Wang Huanzhi 王奐之

Wang Huizhi 王徽之
Wang Qishao 王綦韶
Wang Kentang 王肯堂
"Wang Meirenshan ming" 望美人山銘
Wang shi 汪氏
Wang Shihong 汪士鋐
Wang Shizhen 王世貞
Wang Shu 王澍
Wang Wenzhi 王文治
Wang Xiangzhi 王象之
Wang Xizhi 王羲之
Wang Yuan 王遠
Wang Zan 王瓚
Wang Zongni 汪宗尼
Wangzi Qiao 王子喬
Wei Dan 韋誕
Wei Heng 衛恆
Wei Xizeng 魏錫曾
Wei Xu 韋續
weike 偽刻
Wen Chu 文俶
Wen Jia 文嘉
Wen Peng 文彭
"Wen ye he" 聞夜鶴
Wen Zhengming 文徵明
Wen Zhenheng 文震亨
Weng Danian 翁大年
Weng Fanggang 翁方綱
wenhua mingpian 文化名片
Wenquan ming 溫泉銘
Wenxin diaolong 文心雕龍
Wu Dongfa 吴東發
Wu Ju 吴琚
Wu Ting 吴廷
Wu Yun 吴雲
Wudeng huiyuan 五燈會元
"Wuhe fu" 舞鶴賦

Xianchun 咸淳
Xiang he jing 相鶴經
Xiang Yu 項羽
Xiangfu 祥符
Xiangfu tujing 祥符圖經
Xiangfu zhouxian tujing 祥符州縣圖經
xiangta 響搨
Xianmen 羨門
Xianshan louge tu 仙山樓閣圖
Xianyu Shu 鮮于樞
Xiao Dan 蕭憺
Xiao Gang 蕭綱
Xiao Lun 蕭綸
Xiao Rong 蕭融
Xiao Tong 蕭統
Xiao Xiang 蕭象
Xiao Yan 蕭衍
Xiao Yong 蕭永
xiaosan junyi 蕭散駿逸
Xie Lingyun 謝靈運
Xie Zhuang 謝莊
xiedan 寫丹
xiefa 邪法
xiezi 寫字
Xihongtang fashu 戲鴻堂法書
Xing Tong 邢侗
Xinjuan Hainei qiguan 新鐫海內奇觀
xingshu 行書
Xingshu lin Yuyantang tie 行書臨玉煙堂帖
Xishi 西施
Xiyue Huashan miao bei 西嶽華山廟碑
xu 序
Xu Guocheng 許國誠
Xu Mi 許謐
Xu Xiake 徐霞客
Xue Ji 薛稷
xun 尋
Xun Xian 荀羨

Yan Yannian 顏延年
Yan Zhenqing 顏真卿
Yan Zhitui 顏之推
Yang Bin 楊賓

Yang Han 楊翰
Yang Hu 羊祜
Yang Xi 楊羲
Yang Xin 羊欣
yantai 妍態
Ye Boyin 葉伯寅
Ye Changchi 葉昌熾
yi 意
Yi he ming 瘞鶴銘
Yi he ming bian 瘞鶴銘辨
Yi he ming kao 瘞鶴銘考
yinghuang 硬黃
Yishan 嶧山
yiwen 移文
yizhou shuangji 藝舟雙楫
Yongzhou 永州
You Qingyuanshan shi 遊青原山詩
You Si 游似
Youquan Xian 由拳縣
youzheng shuju 有正書局
Yu hai 玉海
Yu Xin 庾信
Yuan Hongdao 袁宏道
Yuan Jie 元結
Yuan Shu 袁淑
Yuan Zhongdao 袁中道
Yuan Zongdao 袁宗道
Yuandi tie 元帝帖
yuanti 院體
Yudi jisheng 輿地紀勝
Yue Yi lun 樂毅論
yun 韻
Yunfengshan 雲峰山
Yuqingzhai tie 餘清齋帖
yuren 羽人
Yuruihua shi bei 玉蕊花诗碑
Yuyantang Dong tie 玉煙堂董帖
Yuyantang fatie 玉煙堂法帖

Zashu ce 雜書冊
Zeng Xi 曾熙
Zeng Zhang Datong juan bawei 贈張大同卷跋尾
Zengzi 曾子
Zhan Fangsheng 湛方生
zhang 丈
Zhang Bangji 張邦基
Zhang Chao 張弨
Zhang Chou 張丑
Zhang Daqian 張大千
Zhang Huaiguan 張懷瓘
Zhang Jianfu 章簡甫
Zhang Liang 張良
Zhang Min 章岷
Zhang Ruitu 張瑞圖
Zhang Xu 張旭
Zhang Yanyuan 張彥遠
Zhang Yu 張嬰
Zhang Yuanzhi 張元之
Zhang Zhi 張芝
Zhao Jin 趙溍
Zhao Jun 趙均
Zhao Mengfu 趙孟頫
Zhao Mengkui 趙孟奎
Zhao Mingcheng 趙明誠
Zhao Yanwei 趙彥衛
Zhao Yi 趙壹
Zhao Yiguang 趙宧光
Zhao Zhiqian 趙之謙
Zhaoyincha ming 招隱刹銘
zhe 折
zhen 真
zheng 正
Zheng Daozhao 鄭道昭
Zheng Fu 鄭簠
Zheng Qiao 鄭樵
zhengshu 正書
Zhenjiang 鎮江
Zhenjiang fuzhi bieke 鎮江府治別刻
zhenren 真人
Zhenshangzhai tie 真賞齋帖
zhenshu 真書
zhi 質
Zhidun 支遁
zhiming 誌銘
Zhishun 至順

zhong feng 中鋒
Zhong You 鍾繇
Zhongshan 種山
Zhuangguanting bieke 壯觀亭別刻
Zhuangzi 莊子
Zhuanshiting 篆石亭
zhuanshu 篆書
zhuanyi 篆意
Zhufang 朱方
zhushu 注疏
zi 字
ziran 自然

Notes

INTRODUCTION

1 See Zhenjiang Shi Minjian Wenyi Yanjiuhui, *Zhenjiang minjian gushi*, 13–15.

2 For a description of the environment of the island and inscription, see Lu Jiugao, "Jiaoshan fang Yi he ming keshi," 26–33; and Yuan Daojun, *Jiaoshan shike yanjiu*.

3 Zhenjiang Bowuguan, "Zhenjiang Jiaoshan Yi he ming beike fajue jianbao."

4 Mizuno Seiichi's short but informative essay still serves as the best introduction to the inscription and its reception history (Mizuno, "Egakumei ni tsuite").

5 The pre-modern scholarship was compiled in Wang Shihong's (1658–1723) book *Yi he ming kao* and Wu Dongfa (1747–1803), *Yi he ming kao*. For a recent collection of documented materials, see Luo, *Yi he ming yanjiu*.

6 As far back as the late eleventh century, only six extant works of calligraphy by Tao Hongjing were known in the Northern Song imperial collection catalog (see *Xuanhe shupu*, 8.2b–3a). Three other works, all in small script, were reportedly found in private collections in Zhou Mi, *Yunyan guoyan lu*, 2.1b. Among the very few works that show a certain connection to Tao is *Letter of Entering Mountains* (Ru shan tie), also known as *Letter of Emperor Yuan* (Yuandi tie), that appears in *Model Letters of the Halting Cloud Hall* (Tingyunguan tie; published 1537–1560). Its calligraphy, however, bears little resemblance to any sixth-century works and thus has long been dismissed. For a collection of comments on the alleged Tao Hongjing piece, see Zhou Daozhen, *Tingyunguan tie huikao*, 54–56. For a survey of these recorded and extant works, see Lu Renlong, "Tao Hongjing." See also Kōzen Hiroshi's discussion of Tao's calligraphy in relation to his Daoist practice (Kōzen, "Shoga no rekishi").

7 For the two stone well fences, see *SDZS* 5:142–43 and Chen Shihua, "Heming, Tianjian jinglan yu Tao Hongjing shufa." In 1986, bricks said to be from the tomb of Tao were found near Maoshan. The style of the carvings on the bricks, according to the author of the archaeological report, is close to that of *Eulogy for Burying a Crane*. See Chen Shihua, "Tao Hongjing shu muzhuan." For a further study of the bricks, see Mugitani Kunio, "Ryō tenkan juhachi nen kinenmei bosen."

8 Shen Dacheng (1700–1771) attributed the *Eulogy* to Pi Rixiu (ca. 834–ca. 902), a late Tang poet who lived not far away from Maoshan and did write other poems on a dead crane (Shen, *Xuefuzhai ji*, 29a–30b). His theory is echoed in a recent study by Wang Jiakui (Wang, *Tao Hongjing congkao*, 294–312). Some scholars agree on a late Tang date but not the above authorship (Bian Xiaoxuan, *Dongqing shuwu biji*, 352–64; Chen Yaodong, "Yi he ming de shidai," 16–23). The attribution to Wang Xizhi, though dismissed by most premodern and modern scholars, continues to be embraced today (Liu Jianguo and Pan Meiyun, *Yi he ming*).

9 For a review of the compilation of *Essential Records on Calligraphy*, see McNair, "Fa shu yao lu." A recent contextual study of Zhang Yanyuan can be found in Shi Rui, "Tangdai liang jing de shuhua jiancang."
10 See a review and recent discovery of the editions of *Essential Records on Calligraphy* in Chen Zhiping, "Fashu yaolu de liangge banben xitong."
11 See Chiang, *Chinese Calligraphy*, 153–63.
12 See a detailed linguistic discussion of the evolution of script in Qiu, *Chinese Writing*, 29–150.
13 For a classical essay on the script types, see Qi Gong, *Gudai ziti lungao* (available in an English translation in Qi, *Chinese Characters Then and Now*). Examples can be found in many Han dynasty steles, which feature a title in archaic seal script to signify the sacredness of the monument, while the body text is in contemporary clerical script.
14 However, there is no clear distinction in later publications of rubbings; model letters certainly include recarving of the rubbings from inscriptions. Many late Ming model letters include replication of stone inscriptions (see the discussion in chapter 3). For an eighteenth-century example, see Lu Huiwen, "Bei yu tie de jiaohui."
15 See a concise introduction to this topic in Ledderose, *Mi Fu*, 10–12. For the culture of letter writing as calligraphy performance, see Harrist, "A Letter from Wang Hsi-chih."
16 Zhao Yiguang, *Hanshan zhoutan*, 2.30b.
17 For more details and intricate techniques involved, see Starr, *Black Tigers*, chapters 3 and 4.
18 Ma Ziyun and Shi Anchang, *Beitie jianding*, 448–53. See a discussion of the field in Wu, *A Story of Ruins*, 55–59. Often cited modern references for rubbing connoisseurship include Zhang Yansheng, *Shanben beitie lu*; Ma Chengming, *Haiwai suojian shanben beitie lu*; and Zhong Wei, *Zhongguo beitie jianbie tudian*, to name a few.
19 Zeitlin and Liu, *Writing and Materiality in China*; Wu, "On Rubbings."
20 Harrist, *The Landscape of Words*, 18.
21 Clunas, *Empire of Great Brightness*, 84–110; *Screen of Kings*, 63–99.

CHAPTER 1: INSCRIBING THE ISLAND

1 This is the official figure given in the annual report of the Jiaoshan Stone Inscription Museum (provided by Yang Yuanhui).
2 For a discussion of the particular rubbing, see *Zhongguo meishu quanji: Shufa zhuanke bian* 2: 52. A more detailed evaluation of this and other early rubbings of the *Eulogy* can be found in Lu Zongrun, "Yi he ming jiaobu"; Ma Ziyun, *Bei tie jianding*, 134–37; and Wang Zhuanghong, *Zengbu Jiaobei suibi*, 218–21.
3 Wang Shihong, *Yi he ming kao*, 671–778; Zhang Chao, *Yi he ming bian*, 9b–10a.
4 Huayang is an alternative name for Maoshan. *Zhen*, or "perfected," is often added to the aliases of Daoist immortals and adepts. And the "perfected" is considered higher than other immortals in Shangqing Daoism (Robinet, *Taoist Meditation*, 42–48.)
5 The identity of the person is unknown. "Woodcutter" often refers to a recluse in Chinese literature. "Mount Shanghuang" perhaps refers to a local place whose whereabouts are now unknown. It was still known to local people—at least in the late eleventh century—and was mentioned by Mi Fu, the Song dynasty calligrapher who lived in Zhenjiang. See his *Sweet Dew Letter* (Ganlu tie, dated 1102), at the National Palace Museum, Taipei, accessed April 1, 2017, http://catalog.digitalarchives.tw/item/00/11/11/1a.html. For other interpretations about the place name, see Luo Yonglai, *Yi he ming yanjiu*, 197–98.
6 *Renchen* and *jiawu* are two terms for a year in the Chinese sexagenary-cycle calendar. Scholars' debates on the exact years will be discussed in chapter 2.

7 Huating, a town near today's Shanghai. It does not necessarily point to the real place, however. There is a deeper metaphoric meaning. Huating was known mainly for the famous last words of Lu Ji (261–303), a talented scholar who had also succeeded as a military general but eventually fell because of political rivals' incrimination. Before he was executed, he recalled his early peaceful years at Huating, where one can listen to cranes singing, and lamented his poor choices (Liu Yiqing, *Shishuo xinyu jianshu*, 33.896. See translation in Mather, *Shih-shuo hsin-yu: A New Account of Tales of the World*, 471). The "Huating crane" thus became a literary trope for lamenting vanity and the fleeting nature of life.

8 Zhufang was the older name of Zhenjiang in the Spring and Autumn period (770–476 BCE), when it was under the control of the Wu Kingdom. For an analysis of the place names in actual and literary use in these two lines, see Xue Lei, "Yi he ming de wenben yu yujing zaiyi."

9 Daoism holds that the cosmos is ordered by a bureaucracy of deities and immortals officials. As we shall discuss soon, the crane was believed to be the vehicle of immortals in Daoist lore.

10 In Daoist contexts, "black and yellow silk" refers to immortals' robes with shining and colorful decorations. See Edward H. Schafer's discussion in "The Early History of Lead Pigments and Cosmetics in China," 416–20. The image of wrapping the dead crane in this kind of silk may suggest the hoped-for posthumous existence of the bird.

11 The missing characters in lines 11 and 12 likely expressed the hope, common in the conclusions of prose introductions in epitaphs from the medieval period, that the carved stone would endure forever.

12 According to the *Classics on Judging Cranes* (Xiang he jing), a work that survives only partially in a Ming dynasty edition, cranes in medieval times were regarded as viviparous birds (*Xiang he jing*, *CSJCXB* 44: 257).

13 The *Classics on Judging Cranes* is attributed to the Fuqiu Gong, one of the earliest Daoist immortal figures. See Edward H. Schafer's remarks on the history of *Xianghe jing* in "The Cranes of Maoshan," 374–75n12.

14 This line is a speculation by later scholars.

15 "Thunder Gate" was the city gate of Kuaiji, today's Shaoxing, Zhejiang. As the odd story goes, one day, a crane flew into a drum at the gate and hid inside. Since then, the drum produced such a loud sound that it could be heard even in Luoyang, more than a thousand miles away. At a later time, someone broke the drum and saw the crane fly out and disappear, after which, the drum was unable to produce a far-reaching sound. See Sun Shen (fl. mid-fifth century), *Linhai ji*, cited in Ouyang Xun, *Yiwen leiju*, 90.1564–65.

16 *Huabiao* is a pair of ceremonial pillars in front of a palace or city gate. The popular crane-related story refers to that of Ding Lingwei, another ancient Daoist, who became immortal and once revealed himself to people as a white crane hovering and speaking on top of ceremonial pillars. See Tao Qian, *Xu Sou shen ji*, cited in Ouyang Xun, *Yiwen leiju*, 90.1565. For the story of Ding Lingwei, see Campany, *Strange Writing*, 69–75.

17 The paired terms "meaning" (*yi*) and "events" (*shi*) reflect an ancient dichotomy in historical and literary writings. Mencius comments that all history books narrate *shi*, whereas the *Spring and Autumn Annals*, attributed to Confucius, articulates *yi*. See discussions in the section of "*shilei*" in Liu Xie, *Zengding wenxin diaolong jiaozhu*, 472.

18 "Released and transformed" (*jiehua*) refers to the Daoist belief that the body is transformed after death. In Shangqing doctrine, the corpse of the adept is assumed to remain in the coffin and be purified until it disappears, leaving only a staff, a sandal, or, in the highest ranks of adepts, a sword. See Robinet, "Metamorphosis and Deliverance from the Corpse in Taoism." It is reported, for example, that Tao Hongjing eventually

"released" in the form of a sword (Jia, "Huayang Tao Yinju neizhuan," *DZ* 310, 5:509a). It is also reported that when Tao's tomb was opened at a later time, only a sword was found in his coffin (Liu Dabin, *Maoshan zhi*, *DZ* 314, 5:591a).

19 The line has no clear meaning. It was added by Wang Shihong from a suspicious transcription of the *Eulogy* later known as the Jinshan version, which will be discussed in chapter 2, note 114.

20 The two lines may reflect the directional concerns in Daoist burial. Kristofer Schipper suggests that the right and left directions in the text refer to the two parts of the tomb contract that was common in burial practice in the sixth century. See Schipper, "L'Epitaphe pour une Grue (*Yi he ming*) et son Auteur," 413.

21 The "double-layered gate" is often found in mortuary writings to describe the setting of tombs. For another example of the usage, see Xie Zhuang (421–466), "Eulogy to the Honored Consort Xuan of Emperor Xiaowu of the Song" (Song Xiaowu Xuan guifei lei), in Xiao Tong, *Wen xuan*, 57.795.

22 This line was added from unknown sources by Zhang Chao (*Yi he ming bian*, 9b–10a). To my knowledge, "the Kingdom of Cao" does not refer to any literary allusion.

23 Combined with references to the landscape behind and in front of the tomb, this passage completes a tour of the four directions surrounding the site of the inscription. It is unclear whether there are references beyond the literal meaning of the "thorny gate." The phrase also appears in Tao Hongjing's "Records on Searching Mountains" (Xun shan zhi), *Tao Hongjing ji jiaozhu*, 6.

24 Naming the native place of the deceased—here, Huating, the birthplace of the crane—is a convention of medieval epitaphs.

25 *Zhenlü*, or "perfected companions," refers to Daoist practitioners.

26 The second character, *yue* 岳, is speculative, since only its lower part survives. Mount Jiang, not known in other sources, is perhaps a fictitious place name. *Zhengjun* has been an honorific title for scholars without an official career.

27 Danyang is an alternative name for Zhenjiang. The Daoist title Outer Immortal Commandant (Wai Xianwei) is not documented in other extant Daoist texts. In Chinese traditional bureaucratic system, "outer" often refers to officials serving outside of the imperial court.

28 Jiangyin is a nearby town in today's Jiangsu Province. *Zhenzai*, "perfected steward," appears to be a Daoist title but is not documented elsewhere in Daoist writings.

29 This and similar notations following excerpts indicate corresponding Chinese texts in appendix 3.

30 This is one of a pair of bronze *hu* vessels excavated in Xinzheng, Henan, in 1923. See Xia Zhifeng, "Xinzheng qiqun san kao." For the discovery, see also Loewe, *Cambridge History of Ancient China*, 478–81.

31 See Shaanxi Sheng Kaogu Yanjiuyuan, *Qin Shihuangdi lingyuan kaogu baogao*, 161–69.

32 Wang Shumin, *Liexian zhuan jiaojian*, 65. The book is attributed to Liu Xiang (77–6 BCE) but was probably compiled in the first century CE. For a discussion on the immortal Wangzi Qiao, see also Campany, *Strange Writing*, 193–95.

33 For the excavation report on the painted tombs in Tonggou, see Ikeuchi Hiroshi, *Tsūkō*; and Jilin Sheng Bowuguan, "Jilin Ji'an wukui fen sihao he wuhao mu qingli lueji."

34 Numerous studies of the *Eulogy* have addressed the Daoist imagery of the crane. For a few modern examples, see Wang Yuanqing, "Shengming de jisi"; Wang Tongshun, "Shilun Yi he ming de sixiangxing yishuxing jiqi lishi diwei"; and Jin Yuzhe (Kim You Cheol), "Yi he ming de mingwen neirong jiqi lixiang."

35 Legge, *Confucian Analects*, 6.

36 For a study of this genre, see Knechtges, *The Han Rhapsody*.

37 Jia Yi, "Funiao fu," in Xiao Tong, *Wen xuan*, 16a–23b. See also Knechtges's annotated translation in *Wen xuan* 3: 41–49. The same section in *Wen xuan* includes a few other writings about birds, such as Mi Heng's (173–198 CE) "Rhapsody on a Parrot" (Yingwu fu), ibid., 49–57. A case study of bird imagery in medieval literature can be found in Kroll, "The Image of the Halcyon Kingfisher in Medieval Chinese Poetry."

38 The earliest poetic reference to an appearance of a crane understood it as a superior human being and treated it as an auspicious omen; in some poems, cranes were associated with exotic fashions or distant lands. "A Crane Cries" (He ming) appears in *The Book of Songs* and implies the lofty virtue of a gentleman-hermit, whose wisdom spreads across the world. For a translation, see Waley, *The Book of Songs*, 158, poem 184. In addition, the crane is a popular subject for the genre "rhapsody on objects," which focuses on elaborate descriptions of precious things. For an early record of the gathering of cranes as an auspicious omen, see Ban Gu, *Han shu*, 25.1248.

39 Cao Zhi, *Cao Zhi ji jiaozhu*, 238–40.

40 For an account of Cao Zhi's life, see Cutter, "The Incident at the Gate."

41 Cao Zhi, *Cao Zhi ji jiaozhu*, 239.

42 Liu Yiqing, *Shishuo xinyu jianshu*, 136. See also Mather's translation, 69–70.

43 Bao Zhao, "Wuhe fu," *Wen xuan*, 14.8a–10b. See also Knechtges's translation in *Wen xuan*, 75–82. For works by Shen Yue and Yu Xin, see Ouyang Xun, *Yiwen leiju*, 90.1568.

44 For more discussion of the imagery of cranes in Tang Chinese art and literature, see Armstrong, "The Crane Dance in East and West"; and Schafer, "The Cranes of Maoshan." See also Spring, "The Celebrated Cranes of Po Chü-I." For visual representations of cranes in later art, see Song, "Images of the Crane in Chinese Painting" and Sturman, "Cranes above Kaifeng."

45 This line alludes to "A Crane Cries" in *The Book of Songs*. See note 38 above.

46 The "wild court" (*huangting*) is a short form for Court of the Great Wilds (Dahuang zhi ting), which refers to a remote land for immortals recorded in *The Classic of Mountains and Seas* (Shan hai jing). For an explanation of the term, see Strassberg, *A Chinese Bestiary*, 39–42.

47 Zhan Fangsheng, "Dirge for a Crane" (Diao he wen), in Ouyang Xun, *Yiwen leiju*, 90.1568.

48 See an English translation of the poem in Owen, *An Anthology of Chinese Literature*, 162–175. For the literary tradition of "Encountering Sorrow," see Murck, *Poetry and Painting in Song China*, 10–15.

49 More examples can be found in Liu Na (fl. second half of the sixth century), "A Single Crane Flying Over the Cloud" (Fude duhe lingyun qu), and Ruan Zhuo (531–589), "A Yellow Crane Saying Farewell" (Fude huanghu yi yuanbie), both in Ouyang Xun, *Yiwen leiju*, 90.1567.

50 For an overview of the use of epitaphs in Western culture, see Guthke, *Epitaph Culture in the West*. And a study of the materials from the ancient world can be found in Lattimore, *Themes in Greek and Latin Epitaphs*.

51 For a discussion of the origin of epitaph in ancient China, see Huang Zhanyue, "Zaoqi muzhi de yixie wenti."

52 On the origin and ritual function of medieval epitaphs, see Davis, *Entombed Epigraphy*, 92–151. See also Fukuhara Keirou, "Seishin no boshi no igi"; and Liu Tao, *Zhongguo shufashi*, 495–520. For a recent study of mortuary steles, see Brashier, "Text and Ritual in Early Chinese Stelae"; and Wong, *Chinese Steles*, esp. 27–34.

53 Early examples include those for aristocratic clans. Most of these epitaphs were excavated in Nanjing and Zhenjiang region. For a general discussion, see Dien, *Six Dynasties Civilization*, 205–7.

54 Davis, *Entombed Epigraphy*, 126–50.

55 Excavated in 1980, these epitaphs were found in the corridor leading to the tomb chamber. See Ruan Guolin, "Nanjing Liang Guiyangwang Xiao Rong fufu hezangmu."

56 The origin of the epitaph cover is a debatable issue in Chinese archaeology. See Zhao Chao, *Gudai muzhi tonglun*, 102–16. Epitaph decorations have drawn the attention of art historians. For an example, see Bush, "Floral Motifs."

57 The earliest examples of *muzhiming* in written records are found in literary anthologies from the Western Jin. See Fu Xuan (217–278), "Epitaph for Gentleman Ren of Jiangxia" (Jiangxia Ren jun muming), in Yan Kejun, *Quan shanggu sandai Qin Han Sanguo Liuchao wen*, 1726. In the Six Dynasties, *ming* became associated above all with burials and assimilated features of older mortuary genres such as *lei*, *diaowen*, and *aice*. See Huang Jinming, *Han Wei Jin Nanbeichao leibeiwen yanjiu*.

58 See the transcription in Zhao Chao, *Han Wei Nanbeichao muzhi huibian*, 25–26. The English translation of the full text is included in Davis, *Entombed Epigraphy*, 333–40, with a contextual analysis, 340–50.

59 The translation is based on Timothy Davis's, with minor modifications (Davis, *Entombed Epigraphy*, 335).

60 Ji Chang is the name of King Wen of the Zhou dynasty (1152–1056 BCE).

61 The phrase "written in cinnabar" (*xiedan*) refers to the red ink that is reserved for documenting meritorious events in official archives.

62 Lacquer was material for writings at the time. However, here "lacquered documents" may have been used to emphasize the deep tone of the ink which in turn suggests the significance of the documents. For an introduction to above writing materials, see Tsien, *Written on Bamboo and Silk*, 126–44, 187–90.

63 This fashion can be detected in the genre *paixie* (humorous writings) in traditional literary theory. Among the most well-known works are Yuan Shu's (408–453) "Nine Gifts Bestowed on a Rooster" (Ji jiuci wen), Kong Zhigui's (447–501) "Official Letter from the North Mountain" (Beishan yiwen), and Shen Yue's "A Slim Bamboo's Prosecution against a Sugar Cane" (Xiuzhu tan ganzhe wen). See a discussion of this subject in Li Shibiao, *Wei Jin Nanbeichao wentixue*. For a recent study of humorous writings in the Six Dynasties, see Fukui Yoshio, *Rikuchō no yūgi bungaku*. Not all parodic writings are humorous, however, as suggested by the examples here.

64 Yu Xin, *Yu Zishan ji zhu*, 684–95.

65 The "broken-string zither" is a metaphor for the death of one's beloved partner.

66 The "neighbor" refers to the story of the noted scholar Xiang Xiu (ca. 227–272), who once composed "Rhapsody of Thinking of the Past" (Si jiu fu) while listening to a neighbor playing the flute (Xiao Tong, *Wen xuan*, 16.719–22). See English translation and introduction in Knechtges, *Wen xuan*, 167–70.

67 A funerary tent was a common setup during this period. The line may also refer to the famous "Will and Testament" (Yiling) by Cao Cao (155–220), the Three Kingdom warlord who requested a tent be set up for his surviving consorts to dance in front of his soul. For the text and its literary influence, see Tian, *The Halberd at Red Cliff*, 173–81.

68 A comparable phenomenon in ancient Western culture is exemplified by Hellenistic epigrams, in which "inscribed" and "literary" examples fell into different categories; the latter were regarded as literary representations of actual epigrams. See Gutzwiller, *Poetic Garlands*, 7.

69 Yu Xin was a Liang dynasty official who, after the collapse of the Liang, served in the Northern Zhou and was not allowed to return to the south. On the lyrical theme in Yu Xin's works, see Graham, "*The Lament for the South.*"

70 Yu Xin, *Yu Zishan ji zhu*, 936–1091.
71 For an example of an actual inscription, see "Inscription on Buddhist caves at Maijiya in Tianshui Prefecture, Qinzhou" (Qinzhou Tianshui Jun Maijiya fokan ming), which commemorates the completion of the famous Buddhist monument in around 574 CE (Yu Xin, *Yu Zishan ji zhu*, 672–79). Another literary imitation similar to "Inscription on Thinking of the Past" is "Inscription on Watching the Beauty Mountain" (Wang Meirenshan ming), also in Yu Xin, 698–99.
72 For examples, see *Eulogy to Gentleman Chu Constructing the Baoxie Path* (Chu jun kaitong baoxiedao keshi, dated 63 CE) and *Eulogy to the Stone Gate* (Shimen song, dated 148 CE) at a road construction site in today's Hanzhong, Shanxi. For above *moya* inscriptions and a survey of the historical site, see Guo Rongzhang, *Shimen shike daquan*.
73 See Toyama Gunji, "Magai," 23–30.
74 Harrist, *The Landscape of Words*, esp. 93–156.
75 Ibid. See also Shandong Shike Yishu Bowuguan, *Yunfeng keshi yanjiu*.
76 Harrist, *The Landscape of Words*, plate 8.
77 Ibid., 149–54.
78 For a discussion of Daoist beliefs regarding mysterious scripts, see Huang, *Picturing the True Form*, 89–93; and Xie Shiwei, *Tianjie zhi wen*, esp. 87–98.
79 *Taishang dongxuan lingbao zhutian neiyin ziran yuzi* (Inner tones and spontaneous jade script of all heavens), 4, *DZ* 97, 2:235a–b.
80 Many examples of this kind of celestial writings can be found in *Chishu yupian zhenwen tianshu jing* (The scripture of red writings in celestial on jade tablets), 1, *DZ* 22, 1:774–799b.
81 *Shangqing yudi qisheng xuanji huitian jiuxiao jing* (The scripture of the return to the Nine Empyrean Heavens, the mythical records of the seven sages of the Jade Emperor of Higher Clarity), *DZ* 1399, 34:63a. I want to thank Dr. Chang Ch'ao-jan for pointing me to above sources.
82 For this Daoist meditative practice, see Huang, *Picturing the True Form*, 25–27.
83 Xie Shiwei, *Tianjie zhiwen*, 94–97.
84 Tao Hongjing, *Zhen gao*, 2, *DZ* 1039, 20:499a.
85 It may occur in other forms of writing practice, such as copying sutras. See Ledderose, "Some Taoist Elements in the Calligraphy of the Six Dynasties," especially 256–58 for a discussion of Tao Hongjing's case.
86 Other monumental works from the mid-sixth century include the extensive Buddhist sutra carving projects, undertaken in the mountains of northern China. See Lai Fei, *Shandong Beichao fojiao moya kejing: Diaocha yu yanjiu*. See also an analysis of this phenomenon in Harrist, *Landscape of Words*, 157–218; Zhang Qiang and Wei Liya, *Da kong wang fo*.
87 Tao Hongjing, *Zhen gao*, *DZ* 1039, 20: 571a–c.
88 The tombs of Prince Liu Sheng (d. 113 BCE) and his wife at Mancheng in Hebei exemplify this type of mountain burial. For a description of the tombs and the landscape setting, see Zhongguo Shehui Kexueyuan Kaogu Yanjiusuo and Hebei Wenwu Guanlichu, *Mancheng Han mu fajue baogao*, 4–23. For a recent study, see Shi, "The Mancheng Tombs."
89 See Nanjing Bowuyuan, "Jiangsu Danyang Huqiao Nanchao damu jiqi zhuanke bihua."
90 On the emergence of the practice, see Wu, *Monumentality in Early Chinese Art and Architecture*, 112.
91 For a discussion of *que* (towers/pillars) in cemetery configurations, see Paludan, *Chinese Spirit Road*, 31–35, and Wu Hung's discussion of its origin in *Monumentality*, 277–78.

92 Toyama, "Magai," 26.

93 For a short introduction to the school, see Robinet, "Shangqing—Highest Clarity."

94 For the religious and political significance of Maoshan in later periods, see Schafer, *Mao Shan in T'ang Times*. On the tradition of the Highest Clarity at Maoshan, see Robinet, *Taoist Meditation*; and Strickmann, "The Mao-Shan Revelations" and "On the Alchemy of T'ao Hung-ching."

95 For a historical analysis of these *daoguan* monasteries, see Tsuzuki Akiko, "Rikuchō jidai no konan shakai to dōkyō."

96 Da Changuang, *Maoshan zhi*, 2.709–96.

97 See Tao Hongjing, *Zhen gao*, 11, *DZ* 1039, 20: 554b. Tao Hongjing also wrote a poem on the temple (see Liu Dabin, *Maoshan zhi*, 17, *DZ* 314, 5: 677b). This temple was renamed Shengyuanguan in the Song dynasty (Liu Dabin, *Maoshan zhi*, 625c).

98 Liu Dabin, *Maoshan zhi*, 583b.

99 Ibid., 617b.

100 Regarding his childhood name, Lian'er (literally, "little practitioner"), scholars speculate that Liang Wudi was born into a Daoist family. See Zhou Yiliang, "Lun Liang Wudi jiqi shidai," 123–40. See also the emperor's biography in Tian, *Beacon Fire and Shooting Star*, chapter 1.

101 For a summary of the history of the debates between Daoism and Buddhism, see Kohn, *Laughing at the Tao*, 17–21.

102 See "Liang Wuhuangdi shedao chiwen" (Liang Wudi's order on abandoning Daoism), in Falin (572–640), *Bian zheng lun*, 8, *TSZ* 52:2110.549b–549c. The article also appears under the title "She shi Lilao daofa zhao" (Imperial command on abandoning the belief in Master Li's Daoism) in Daoxuan (596–667), *Guang hongming ji*, 4, *TSZ* 52:2103.111c–112c.

103 Li Yanshou, *Nan shi*, 76.1897. The same text, with a little variation, appears also in Yao Silian, *Liang shu*, 51.742.

104 Li Yanshou, *Nan shi*, 76.1898–99.

105 See summary of the scholarly debates in Strickmann, "A Taoist Confirmation."

106 Jia Song, "Huayang Tao Yinju neizhuan," *DZ* 310, 5:501–12. Other major sources of Tao's career include Tao Yi (fl. ca. 492), "Huayang Yinju xiansheng benqi lu" (Biography of the Hermit from Huayang), in *Yunji qiqian*, 107 (*DZ* 1055, 22:730b–733c); Xiao Lun (ca. 507–551), "Yinju Zhenbai xiansheng Tao jun bei" (Stele to Yinju the honorable master Zhenbai), in Li Fang, *Wenyuan yinghua*, 873.4604b–4606a.

107 See Tao Hongjing, "Nan Zhenjun's 'Junsheng lun'" (Disputation of Zhenjun's [Shen Yue] "On Equal Sages"), in *Guang Hongming ji*, 5, *TSZ* 52:2013.122a–123a.

108 See Wang Jiakui, *Tao Hongjing congkao*, 23–41.

109 Jia, "Huayang Tao Yinju neizhuan," *DZ* 310, 5:505b. The tension between Liang Wudi and Tao is also discussed in Bokenkamp, "Answering a Summons." For the detailed process of his method of alchemy, see Strickmann, "On the Alchemy of T'ao Hung-ching," 143–51.

110 Jia, "Huayang Tao Yinju neizhuan," *DZ* 310, 5:501–12.

111 Ibid., 506c.

112 Ibid.

113 Ibid., 508b. According to the same text, it was as late as 525 CE that Tao finally achieved success, but the vague and brief narrative makes the statement questionable (ibid., 508c).

114 Liu Dabin, *Maoshan zhi*, *DZ* 314, 5: 600b. Yao Silian, *Liang shu*, 51.743. For a detailed discussion of this event, see Funayama Tōru, "Tō Kōkei to bokkyō no kairitsu."

115 Xiao Lun, "Yinju Zhenbai Xiansheng Tao jun bei" (Stele to Yinju the honorable master Zhenbai), in Li Fang, *Wenyuan yinghua*, 873.4605b.

116 See Falin, *Bianzheng lun*, 8, *TSZ* 52:2110.547c. According to Falin, these lines were cited from "Internal Biography," but they are not found in the extant edition of the latter.

117 Liu Dabin, *Maoshan zhi*, 20, *DZ* 314, 5: 633c. The stele is dedicated to the Shangqing patriarch Xu Mi. For a study of the stele, see Weng Danian, *Jiu guan tan bei kao*. See also Strickmann, "On the Alchemy of T'ao Hung-ching," 129–30.

118 For the *tan* structure and related Daoist rituals, see Huang, *Picturing the True Form*, 192–95.

119 These structures do not survive, though the site is known as the location of the Yuchen Temple (Yuchenguan), a monastery built in 1008 that survives to this day. Jurong Shi Difangzhi Bangongshi, *Jurong Maoshan zhi*, 92–93.

120 Li Yanshou, *Nan shi* 76.1900.

121 Tao's own writings, such as *Zhou [Ziliang]'s Records of His Communication with the Invisible World* (Zhoushi mingtong ji), demonstrate an effort to incorporate Buddhist concepts such as incarnation into his Daoist theory. See Funayama Tōru, "Tō Kōkei to bokkyō no kairitsu."

122 Li Yanshou, *Nan shi*, 76.1898.

123 For the emperor's edict, see Zhipan, *Fozu tongji*, 54, in *TSZ* 49: 2035.471a. In contrast, Deng Yu (d. 515), a contemporary Daoist master who was also charged with conducting alchemical experiments for Liang Wudi, ended up consuming his elixir and died in 515—a likely suicide. Deng's experience is recorded in Tao Hongjing's biography (Jia Song, "Huayang Tao Yinju neizhuan," DZ 310, 5: 507c–508a). In his official biography in the *Southern History*, Deng Yu is also pictured as a successful Daoist who received reverence from the emperor until his "transcendence" (Li Yanshou, *Nan shi* 76.1896). See also James Robson's discussion of Deng's career in *Power of Place*, 150–54. For the flourishing Daoist community at Maoshan in the Tang era, see Schafer, *Mao Shan in T'ang Times*.

124 Huan Kai, "Huan Zhenren shengxian ji" (Record of the perfected man Huan becoming an immortal), *DZ* 311, 5:514b.

125 Tao Hongjing, *Zhoushi mingtong ji*, 3, *DZ* 312, 5:534c.

126 Jia Song, "Huayang Tao Yinju neizhuan," *DZ* 310, 5:508c.

127 For a description of the environment of the island and inscription, see Lu Jiugao, "Jiaoshan fang Yi he ming keshi"; and Yuan Daojun, *Jiaoshan shike yanjiu*.

128 For the historical changes to the coastline of the region, see Jiangsu Sheng Difangzhi Bianzhuan Weiyuanhui, *Jiangsu Sheng zhi: Dili zhi*, 212–14.

129 See Wu Yun, *Tongzhi Jiaoshan zhi*, 1.5a–5b. Only one rock still stands in the river today.

130 Liu Yiqing, *Shishuo xinyu jianshu*, 135. See English translation in Mather, *Shih-shuo Hsin-yu*, 68–69.

131 For the two emperors' search for immortals, see Sima Qian, *Shiji*, 28.1369–70, 1397–1404. See Burton Watson's translation of the above passages, "Treatise on the Feng and Shan Sacrifices," in Sima Qian, *Records of the Grand Historian: Han Dynasty*, vol. 2, 3–52. Another early source is found in *The Classic of Mountains and Seas* (see a commentary and translation in Strassberg, *A Chinese Bestiary*, 204–5).

132 Li Bai, *Li Bai ji Jiaozhu*, 21.1218.

133 See Liu Mingfang, *Qianlong Jiaoshan zhi*, 3.1a–2b.

134 It is probably a variation of the title Taishang Laojun (the Most High Lord Lao), the deified Laozi in Daoist pantheon.

135 Tao, *Zhen gao*, 5, *DZ* 1039, 20:518a.

136 Ibid.

137 Liang Wudi, "Ascending the Beigu Tower" (Deng Beigulou shi), in Ouyang Xun, *Yiwen leiju*, 63.1131.

CHAPTER 2: DISCOVERING THE PAST

1 For the last years of Liang Wudi's life, see Tian, *Beacon Fire and Shooting Star*, 67–76.
2 For Qian's biography, see Su Song, "Qian Qiju shendaobei," in *Su Weigong wenji*, 52.13a–23b.
3 According to a local gazetteer, the other inscriptions are a carved *Dharani Sutra* stone banner with the "collected characters" of Wang Xizhi's calligraphy, a stele with the "Poems of Jade Blossoms" (Yuruihua shi bei) by Li Deyu (787–850), the Tang dynasty statesman and poet, and the *Inscription on the Zhaoyin Temple* (Zhaoyincha ming) by Prince Xiao Lun of the Liang dynasty. See Lu Xian, *Jiading Zhenjiang zhi*, 6.6b–7a and Yu Xilu, *Zhishun Zhenjiang zhi*, 21. None of these inscriptions survive today, however. The exact date of the event is unknown, but based on the careers of the people involved, it can be dated roughly to 1047 or 1048. See the discussion on the date in Luo Yonglai, "Yi he ming xinzheng san ti," 41.
4 One famous anecdote about Wang Xizhi, the Sage of Calligraphy, is that when he lived in Shanyin, today's Shaoxing, he made a copy of the Daoist sutra *Yellow Court* in exchange for geese (Fang Xuanling, *Jin shu*, 80.2100).
5 This refers to another piece written by Zhang Min (*jinshi* degree earned in [hereafter noted as *jinshi*] 1027), a scholar and native of Zhenjiang, for the same event. The Jixian Academy was the imperial court institution for cultural affairs.
6 The two poems refer to the stele by Li Deyu. An account of the poems and their inscription on a stele can be found in Hu Zi, *Tiaoxi yuyin conghua qianji*, 322.
7 Su Shunqin, *Su Shunqin ji biannian jiaozhu*, 164–65.
8 See Su Song, "Runzhou Qian Cibu xinjian Baomoting," in *Su Weigong wenji*, 6.3b. For Su Song's career, see Tuotuo, *Song shi*, 340.10859–68. Based on the reconstruction of the whole inscription, Luo Yonglai suggests that it was the central area of the inscription (see Luo Yonglai, "Yi he ming xinzheng san ti," 41–44).
9 According to a local monk, Ruyu (fl. mid-thirteenth century), most of the inscription did not fall until the Jingde reign (1004–7) of the Song dynasty (Yu Xilu, *Zhishun Zhenjiang zhi*, 21.10a).
10 Ouyang Xiu was aware of the *Dharani Sutra* inscription in Treasured Ink Pavilion too. See Ouyang Xiu, *Jigu lu bawei*, in *Ouyang Xiu quanji*, 143.2306.
11 Ibid., 143.2308–09. There are a few problems in the text, however, perhaps a result of the corruption during transmission. The character *ji* 幾 is probably a typographical error for *ji* 紀. And "six hundred" is likely a typo for "sixty."
12 Dong You, "Shu Yi he ming hou" in *Guangchuan shuba*, 6.78.
13 As the catalogs of the Tang imperial library indicate, only a small part of the collection survived the devastation of the rebellions of An Lushan (755–63) and Huang Chao (875–84). The loss of books in the Tang is recorded in the preface of "Jingji zhi" section in Liu Xu, *Jiu Tang shu*, 46.1962–66. More accounts about the loss can be found in Chen Dengyuan, *Gujin dianji jusan kao*.
14 For a Tang study of the classics, see Pi Xirui, *Jingxue lishi*, 205–36.
15 For a comprehensive study of the phenomenon, see Fu Xuancong, *Tangdai keju yu wenxue*. For a critical discussion of Tang scholarship in English, see McMullen, *State and Scholars in T'ang China*, 67–112.
16 For a study of the *guwen* movement, see Bol, *"This Culture of Ours,"* 123–47.

17 The discovery of the Stone Drums and the response of Tang scholars are discussed in Mattos, *The Stone Drums of Ch'in*, 37–42.

18 For a biography of Han Yu, see Hartman, *Han Yu*.

19 Han Yu, *Han Changli shi jinian jishi*, 794–807.The English translation is based on Innes Herdan's, with my minor modification. See Minford and Lau, *Classical Chinese Literature*, 857–59. See also Stephen Owen's translation and discussion in *The Poetry of Meng Chiao and Han Yu*, 246–54.

20 For Han Yu's selected definition of *gu*, or antiquity, see Bol, *This Culture of Ours*, 124–25.

21 See McNair, "Engraved Calligraphy in China," 109–12.

22 See a list of the cited steles in Shi Zhecun, *Shuijingzhu bei lu*.

23 For the early history of gazetteers, see Zhang Guogan, *Zhongguo gufangzhi kao*, 2–3. Few Tang gazetteers have survived, but fragments from these early books were preserved in Dunhuang. One of them, a fragmentary manuscript of *Illustrated Records of Shazhou Area Command* (Shazhou Dudufu tujing, P.2005, seventh to eighth century) provides the visual evidence for this early genre, though the illustration section is not included. For a recent study of *tujing*, see Hua Linfu, "Sui Tang tujing jikao."

24 The monumental project, in 1,566 volumes, was supervised by Li Zong'e (964–1012) (Wang Yinglin, *Yu hai*, 14.31b–35a). Although the whole collection has been lost, partial contents are available through later local gazetteers such as *Jiading Zhenjiang zhi* (see page 2.4a). For a survey of the Song gazetteers, see Hargett, "Song Dynasty Local Gazetteers and Their Place in the History of Difangzhi Writing." For a broader discussion of geopolitics in the Song, see Mostern, *"Dividing the Realm in Order to Govern."*

25 The Song gazetteer might be based on an older Tang version, ascribed to Sun Chuxuan (fl. ca. 705), which is recorded in the "Jingji zhi" section in Liu Xu, *Jiu Tang shu*, 46.2015.

26 For the cultural-political context of the rise of antiquarianism in the Northern Song, see Rudolph, "Preliminary Notes on Sung Archaeology." More recent studies of this particular topic include Chen Fangmei, "Song guqiwuxue de xingqi yu song fanggu tongqi"; Sena, *Bronze and Stone*; and Hsu, "Songdai shidafu de jinshi shoucang yu liyi shijian" and "Antiquities, Ritual Reform, and the Shaping of New Taste at Huizong's Court."

27 For a critical review of Ouyang Xiu's epigraphic research, see Egan, *The Problem of Beauty*, 7–59.

28 His first name, Yu 嶨, has been mistakenly read as Xue 壆 in many editions. An official biography of Zhang Yu is included in the section of "hermits" in Tuotuo, *Song shi*, 458.13454–55.

29 A recent study of Dong's biography can be found in Wang Hongsheng, "Dong You shengping kaolüe."

30 Cited in Dong You, *Guangchuan shuba*, 6.77. Dong had also visited Jiaoshan in person but reported no new findings.

31 For Shao Kang's biography, see Tuotuo, *Song shi*, 317.10335–37.

32 Dong You, "Shu Huang Xueshi Yi he ming hou," *Guangchuan shuba*, 6.79. Dong You and Huang Bosi were coworkers in the Palace Library. For their collaborative activities, see Ebrey, *Accumulating Culture*, 136–38.

33 Huang Bosi, "Ba Yi he ming hou," in *Dongguan yulun*, 886. Huang includes only the Shao Kang reconstruction and seems to be unaware of Zhang Yu's. The reconstructed text attached to the published book, however, is most likely a mixture of various sources because it also includes Zhang Yu's discovery. A later editing is possible, given the fact that the book was compiled later by Huang's son and published in 1147 (ibid., 892).

34 Ibid., 886.

35 Ouyang Xiu, *Jigu lu baowei*, in *Ouyang Xiu quanji*, 143.2308.

36 For the history of the work, see He Yanquan, "Ouyang Xiu Jigu lu ba moji juan de xiangguan wenti yu liuchuan."
37 For the image of this entry in the manuscript of *Collection of Antiquities* at the National Palace Museum, Taipei, see http://painting.npm.gov.tw/Painting_Page.aspx?dep=P&PaintingId=675, accessed January 10, 2019.
38 For a historical survey of the epigraphic research on the stele, see Wu, "On Rubbings," 37–45.
39 See Huang Bosi, *Dongguan yulun*, 64b.
40 Huang Tingjian, "Shu Yijiao jing hou," in *Shangu tiba*, 4.36. *Stele for Song Kaifu* (dated 772) refers to the stele erected for the Tang statesman Song Jing (663–737), which survives in Xingtai, Hebei. See *SDZS* 10: plates 48–51, 161.
41 For Huang's association with Chan Buddhism, see Chen Zhiping, *Huang Tingjian shuxue yanjiu*, esp. 11–19 and 34–41. See also Nakata Yūjirō, "Kō Teiken no sanzen to bokuseki," in Nakata, *Kō Teiken*, 68–76.
42 The term *fa* would be adopted by Dong Qichang as the "period style" of the Tang and eventually became one of the most familiar notions in later writings about Chinese calligraphy. Dong Qichang, *Rongtai bieji*, 4.23b.
43 This genealogy of *bifa* is recorded in Zhang Yanyuan's "Chuanshou bifa renming," in *Fashu yaolu*, *ZGSHQS* 1:34–35.
44 Although mentioned in textual sources, few material examples of rubbing survive from the Tang dynasty, not to mention earlier times. An alleged Tang rubbing of *Inscriptions on the Hot Spring* (Wenquan ming) was found in Dunhuang, but the date is still debatable. For the origin of rubbings, see Starr, *Black Tigers*, 8–24.
45 Chunhua (r. 990–94) is the reign title of Emperor Taizong of the Song and the *bige* is the palace institute for archives that include calligraphy works. See McNair, "The Engraved Model-Letters Compendia of the Song Dynasty." For the collecting of calligraphy in early Song, see also Ebrey, *Accumulating Culture*, 204–56.
46 McNair, "The Engraved Model-Letters Compendia of the Song Dynasty," 218
47 See Egan, "To Count Grains of Sand on the Ocean Floor." For a study of Huang Tingjian's poetry in relation to the new print culture, see Wang, *Ten Thousand Scrolls*, 173–94.
48 Tuotuo, *Song shi*, 319.10375.
49 Ouyang Xiu, "Xue shu wei le" (Enjoyment of learning calligraphy), in *Ouyang Xiu quanji*, 130.1977.
50 For a discussion of Cai Xiang's calligraphy, see Sturman, *Mi Fu*, 41–44.
51 McNair, "The Engraved Model-Letters Compendia of the Song Dynasty," 210. For a collection of the Song scholar's criticism toward the *Chunhua Model Letters*, see Shui Laiyou, *Chunhuage tie jishi*.
52 For the reception and criticism on *Preface to the Holy Teaching of Tripitaka of the Great Tang*, see Gao Mingyi, "Moluo de dianfan;" and Luo Feng, "Huairen ji Wang Xizhi Shengjiao xu bei."
53 The rise of Yan Zhenqing style in the Northern Song is discussed in McNair, *The Upright Brush*, 7–15.
54 For the Song scholars' effort of revising (or even remaking) the classical tradition, see Lu Huiwen, "Tang zhi Song de Liuchao shushiguan zhi bian."
55 See Shui Laiyou, *Songdai tiexue yanjiu*, 10–14. For an introduction to the debates on *Preface of Gathering of the Orchid Pavilion*, see Ledderose, *Mi Fu*, 19–24.
56 See Fong, "Northern Sung Calligraphy: The Picture of the Mind," in *Images of the Mind*, 74–91.
57 For a discussion of the term *yi*, see Sturman, *Mi Fu*, 21.

58 For a discussion of Mi Fu's calligraphic theory, see ibid., 150–72.
59 Huang Tingjian, "Ba yu Zhang Xizai shu juanwei," in *Shangu tiba,* 5.49. Susan Bush suggests that the phrase "*rushen*" in this passage is related to Chan practice. See Bush, *The Chinese Literati on Painting,* 50.
60 See the discussion of the term in Clunas, *Pictures and Visuality in Early Modern China,* 117–19.
61 For the Linji Chan notion of dharma eye, see Dumoulin, *Zen Buddhism,* 200.
62 See Huang Tingjian, "Ba Fatie" and "Ti jiangben Fatie," in *Shangu tiba,* 4.32–36. "Zi ping yuanyou jian zi," ibid., 5.48b–49a. For the Chan Buddhist origin of the term *yan* (eye), see Zhou Yukai, *Wenzichan yu Songdai shixue,* 114–15. In other contexts, Huang Tingjian replaces this Buddhist term with *yun,* or resonance, a term from traditional art criticism, and contrasts it with the term *su,* or vulgarity, which denotes a cliché or straightforward imitation. For a comprehensive study from this perspective, see Chen Zhiping, *Huang Tingjian shuxue yanjiu,* esp. 42–120.
63 See Ouyang Xiu, "Shigu wen," *Jigu lu bawei,* in *Ouyang Xiu quanji,* 134.2079; and Dong You, "Shigu wen bian," in *Guangchuan shuba,* 2.13–14.
64 Huang Tingjian, "Ba Zhaigong Xun suocang shike," in *Shangu tiba,* 4.39.
65 Huang's influence on calligraphy in the Zen community, however, can be seen only among his followers in Japan, in the works of the Zen monk-calligraphers from the twelfth to the sixteenth centuries (Fu, "Huang T'ing-Chien's Calligraphy and His Scroll for Chang Ta-T'ung," 242–43). In a completely different historical context, this association between the *Eulogy*'s calligraphy and Zen Buddhism was echoed by the monk, poet, and calligrapher Ryōkan (1758–1831) in his idiosyncratic calligraphy. See Morita Shiryū, "Eigakumei nōto," and Katō Kiichi, *Ryōkan's Calligraphy,* 3–12. This cross-cultural phenomenon awaits further analysis. For images of Ryōkan's works, see *SDZS* 23: plates 38–45.
66 *Sutra of Buddha's Bequeathed Teaching* (Fo yijiao jing) is another work later attributed to Wang Xizhi, but its authenticity has been widely challenged by Ouyang Xiu and other Song scholars. See Ouyang Xiu's comments on the work in *Ouyang Xiu quanji,* 2311.
67 Zhang Zhi (d. 192 CE) is the Eastern Han calligrapher who has been admired as the Sage of Cursive Calligraphy, though no reliable works survive.
68 Huang Tingjian, "Yi Youjun shu shuzhong zeng Qiu Shisi," in *Shangu shi jizhu,* 1212.
69 Huang Tingjian, "Ba Zhaigong Xun cang shike" in *Shangu tiba,* 4.40. A similar comment is also found in his colophon to a copy of *Essay on Yue Yi* (ibid., 4.32).
70 For the exchange of the two major culture figures, see Yang Qingcun, "Su Shi yu Huang Tingjian jiaoyou kaoshu."
71 Huang Tingjian, "Shu Wang Zhouyan Dongpo tie" (dated 1101), in *Shangu ji, Shangu waiji, Shangu bieji,* 12.9b, 657. For Su Shi's comment about large-size calligraphy, see Su Shi, "Ba Wang Jinqing suo cang Lianhua jing," in *Dongpo tiba,* 4.86.
72 Huang Tingjian, "Shuzeng Fuzhou Chen Jiyue," in *Shangu tiba,* 5.49.
73 These early legendary calligraphers are documented in Wei Heng's (d. 291 CE), "Momentum of Calligraphy of the Four Script Types" (Si ti shushi) (Fang Xuanling, *Jin shu,* 36.1064).
74 Wang Sengqian, "Cai gu lai neng shu ren ming," in *Fashu yaolu, ZGSHQS* 1: 33–34.
75 See Wang Xianzhi's biography in Fang Xuanling, *Jin shu,* 80.2105. The same biography reports that young Wang Xianzhi have once written characters as large as one *zhang* on a wall, which fascinated an audience of hundreds of people.
76 See a discussion of screen calligraphy in Shi Rui, "Sui Tang fashu pingfeng kao," especially 350–59.

77 For images of the screens, see "Bird-Feather Seal-Script Calligraphy Folding Screen, no. 1," Imperial Household Agency, accessed April 13, 2018, http://shosoin.kunaicho.go.jp/ja-JP/Treasure?id=0000020014.

78 For extensive research on the special script, see Rong Geng, "Feibai kao" (On flying-white), in *Songzhai shulin*, 189–234. See a study of Wu Zetian's calligraphy enterprise in Lee, *Empresses, Art, and Agency*, 70–76.

79 Li Bai, "Caoshu gexing," in *Li Bai ji jiaozhu*, 587–91. Although some scholars have challenged the authenticity of the poem, most agree that it is dated to the Tang and thus still reflects the influence of Huaisu's calligraphy. For historical accounts of Huaisu's popular calligraphy screen, see Shi Zhongping, "Tang dai pingfeng shufa xiaokao." For a contextual study of the cursive calligraphy tradition, see Lu, "Wild Cursive Calligraphy, Poetry, and Chan Monks in the Tenth Century."

80 For Emperor Taizong's calligraphy, see Huang Xiuzhu, "Yi shu zhi zhi yu zuzong zhi fa," 31–35.

81 An example of such a screen can be found in a waterside wine shop in the lower left corner of the tenth-century landscape masterpiece *A Solitary Temple amid Clearing Peaks*, Nelson-Atkins Museum of Art, Kansas City, accessed January 10, 2019, https://art.nelson-atkins.org/objects/641/a-solitary-temple-amid-clearing-peaks.

82 He Yanquan studies the fashion of writing large calligraphy from a material perspective; see He Yanquan, "Bei Song maobi fazhan yu shufa chicun de guanxi."

83 Fu, "Huang T'ing-Chien's Calligraphy and His Scroll for Chang Ta-T'ung," 229–33. A work attributed to Huang Tingjian that demonstrates a more striking similar style is *Poems on Visiting the Qingyuan Mountain* (You Qingyuanshan shi, dated 1083). The calligraphy is said to have been carved into stone in 1101 at the sacred mountain for Chan Buddhism in Jiangxi. The inscription has been long lost and is known only through later rubbings. It is unclear, however, how much the existing rubbing reflects the original work by Huang Tingjian. Some characters appear almost identical to those in the *Eulogy*—it is not impossible that someone took characters from the latter and forged the entire work. For an introduction and images of the work, see Shanghai Tushuguan, *Huang Tingjian Qingyuanshan shi keshi*.

84 Fu, "Huang T'ing-Chien's Calligraphy and His Scroll for Chang Ta-T'ung," 224.

85 See Huang Tingjian, "Ziping yuanyou jian zi," in *Shangu tiba*, 5.49.

86 This feature in Huang Tingjian's brushwork was first pointed out by Kang Youwei (*Guang Yizhou shuang ji*, 859) and discussed in Fu, "Huang T'ing-Chien's Calligraphy," 228–29. See also Fong, *Images of the Mind*, 78–80.

87 The original Yishan stele, erected in 219 BCE, is long gone. The Song copy was made by Xu Xuan (916–991), the early Song court calligrapher, and was carved into stone in 993. More replicas have since been produced. For a recent study of the Yishan stele, see Zhang Tao, "Yishan keshi kaolüe." For the content of the original stele and its historical context, see Kern, *The Stele Inscriptions of Ch'in Shih-huang*, 10–15, 106–18.

88 Ouyang Xiu, "Qin Yishan keshi," in *Ouyang Xiu quanji*, 134.2083.

89 For an analysis of Yan Zhenqing's calligraphic style, see McNair, *The Upright Brush*, 118–20.

90 Ouyang Xiu, *Ouyang Xiu quanji*, 140.2243. Yan's robust standard script provided an alternative to the style of Wang Xizhi that had been promoted by the early Song imperial court through the publication of model letters. See McNair, *The Upright Brush*, 120–39. The socio-political context of this attitude has been reviewed in Egan, "Ou-yang Hsiu and Su Shih on Calligraphy." The Northern Song and the Southern Song calligraphers' responses to the Yan Zhenqing tradition is discussed in Sturman, *Mi Fu*, 18–53.

91 McNair, *The Upright Brush*, 53–59. Although Huang Tingjian studied Yan Zhenqing's style closely, it was not until 1104 that he finally got a chance to visit the *Hymn* inscription on site. He left a poem, which was inscribed later right next to *Hymn*, to lament the tragic historical episodes in *Hymn* but, curiously enough, did not comment on the calligraphy at all. Huang Tingjian, "Shu moyabei hou," in *Shangu ji, Shangu waiji, Shangu bieji*, 8.9b, 63. For a translation, see McNair, ibid., 52. The rubbing of the poem was published in Nakata Yūjirō, *Kō Teiken*, vol. 2, 168.

92 A recent study on *Hymn to the Revival of the Great Tang Dynasty* suggests that the unusual layout may imply a criticism to the emperor. See Deng Xiaojun, "Yuan Jie zhuan Yan Zhenqing shu Da Tang zhongxing song kaoshi."

93 Huang Tingjian, "Ti Yi he ming ba hou," *Shangu tiba*, 4.32. The "dragon-claw writing" script is mentioned and attributed to Wang Xizhi in a late Tang source, which states that "Youjun was once drunk and wrote a few characters. The strokes resemble [a] dragon claw. Then there was dragon-claw writing" (Li Chuo, *Shangshu gushi*, 1.13b). The script is also listed in "Wushiliu zhong shu bing xu" (Fifty-six script types with a preface), which, although attributed to Tang scholar Wei Xu (dates unknown), is perhaps a much later source. For the text, see Huadong Shifan Daxue Guji Zhengli Yanjiushi, *Lidai shufa lunwenxuan*, 305.

94 Huang Tingjian, "Ti Yan Lugong tie," in *Shangu ji, Shangu waiji, Shangu bieji*, 28.16a, 297.

95 Huang Tingjian, "Ba Hong Jufu zhu jia shu," ibid., 23a, 300.

96 Ibid.

97 An exception might be Li Gonglin (ca. 1042–1106). Li's calligraphic style, as Wen Fong and other scholars note, shows features of ancient inscriptions, probably from Li's collection of bronze vessels. See Fong, *Beyond Representation*, 139. Hui-liang Chu argues that Li also studied calligraphic style of Han dynasty steles (Chu Hui-liang, "The Calligraphy of Li Kung-lin in the Classic of Filial Piety," especially 58–62).

98 The beginning entries of *Hanyue mingyan* (Famous sayings of the Haiyue [studio]), a collection of Mi's calligraphy criticism, are all dedicated to large-size calligraphy. See Mi Fu, *Haiyue mingyan*, *ZGSHQS* 1:976–77.

99 According to local gazetteers, besides the *Eulogy*, there are only two surviving inscriptions on Jiaoshan arguably predating the Song inscriptions. One is an excerpt from the *Diamond Sutra*, which is believed to have been carved by a Tang monk. The other, which drew attention from the Song scholars, is a poem by a certain Wang Zan (ca. seventh century), a local official in Zhenjiang in the Tang dynasty. The poem inscription, according to many eyewitnesses, was carved alongside the *Eulogy* with a similar calligraphy style. This inscription was reportedly still extant yet badly worn in the eighteenth century. It was moved out of the water with the fragments of the *Eulogy* and lost soon after that. Accounts of these inscriptions can be found in Liu Mingfang, *Qianlong Jiaoshan zhi*, 5.10b.

100 The early *timing* inscriptions in the Tang dynasty, mainly known through textual sources, seemed written in ink. The most famous example is *Timing Inscriptions at the Great Geese Pagoda* (Yanta timing), Tang visitors' ink-written inscriptions on the famous pagoda in Xi'an, which was reportedly discovered in the early twelfth century. Perhaps partly due to the rising *timing* fashion, in the year of 1119, a local official had the ink traces carved into stone, and rubbings were made and widely circulated. See Li Yumin, "Yan ta timing yanjiu." For a study of the origin of *timing* as a literary genre, see Wang Xiaoli, "Songdai timing yu timingji kaolun," esp. 70–71. Another famous site of *timing* is the Dragon Hidden Cave (Longyindong) in Guilin, Guangxi, where more than a hundred inscriptions are left from the Song dynasty. See Guilin Shi Wenwu Guanli Weiyuanhui, *Guilin shike*.

101 Richard E. Strassberg has discussed the phenomena in his study of Chinese travel writing, *Inscribed Landscape*, 5–7.
102 For the historical events and the people, including the Buddhist monk Master Yuan of Jiaoshan, see Yu Beishan, *Lu You nianpu*, 124–25.
103 See a survey of Lu You's extant works of calligraphy in Liu Zhengcheng, ed., *Zhongguo shufa quanji* 40: 86–141.
104 For an account of the history, see Twitchett and Smith, *The Cambridge History of China*, vol. 5, part 1, *The Sung Dynasty and its Precursors, 907-1279*, 713–20. For a biography of Lu You and his poetry, see Duke, *Lu You*, esp. chapters 1 and 3.
105 Zhao Yanwei, *Yunlu manchao*, 2.26.
106 See a study of Zhao Yanwei's career by Fu Genqing, "Zhao Yanwei shengping kaosuo."
107 For Emperor Gaozong's interest in calligraphy and cultural policy, see Murray, "The Role of Art in the Southern Sung Dynastic Revival"; and *Ma Hezhi and the Illustration of the Book of Odes*, chapter 2.
108 See Wu Yun, *Tongzhi Jiaoshan zhi*, 1.14b.
109 For a general discussion of the replication of steles, see Ye Changchi and Ke Changsi, *Yu shi, Yu shi yitong ping*, 539–45.
110 Some scholars believe that the replica might be as it is and the rest was never carved. Luo Yonglai, *Yi he ming yanjiu*, 22–30.
111 "Guzhou Ma Ziyan ti," cited in Wang Shihong, *Yi he ming kao*, 16b–17a.
112 It is recorded as *Fuzhi hou shike linben* (the engraved replica behind the prefecture building) in Yu Xilu, *Zhishun Zhenjiang zhi*, 21.9b.
113 See Liu Changshi, *Lupu biji*, 45.
114 The transcription, later known as the "Jinshan version," was recorded in Dong You's note "Yi he ming hou" in *Guangchuan shuba*, 6.78a–79a. According to Dong, the inscription was found by a local scholar Diao Yue (994–1077) on the back of a sheet of sutra copy in the nearby Jinshan Temple. Despite being a possible Tang transcription, Dong argues, the text by no means reflects the original inscription.

CHAPTER 3: REMAKING THE MODEL

1 Mote, "A Millennium of Chinese Urban History," 51.
2 A long entry on the *Eulogy* is found in a revised local gazetteer *Zhishun Zhenjian zhi*, published in 1332. It preserves much otherwise-lost information but mentions no contemporary visits or studies. See Yu Xilu, *Zhishun Zhenjian zhi*, 21.5a–7b.
3 See Du Mu, "You Jiaoshan ji," in Wu Yun, *Tongzhi Jiaoshan zhi*, 13.1a–2b.
4 Here, Du Mu must have put a wrong date for Lu You's inscription, which is dated 1165 instead.
5 Cited in Gu Yuanqing, *Yi he ming kao*, 8b–9a. Gu indicates that the source was Du Mu's writing collection *Jinxie linlang*, but the entry is not found in the current edition of Du's book, which is published before 1517 (Li Yuqi, "Jinxie linlang chengshu niandai ji banben kao"). The entry was probably supposed to be published in an enlarged edition later. Gu may have asked for his teacher's permission to publish the entry in his own book, which came out the year after Du Mu's "rediscovery" of the stone.
6 For Gu Yuanqing's career, see Zhong Laiyin and Zhu Yaping, "Gu Yuanqian yanjiu."
7 See the introduction to the volume in Yongrong, *Siku quanshu zongmu*, 87.747a–b.
8 This scholarly trend has been pointed out by Zhu Jianxin, *Jinshixue*, 29–33. See also discussion of a "consumerist approach" to the antique in Craig Clunas, *Superfluous Things*, 97–98. For a critical review of the general background of the evidential scholarship in the

Ming, see Lin Qingzhang, *Mingdai kaojuxue yanjiu*. This casual attitude toward ancient remains, as well as its manifestation in everyday lifestyle, had been identified in Southern Song writings. See Chen Fangmei, *Qingtongqi yu Song dai wenhuashi*, 121–25.

9 Wang Shizhen, "Yi he ming," in *Yanzhou sibu gao*, 134.20a.

10 Ibid.

11 Wang Shizhen, "Yu Shen Jiaze shu," in *Yanzhou sibu gao*, 117.17b.

12 Wang Shizhen's trip was documented in a series of journals under the title "Jiang xing ji shi" (Records on traveling along the Yangzi River), in *Yanzhou sibu gao*, 78.2b.

13 Ibid.

14 For an analysis of the term *qi* in late Ming culture and calligraphy, see Bai, *Fu Shan's World*, 10–20.

15 Wang Zongni and Cheng Yingqu were book editors and publishers. Wang is known for editing and republishing *Graded Compendium of Tang poetry* (Tangshi pinhui, originally published 1393), a popular book on Tang poems at the time. Mao Zhen, a native of Zhenjiang, was known as a writer of popular *sanqu* songs. Chen Yangchan might be the only *jinshi* degree holder (1574) among the party.

16 For a discussion of the culture of pleasure seeking in the late Ming, see Brook, *The Confusions of Pleasure*; and Li, "The Late Ming Courtesan."

17 For the history and character of tourism in the late Ming, see Wu Renshu, *Pinwei shehua*, 169–204.

18 Wang Shi, *Shiyu huapu*, 367–68. For a historical survey and discussion of the mixed genre "painting manuals," see Park, *Art by the Book*, 30–83.

19 For the poem and its pictorialization in later visual culture, especially in woodblock prints, see Lin Li-chiang, "You shanggan erzhi fengyue."

20 See a contextual study of the book in Lin, "A Study of the *Xinjuan Hainei qiguan*."

21 Yang Erzeng, *Xinjuan Hainei qiguan*, 2.28a.

22 Ibid., 2.28a–b.

23 Examples of such works can be found in Xu Wenmei, *Hechu shi Penglai*, a recent exhibition catalogue of immortal mountain paintings in the collection of National Palace Museum.

24 For the cultural turn in the late Ming, see Rawski, "Economic and Social Foundations of Late Imperial Culture." Urbanization of Jiangnan cities, in particular Nanjing, in the late Ming is discussed in Fei, *Negotiating Urban Space*.

25 See essays in Brokaw and Chow, *Printing and Book Culture in Late Imperial China*; and Ōki Yasushi, "Minmatsu konan ni okeru shuppan bunka no kenkyu." For studies of the economic aspect of the publishing industry, see Chow, *Publishing, Culture, and Power in Early Modern China*. For works addressing publishing from other cultural perspectives, see Dorothy Ko's first chapter in *Teachers of the Inner Chambers*; Lin, "The Proliferation of Images"; Hegel, *Reading Illustrated Fiction in Late Imperial China*; and Chia, *Printing for Profits*, chapter 5.

26 The incorporation of reproduced handwriting in the prefaces to books is the subject of Hung-lam Chu, "Calligraphy's New Importance in Later Ming Printing." The phenomenon begins in publishing at least in the middle of the Southern Song dynasty. See Xu Zheying, "Gushu zhong de tuijianwen"; and Liu Yuantang, "Songdai banke shufa yanjiu," especially 91–106. A more comprehensive survey of printed calligraphy in books can be found in Qi Xiaochun, *Guji banke shuji lishuo*.

27 Wang Cheng-hua, "Shenghuo, zhishi, yu wenhua shangpin." Such a publication can be traced to *Comprehensive Records of Assorted Affairs* (Shilin guangji, earliest extant edition published 1328–32), if not earlier. For the origins of vernacular *leishu*, see Sakai

Tadao, *Chūgoku nichiyō ruishoshi no kenkyū*, especially 53–91. Focusing on the inclusion of Mongol scripts, Shane McCausland discusses the calligraphy component in *Shilin guangji* (McCausland, *The Mongol Century*, 201–5).

28 Wang Cheng-hua, "Shenghuo, zhishi, yu wenhua shangpin," 31–32.

29 For a discussion of *Painting Manual of the Gu Family*, see Clunas, *Pictures and Visuality in Early Modern China*, 138–48. The prevailing poem-painting album and its relationship to collecting culture in mid-Ming is discussed in Liu, "Collecting the Here and Now."

30 Wang Shi, *Shiyu huapu*, 312.

31 Ibid., 478.

32 Huang Mianzhong, "Shiyu huapu ba," in Wang Shi, *Shiyu huapu*, 291.

33 See ibid., 308 and 434.

34 The same issue may be raised for the publisher of *Painting Manual of the Gu Family*, who also claimed to have recruited celebrities to transcribe texts. Similar phenomena were found in printed books, which often began with alleged prefaces by celebrities. See Hung-lam Chu's discussion of "Wang Shizhen" calligraphy (Chu, "Calligraphy's New Importance in Later Ming Printing," 176–77).

35 For an example, see the "Eight Views of Xiao and Xiang Rivers" series in Yang Erzeng, *Xinjuan Hainei qiguan*, 8.

36 Shi Zhangyan, "Tangshi huapu yanjiu."

37 Huang Fengchi, *Tang Liuru huapu*, in Wu Shuping, *Zhongguo lidai huapu huibian* 1:24.

38 Clunas's comments are on *Painting Manual of the Gu Family*. See Clunas, *Pictures and Visuality in Early Modern China*, 138.

39 Ibid., 134–48.

40 Roughly 10 percent of the male population in late Ming may have had a high level of educational achievement. In the Jiangnan region, this number was probably higher. See Peterson, "Confucian Learning in Late Ming Thought," 715. In contrast, the passing rate of civil examination at the provincial level in Nanjing dropped to as low as 2.4 percent in 1603 (Wu Renshu, *Pinwei shehua*, 57). For a general discussion of social classes in the late Ming, see Johnson, "Communication, Class, and Consciousness in Late Imperial China."

41 For the contemporary book industry in Nanjing, see Chia, "Of Three Mountains Street."

42 The painting scroll illustrated in figure 3.6 itself was very likely made for the low-end customers at the time and probably cost no more than one *tael*. See Wang Cheng-hua, "Guoyan fanhua," 432–33.

43 Dong Qichang, "Preface to *Model Letters of the Jade Smoke Hall*," cited in Rong Geng, *Congtie mu*, 309–10.

44 For the content of the collection, see ibid., 297–311. Another large volume of *Model Letters of the Late Fragrance Hall* (Wanxiangtang fatie) in thirty volumes and all Su Shi calligraphy, would be published in 1616 by Chen Jiru (1558–1639), one of Dong's close friends.

45 See Xue, "From Dots and Strokes to Lines."

46 For a survey of model-letters production in the Ming dynasty, see Huang Dun, *Zhongguo shufa shi: Yuan Ming juan*, 451–72; Wang Jingxian, "Mingdai congtie zongshu." And a more comprehensive study in Yu Bo, *Mingdai ketie yanjiu*. Craig Clunas analyzes the cultural politics of major "official compendia" in *Screen of Kings*, 63–99.

47 Despite limited sources, we know that a similar phenomenon had been observed in the Southern Song, when the publication of model letters was part of the publishing industry. See Mo Jialiang, "Nan Song ketie wenhua guankui," 69–76.

48 For images of *Model Letters of the True Appreciation Studio*, see Qi Gong, *Zhongguo fatie quanji*, 13.
49 Qi Gong, *Zhongguo fatie quanji* 13:49–53.
50 The publication of model letters as "cultural capital" is discussed in Fang Bo, "Wenhua ziben yu wenhua shangpin."
51 For the records of sales of calligraphic compendia in the Song dynasty, see Shui Laiyou, *Songdai tiexue yanjiu*, 31–32. For records of prices of calligraphic compendia in the late Ming, see Ye Kangning, *Fengya zhihao*, 182–94.
52 Shi Anchang, "Hua Xia yu *Zhenshangzhai tie*," in *Shanben beitie lunji*, 230–39.
53 Gu Congyi's statement, dated 1568, is cited in Rong Geng, *Congtie mu*, 17.
54 For a study on the production of model letters and the prestige of the Wen family, see Masuda Tomoyuki, "Meidai ni ogeru hōjō no kangyō to Sushū Bunji yichizoku."
55 For a historical study of the stone carver, see Cheng Zhangcan, *Shike kegong yanjiu*, 146–62.
56 For a recent study of *Model Letter of the Halting Clouds Studio*, see Zhou Daozhen, *Tingyunguan tie huikao*; and Guo Weiqi, *Tingyun mokai*, 57–97.
57 Rong Geng, *Congtie mu*, 249–53.
58 Clunas, *Fruitful Sites*, 104–36.
59 For a recent study of Wen Chu and the Zhao family, as well as the latter's economic activities, see Lee, "For 'Co-Branding' a *Cainü* and a Garden."
60 At the time, a half *tael* of silver could buy 1 *dan* (about 133 pounds) of rice. For a discussion of the prices of books and other goods in the late Ming, see Chow, *Publishing, Culture, and Power in Early Modern China*, 38–56, 255–63.
61 Cited in Rong Geng, *Congtie mu*, 242–44.
62 Shen Jin, "Mingdai fangke tushu zhi liutong yu jiage."
63 See Wu, "On Rubbings," 30.
64 Benjamin, "The Work of Art in the Age of Mechanical Reproduction," 220.
65 Harrist, "Copies, All the Way Down," especially 181–82.
66 Wang Kentang, *Yugangzhai bichen*, 4.33a.
67 The anecdote is recorded in Shen Defu, *Wanli yehuo bian*, 26.658. The work mentioned in the anecdote is a copy of Daoist sutra *Inner Landscape of the Yellow Court* (Huangting neijing jing), which is reproduced in *Model Letters of the Frolicking Geese Hall*. The original is lost, however. Amy McNair also notes that a Yan Zhenqing's letter reproduced in *Frolicking Geese* appears to be a freehand copy (McNair, "Letters as Calligraphy Exemplars," especially 78–81).
68 For a study of extant copies of *Model Letters of the Frolicking Geese Hall*, see Yin Yimei, "Xihongtang fashu kaolüe."
69 For the transmission history of *Poems on Cold Food Festival in Huangzhou*, see Fu Shen, "Tianxia diyi Su Dongpo." Dong actually wrote a colophon on the scroll: "I have had it copied into my *Frolicking Geese*." For a study of Han family's collection, see Han Jin, "Nanyang shuhua biao kaobian."
70 Zhao Yiguang, *Hanshan zhoutan*, 2.30b.
71 For a close study of its content, see Qi Gong, "Cong Xihongtang tie kan Dong Qichang dui fashu de jianding." For a survey of Dong's model-letters production, see Wang Qingzheng, "Dong Qichang fashu ketie jianshu."
72 See a publisher's note in a new edition of *Frolicking Geese*, cited in Rong Geng, *Congtie mu*, 269.
73 See Yin Yimei, "Xihongtang fashu kaolüe," 220.

74 A later manifestation of the tension between printed images and rubbings is discussed in Tseng, "Between Printing and Rubbing."

75 For a recent discussion of the late Ming cultural distinctions, see Park, *Art by the Book*, 117–19.

76 An example is the compilation of *Model Letters of Clear Mountains Hall* (Qingshantang fatie), a collection that Xu Xiake (1587–1641), the noted travel writer, began to put together in 1624 in celebration of his mother's eightieth birthday. All works in the final product, dating from 1370 to 1629, are from the family collection and dedicated to family members over the generations. For an introduction to the compendium, see Wang Xiaoling, "Qingshantang fatie yu Xu shi jiazu shangyong yaji huodong."

77 Guoli Gugong Bowuyuan Bianji Weiyuanhui, *Gugong lidai fashu quanji*, 27:41.

78 The only source about Chen Huan is found in a short of entry in the local gazetteer (Zhou Guangye, *Haichang beizhi*, 29.9b). For a recent study of the calligraphy of the Chen family, see Li Hui, "Ming mo Qing chu Haining Chen shi jiazu shufa yanjiu."

79 It is reported that Dong Qichang served as a private tutor in Chen's house before starting his successful official career (See Chen Qiyuan, *Yongxianzhai biji*, 10–11). It is known that Chen Huan had a vast collection of Dong's calligraphy. A few years after the publication of *Model Letters of the Jade Smoke Hall*, Chen Huan published *Model Letters of Dong (Qichang) at the Jade Smoke Hall* (Yuyantang Dong tie, 1616–1630), an exclusive collection of Dong Qichang's calligraphy written over the years from 1589 to 1630 (See Rong Geng, *Congtie mu*, 1249–51; and Wang Qingzheng, "Dong Qichang fashu ketie jianshu," 339). And certainly more of Dong's works would be published by Chen's house later, when the demand for Dong's calligraphy model was even higher.

80 Other major sources of *Model Letters of the Jade Smoke Hall* include earlier model letters such as *Model Letters of the Treasuring Jin Studio* (Baojinzhai fatie) and *Model Letters of the Clarity and Purity Hall* (Chengqingtang tie). See Nakata Yūjirō, "Min Shin jidai no shūjō," in Nakata, *Shinkashitsu shū*, 4:330.

81 See "Cheng Kangzhuang [1613–1679] chongke Yuyantang ben" in Wu Yun, *Tongzhi Jiaoshan zhi*, 5.8a-b. Another copy was carved into stone in 1665 by Qian Sheng (dates unknown), who claimed that the original was a "thousand year old" rubbing owned by Gu Chen (1607–1674), a noted collector in Wuxi. It turns out to be a rubbing from the *Alternative Carving at the Grand View Pavilion* (ibid., 5.8b–10a).

82 For imported calligraphic model letters from China, including *Frolicking Geese Hall* and *Jade Smoke*, in Edo Japan, see Ōba Osamu, *Edo jidai ni okeru Chūgoku bunka juyō no kenkyū*, 406–20; and Ma Chengfen, *Tōsen hōjō no kenkyū*. It might have been through these model letters that knowledge of the *Eulogy* reached Ryōkan and other Edo calligraphers.

83 A series of works by Dong Qichang, mounted as a scroll titled "Running Calligraphy after *Jade Smoke Model Letters*" (Xingshu lin Yuyangtang tie, 1612), is in the Capital Museum of Beijing (Zhongguo Gudai Shuhua Jiandingzu, *Zhongguo gudai shuhua tumu* 1:393, jing 5–230). Dong is also known to have used *Frolicking Geese* often as reference. See a collection of such colophons in Yin Yimei, "Xihongtang fashu kaolüe," 221–23.

84 Wang Shizhen, *Yanzhou sibu gao*, 134.19a–b. The "neighbor lady" refers to a well-known story in *Zhuangzi* about an ugly woman who tried to imitate the manner of the beautiful Xi Shi (ca. 503–ca. 473 BCE) next door and only made her own appearance worse.

85 See an account of Zhao's life and his role in the history of calligraphy in McCausland, *Zhao Mengfu*, 11–112.

86 For analysis of Wang's archaism, see Hammond, "Beyond Archaism."

87 For a comprehensive study of Wang's calligraphic theory, see Xiong Peijun, "Wang Shizhen shulun yanjiu," especially 77–82.

88 The quotation is not accurate. Dong must have cited Huang Tingjian's poem from memory. See chapter 2 for Huang Tingjian's original text, which mentions *Essay on Yue Yi* as the model for small-character calligraphy. Dong's additional comments on Huang Tingjian's calligraphy and the latter's connection to the *Eulogy* can be found in Huang Dun, *Dong Qichang shufa lunzhu*, 283–88.

89 Dong Qichang, *Huachanshi suibi*, *ZGSHQS* 3:1008.

90 Reprinted in Lu Jiaming, *Rong Geng cangtie* 14, no. 102.

91 For more examples, see Chu Hui-liang, *Dong Qichang fashu tezhan yanjiu tulu*, 29. For a close examination of the phenomenon, see Tseng Lan-ying, "Dong Qichang de shuxue lilun yu shijian." A similar expression appears in his inscription on a painting: "Once I borrowed Ni Yuanzhen's [Ni Zan] *Hills and Valleys of Shanyin* to study, but did not have time to make a sketch copy. Now I try to make it with the [model] of Juran's *Snow Clearing over the Mountain Passes*." (Fong, "Tung Ch'i-Ch'ang and Artistic Renewal," 53). The painting mentioned here is in the National Palace Museum, Taipei.

92 For an analysis of Dong's *fang* manner, see James Cahill, *The Compelling Image: Nature and Style in Seventeenth-Century Chinese Painting*, 36–69. For a recent case study, see Huang Dun, "Mingdai fangshu chuangzuo moshi de chuxian."

93 See Dong Qichang, *Huachanshi suibi*, *ZGSHQS*, 3:1002b.

94 Ho and Smith, *The Century of Tung Ch'i-Ch'ang*, 2:32–34, 213–17. Another similar large-character scroll by Dong Qichang is "Inscription for the Yanran Mountain" (Yanranshan ming), dated 1611, in the Capital Museum, Beijing (Li Wenqi, "Dong Qichang Yanranshan ming qianlun").

95 See the website for the Taiwan Digital Archives, accessed April 1, 2017, http://catalog.digitalarchives.tw/item/00/11/0c/b2.html. The text is a transcription of an excerpt from the biography of the renowned Han dynasty Confucius scholar Ni Kuan (d. 103 BCE) in Ban Gu, *Han shu*, 58.2633–34.

96 For the publication of the imperial model-letters, see *Sanxitang fatie*, 1–5.

97 Ibid., 2206.

98 An active member of the avant-garde circle, Dong Qichang also participated in the debate on cultural revivalism. This intellectual background is discussed in Ho, "Tung Ch'i-Ch'ang's New Orthodoxy and the Southern School Theory." For a critical review of Yuan Hongdao, see Chaves, "The Panoply of Images."

99 Bai, *Fu Shan's World*, 44–50.

100 For a discussion of Dong's approaches, see Chu Hui-liang, "Lingu zhi xinlu." See also Bai, *Fu Shan's World*, 35–40.

CONCLUSION

1 Zhang Chao, *Yi he ming bian*, 2a–b.

2 Ibid., 10a.

3 Zhang Chao's description was confirmed by Yang Bin (1650–1720), another antiquarian scholar and calligrapher who visited the same site in 1704 and made rubbings from the stones. See Yang Bin, *Dapiao oubi*, 456.

4 The social and intellectual foundation of this phenomenon has been well studied by Benjamin Elman, among other scholars. See Elman, *From Philosophy to Philology*, especially 177–98.

5 Bai, *Fu Shan's World*, 153–208, especially 172–84, on the scholarly enthusiasm for visiting steles. See also a discussion of the representation of visiting steles in painting in von Spee, "Visiting Steles." Lilian Lan-ying Tseng, in "Between Printing and Rubbing," discusses a renewed attention to materiality in publication of rubbings. See also Lu Huiwen's study of a later conjunction of stele study and the model-letters tradition in "Bei yu tie de jiaohui." For a general historical review, see also Brown, *Pastimes*, 24–32.

6 Zhang Chao, *Yi he ming bian*, 2a–b.

7 Chen Pengnian, "Record of Re-erecting the Stele *Eulogy for Burying a Crane* (Chongli Yi he ming beiji), in Wu Yun, *Tongzhi Jiaoshan zhi*, 5.43a–44b. The stele is still in the Jiaoshan Stone Inscription Museum.

8 Wang Shihong, *Yi he ming kao*, 1b.

9 Wu Yun, *Tongzhi Jiaoshan zhi*, 5.43a–44b.

10 See reports of damage in Weng Fanggang, *Yi he ming kaobu*, 12b.

11 My major references in judging the dates of these rubbings include Weng Fanggang, *Yi he ming kaobu*; Wang Zhuanghong, *Zengbu Jiaobei suibi*, 217–21; Ma Ziyun and Shi Anchang, *Beitie jianding*, 134–36; Zhang Yansheng, *Shanben beitie lu*, 58; Weng Kaiyun, "Yi he ming Tan"; and Lu Zongrun, "Yi he ming jiaobu."

12 Wang Shu, *Zhuyun tiba*, 2.32a.

13 Qianlong's southern inspection and the visual products around it can be found in numerous studies. See an introduction in Elliott, *Emperor Qianlong*, 78–85.

14 For the visit of the emperor, see Wu Yun, *Tongzhi Jiaoshan zhi*, 5.1a.

15 According to *Tongzhi Jiaoshan zhi*, the stele was covered by a new pavilion next to the Jiao Guang Shrine (ibid., 0.14a–15a).

16 For image of the jade desk screen, see SINA Auction Record Database, accessed April 15, 2019, http://data.collection.sina.com.cn/index.php?p=data&s=default&a=item&id=186791. The inscription in figure 3.13, now found in the Jiaoshan Stone Inscription Museum, has been attributed to Qianlong's copy. As I demonstrated in the previous chapter, it is instead most likely a replica of the *Jade Smoke* edition.

17 Weng Fanggang, *Yi he ming kaobu*, 14b–15a.

18 See Qianshen Bai's discussion in *Fu Shan's World*, 167–71, 185–208. For Zheng Fu's calligraphy and the trend of epigraphic calligraphy in the Qing dynasty, see also Xue Longchun, *Zheng Fu yanjiu*, especially 107–50.

19 This phenomenon is discussed in Ledderose, "Aesthetic Appropriation of Ancient Calligraphy in Modern China."

20 Weng Fanggang, "Ziti kaoding jinshi tu hou," in *Fuchuzhai wenji*, 6.281.

21 For a general discussion of Weng Fanggang's calligraphic theory, see Zhu Youzhou, "Weng Fanggang de shuxue sixiang yanjiu." See also Liu Zhonghua, *Han Song zhijian: Weng Fanggang xueshu sixiang yanjiu*.

22 A recent comprehensive study of Ruan Yuan in English is found in Wei, *Ruan Yuan*, especially chapter 3 for Ruan's scholarly activities.

23 Ruan Yuan, "Nan bei shupai lun," in *Yanjingshi ji*, 591–96.

24 For a comprehensive study of Ruan's calligraphic theory, see Jin Dan, *Ruan Yuan shuxue yanjiu*, especially 121–38.

25 Ruan Yuan, "Beibei nantie lun," in *Yanjingshi ji*, 596–98.

26 Ruan's fascination with the *Eulogy* is not in question. When helping to build a famous library at Jiaoshan, he even catalogued the collection by using the text of the *Eulogy*. See Ruan Yuan, "Record of the Book Collection at Jiaoshan (Jiaoshan shuzang ji) in *Yanjingshi ji*, 618–19. For Ruan Yuan's study of inscriptions at Could Peak Mountain, see *Shanzuo jinshi zhi*, 9.1a–8b.

27 Bao Shichen, "Shu shu" (On calligraphy), in Huangdong Shifan Daxue Guji Zhengli Yanjiushi, *Lidai shufa lunwen xuan*, 649.
28 Bao Shichen, "Li xia bi tan," ibid., 651.
29 Bao Shichen, "Da Xizhai jiu wen," ibid., 664.
30 For an introduction to the large engraved *Diamond Sutra* in Mount Tai, see Harrist, *The Landscape of Words*, 174–75. And see also a recent study of the site in Wenzel, "Monumental Stone Sutra Carvings in China and Indian Pilgrim Sites."
31 The absence is unusual, considering that he was the disciple of Deng Shiru (1743–1805), one of the most noted specialists of seal-script calligraphy. For the latter and the revival of seal-script calligraphy in the Qing dynasty, see Ledderose, "Calligraphy at the Close of China's Empire"; and *Die Siegelschrift (Chuan-shu) in der Ch'ing-Zeit*.
32 For examples of Bao Shichen's calligraphic style, see *SDZS* 24: plates 36–39.
33 *Stele of the Huadu Temple* is also a topic of heated debate among rubbing scholars. See Zhong Wei, "Huadusi taming chuanshi cangben kao."
34 He Shaoji, *He Shaoji shiwenji*, 880-81. For Zhiyong's piece, see Qi Gong, "Shuo Qian zi wen"; and Liu Tao, "Liangchao de liang ben Qian zi wen ji shufa." For a study of "A Thousand-Character Text" in English, see Nugent, "Structured Gaps."
35 There was a long tradition of couplets as the major medium of calligraphy. For the cultural tradition of couplets, see Liu, "Calligraphic Couplets as Manifestations of Deities and Markers of Buildings." For a survey of the fashion of incorporating the text of *Eulogy for Burying a Crane* in collated couplets, see Wang Yaoyao, "Qingdai zhi minguo Yi he ming jilian yanjiu."
36 Yuan Jie, "Chaoyangyan ming," in *Yuan Cishan ji*, 6. For a survey of the historical site and *moya* inscriptions at Chaoyang Rock, see Zhang Jinghua, *Hunan Chaoyangyan shike kaoshi*.
37 For a review of the method, see Zhang Yingxiu, "He Shaoji shufa jiqi shuxue sixiang yanjiu," 73–77.
38 My following interpretation was inspired by Lothar Ledderose's discussion in "Aesthetic Appropriation of Ancient Calligraphy in Modern China."
39 Liu Zhengcheng, *Zhongguo shufa quanji* 71: plate 9.
40 For Zhao's stylistic change, see Zou Tao, "Zhao Zhiqian shufa pingzhuan."
41 Cited in Zou Tao, *Zhao Zhiqian nianpu*, 192.
42 For a recent study of Kang's calligraphy theory in relation to his political agenda, see Wong, *The Other Kang Youwei*, especially 16–35.
43 Kang Youwei, *Guang Yizhou shuangji*, 827. It is reported that there were as many as eighteen print runs in the seven years since the first publication of *Extended Paired Oars for the Boat of Art*. For the reception of Kang Youwei's book, see Wong, *The Other Kang Youwei*, 26–35.
44 See Kano Chiaki, *Kindai Chūgoku no shu bunka*, 194. For the history of Youzheng Shuju and its founder Di Baoxian (1872–1941), see Vinograd, "Patrimonies in Press."
45 Ledderose, "Aesthetic Appropriation of Ancient Calligraphy in Modern China," 242.
46 See a short biography of Kang Youwei in Lo, *Kang Yu-wei*, 13–17.
47 See the accounts of the disastrous events during the Taiping Rebellion (1850–64) in Chen Renyang, *Jiaoshan xuzhi*, 5.1a–5a.
48 For brief biographies of these two calligraphers, see entries no. 42 and 43 in Harrist and Fong, *The Embodied Image*, 202–4.
49 The rubbing mentioned in the colophon might be the one in the former Robert Hatfield Ellsworth collection. See An Siyuan, *An Siyuan cang shanben beitie xuan*, 80–82. For Duanfang's collecting activities, see Brown, *Pastimes*, 51–72.

50 The phenomenon may be compared to the "eight-brokens" painting that depicts a collage of fragmentary rubbings and ink-written works of calligraphy. See Berliner, "The 'Eight Brokens.'"

51 See examples in Zeng Yingsan, *Zeng Xi, Li Ruiqing, Zhang Daqian Yi he ming yaji.*

52 For more on Zhang Daqian's early career, see Fong, *Between Two Cultures*, 52–56, 178–80.

53 Another very similar album, dated January 11, 1959, was published in Zhang Daqian, *Daqian Jushi lin Yi he ming*. The colophon of the copy indicates that it was the sixth copy that Zhang made in the same day (ibid., 47)

54 Zhang adds a colophon, dated January 22, 1959, saying it was the third copy he made that day. See Zeng Yingsan, *Zeng Xi, Li Ruiqing, Zhang Daqian Yi he ming yaji*, 189.

55 Qi Gong, *Qi Gong yunyu ji*, 221.

56 For a recent collection of essays on this topic, see Wu Hung, *Reinventing the Past.*

57 For a review of the "culture fever" in late 1989s and 1990s, see Wang, *High Culture Fever.*

58 It is reported that an excavation in 1996 yielded two characters. For the excavation report, see Zhenjiang Bowuguan, "Zhenjiang Jiaoshan *Yi he ming* beike fajue jianbao." Four small fragments, carrying a few more characters, were discovered in 2009. See Ding Chao, "Yi he ming si kuai canshi chongjian tianri."

59 See CCTV's archived video clip, accessed July 9, 2018, http://news.cntv.cn/program/news20/20100604/103119.shtml.

60 A few days later, an essay questioning the program appeared in a state media. See Li Yun, "San wen Yi he ming zhi dalao."

61 See Zhenjiang Shi Minjian Wenyi Yanjiuhui, *Zhenjiang minjian gushi*, 15.

Bibliography

ABBREVIATIONS

CSJC	*Congshu jicheng chubian* 叢書集成初編. Beijing: Zhonghua Shuju, 1985–91.
CSJCXB	*Congshu jicheng xinbian* 叢書集成新編. Taipei: Xinwenfeng Chuban Gufen Youxian Gongsi, 1985.
DZ	*Daozang* 道藏. Beijing: Wenwu Chubanshe; Shanghai: Shanhai Shudian; Tianjin: Tianjin Guji Chubanshe, 1988.
SDZS	*Shodō zenshū* 書道全集. Tokyo: Heibonsha, 1957.
SKQS	*Yingyin Wenyuange Siku quanshu* 景印文淵閣四庫全書. Taipei: Taiwan Shangwu Yinshuguan, 1983.
SKSL	*Shike shiliao xinbian* 石刻史料新編. Taipei: Xinwenfeng Chuban Gufen Youxian Gongsi, 1982.
TSZ	*Taishō shinshū Daizōkyō* 大正新脩大藏經. Tokyo: Taishō Shinshū Daizōkyō Kankōkai, 1969.
XSKQS	*Xuxiu Siku quanshu* 續修四庫全書. Shanghai: Shanghai Guji Chubanshe, 2003.
ZGSHQS	Lu Fusheng 盧輔聖, ed. *Zhongguo shuhua quanshu* 中國書畫全書. Shanghai: Shanghai Shuhua Chubanshe, 1993–98.

SOURCES

An Siyuan [Robert Hatfield Ellsworth]. *An Siyuan cang shanben beitie xuan* 安思遠藏善本碑帖選. Beijing: Wenwu Chubanshe, 1996.

Armstrong, Edwards A. "The Crane Dance in East and West." *Antiquity* 17 (1943): 71–76.

Bai, Qianshen. *Fu Shan's World: The Transformation of Chinese Calligraphy in the Seventeenth Century*. Cambridge, MA: Harvard University Asia Center, 2003.

Ban Gu 班固. *Han shu* 漢書. Beijing: Zhonghua Shuju, 1995.

Benjamin, Walter. "The Work of Art in the Age of Mechanical Reproduction." In *Illuminations*, 217–52. New York: Harcourt, Brace & World, 1968.

Berliner, Nancy. "The 'Eight Brokens': Chinese Trompe-l'oeil Painting." *Orientations* 23, no. 2 (1992): 61–70.

Bian Xiaoxuan 卞孝萱. *Dongqing shuwu biji* 冬青書屋筆記. Shanghai: Dongfang Chuban Zhongxin, 1999.

Bokenkamp, Stephen R. "Answering a Summons." In *Religions of China in Practice*, edited by Donald S. Lopez, 188–202. Princeton: Princeton University Press, 1996.

Bol, Peter. *"This Culture of Ours": Intellectual Transitions in T'ang and Sung China*. Stanford: Stanford University Press, 1992.

Brashier, Kenneth E. "Text and Ritual in Early Chinese Stelae." In *Text and Ritual in Early China*, edited by Martin Kern, 249–84. Seattle: University of Washington Press, 2005.

Brokaw, Cynthia J, and Kai-wing Chow, eds. *Printing and Book Culture in Late Imperial China*. Berkeley: University of California Press, 2005.

Brook, Timothy. *The Confusions of Pleasure: Commerce and Culture in Ming China*. Berkeley: University of California Press, 1998.

Brown, Shana J. *Pastimes: From Art and Antiquarianism to Modern Chinese Historiography*. Honolulu: University of Hawai'i Press, 2011.

Bush, Susan. *The Chinese Literati on Painting: Su Shih (1037–1101) to Tung Ch'i-Ch'ang (1555–1636)*. Cambridge, MA: Harvard University Press, 1971.

———. "Floral Motifs and Vine Scrolls in Chinese Art of the Late Fifth to Early Sixth Centuries A.D." *Artibus Asiae* 38, no. 1 (1976): 49–83.

Cahill, James. *The Compelling Image: Nature and Style in Seventeenth-Century Chinese Painting*. Cambridge, MA: Harvard University Press, 1982.

Campany, Robert F. *Strange Writing: Anomaly Accounts in Early Medieval China*. Albany: State University of New York Press, 1996.

Cao Zhi 曹植. *Cao Zhi ji jiaozhu* 曹植集校注. Annotated by Zhao Youwen 趙幼文. Beijing: Renmin Wenxue Chubanshe, 1984.

Chaves, Jonathan. "The Panoply of Images: A Reconsideration of the Literary Theory of the Kung-an School." In *Theories of the Arts in China*, edited by Susan Bush and Christian Murck, 341–64. Princeton: Princeton University Press, 1983.

Chen Dengyuan 陳登原. *Gujin dianji jusan kao* 古今典籍聚散攷. Shanghai: Shangwu Yinshuguan, 1936.

Chen Fangmei 陳芳妹. "Song guqiwuxue de xingqi yu song fanggu tongqi" 宋古器物學的興起與宋仿古銅器. *Guoli Taiwan Daxue meishushi yanjiu jikan* 國立台灣大學美術史研究集刊 10 (2000): 37–160.

———. *Qingtongqi yu Song dai wenhuashi* 青銅器與宋代文化史. Taipei: Taida Chuban Zhongxin, 2016.

Chen Qiyuan 陳其元. *Yongxianzhai biji* 庸閑齋筆記. Beijing: Zhonghua Shuju, 1989.

Chen Renyang 陳任暘. *Jiaoshan xuzhi* 焦山續志. Reprinted in *Gugong zhenben congkan* 故宮珍本叢刊, no. 247. Haikou: Hainan Chubanshe, 2001.

Chen Shihua 陳世華. "Heming, Tianjian jinglan yu Tao Hongjing shufa" 鶴銘、天監井欄與陶弘景書法. *Shufa yanjiu* 書法研究, no. 4 (1985): 24–30.

———. "Tao Hongjing shu muzhuan mingwen faxian ji kaozheng" 陶弘景書墓磚銘文發現及考證. *Dongnan wenhua* 東南文化, no. 3 (1987): 54–59.

Chen Yaodong 陳耀東. "Yi he ming de shidai ji zuozhe kaobian" 瘞鶴銘的時代及作者考辨. *Shufa yanjiu*, no. 4 (1985): 16–23.

Chen Zhiping 陳志平. *Huang Tingjian shuxue yanjiu* 黃庭堅書學研究. Beijing: Zhonghua Shuju, 2006.

———. "Fashu yaolu de liangge banben xitong ji xiangguan wenti kaoshu" 法書要錄的兩個版本系統及相關問題考述. *Wenyi yanjiu* 文藝研究, no. 2 (2018): 130–45.

Cheng Zhangcan 程章燦. "Muzhi qiyuan kao: Jian dui guanyu muzhi qiyuan de zhuzhong chuantong shuofa de kaocha" 墓誌起源考—兼對關於墓誌起源的諸種傳統説法的考察. In *Shixue luncong* 石學論叢, 1–20. Taipei: Da'an Chubanshe, 1999.

———. *Shike kegong yanjiu* 石刻刻工研究. Shanghai: Shanghai Guji Chubanshe, 2008.

Chia, Lucille. *Printing for Profits: The Commercial Publishers of Jianyang, Fujian (11th–17th Centuries)*. Cambridge, MA: Harvard University Press, 2003.

———. "Of Three Mountains Street: The Commercial Publishers of Ming Nanjing." In *Printing and Book Culture in Late Imperial China,* edited by Cynthia J. Brokaw and Kai-wing Chow, 107–51. Berkeley: University of California Press, 2005.

Chia, Lucille, and Hilde De Weerdt, eds. *Knowledge and Text Production in an Age of Print China, 900–1400*. Leiden: Brill, 2011.

Chiang, Yee. *Chinese Calligraphy; An Introduction to Its Aesthetic and Technique.* 3rd ed. Cambridge, MA: Harvard University Press, 1973.

Chow, Kai-wing. *Publishing, Culture, and Power in Early Modern China*. Stanford: Stanford University Press, 2004.

Chu, Hung–lam. "Calligraphy's New Importance in Later Ming Printing." In *Calligraphy and the East Asian Book,* edited by Howard L. Goodman, 167–202. Boston: Shambhala, 1989.

Chu Hui-liang 朱惠良. "The Calligraphy of Li Kung-lin in the Classic of Filial Piety." In *Li Kung-lin's Classic of Filial Piety,* edited by Richard M. Barnhart, 53–71. New York: Metropolitan Museum of Art, 1993.

———. "Dong Qichang shufa yishu" 董其昌書法藝術. In *Dong Qichang fashu tezhan yanjiu tulu* 董其昌法書特展研究圖錄, 6–38. Taipei: Guoli Gugong Bowuyuan, 1993.

———. "Lingu zhi xinlu: Dong Qichang yihou shufa fazhan yanjiu zhiyi" 臨古之新路：董其昌以後書法發展研究之一. *Gugong xueshu jikan* 故宮學術季刊 10, no. 3 (1993): 51–94.

Clunas, Craig. *Superfluous Things: Material Culture and Social Status in Early Modern China.* Cambridge, UK: Polity Press, 1991.

———. *Fruitful Sites: Garden Culture in Ming Dynasty China*. Durham, NC: Duke University Press, 1996.

———. *Pictures and Visuality in Early Modern China.* London: Reaktion Books, 1997.

———. *Empire of Great Brightness: Visual and Material Cultures of Ming China, 1368–1644*. Honolulu: University of Hawai'i Press, 2007.

———. *Screen of Kings: Royal Art and Power in Ming China*. Honolulu: University of Hawai'i Press, 2013.

Cutter, Robert Joe. "The Incident at the Gate: Cao Zhi, the Succession, and Literary Fame." *T'oung Pao* 71, no. 4/5 (1985): 228–62.

Da Changuang 笪蟾光. *Maoshan zhi* 茅山志. Taipei: Wenhai Chubanshe, 1971.

Daoxuan 道宣. *Guang hongming ji* 廣弘明集. *TSZ* 52.

Davis, Timothy M. *Entombed Epigraphy and Commemorative Culture in Early Medieval China: A Brief History of Early Muzhiming.* Leiden: Brill, 2015.

Deng Xiaojun 鄧小軍. "Yuan Jie zhuan Yan Zhenqing shu Da Tang zhongxing song kaoshi" 元結撰顏真卿書大唐中興頌考釋. *Jinyang xuekan* 晉陽學刊, no. 2 (2012): 125–30.

Dien, Albert E. *Six Dynasties Civilization.* New Haven: Yale University Press, 2007.

Ding Chao 丁超. "Yi he ming si kuai canshi chongjian tianri" 瘞鶴銘四塊殘石重見天日, *Zhongguo wenhua bao* 中國文化報, May 28, 2009, 6.

———, ed. *Zhongguo Zhenjiang Yi he ming guoji xueshu yantaohui lunwen huibian* 中國鎮江瘞鶴銘國際學術研討會論文彙編. Zhenjiang: Jiangsu Daxue Chubanshe, 2009.

Dong Qichang 董其昌. *Huachanshi suibi* 畫禪室隨筆. *ZGSHQS*, 3.

———. *Rongtai bieji* 容臺別集. Chongzhen ed.

Dong You 董逌. *Guangchuan shuba* 廣川書跋. *CSJC*, 1511–12.

Du Mu 都穆. *Jinxie linlang* 金薤琳琅. *SKSL*, s. 1, no. 10.

Duke, Michael S. *Lu You.* Boston: Twayne Pubishers, 1977.

Dumoulin, Heinrich. *Zen Buddhism: A History.* Vol. 1, *India and China*, translated by James W. Heisig and Paul Knitter. New York: Collier Macmillan, 1988.

Ebrey, Patricia Buckley. *Accumulating Culture: The Collections of Emperor Huizong.* Seattle: University of Washington Press, 2008.

Egan, Ronald C. "Ou-yang Hsiu and Su Shih on Calligraphy." *Harvard Journal of Asiatic Studies* 49, no. 2 (December 1989): 365–419.

———. *The Problem of Beauty: Aesthetic Thought and Pursuits in Northern Song Dynasty China.* Cambridge, MA: Harvard University Press, 2006.

———. "To Count Grains of Sand on the Ocean Floor: Changing Perceptions of Books and Learning in the Song Dynasty." In *Knowledge and Text Production in an Age of Print China, 900–1400*, edited by Lucille Chia and Hilde Godelieve Dominique De Weerdt, 33–62. Leiden: Brill, 2011.

Elliott, Mark C. *Emperor Qianlong: Son of Heaven, Man of the World.* New York: Pearson Longman, 2009.

Elman, Benjamin. *From Philosophy to Philology: Intellectual and Social Aspects of Change in Late Imperial China.* Cambridge, MA: Harvard University Asia Center, 1984.

Fang Bo 方波. "Wenhua ziben yu wenhua shangpin: Mingdai Jiangnan sijia ketie de yige mianxiang" 文化資本與文化商品：明代江南私家刻帖的一個面向. *Wenyi yanjiu*, no. 12 (2012): 110–16.

Fang Xuanling 房玄齡. *Jin shu* 晉書. Beijing: Zhonghua Shuju, 1995.

Fei, Si-yen. *Negotiating Urban Space: Nanjing and Late Ming Urbanization.* Cambridge, MA: Harvard University Asia Center, 2010.

Fong, Wen C. *Images of the Mind: Selections from the Edward L. Elliott Family and John B. Elliott Collections of Chinese Calligraphy and Painting at the Art Museum, Princeton University*. Princeton: The Art Museum, Princeton University, 1984.

———. *Beyond Representation: Chinese Painting and Calligraphy, 8th–14th Century*. New Haven: Yale University Press, 1992.

———. "Tung Ch'i-Ch'ang and Artistic Renewal." In *The Century of Tung Ch'i-Ch'ang, 1555–1636*, edited by Wai–Kam Ho, 43–54. Seattle: University of Washington Press, 1992.

———. *Between Two Cultures: Late Nineteenth- and Twentieth-Century Chinese Paintings from the Robert H. Ellsworth Collection in the Metropolitan Museum of Art*. New Haven: Yale University Press, 2001.

Fu, Shen. "Huang T'ing-Chien's Calligraphy and His Scroll for Chang Ta-T'ung: A Masterpiece Written in Exile." PhD diss., Princeton University, 1976. ProQuest Dissertations and Theses.

Fu Genqing 傅根清. "Zhao Yanwei shengping kaosuo" 趙彥衛生平考索. *Shandong Daxue xuebao* 山東大學學報, no. 3 (1988): 107–11.

Fu Shen 傅申. "Tianxia diyi Su Dongpo: Hanshi tie" 天下第一蘇東坡寒食帖. In *Shushi yu shuji* 書史與書跡, 79–96. Taipei: Guoli Lishi Bowuguan, 1996.

Fu Xuancong 傅璇琮. *Tangdai keju yu wenxue* 唐代科舉與文學. Xi'an: Shanxi Renmin Chubanshe, 1986.

Fukuhara Keirou 福原啓郎. "Seishin no boshi no igi" 西晋の墓誌の意義. In *Chūgoku kizokusei shakai no kenkyū* 中国貴族制社会の研究, edited by Kawakatsu Yoshio 川勝義雄 and Tonami Mamoru 礪波護, 315–69. Kyoto: Kyoto Daigaku Jinbun Kagaku Kinkyūjo, 1987.

Fukui Yoshio 福井佳夫. *Rikuchō no yūgi bungaku* 六朝の遊戲文学. Tokyo: Kyūko Shoin, 2007.

Funayama Tōru 船山徹. "Tō Kōkei to bokkyō no kairitsu" 陶弘景と仏教の戒律. In *Rokochō dōkyō no kenkyū* 六朝道教の研究, edited by Yoshikawa Tadao, 353–76. Tokyo: Shunjūsha, 1998.

Gao Mingyi 高明一. "Moluo de dianfan: Ji Wang xingshu zai bei Song de liuchuan yu gaibian" 沒落的典範—「集王行書」在北宋的流傳與改變. *Guoli Taiwan Daxue meishushi yanjiu jikan* 國立臺灣大學美術史研究集刊 23 (2007): 81–113.

Graham, William T., and Xin Yu. *"The Lament for the South": Yü Hsin's "Ai Chiang-nan Fu."* Cambridge: Cambridge University Press, 1980.

Gu Yuanqing 顧元慶. *Yi he ming kao* 瘞鶴銘考. In *Siku quanshu cunmu congshu* 四庫全書存目叢書, 278:90–95. Tainan: Zhuangyan Wenhua Shiye Youxian Gongsi, 1997.

Guilin Shi Wenwu Guanli Weiyuanhui 桂林文物管理委員會. *Guilin shike* 桂林石刻. 1977

Guo Pu 郭璞. *Shanhai jing* 山海經. *CSJC*, 2994–96.

Guo Rongzhang 郭榮章. *Shimen shike daquan* 石門石刻大全. Xi'an: San Qin Chubanshe, 2001.

Guo Weiqi 郭偉其. *Tingyun mokai: Guanyu Wen Zhengming yu shiliu shiji wumen fengge guifan de yizhong jiashe* 停雲模楷：關於文徵明與十六世紀吳門風格規範的一種假設. Hangzhou: Zhongguo Meishu Xueyuan Chubanshe, 2012.

Guoli Gugong Bowuyuan Bianji Weiyuanhui 國立故宮博物院編輯委員會. *Gugong lidai fashu quanji* 故宮歷代法書全集. Taipei: Guoli Gugong Bowuyuan, 1973.

Guthke, Karl S. *Epitaph Culture in the West: Variations on a Theme in Cultural History*. Lewiston: Edwin Mellen Press, 2003.

Gutzwiller, Kathryn J. *Poetic Garlands: Hellenistic Epigrams in Context.* Berkeley: University of California Press, 1998.

Hammond, Kenneth J. "Beyond Archaism: Wang Shizhen and the Legacy of the Northern Song." *Ming Studies* 36 (1996): 6–28.

Han Jin 韓進. "Nanyang shuhua biao kaobian" 南陽書畫表考辨. *Tushuguan zazhi* 圖書館雜誌29 no. 3 (2010): 70–75.

Han Yu 韓愈. *Han Changli shi xi'nian jishi* 韓昌黎詩繫年集釋. Annotated by Qian Zhonglian 錢仲聯. Shanghai: Shanghai Guji Chubanshe, 1984.

Hargett, James M. "Song Dynasty Local Gazetteers and Their Place in the History of Difangzhi Writing." *Harvard Journal of Asiatic Studies* 56, no. 2 (1996): 405–42.

Harrist, Robert E., Jr. "Eulogy on Burying a Crane: A Ruined Inscription and Restoration." *Oriental Art* no. 3 (1998): 2–10.

———. "A Letter from Wang Hsi-chih and the Culture of Chinese Calligraphy." In *The Embodied Image: Chinese Calligraphy from the John B. Elliott Collection*, edited by Robert E. Harrist Jr. and Wen Fong, 241–59. Princeton: Princeton University Press, 1999.

———. "Copies, All the Way Down: Notes on the Early Transmission of Calligraphy by Wang Xizhi." *East Asian Library Journal* 10, no. 1 (2001): 176–96.

———. *The Landscape of Words: Stone Inscriptions from Early and Medieval China.* Seattle: University of Washington Press, 2008.

Harrist, Robert E., Jr., and Wen Fong. *Embodied Image: Chinese Calligraphy from the John B. Elliott Collection*. Princeton: Princeton University Press, 1999.

Hartman, Charles. *Han Yu and the T'ang Search for Unity*. Princeton: Princeton University Press, 1986.

He Shaoji 何紹基. *He Shaoji shiwenji* 何紹基詩文集. Changsha: Yuelu Shushe, 1992.

He Yanquan 何炎泉. "Ouyang Xiu Jigu lu ba moji juan de xiangguan wenti yu liuchuan" 歐陽修集古錄跋墨蹟卷的相關問題與流傳. *Gugong wenwu yuekan* 23, no. 271 (2005): 94–102.

———. "Bei Song maobi fazhan yu shufa chicun de guanxi" 北宋毛筆發展與書法尺寸的關係. In *Qing xun qi ben: Gudai shufa chuangzuo yanjiu guoji xueshu yantaohui lunwen ji* 請循其本：古代書法創作研究國際學術研討會論文集, edited by Sun Xiaoyun 孫曉雲 and Xue Longchun 薛龍春, 108–19. Nanjing: Nanjing Daxue Chubanshe, 2010.

Hegel, Robert. *Reading Illustrated Fiction in Late Imperial China.* Stanford: Stanford University Press, 1998.

Ho, Wai-kam. "Tung Ch'i-Ch'ang's New Orthodoxy and the Southern School Theory." In *Artists and Traditions: Uses of the Past in Chinese Culture*, edited by Christian F. Murck, 113–29. Princeton: Princeton University Press, 1976.

Ho, Wai-kam, and Judith G. Smith, ed. *The Century of Tung Ch'i-Ch'ang*. Seattle: University of Washington Press, 1992.

Hsu, Ya-Hwei. "Antiquities, Ritual Reform, and the Shaping of New Taste at Hizong's Court." *Artibus Asiae* 73, no. 1 (2013): 137–80.

Hsu Ya-Hwei 許雅惠. "Songdai shidafu de jinshi shoucang yu liyi shijian: Yi Lantian Lü shi jiazu weili" 宋代士大夫的金石收藏與禮儀實踐–以藍田呂氏家族為例. *Zhejiang Daxue yishu yu kaogu yanjiu* 浙江大學藝術與考古研究 3 (2018): 131–64.

Hu Zi 胡仔. *Tiaoxi yuyin conghua qianji* 苕溪漁隱叢話前集. Beijing: Renmin Wenxue Chubanshe, 1962.

Hua Linfu 華林甫. "Sui Tang tujing jikao" 隋唐圖經輯攷. *Guoli Zhengzhi Daxue lishi xuebao* 27 (2007): 141–213; 28 (2007): 1–92.

Huadong Shifan Daxue Guji Zhengli Yanjiushi 华东师范大学古籍整理研究室. *Lidai shufa lunwen xuan* 歷代書法論文選. Shanghai: Shanghai Shuhua Chubanshe, 1979.

Huang, Susan Shih-Shan. *Picturing the True Form: Daoist Visual Culture in Traditional China*. Cambridge, MA: Harvard University Asia Center, 2015.

Huang Bosi 黄伯思. *Dongguan yulun* 東觀餘論. Published in 1210. Reprinted in Zhonghua zaizao shanben 中華再造善本. Beijing: Beijing Tushuguan Chubanshe, 2004.

———. *Dongguan yulun* 東觀餘論. *ZGSHQS*, 1.

Huang Dun 黄惇, ed. *Dong Qichang shufa lunzhu* 董其昌書法論著. Nanjing: Jiangsu Meishu Chubanshe, 1993.

———. *Zhongguo shufa shi: Yuan Ming juan* 中國書法史•元明卷. Nanjing: Jiangsu Jiaoyu Chubanshe, 2001.

———. "Mingdai fangshu chuangzuo moshi de chuxian: Cong Zhu Yunming dao Dong Qichang shu 'Gushi shijiu shou juan' de taolun" 明代仿書創作模式的出現：從祝允明到董其昌書《古詩十九首卷》的討論. In *Shanggu yu shangyi* 尚古與尚意, edited by Li Yuzhou 李郁周, 359–95. Taipei: Wanjuan Lou, 2013.

Huang Jinming 黄金明. *Han Wei Jin Nanbeichao leibeiwen yanjiu* 漢魏晉南北朝誄碑文研究. Beijing: Renmin Wenxue Chubanshe, 2005.

Huang Tingjian 黄庭堅. *Shangu ji, Shangu waiji, Shangu bieji*, 山谷集 山谷外集 山谷別集. *SKQS*, 1113.

———. *Shangu Tiba* 山谷題跋. *CSJC*, 1564.

———. *Shangu shi jizhu* 山谷詩集注. Annotated by Ren Yuan 任淵, Shi Rong 史蓉, and Shi Jiwen 史季温. Edited by Huang Baohua 黄寶華. Shanghai: Shanghai Guji Chubanshe, 2003.

Huang Xiuzhu 黄脩珠. "Yi shu zhi zhi yu zuzong zhi fa: Song Taizong de wenzhi yu shufa" 以書致治與祖宗之法: 宋太宗的文治與書法. PhD diss., Nanjing Yishu Xueyuan, 2016. http://nvsm.cnki.net/kns/detail/detail.aspx?FileName=1016214749.nh&DbName=CDFD2017.

Huang Zhanyue 黃展岳. "Zaoqi muzhi de yixie wenti" 早期墓誌的一些問題. *Wenwu*, no. 12 (1995): 51–58.

Ikeuchi Hiroshi 池内宏. *Tsūkō* 通溝. Tokyo: Nichiman Bunka Kyōkai, 1938–40.

Jia Song 賈嵩. "Huayang Tao Yinju neizhuan" 華陽陶隱居内傳. *DZ* 310, 5:499–512.

Jiangsu Sheng Difangzhi Bianzuan Weiyuanhui 江蘇省地方志編纂委員會. *Jiangsu Sheng zhi: Dili zhi* 江蘇省志：地理志. Nanjing: Jiangsu Guji Chubanshe, 1999.

Jilin Sheng Bowuguan 吉林省博物館. "Jilin Ji'an wukui fen sihao he wuhao mu qingli lüeji" 吉林集安五盔墳四號和五號墓清理略記. *Kaogu*, no. 2 (1964): 59–66.

Jin Dan 金丹. *Ruan Yuan shuxue yanjiu* 阮元書學研究. Beijing: Rongbaozhai, 2012.

Jin Yuzhe 金裕哲 [Kim You Cheol]. "Yi he ming de mingwen neirong jiqi lixiang: Tao Hongjing yu Jiaoshan daojiao" 瘞鶴銘的銘文內容及其理想：陶弘景與焦山道教. In *Daojia Yu Daojiao: Daojiao Juan* 道家與道教•道教卷, edited by Chen Guying 陳鼓應 and Feng Dawen 馮達文, 141–155. Guangzhou: Guangdong Renmin Chubanshe, 2001.

Johnson, David. "Communication, Class, and Consciousness in Late Imperial China." In *Popular Culture in Late Imperial China*, edited by David Johnson, Andrew J. Nathan, and Evelyn S. Rawski, 34–72. Berkeley: University of California Press, 1985.

Jurong Shi Difangzhi Bangongshi 句容市地方誌辦公室. *Jurong Maoshan zhi* 句容茅山志. Hefei: Huangshan Shushe, 1998.

Kang Youwei 康有為. *Guang Yizhou shuangji* 廣藝舟雙楫. In *Lidai shufa lunwen xuan* 歷代書法論文選. Shanghai: Shanghai Shuhua Chubanshe, 1979.

Kano Chiaki 菅野智明. *Kindai chūgoku no shu bunka* 近代中国の書文化. Tsukuba: Tsukuba University Press, 2009.

Katō Kiichi 加藤僖一. *Ryōkan's Calligraphy*. Niigata: Kōkodō Shoten, 1997.

Kern, Martin. *The Stele Inscriptions of Ch'in Shih-huang: Text and Ritual in Early Chinese Imperial Representation*. New Haven: American Oriental Society, 2000.

Knechtges, David R. *The Han Rhapsody: A Study of the Fu of Yang Hsiung (53 B.C.–A.D. 18)*. Cambridge: Cambridge University Press, 1976.

———. *Wen Xuan or Selections of Refined Literature*. Princeton: Princeton University Press, 1996.

Ko, Dorothy. *Teachers of the Inner Chambers: Women and Culture in the Seventeenth Century China*. Stanford: Stanford University Press, 1994.

Kohn, Livia. *Laughing at the Tao: Debates among Buddhists and Taoists in Medieval China*. Princeton: Princeton University Press, 1995.

Kōzen Hiroshi 興膳宏. "Shoga no rekishi no naga de no Tō Kōkei to Shin ko" 書寫の歷史の中での陶弘景と真誥. In *Rokochō dōkyō no kenkyū*, 六朝道教の研究, edited by Yoshikawa Tadao, 331–52. Tokyo: Shunjūsha, 1998.

Kroll, Paul W. "The Image of the Halcyon Kingfisher in Medieval Chinese Poetry." *Journal of the American Oriental Society* 104, no. 2 (1984): 237–51.

Lai Fei 賴非. *Shandong Beichao fojiao kejing: Diaocha yu yanjiu* 山東北朝佛教刻經：調查與研究. Beijing: Kexue Chubanshe, 2007.

Lattimore, Richmond A. *Themes in Greek and Latin Epitaphs*. Urbana: University of Illinois Press, 1962.

Ledderose, Lothar. *Die Siegelschrift (Chuan-shu) in der Ch'ing-Zeit: Ein Beitrag zur Geschichte der chinesischen Schriftkunst*. Wiesbaden: Steiner, 1970.

———. *Mi Fu and the Classical Tradition of Chinese Calligraphy*. Princeton: Princeton University Press, 1979.

———. "Some Taoist Elements in the Calligraphy of the Six Dynasties." *T'oung Pao* 70 (1984): 246–78.

———. "Calligraphy at the Close of China's Empire." In *Art at the Close of China's Empire*, edited by Ju-hsi Chou, 189–208. Tempe: Arizona State University, 1998.

———. "Aesthetic Appropriation of Ancient Calligraphy in Modern China." In *Chinese Art: Modern Expression*, edited by Maxwell K. Hearn and Judith G. Smith, 212–45. New York: Metropolitan Museum of Art, 2001.

Lee, Hui-shu. *Empresses, Art, and Agency in Song Dynasty China*. Seattle: University of Washington Press, 2010.

Lee, Silvia W. S. "For 'Co-Branding' a *Cainü* and a Garden: How the Zhao Family Established Identities for Wen Shu and Their Garden Residence, Hanshan." *Nan Nü: Men, Women, and Gender in Early and Imperial China* 18, no. 1 (2016): 49–83.

Legge, James. *"Confucian Analects," "The Great Learning," and "The Doctrine of the Mean"*. New York: Dover, 1971.

Li, Wai-yee. "The Late Ming Courtesan: Invention of a Cultural Ideal." In *Writing Women in Late Imperial China*, edited by Ellen Widmer and Chang Sun Kang-I, 46–73. Stanford: Stanford University Press, 1997.

Li Bai 李白. *Li Bai ji jiaozhu* 李白集校注. Shanghai: Shanghai Guji Chubanshe, 1980.

Li Chuo 李綽. *Shangshu gushi* 尚書故實. *SKQS*, 862.

Li Fang 李昉. *Wenyuan yinghua* 文苑英華. Beijing: Zhonghua Shuju, 1966.

Li Hui 李慧. "Ming mo Qing chu Haining Chen shi jiazu shufa yanjiu 明末清初海寧陳氏家族書法研究." Master's thesis, Nanjing Yishu Xueyuan, 2015. http://nvsm.cnki.net/kns/detail/detail.aspx?FileName=1015643066.nh&DbName=CMFD2016.

Li Shibiao 李士彪. *Wei Jin Nanbeichao wentixue* 魏晋南北朝文體學. Shanghai: Shanghai Guji Chubanshe, 2004.

Li Wenqi 李文琪. "Dong Qichang Yanranshan ming qianlun" 董其昌《燕然山銘》淺論. *Zhongguo Guojia Bowuguan guankan* no. 11 (2018): 117–27.

Li Yanshou 李延壽. *Nan shi* 南史. Beijing: Zhonghua Shuju, 1995.

Li Yumin 李裕民. "Yan ta timing yanjiu" 雁塔題名研究. *Chang'an Daxue xuebao* 長安大學學報 12, no. 2 (2010): 1–7.

Li Yuqi 李玉奇. "Jinxie linlang chengshu niandai ji banben kao" 《金薤琳琅》成書年代及版本考. *Guji zhengli yanjiu xuekan* 古籍整理研究學刊, no. 2 (1994): 37–39.

Li Yun 李韻. "San wen Yi he ming zhi dalao" 三問瘞鶴銘之打撈. *Guangming ribao*, June 8, 2010, 7.

Lin, Li-chiang. "The Proliferation of Images: The Ink–Stick Designs and the Printing of the Fang-shih mo-p'u and the Ch'eng-shih mo-yuan." PhD diss., Princeton University, 1998. ProQuest Dissertations and Theses.

———. "A Study of the *Xinjuan Hainei qiguan,* a Ming Dynasty Book of Famous Sites." In *Bridges to Heaven: Essays on East Asian Art in Honor of Professor Wen C. Fong,* edited by Jerome Silbergeld, Dora C. Y. Ching, Judith G. Smith, and Alfreda Murch, 779–812. Princeton: Princeton University Press, 2011.

Lin Li-chiang 林麗江. "You shanggan erzhi fengyue: Bai Juyi 'Pipa xing' shi zhi tuwen zhuanyi" 由傷感而至風月—白居易《琵琶行》詩之圖文轉繹. *Gugong xueshu jikan* 20, no. 3 (2003): 1–50.

Lin Qingzhang 林慶彰. *Mingdai kaojuxue yanjiu* 明代考據學研究. Taipei: Xuesheng Shuju, 1986.

Liu, Cary Y. "Calligraphic Couplets as Manifestations of Deities and Markers of Buildings." In *The Embodied Image: Chinese Calligraphy from the John B. Elliott Collection,* edited by Robert E. Harrist, Jr., and Wen Fong, 360–79. Princeton: Princeton University Press, 1999.

Liu, Lihong. "Collecting the Here and Now: Birthday Albums and the Aesthetics of Association in Mid-Ming China." *Journal of Chinese Literature and Culture* 2, no. 1 (2015): 43–91.

Liu Changshi 劉昌詩. *Lupu biji* 蘆浦筆記. Beijing: Zhonghua Shuju, 2005.

Liu Dabin 劉大彬. *Maoshan zhi* 茅山志. *DZ* 314, 5:584–702.

Liu Jianguo 劉建國 and Pan Meiyun 潘美雲. *Yi he ming shike kaozheng* 瘞鶴銘石刻考證. Nanjing: Jiangsu Renmin Chubanshe, 2006.

Liu Mingfang 劉名芳. *Qianlong Jiaoshan zhi* 乾隆焦山志. Reprinted in *Gugong zhenben congkan* 故宮珍本叢刊, no. 247. Haikou: Hainan Chubanshe, 2001.

Liu Tao 劉濤. *Zhongguo shufashi: Wei Jin Nanbeichao juan* 中國書法史•魏晉南北朝卷. Nanjing: Jiangsu Guji Chubanshe, 2002.

Liu Xie 劉勰. *Zengding Wenxin diaolong jiaozhu* 增订文心雕龍校注. Annotated by Huang Shulin 黄叔琳, Li Xiang李祥, and Yang Mingzhao 杨明照. Beijing: Zhonghua Shuju, 1999.

Liu Xu 劉昫. *Jiu Tang shu* 舊唐書. Beijing: Zhonghua Shuju, 1995.

Liu Yiqing 劉義慶. *Shishuo xinyu jianshu* 世說新語箋疏. Annotated by Yu Jiaxi 余嘉錫. Beijing: Zhonghua Shuju, 1983.

Liu Yuantang 劉元堂. "Songdai banke shufa yanjiu," 宋代版刻書法研究. PhD diss., Nanjing Yishu Xueyuan, 2012. http://nvsm.cnki.net/kns/detail/detail.aspx?FileName=1012506901.nh&DbName=CDFD2013.

Liu Zhengcheng 劉正成, ed. *Zhongguo shufa quanji* 中國書法全集. Beijing: Rongbaozhai, 1995.

Liu Zhonghua 劉仲華. *Han Song zhijian: Wen Fanggang xueshu sixiang yanjiu* 漢宋之間：翁方綱學術思想研究. Beijing: Renmin Daxue Chubanshe, 2010.

Lo, Jung-Pang. *Kang Yu-wei: A Biograohy and A Symposium. The Association for Asian Studies: Monographs and Papers,* no. 23. Tuscon: University of Arizona Press, 1967.

Loewe, Michael, and Edward L Shaughnessy. *The Cambridge History of Ancient China: From the Origins of Civilization to 221 B.C.* Cambridge: Cambridge University Press, 1999.

Lu, Hui-wen. "Calligraphy of Stone Engravings in Northern Wei Luoyang." In *Character and Context in Chinese Calligraphy,* edited by Cary Yee–Wei Liu, Dora C. Y. Ching, and Judith G. Smith, 78–103. Princeton: Art Museum, Princeton University, 1999.

———. "Wild Cursive Calligraphy, Poetry, and Chan Monks in the Tenth Century." In *Tenth Century China and Beyond: Art and Visual Culture in a Multi–centered Age,* edited by Wu Hung, 364–90. Chicago: Center for the Art of East Asia, University of Chicago, 2012.

Lu Huiwen 盧慧紋. "Bei yu tie de jiaohui—Qian Yong Panyunge tie zai Qing dai shushi Zhong de yiyi" 碑與帖的交會—錢泳《攀雲閣帖》在清代書史中的意義. *Guoli Taiwan Daxue meishushi yanjiu jikan* 31 (2011): 205–60.

———. "Tang zhi Song de Liuchao shushiguan zhi bian: Yi Wang Xizhi 'Yue Yi lun' zai Song dai de moke ji bianmao wei li" 唐至宋的六朝書史觀之變：以王羲之樂毅論在宋代的摹刻及變貌為例. *Gugong xueshu jikan* 31, no. 3 (2015): 1–56.

Lu Jiaming 盧家明, ed. *Rong Geng cangtie* 容庚藏帖. Guangzhou: Guangdong Renmin Chubanshe, 2016.

Lu Jiugao 陆九皋. "Jiaoshan fang Yi he ming keshi" 焦山訪瘞鶴銘刻石. *Shufa* 書法, no. 6 (1979): 26–33.

Lu Renlong 盧仁龍. "Tao Hongjing yu shufa shiliao gouchen" 陶弘景與書法史料鉤沉. *Wenxian* 文獻, no. 1 (1991): 160–74.

Lu Xian 盧憲. *Jiading Zhenjiang zhi* 嘉定鎮江志. In *Song Yuan difangzhi congshu* 宋元方志叢書. Taipei: Dahua Shuju, 1987.

Lu Zongrun 陸宗潤. "Yi he ming jiaobu" 瘞鶴銘校補. *Lishi wenwu yuekan* 歷史文物月刊, no. 166 (2007): 36–49.

Luo Feng 羅豐. "Huairen Ji Wang Xizhi Shengjiao xu bei—yige Wang zi chuantong de jiangou yu liuxing" 懷仁集王羲之聖教序碑—一個王字傳統的建構與流行. *Tang yanjiu* 23 (2017): 1–108.

Luo Yonglai 羅勇來. "Yi he ming xinzheng san ti" 瘞鶴銘新証三題. *Shufa yanjiu,* no. 3 (2002): 32–47.

———. *Yi he ming yanjiu* 瘞鶴銘研究. Shanghai: Baijia Chubanshe, 2006.

Ma Chengfen 馬成芬. *Tōsen hōjō no kenkyū* 唐船法帖の研究. Osaka: Seibundo, 2017.

Ma Chengming 馬成名. *Haiwai suojian shanben beitie lu* 海外所見善本碑帖錄. Shanghai: Shanghai Shuhua Chubanshe, 2014.

Ma Ziyun 馬子雲 and Shi Anchang 施安昌. *Beitie jianding* 碑帖鑑定. Guilin: Guangxi Shifan Daxue Chubanshe, 1993.

Masuda Tomoyuki 増田知之. "Meidai ni ogeru hōjō no kangyō to Sushū Bunji yichizoku" 明代における法帖の刊行と蘇州文氏一族. *Tōyōshi kenkyū* 62, no. 1 (2003): 39–74.

Mather, Richard B. *Shih-shuo Hsin-yu: A New Account of Tales of the World.* 2nd ed. Ann Arbor: Center for Chinese Studies, University of Michigan, 2002.

Mattos, Gilbert L. *The Stone Drums of Ch'in*. Nettetal: Steyler Verlag-Wort und Werk, 1988.

McCausland, Shane. *Zhao Mengfu: Calligraphy and Painting for Khubilai's China*. Hong Kong: Hong Kong University Press, 2011.

———. *The Mongol Century: Visual Culture of Yuan China, 1271–1368*. Honolulu: University of Hawai'i Press, 2014.

McMullen, David. *State and Scholars in T'ang China*. Cambridge: Cambridge University Press, 1988.

McNair, Amy. "Fa shu yao lu, a Ninth-Century Compendium of Texts on Calligraphy." *T'ang Studies* 5 (1987): 69–86.

———. "The Engraved Model-Letters Compendia of the Song Dynasty." *Journal of the American Oriental Society* 114, no. 2 (1994): 209–25.

———. "Engraved Calligraphy in China: Recension and Reception." *The Art Bulletin* 77, no. 1 (March 1995): 106–14.

———. *The Upright Brush: Yan Zhenqing's Calligraphy and Song Literati Politics*. Honolulu: University of Hawai'i Press, 1998.

———. "Letters as Calligraphy Exemplars: The Long and Eventful Life of Yan Zhenqing's (709–785) *Imperial Commissioner Liu Letter*." In *A History of Chinese Letters and Epistolary Culture*, edited by Antje Richter, 53–96. Leiden: Brill, 2016.

Mi Fu 米芾. *Haiyue mingyan 海岳名言*. *ZGSHQS*, 1.

Minford, John, and Joseph S. M. Lau, eds. *Classical Chinese Literature: An Anthology of Translations*. New York: Columbia University Press, 2000.

Mizuno Seiichi 水野清一. "Egakumei ni tsuite" 瘞鶴銘について. In *SDZS*, 5:19–23.

Mo Jialiang 莫家良. "Nan Song ketie wenhua guankui" 南宋刻帖文化管窺. In *Zhongguo beitie yu shufa guoji yantaohui lunwenji 中國碑帖與書法國際研討會論文集*, 69–76. Hong Kong: Xianggang Zhongwen Daxue Wenwuguan, 2001.

Morita Shiryū 森田子龍. "Eigakumei nōto" 瘞鶴銘ノート. In *Bokubi 墨美*, no. 246 (1974): 2.

Mostern, Ruth. "*Dividing the Realm in Order to Govern*": *The Spatial Organization of the Song State*. Cambridge, MA: Harvard University Asia Center, 2011.

Mote, Frederick W. "A Millenium of Chinese Urban History: Form, Time, and Space Concepts in Soochow." *Rice Institute Pamphlet—Rice University Studies* 59, no. 4 (1973): 35–65.

Mugitani Kunio 麥谷邦夫. "Tō Kōkei nenpo kōryaku" 陶弘景年谱考略. *Tōhō shūkyō 东方宗教*, no. 47, no. 48 (1976).

———. "Ryō tenkan jūhachi nen kinenmei bosen to tankan nenkan no Tō Kōkei" 梁天監十八年紀年銘墓磚と天監年間の陶弘景. In *Chūgoku chūsei no bunbutsu 中國中世の文物*, 291–314. Kyoto: Kyōto Daigaku Jinbun Kagaku Kenkyūjo, 1993.

——— and Yoshikawa Tadao 吉川忠夫. *Shū-shi meitsūki kenkyū: Yakuchū hen 周氏冥通記研究: 譯注篇*. Kyoto: Kyōto Daigaku Jinbun Kagaku Kenkyūjo, 2003.

Murck, Alfreda. *Poetry and Painting in Song China: The Subtle Art of Dissent*. Cambridge, MA: Harvard University Asia Center for the Harvard-Yenching Institute, 2000.

Murray, Julia. "The Role of Art in the Southern Sung Dynastic Revival." *Bulletin of Sung-Yuan Studies* 18 (1986): 41–59.

———. *Ma Hezhi and the Illustration of the Book of Odes*. Cambridge: Cambridge University Press, 1993.

Nakata Yūjirō 中田勇次郎 *Shinkashitsu shū: Nakata Yūjirō chosakushū* 心花室集: 中田勇次郎著作集. Tokyo: Nigensha, 1984.

———, ed. *Kō Teiken* 黄庭堅. Tokyo: Nigensha, 1994.

Nanjing bowuyuan 南京博物院. "Jiangsu Danyang Huqiao Nanchao damu jiqi zhuanke bihua" 江蘇丹陽胡橋南朝大墓及其磚刻壁畫. *Wenwu*, no. 2 (1974): 44–56.

Nugent, Christopher M. B. "Structured Gaps: The Qianzi wen and Its Paratexts as Mnemotechnics." In *Memory in Medieval China: Text, Ritual, and Community*, edited by Wendy Swartz and Robert Ford Campany, 158–92. Leiden: Brill, 2018.

Ōba Osamu 大庭修. *Edo jidai ni okeru Chūgoku bunka juyō no kenkyū* 江戸時代における中国文化受容の研究. Tokyo: Dōhōsha, 1986.

Ōki Yasushi 大木康. "Minmatsu konan ni okeru shuppan bunka no kenkyu" 明末江南における出版文化の研究. *Hiroshima daigaku bungakubu kiyo* 広島大学文学部紀要 50 (1991): 1–153.

Ouyang Xiu 歐陽修. *Ouyang Xiu quanji* 歐陽脩全集. Beijing: Zhonghua Shuju, 2001.

Ouyang Xun 歐陽詢. *Yiwen leiju* 藝文類聚. Beijing: Zhonghua Shuju, 1959.

Owen, Stephen. *The Poetry of Meng Chiao and Han Yu*. New Haven: Yale University Press, 1975.

———. *An Anthology of Chinese Literature: Beginnings to 1911*. New York: W. W. Norton, 1996.

Paludan, Ann. *The Chinese Spirit Road: The Classical Tradition of Stone Tomb Statuary*. New Haven: Yale University Press, 1991.

Park, J. P. *Art by the Book: Painted Manuals and the Leisure Life in Late Ming China*. Seattle: University of Washington Press, 2012.

Peterson, Willard. "Confucian Learning in Late Ming Thought." In *The Ming Dynasty, 1368–1644*, edited by Denis C. Twitchett and Frederick W. Mote, 708–88. Vol. 8, part 2, of *The Cambridge History of China*. Cambridge: Cambridge University Press, 1998.

Pi Xirui 皮錫瑞. *Jingxue lishi* 經學歷史. Taipei: Yiwen Chubanshe, 2004.

Qi, Gong. *Chinese Characters Then and Now*. New York: Springer, 2004.

Qi Gong 啟功. "Cong Xihongtang tie kan Dong Qichang dui fashu de jianding" 從戲鴻堂帖看董其昌對法書的鑑定. In *Qi Gong conggao: Lunwen juan* 啟功叢稿·論文卷, 126–35. Beijing: Zhonghua Shuju, 1999.

———. *Gudai ziti lungao* 古代字體論稿. Beijing: Wenwu Chubanshe, 1999.

———. "Shuo Qian zi wen" 說千字文. In *Qi Gong conggao: Lunwen juan*, 252–67. Beijing: Zhonghua Shuju, 1999.

———, ed. *Zhongguo fatie quanji* 中國法帖全集. Wuhan: Hubei Meishu Chubanshe, 2002.

———. *Qi Gong yunyu ji* 啓功韻語集. Beijing: Beijing Shifan Daxue Chubanshe, 2004.

Qi Xiaochun 祁小春. *Guji banke shuji lishuo* 古籍版刻書跡例說. Hangzhou: Zhejiang Renmin Meishu Chubanshe, 2018.

Qiu, Xigui. *Chinese Writing.* Tranlsated by Gilbert L. Mattos and Jerry Norman. New Haven: Society for the Study of Early China, 2000.

Rawski, Evelyn S. "Economic and Social Foundations of Late Imperial Culture." In *Popular Culture in Late Imperial China*, edited by David Johnson, Andrew J. Nathan, and Evelyn S. Rawski, 3–33. Berkeley: University of California Press, 1985.

Robinet, Isabelle. "Metamorphosis and Deliverance from the Corpse in Taoism." *History of Religions*, no. 1 (1979): 37–70.

———. *Taoist Meditation: The Mao-shan Tradition of Great Purity*. Albany: State University of New York Press, 1993.

———. "Shangqing—Highest Clarity." In *Daoism Handbook*, edited by Livia Kohn, 196–224. Leiden: Koninklijke Brill, 2000.

Robson, James. *Power of Place: The Religious Landscape of the Southern Sacred Peak (Nanyue) in Medieval China*. Cambridge, MA: Harvard University Asian Center, 2009.

Rong Geng 容庚. *Congtie mu* 叢帖目. Hong Kong: Zhonghua Shuju, 1980.

———. *Songzhai shulin* 頌齋述林. Hong Kong: Hanmoxuan, 1994.

Ruan Guolin 阮國林. "Nanjing Liang Guiyangwang Xiaorong fufu hezangmu" 南京梁桂陽王蕭融夫婦合葬墓. *Wenwu*, no. 12 (1981): 8–13.

Ruan Yuan 阮元. *Yanjingshi ji* 揅經室集. Beijing: Zhonghua Shuju, 1993.

Ruan Yuan 阮元 and Bi Yuan 畢沅. *Shanzuo jinshi zhi* 山左金石志. *SKSL*, s. 1, no. 19.

Rudolph, R. C. "Preliminary Notes on Song Archaeology." *Journal of Asian Studies* 22 (1962–63): 169–77.

Sakai Tadao 酒井忠夫. *Chūgoku nichiyō ruishoshi no kenkyū* 中國日用類書史の研究. Tokyo: Kokusho Kankōkai, 2011.

Sanxitang fatie 三希堂法帖. Beijing: Beijing Ribao Chubanshe, 1984.

Schafer, Edward H. "The Early History of Lead Pigments and Cosmetics in China." *T'oung Pao* 44 (1956): 416–20.

———. *Mao Shan in T'ang Times.* Boulder: Society for the Study of Chinese Religions, Monograph no. 1, 1980.

———. "The Cranes of Maoshan." In *Tantric and Taoist Studies in Honour of R. A. Stein*, Vol. 2, edited by Michel Strickmann, 372–93. Bruxelles: Institut belge des hautes études chinoises, 1983.

Schipper, Kristofer. "L'Epitaphe pour une Grue (*Yi he ming*) et son Auteur." In *A festschrift in Honour of Professor Jao Tsung-i on the Occasion of his Seventy-fifth Anniversary*, 409–21. Hong Kong: Chinese University Press, 1993.

Sena, Yuchiahn C. *Bronze and Stone: The Cult of Antiquity in Song Dynasty China.* Seattle: University of Washington Press, 2019.

Shaanxi Sheng Kaogu Yanjiuyuan 陝西省考古研究院, ed. *Qin Shihuangdi lingyuan kaogu baogao* 秦始皇帝陵园考古报告 (2001–03). Beijing: Wenwu Chubanshe, 2007.

Shandong Shike Yishu Bowuguan 山東石刻藝術博物館, Laizhou Shi Bowuguan 萊州市博物館, ed. *Yunfeng ke shi quan ji* 雲峰刻石全集. Jinan: Qilu Shushe, 1989.

Shanghai Tushuguan 上海圖書館. *Huang Tingjian Qingyuanshan shi keshi* 黄庭堅青原山詩刻石. Shanghai: Shanghai Guji Chubanshe, 2006.

Shen Dacheng 沈大成. *Xuefuzhai ji* 學福齋集. 1774. *XSKQS*, 1428.

Shen Defu 沈德符. *Wanli yehuo bian* 萬曆野獲編. Beijing: Zhonghua Shuju, 1959.

Shen Jin 沈津. "Mingdai fangke tushu zhi liutong yu jiage" 明代坊刻圖書之流通與價格. *Guojia Tushuguan guankan* 國家圖書館館刊 85, no. 1 (1996): 101–18.

Shi, Jie. "The Mancheng Tombs: Shaping the Afterlife of the 'Kingdom Within Mountains' (Zhongshan) in Western Han China (206 BCE–8CE)." Phd diss. University of Chicago, 2017. ProQuest Dissertations and Theses.

Shi Anchang 施安昌. *Shanben beitie lunji* 善本碑帖論集. Beijing: Zijincheng Chubanshe, 2002.

Shi Rui 史睿. "Tangdai liang jing de shuhua jiancang yu shiren jiaoyou: Yi Zhang Yanyuan jiazu wei hexin" 唐代兩京的書畫鑑藏與士人交遊：以張彥遠家族為核心. *Tang yanjiu* 21 (2015): 95–130.

———. "Sui Tang fashu pingfeng kao: Cong Mogao ku 220 ku Weimoji jingbian tanqi" 隋唐法書屏風考：從莫高窟220窟維摩詰經變談起. *Tang yanjiu* 23 (2017): 339–60.

Shi Zhangyan 石張燕. "Tangshi huapu yanjiu" 《唐詩畫譜》研究. Master's thesis, Nanjing Shifan Daxue, 2014. http://nvsm.cnki.net/kns/detail/detail.aspx?FileName=1014344827.nh&DbName=CMFD2015.

Shi Zhecun 施蟄存. *Shuijingzhu bei lu* 水經注碑錄. Tianjin: Tianjin Guji Chubanshe, 1987.

Shi Zhongping 史中平. "Tangdai pingfeng shufa xiaokao" 唐代屏風書法小考. *Zhongguo shufa* 中國書法, no. 267 (2015): 191–93.

Shui Laiyou 水賚佑. *Songdai tiexue yanjiu* 宋代帖學研究. Shanghai: Shanghai Renmin Meishu Chubanshe, 2001.

———. *Chunhuage tie jishi* 淳化閣帖集釋. Shanghai: Shanghai Guji Chubanshe, 2009.

Sima, Qian. *Records of the Grand Historian: Han Dynasty*, vol. 2. Translated by Burton Watson. Revised edition. New York: Columbia University Press, 1993.

Sima Qian 司馬遷. *Shiji* 史記. Beijing: Zhonghua Shuju, 1995.

Song, Houmei. "Images of the Crane in Chinese Painting." *Oriental Art* 44, no. 3 (1998): 11–23.

Spring, Madeline K. "The Celebrated Cranes of Po Chü-i." *Journal of the American Oriental Society* 111, no. 1 (1991): 8–18.

Starr, Kenneth. *Black Tigers: A Grammar of Chinese Rubbings.* Seattle: University of Washington Press, 2008.

Strassberg, Richard E. *Inscribed Landscape: Travel Writing from Imperial China.* Berkeley: University of California Press, 1994.

———. *A Chinese Bestiary: Strange Creatures from the Guideways through Mountains and Seas.* Berkeley: University of California Press, 2002.

Strickmann, Michel. "The Mao-Shan Revelations: Taoism and the Aristocracy." *T'oung Pao* 63 (1977): 1–63.

———. "A Taoist Confirmation of Liang Wu Ti's Suppression of Taoism." *Journal of the American Oriental Society* 98, no. 4 (1978): 467–75.

———. "On the Alchemy of T'ao Hung-Ching." In *Facets of Taoism: Essays in Chinese Religion*, edited by Holmes Welch and Anna Seidel, 123–92. New Haven: Yale University Press, 1981.

Sturman, Peter C. "Cranes above Kaifeng: The Auspicious Image at the Court of Huizong." *Ars Orientalis* 20 (1990): 33–68.

———. *Mi Fu: Style and the Art of Calligraphy in Northern Song China*. New Haven: Yale University Press, 1997.

Su Shi 蘇軾. *Dongpo tiba* 東坡題跋. *CSJC*, 1590–91.

Su Shunqin 蘇舜欽. *Su Shunqin ji biannian jiaozhu* 蘇舜欽集編年校注. Annotated by Fu Pingxiang 傅平驤 and Hu Wentao 胡問陶. Chengdu: Bashu Shushe, 1991.

Su Song 蘇頌. *Su Weigong wenji* 蘇魏公文集. In *Songji zhenben congkan* 宋集珍本叢刊 12, 190. Beijing: Xianzhuang Shuju, 2004.

Tao Hongjing 陶弘景. *Deng zhen yin jue* 登真隱訣. *DZ* 431, 6:606–25.

———. *Zhen gao* 真誥. *DZ* 1039, 20:490–609.

———. *Zhoushi mingtong ji* 周氏冥通記. *DZ* 312, 5:518–41.

———. *Tao Hongjing ji jiaozhu* 陶弘景集校注. Shanghai: Shanghai Guji Chubanshe, 2009.

Thompson, John. *Illustrations of China and Its People: A Series of Two Hundred Photographs, with Letterpress Descriptive of the Places and People Represented*. London: Marston, Low, and Searle, 1873–74.

Tian, Xiaofei. *Beacon Fire and Shooting Star: The Literary Culture of the Liang (502–557)*. Cambridge, MA: Harvard University Asia Center, 2007.

———. *The Halberd at Red Cliff: Jian'an and the Three Kingdoms*. Cambridge, MA: Harvard University Asia Center, 2018.

Tingyunguan tie 停雲館帖. Taipei: Shufa Wenwu Guan 書法文物館, 1979.

Toyama Gunji 外山軍治. "Magai" 摩崖. *SDZS* 6:23–30.

Tseng, Lilian Lan-ying. "Between Printing and Rubbing: Chu Jun's Illustrated Catalogues of Ancient Monuments in Eighteenth-Century China." In *Reinventing the Past: Archaism and Antiquarianism in Chinese Art and Visual Culture*, edited by Wu Hung, 255–90. Chicago: The Center for the Arts of East Asia, University of Chicago, 2010.

Tseng Lan-ying 曾藍瑩. "Dong Qichang de shuxue lilun yu shijian—Yi Jilin sheng bowuguan cang *Shujintangji* wei li" 董其昌的書學理論與實踐—以吉林省博物館藏書錦堂記為例. *Yishu xue* 藝術學, no. 6 (1991): 75–118.

Tsien, Tsuen-hsuin. *Written on Bamboo and Silk: The Beginnings of Chinese Books and Inscriptions*. 2nd ed. Chicago: University of Chicago Press, 2004.

Tsuzuki Akiko 都築晶子. "Rokuchō jidai no konan shakai to dōkyō" 六朝時代の江南社會と道教. In *Gi Shin Nanbokuchō Zui Tō jidaishi no kihon mondai* 魏晉南北朝隋唐時代史の基本問題, 448–55. Tokyo: Kyūko Shoin, 1997.

Tuotuo 脫脫. *Song shi* 宋史. Beijing: Zhonghua Shuju, 1995.

Twitchett, Denis, and John K. Fairbank, eds. *The Ming Dynasty, 1368–1644*. Vol. 8, part 2, of *The Cambridge History of China*. Cambridge: Cambridge University Press, 1998.

Twitchett, Denis, and Paul Jakov Smith, eds. *The Sung Dynasty and its Precursors, 907–1279*. Vol. 5, part 1, of *The Cambridge History of China*. Cambridge: Cambridge University Press, 2009.

Vinograd, Richard. "Patrimonies in Press: Art Publishing, Cultural Politics, and Canon Construction in the Career of Di Baoxian." In *The Role of Japan in Modern Chinese Art*, edited by Johsua A. Fogel, 245–72. Berkeley: University of California Press, 2013.

von Spee, Clarissa. "Visiting Steles: Variations of a Painting Theme." In *On Telling Images of China: Essays in Narrative Painting and Visual Culture,* edited by Shane McCausland and Yin Hwang, 213–36. Hong Kong: Hong Kong University Press, 2014.

Waley, Arthur, trans. *The Book of Songs: The Ancient Chinese Classic of Poetry*. New York: Grove Press, 1996.

Wang, Jing. *High Culture Fever: Politics, Aesthetics, and Ideology in Deng's China*. Berkeley: University of California Press, 1996.

Wang, Yugen. *Ten Thousand Scrolls: Reading and Writing in the Poetics of Huang Tingjian and the Late Northern Song*. Cambridge, MA: Harvard University Asia Center, 2011.

Wang Cheng-hua 王正華. "Shenghuo, zhishi, yu wenhua shangpin: Wan Ming Fujian ban 'riyong leishu' yu qi shuhuamen" 生活，知識，與文化商品：晚明福建版"日用類書"與其書畫門. *Zhongyang Yanjiuyuan Jindaishi Yanjiusuo jikan* 中央研究院近代史研究所集刊 41 (2003): 1–85.

———. "Guoyan fanhua: Wan Ming chenhshi tu, chengshi guan, yu wenhua xiaofei de yanjiu" 過眼繁華：晚明城市圖、城市觀與文化消費的研究. In *Yishu, quanli, yu xiaofei* 藝術、權力與消費, 397–446. Hangzhou: Zhongguo Meishu Xueyuan Chubanshe, 2011.

Wang Hongsheng 王宏生. "Dong You shengping kaolüe" 董逌生平考略. *Guji yanjiu* 古籍研究, no. 1 (2015): 221–26.

Wang Jiakui 王家葵. *Tao Hongjing congkao* 陶弘景叢考. Ji'nan: Qilu Shushe, 2003.

Wang Jingxian 王靖憲. "Mingdai congtie zongshu" 明代叢帖綜述. In *Zhongguo fatie quanji*, vol. 13, edited by Qi Gong, 1–24. Wuhan: Hubei Meishu Chubanshe, 2002.

Wang Kentang 王肯堂. *Yugangzhai bichen* 鬱岡齋筆塵. *XSKQS*, 1130.

Wang Qingzheng 汪慶正. "Dong Qichang fashu ketie jianshu" 董其昌法書刻帖簡述. In *The Century of Tung Ch'i-Ch'ang, 1555–1636*, Vol. 2, edited by Wai-kam Ho, 335–48. Seattle: University of Washington Press, 1992.

Wang Shi 汪氏. *Shiyu huapu* 詩餘畫譜. Reprinted in Zheng Zhenduo 鄭振鐸. *Zhongguo banhuashi tulu* 中國版畫史圖錄, Vol. 5. Beijing: Zhongguo Shudian, 2012.

Wang Shihong 汪士鋐. *Yi he ming kao* 瘞鹤铭考. Songnan shuwu 松南書屋, 1714. Reprinted in *Jinshi congkan* 金石叢刊, Vol. 2, edited by Xu Dongfang 許東方, 671–778. Taipei: Xinyi Shuju, 1975.

Wang Shizhen 王世貞. *Yanzhou sibu gao* 弇州四部稿. *SKQS*, 1279–81.

Wang Shu 王澍. *Zhuyun tiba* 竹雲題跋. *SKSL*, s. 2, no. 19.

Wang Shumin 王叔岷. *Liexian zhuan jiaojian* 列仙傳校箋. Taipei: Zhongyang Yanjiuyuan Zhongguo Wenzhe Yanjiusuo Choubeichu, 1995.

Wang Tongshun 王同顺. "Shilun Yi he ming de sixiangxing yishuxing jiqi lishi diwei" 試論瘞鶴銘的思想性藝術性及其歷史地位. In *Di wu jie zhongguo shufa shilun guoji yantaohui lunwenji* 第五屆中國書法史論國際研討會論文集, 187–94. Beijing: Wenwu Chubanshe, 2002.

———. *Zhenjiang gudai shike ji jiaoshan beilin shufa yanjiu* 鎮江古代石刻及焦山碑林書法研究. Tianjin: Tianjin Renmin Meishu Chubanshe, 2005.

Wang Xiaoli 王曉驪. "Songdai timing yu timingji kaolun: Yuanqi, xinbian, he shenmei jiazhi" 宋代題名與題名記考論：緣起、新變和審美價值. *Beijing shehui kexue*, no. 2 (2016): 70–75.

Wang Xiaoling 王曉玲. "Qingshantang fatie yu Xu shi jiazu shangyong yaji huodong" 晴山堂法帖與徐氏家族觴詠雅集活動. *Zhongguo shufa*, no. 5 (2016): 55–59.

Wang Yaoyao 王尧瑶. "Qingdai zhi minguo Yi he ming jilian yanjiu" 清代至民國瘞鶴銘集聯研究. Master's thesis, Hangzhou Shifan Daxue, 2017. http://nvsm.cnki.net/kns/detail/detail.aspx?FileName=1017195949.nh&DbName=CMFD2018.

Wang Yinglin 王應麟. *Yu hai* 玉海. *SKQS*, 943–48.

Wang Yuanqing 王淵清. "Shengming de jisi: Cong Yi he ming de yishu tese tan Zhongguo daojia jingshen" 生命的祭祀—從瘞鶴銘的藝術特色談中國道家藝術精神. *Shufa yanjiu*, no. 1 (1993): 92–110.

Wang Zhuanghong 王壯弘. *Zengbu Jiaobei suibi* 增補校碑隨筆. Shanghai: Shanghai Shuhua Chubanshe, 1981.

Wei, Betty Peh-T'i. *Ruan Yuan, 1764–1849: The Life and Work of a Major Scholar-Official in Nineteenth-Century China before the Opium War*. Hong Kong: Hong Kong University Press, 2006.

Wenwu chubanshe 文物出版社, ed. *Di wu jie zhongguo shufa shilun guoji yantaohui lunwenji* 第五屆中國書法史論國際研討會論文集. Beijing: Wenwu Chubanshe, 2002.

Weng Danian 翁大年. *Jiu guan tan bei kao* 舊館壇碑考. *SKSL*, s. 3, no. 34.

Weng Fanggang 翁方纲. *Yi he ming kaobu* 瘞鹤铭考補. In *Suzhai congshu* 蘇齋叢書. Shanghai: Boguzhai, 1924.

———. *Fuchuzhai wenji* 復初齋文集. *XSKQS*, 1445.

Weng Kaiyun 翁闿運. "Yi he ming Tan" 瘞鶴銘談. *Shupu* 書譜, no. 3 (1979): 16–21.

Wenzel, Claudia. "Monumental Stone Sutra Carvings in China and Indian Pilgrim Sites." *Zhonghua foxue xuebao* 中華佛學學報, 29 (2016): 51–89.

Wong, Aida Yuen. *The Other Kang Youwei: Calligrapher, Art Activist, and Aesthetic Reformer in Modern China*. Leiden: Brill, 2016.

Wong, Dorothy C. *Chinese Steles: Pre-Buddhist and Buddhist Use of a Symbolic Form*. Honolulu: University of Hawai'i Press, 2004.

Wu, Hung. *Monumentality in Early Chinese Art and Architecture*. Stanford: Stanford University Press, 1995.

———. "On Rubbings: Their Materiality and Historicity." In *Writing and Materiality in China: Essays in Honor of Patrick Hanan*, edited by Judith. T. Zeitlin, Lydia H. Liu, and Ellen Widmer, 29–71. Cambridge, MA: Harvard University Asia Center, 2003.

———, ed. *Reinventing the Past: Archasim and Antiquarianism in Chinese Art and Visual Culture*. Chicago: Center for the Arts of East Asia, University of Chicago, 2010.

———. *A Story of Ruins: Presence and Absence in Chinese Art and Culture*. Princeton: Princeton University Press, 2012.

Wu Dongfa 吴東發. *Yi he ming kao* 瘞鶴銘考. *CSJC*, 1611.

Wu Hao 吳鎬. *Han Wei Liuchao Tangdai zhimu jinshi li* 漢魏六朝唐代志墓金石例. *CSJC*, 2631.

Wu Renshu 巫仁恕. *Pinwei shehua: Wan Ming de xiaofei shehui yu shidafu* 品味奢華：晚明的消費社會與士大夫. Beijing: Zhonghua Shuju, 2008.

Wu Shuping 吳樹平, ed. *Zhongguo lidai huapu huibian* 中國歷代畫譜彙編. Tianjin: Tianjin Guji Chubanshe, 1997.

Wu Yun 吳雲. *Tongzhi Jiaoshan zhi* 同治焦山志. Preface, 1870. Reprinted in *Gugong zhenben congkan* 故宮珍本叢刊, no. 247. Haikou: Hainan Chubanshe, 2001.

Xia Zhifeng 夏志峰. "Xinzheng qiqun san kao" 新鄭器群三考. In *Xinzheng Zhenggong damu qingtongqi* 新鄭鄭公大墓青銅器, edited by Henan Bowuyuan 河南博物院, 38–47. Zhengzhou: Daxiang Chubanshe, 2001.

Xiao Tong 蕭統. *Wen xuan* 文選. Annotated by Li Shan 李善. Beijing: Zhonghua Shuju, 1977.

Xie Shiwei [Hsieh Shu-wei] 謝世維. *Tianjie zhi wen: Weijin nanbeichao lingbao jingdian yanjiu* 天界之文：魏晉南北朝靈寶經典研究. Taipei: Shangwu Yinshuguan, 2010.

Xiong Peijun 熊沛軍. "Wang Shizhen shulun yanjiu" 王世貞書論研究. PhD diss., Shoudu Shifan Daxue, Beijing, 2008. http://nvsm.cnki.net/kns/detail/detail.aspx?FileName=2008144510.nh&DbName=CDFD2009.

Xu Guocheng 許國誠. *Jingkou sanshan quan zhi* 京口三山全志. Reprinted in *Zhongguo difangzhi congshu* 中國地方志叢書, 459. Taipei: Chengwen Chubanshe, 1983.

Xu Wenmei 許文美. *Hechu shi Penglai: Xianshan tu tezhan* 何處是蓬萊：仙山圖特展. Taipei: National Palace Museum, 2018.

Xu Zheying [Hsu Che-ying] 許哲瑛. "Gushu zhong de tuijianwen: Yi Nan Song Wei Liaoweng diaoban shufa wei zhongxin" 古書中的推薦文–以南宋魏了翁雕版書法為中心. *Gugong xueshu jikan* 35, no. 3 (2017): 93–140.

Xuanhe shupu 宣和書譜. *SKQS*, 813.

Xue, Longchun. "From Dots and Strokes to Lines: On Changes Great and Small in Late Ming Calligraphy." In *Out of Character: Decoding Chinese Calligraphy*, edited by Michael Knight and Joseph P. Chang, 221–53. San Francisco: Asian Art Museum, 2012.

Xue Lei 薛磊. "Yi he ming de wenben yu yujing zaiyi" 瘞鶴銘的文本與語境再議. In *Yi he ming guoji xueshu yantaohui lunwenji* 瘞鶴銘國際學術研討會論文集, edited by Ding Chao, 221–25. Zhenjiang: Jiangsu Daxue Chubanshe, 2009.

Xue Longchun 薛龍春. *Zheng Fu yanjiu* 鄭簠研究. Beijing: Rongbaozhai, 2007.

Yan Kejun 嚴可均. *Quan shanggu sandai Qin Han Sanguo Liuchao wen* 全上古三代秦漢三國六朝文. Shanghai: Zhonghua Shuju, 1958.

Yang Bin 楊賓. *Dapiao oubi* 大瓢偶筆. In *Lidai shufa lunwenxuan xubian* 歷代書法論文選續編, 447–596. Shanghai: Shanghai Shuhua Chubanshe, 1993.

Yang Dunli 楊敦禮. "Tan Gugong yuancang de 'Yi he ming kaobu'" 談故宮院藏的《瘞鶴銘考補》. *Gugong wenwu yuekan* 4, no. 4 (1986): 116–21.

Yang Erzeng 楊爾曾. *Xinjuan Hainei qiguan* 新鐫海內奇觀. Qiantang Yang shi Yibaitang kanben 錢塘楊氏夷白堂刊本, 1610.

Yang Qingcun 楊慶存. "Su Shi yu Huang Tingjian jiaoyou kaoshu" 蘇軾與黃庭堅交遊考述. *Qilu xuekan* 齊魯學刊, no. 4 (1995): 33–37.

Yao Silian 姚思廉. *Liang shu* 梁書. Beijing: Zhonghua Shuju, 1974.

Ye Changchi 葉昌熾 and Ke Changsi 柯昌泗. *Yu shi, Yu shi yitong ping* 語石•語石異同評. Beijing: Zhonghua Shuju, 1994.

Ye Kangning 葉康寧. *Fengya zhihao: Ming dai Jia Wan nian jian de shuhua xiaofei* 風雅之好：明代嘉萬年間的書畫消費. Beijing: Shangwu Yinshuguan, 2017.

Yin Yimei 尹一梅. "Xihongtang fashu kaolüe" 戲鴻堂法書考略. In *Nanzong beidou: Dong Qichang de shuhua yishu* 南宗北斗：董其昌的書畫藝術, edited by Macau Art Museum, 212–23. Beijing: Zijincheng Chubanshe, 2015.

Yongrong 永瑢, ed. *Siku quanshu zongmu* 四庫全書總目. Beijing: Zhonghua Shuju, 1963.

Yu Beishan 于北山. *Lu You nianpu* 陸游年譜. Shanghai: Shanghai Guji Chubanshe, 1985.

Yu Bo 于博. "Mingdai ketie yanjiu" 明代刻帖研究. PhD diss., Jilin University, Changchun, 2017.

Yu Xilu 俞希魯. *Zhishun Zhenjiang zhi* 至順鎮江志. Reprinted in *Zhonghua wenshi congshu* 中華文史叢書. Taipei: Huawen Shuju, 1968.

Yu Xin 庾信. *Yu Zishan ji zhu* 庾子山集注. Annotated by Ni Pan 倪璠. Edited by Xu Yimin 許逸民. Beijing: Zhonghua Shuju, 1980.

Yuan Daojun 袁道俊. *Jiaoshan shike yanjiu* 焦山石刻研究. Nanjing: Jiangsu Meishu Chubanshe, 1996.

Yuan Jie 元結. *Yuan Cishan ji* 元次山集. Beijing: Zhonghua Shuju, 1960.

Zeitlin, Judith T., and Lydia H. Liu, eds. *Writing and Materiality in China: Essays in Honor of Patrick Hanan*. Cambridge, MA: Harvard University Asia Center for the Harvard–Yenching Institute, 2003.

Zeng Yingsan 曾迎三, ed. *Zeng Xi, Li Ruiqing, Zhang Daqian Yi he ming yaji* 曾熙、李瑞清、張大千瘞鶴銘雅集. Shanghai: Shanghai Cishu Chubanshe, 2013.

Zhang Boying 張伯英. *Fatie tiyao* 法帖提要. In *Xuxiu Siku quanshu zongmu tiyao gaoben* 續修四庫全書總目提要稿本, 18. Jinan: Qilu Shushe, 1996.

Zhang Chao 張弨. *Yi he ming bian* 瘞鶴銘辨. In *Zhaodai congshu* 昭代叢書, 1700. Reprinted in *Siku quanshu cunmu congshu* 四庫全書存目叢書, 278:90–95. Tainan: Zhuangyan Wenhua Shiye Youxian Gongsi, 1997.

Zhang Daqian 張大千. *Daqian Jushi lin Yi he ming* 大千居士臨瘞鶴銘. Taipei: Huazheng Shuju, 1987.

Zhang Guogan 張國淦. *Zhongguo gufangzhi kao* 中國古方志考. Beijing: Zhonghua Shuju, 1962.

Zhang Jinghua 張京華, Hou Yonghui 侯永慧, and Tang Jun 湯軍. *Hunan Chaoyangyan shike kaoshi* 湖南朝陽岩石刻考釋. Beijing: Zhongguo Shehui Kexue Chubanshe, 2018.

Zhang Qiang 張強 and Wei Liya 魏離雅. *Da kong wang fo: Seng An Daoyi kejing yu Beichao shijue wenhua* 大空王佛：僧安道壹刻經與北朝視覺文化. Beijing: Wenwu Chubanshe, 2017.

Zhang Tao 張韜. "Yishan keshi kaolüe" 嶧山刻石考略. *Zhongguo shufa*, no. 23 (2015): 133–35.

Zhang Yansheng 張彥生. *Shanben beitie lu* 善本碑帖錄. Beijing: Zhonghua Shuju, 1984.

Zhang Yingxiu 張盈袖. "He Shaoji shufa jiqi shuxue sixiang yanjiu" 何紹基書法及其書學思想研究. PhD diss., Jilin University, Changchun, 2013. http://nvsm.cnki.net/kns/detail/detail.aspx?FileName=1013187823.nh&DbName=CDFD2013.

Zhao Chao 趙超. *Han Wei Nanbeichao muzhi huibian* 漢魏南北朝墓誌彙編. Tianjin: Tianjin Guji Chubanshe, 1992.

———. *Gudai muzhi tonglun* 古代墓誌通論. Beijing: Zijincheng Chubanshe, 2003.

Zhao Wanli 趙萬里. *Han Wei Nanbeichao muzhi jishi* 漢魏南北朝墓誌集釋. Beijing: Kexue Chubanshe, 1956.

Zhao Yanwei 趙彥衛. *Yunlu manchao* 雲麓漫抄. Beijing: Zhonghua Shuju, 1996.

Zhao Yiguang 趙宧光. *Hanshan zhoutan* 寒山帚談. *SKQS*, 816.

Zheng Zhenduo 鄭振鐸. *Zhongguo banhuashi tulu* 中國版畫史圖錄. Reprinted. Beijing: Zhongguo Shudian, 2012.

Zhenjiang Bowuguan 鎮江博物館. "Zhenjiang Jiaoshan Yi he ming beike fajue jianbao" 鎮江焦山瘞鶴銘碑刻發掘簡報. *Dongnan wenhua*, no. 11 (2001): 44–48.

Zhenjiang Shi Minjian Wenyi Yanjiuhui 鎮江市民間文藝研究會. *Zhenjiang minjian gushi* 鎮江民間故事. Beijing: Zhongguo Minjian Wenyi Chubanshe, 1982.

Zhipan 志磐. *Fozu tongji* 佛祖統紀, *TSZ* 49.

Zhong Laiyin 鍾來因 and Zhu Yaping 朱亞平. "Gu Yuanqian yanjiu" 顧元慶研究. *Ming Qing xiaoshuo yanjiu* 明清小說研究 6 (1987): 183–204.

Zhong Wei 仲威. "Huadusi taming chuanshi cangben kao" 化度寺塔銘傳世藏本考. *Shoucangjia*, no. 2 (2007): 83–90.

———. *Zhongguo beitie jianbie tudian* 中國碑帖鑑別圖典. Beijing: Wenwu Chubanshe, 2010.

Zhongguo Gudai Shuhua Jiandingzu 中國古代書畫鑑定組. *Zhongguo gudai shuhua tumu* 中國古代書畫圖目. Beijing: Wenwu Chubanshe, 2000.

Zhongguo meishu quanji: Gongyi meishu bian 中國美術全集：工藝美術編. Beijing: Renmin Meishu Chubanshe, 1986.

Zhongguo meishu quanji: Huihua bian 中國美術全集：繪畫編. Beijing: Renmin Meishu Chubanshe, 1986.

Zhongguo meishu quanji: Shufa zhuanke bian 中國美術全集：書法篆刻編. Beijing: Renmin Meishu Chubanshe, 1986.

Zhongguo Shehui Kexueyuan Kaogu Yanjiusuo 中國社會科學院考古研究所and Hebei Wenwu Guanlichu 河北文物管理處. *Mancheng Han mu fajue baogao*滿城漢墓發掘報告. Beijing: Wenwu Chubanshe, 1980.

Zhou Daozhen 周道振. *Tingyunguan tie huikao* 停雲館帖彙考. Zhengzhou: Henan Meishu Chubanshe, 2012.

Zhou Guanye 周廣業. *Haichang beizhi* 海昌備志. Zunjingge尊經閣, 1847.

Zhou Mi 周密. *Yunyan guoyan lu* 雲煙過眼錄. *CSJC*, 1553.

Zhou Yiliang 周一良. "Lun Liang Wudi jiqi shidai" 論梁武帝及其時代. In *Zhonghua xueshu lunwenji* 中華學術論文集, edited by Zhonghua Shuju bianjibu, 123–40. Beijing: Zhonghua Shuju,1981.

Zhou Yukai 周裕鍇. *Wenzichan yu Songdai shixue* 文字禪與宋代詩學. Beijing: Gaodeng Jiaoyu Chubanshe, 1998.

Zhu Jianxin 朱劍心. *Jinshixue* 金石學. Hong Kong: Shangwu Yinshuguan, 1964.

Zhu Youzhou 朱友舟. "Weng Fanggang de shuxue sixiang yanjiu" 翁方綱的書學思想研究. *Shufa yanjiu*, no. 129 (2006): 1–54.

Zou Tao 鄒濤. *Zhao Zhiqian nianpu* 趙之謙年譜. Beijing: Rongbaozhai, 2003.

———. "*Zhao Zhiqian shufa pingzhuan*" 趙之謙書法評傳. In *Zhongguo shufa quanji: Zhao Zhiqian juan* 中國書法全集•趙之謙卷, edited by Liu Zhengcheng, 1–22. Beijing: Rongbaozhai, 2004.

Index